The Rational Practitioner

Sport and exercise psychology has grown exponentially as an academic discipline and profession in the past decade. The dominant approach to sport and exercise psychology practice is the cognitive-behavioural approach that stems from cognitive behavioural therapies (CBTs). CBTs are the most widely used counselling approaches in the world. Through this approach developed rational emotive behaviour therapy (REBT), a cognitive-based theory and therapy that incorporates many of the techniques that defines CBTs to this day (e.g., cognitive restructuring, rehearsal, imagery, self-talk).

The Rational Practitioner: The Sport and Performance Psychologist's Guide to Practicing Rational Emotive Behaviour Therapy develops innovative concepts that are particular to the performance milieu, whilst sticking rigorously to core theory. This book is fundamental to applied practice and offers practitioners, scholars, and researchers of sport psychology and REBT, theoretical and detailed practical information from an experienced and qualified sport and exercise psychologist.

This book provides a comprehensive portrayal of REBT applied within sport and performance and is key reading for current and trainee sport and exercise psychologists, but also to psychologists from other disciplines who wish to work with athletes and other performers.

Martin Turner, PhD is a Reader in Psychology at Manchester Metropolitan University. He is a BPS Chartered and HCPC Registered Sport and Exercise Psychologist, and an Associate Fellow of the BPS. He holds an Advanced Practicum Certificate in REBT from the Albert Ellis Institute, who also awarded him the Albert Ellis Award for research in 2018 and 2020. He also received the Outstanding Achievement Award from the U.K. Association for REBT. As a practitioner, he has worked within professional football and cricket, as well as within a vast range of sports both at team and individual levels. He also works with non-sporting organisations applying performance psychology to enhance wellbeing and performance. He is currently lead psychologist for Scarlets Rugby.

The Rational Practitioner

The Sport and Performance Psychologist's Guide to Practicing Rational Emotive Behaviour Therapy

Martin Turner

NEW YORK AND LONDON

Cover image: Mr. Casper Essam

First published 2023
by Routledge
605 Third Avenue, New York, NY 10158

and by Routledge
4 Park Square, Milton Park, Abingdon, Oxon, OX14 4RN

Routledge is an imprint of the Taylor & Francis Group, an informa business

ISBN: 978-1-032-06044-6 (hbk)
ISBN: 978-1-032-06040-8 (pbk)
ISBN: 978-1-003-20043-7 (ebk)

DOI: 10.4324/9781003200437

Typeset in Baskerville
by codeMantra

This book is dedicated to my friend Dr. Andrew Wood.

Contents

List of Figures

Foreword

Sport is emotional. Whether you are a competitor, coach, official, or supporter you will be familiar with the demands that sport places on those directly engaged or observing. Sport is also a competition and success matters, indeed legendary American Football Coach Vince Lombardi said "winning isn't everything, it's the only thing". But the biggest competition in sport is often internal – within the athlete themselves. This timely and comprehensive book addresses that very issue. How those involved in sport can manage their thoughts, emotions, and behaviours to grow and perform to their potential.

This book begins by outlining the origins and underpinning central tenets of Rational Emotive Behaviour Therapy (REBT), along with current REBT-related research in sport. Then 13 detailed chapters provide a guide to applying and practising REBT in sport. There is much that is new in these chapters but as Martin himself reminds us, REBT is foundational to the cognitive-behavioural approach which underpins many of the psychological skills used in sport psychology. As a sport psychologist I enjoyed reading these chapters. I am a better practitioner for having read this guide, even as someone who does not specialise in REBT. It made me think deeply about my consultancy, outlined new techniques, and reinforced a sense of 'place' of where many techniques used in sport psychology practice are rooted.

Praise should (I need to work on recognising my demands!) always come with a qualification. And mine is that I have known Martin for more than 15 years and was his PhD supervisor. Martin's PhD was not in REBT but rather in challenge and threat states under stress in sport, for which he received an award from the British Psychological Society's Division of Sport and Exercise Psychology for the best PhD in 2013. Martin will say – as he frequently does – that these areas are complimentary. But it is testament to his motivation, and interest in human behaviour, that he should be a leader in both fields, and also award-winning in both. He has also won awards for his research in REBT including the 2018 and 2020 Albert Ellis Award, and the 2019 Outstanding Achievement Award for Research from the United Kingdom Association for REBT. Indeed, he mentions in this book that the study and application of REBT in sport is growing, which is correct. But he does not say that he has been a significant factor in leading that growth, and as such there is no one better to write this book. I know that it has long been a personal goal for Martin to complete this work, and in addition to being impressed with the quality of this book, I am pleased that Martin's personality comes though, both with his deep thinking and humour. It is difficult to write a book in your own voice but for me, when I read this book, I hear Martin speaking.

I have also consulted with Martin across a number of different settings, and I have seen first-hand, both how well received his approach is, but also the challenges of applying an REBT approach in sport. People do sometimes like 'positive thinking' rather than dealing with the world as it actually is, in order to make it better. Some also bristle at the idea that there is no such thing as a 'must-win game', or that in order to win there is no need to be 'perfect'. For them "winning isn't everything, it's the only thing" as Vince Lombardi said. However, sport is nuanced, complicated, and uncertain. And dogmatic, rigid beliefs that some in the sports world hold do not help, certainly not in the long term for either performance or well-being. Of course, as a highly successful coach Vince Lombardi knew this, and he never meant for his quote to be used as a mantra for an unthinking narrow view of success. Indeed, he said, "I wish to hell I'd never said the dammed thing. I meant the effort, I meant having a goal. I sure as hell didn't mean for people to crush human values and morality". This book, and the approach outlined, is an excellent guide to help those in sport direct their effort to navigate the uncertain, emotional, demanding world of sport, and to achieve their goals.

Professor Marc Jones
Sport Psychologist
Newcastle under Lyme
5th May, 2022

Illustrations Credit

Illustrations 'A Journey of Discovery' by Mr. Casper Essam, Freelance illustrator, Milton Keynes.

Acknowledgements

This is just a book, isn't it? Not for me. Not only has this book taken me much time and effort to write (as it should!), it also represents the collective contributions of many people I have had the pleasure to work with whilst writing this book.

This book could not have come into being without a wide network of supportive colleagues off of whom I bounce ideas. I bore them constantly with my REBT ramblings. I extend my thanks to anybody with whom I have conversed about REBT in sport and performance settings, even those with whom my discussions have been adversarial. I am very appreciative of colleagues who sent me their positive comments on the book – this community of academics, teachers, and practitioners provides me with continual sources of inspiration, and I have had the opportunity to work with some brilliant individuals.

I am grateful to the many athletes, coaches, performance directors, sport scientists, and fellow psychologists I have worked alongside over the years. You have challenged me to stay at the applied end of theory, have questioned and contested theory itself, and therefore have helped me to refine my application and conceptualisation of REBT. The examples I draw upon in this book come from our work together.

I especially thank Andrew Wood. In the beginnings of this book, Andrew was my partner in crime, and had global circumstances been different, he would have been my co-author. Andrew's temperance, balance, and enquiring nature have helped shape my thinking, and hence, have helped shape this book. I also extend my gratitude to Rebecca Levett, Dr. Josephine Perry, and Dr. Chris Shambrook, for their early feedback on the book, which helped to shape my thoughts and helped me to maintain a practitioner focus.

I thank Prof. Marc Jones, who in my career has been a rock of humility, diplomacy, and friendship. Many times whilst writing this book I asked myself 'what would Marc say here?' – I can only hope to live up to the standards of my PhD supervisor. I thank Prof. Stephen Palmer for his support and encouragement of my work, and particularly for the role he plays in training and engaging with sport psychologists entering into the world of REBT. I also thank the staff at the Albert Ellis Institute New York with whom I completed my training, for their continued dedication to the work and teaching of Dr. Albert Ellis.

To my past and current PhD students and to the professional doctorate students whose research I have had the pleasure to supervise. Thank you for showing me that I know less than I think I do, and for pushing me to know more. Through you REBT lives and thrives in sport and performance settings.

A big thank you goes to Megan Smith and David Varley at Routledge for their support and assistance in bringing this book into existence, and for having confidence in the project amidst various setbacks and delays.

A special thank you goes to Casper Essam for the astounding illustrations to this book. It is a real pleasure to work with somebody who not only has a creative spirit, but also has the talent to bring it to fruition. May this book signal the start of great things for you and your work.

Thank you Keith Jarrett (pianist) for recording 'The Köln Concert', which frequently accompanied me whilst I was writing this book.

Most importantly, I thank my wife Jayne, without whom my existence would be aimless and meaningless. You listen to my daily drivel, never (or hardly ever) yawning or telling me to abscond. Each day, I strive to earn your love.

Praise

In this book Martin goes deep into REBT and excavates key elements that can be applied in sport and performance environments. As well as offering important theoretical clarifications, there is also a wealth of practitioner tools and techniques in this book. As a sport psychologist who utilises an REBT approach in my own practice, I'm always looking for resources to aid my consultancy practice. Martin's book is a keen addition to my library and one that will continue to guide my use of this important and powerful approach to behaviour change.

Dan Abrahams
Sport Psychologist

Sport psychology publications are too frequently characterised by ideas and approaches that are light on evidence and heavy on the superficial charm of buzzwords or personality. This is not one of those publications. It is both refreshing and reassuring to see the author dig deep into the rich history of psychotherapy, providing a sound philosophical and scientific rationale for the application of REBT to the field of sport and performance.

Dr. Richard Bennett
Clinical Psychologist
Lecturer in the Centre for Applied Psychology at the University of Birmingham
Co-author of *Acceptance and Commitment Therapy: 100 Key Points and Techniques* and *The Mindfulness and Acceptance Workbook for Self-esteem*

True to REBT's nature, Dr. Turner adopts a no-nonsense and reality-based approach in articulating the practical application of REBT to sport and high-performance settings. A premier expert in the field of sport and exercise psychology, Dr. Turner has been a forerunner in demonstrating the empirical support of REBT for athletes and performers. He has devoted his career to disseminating the evidence base of REBT for these populations. This book is a prodigious culmination of his life's work and is a must-read for sport and performance psychologists.

Dr. Angela Breitmeyer
Associate Professor, and Licensed Clinical Psychologist, and
Certified Mental Performance Consultant
Midwestern University, Glendale, Arizona

This book is an informative and invaluable resource for practitioners who are interested in applying REBT within the sport and performance setting. This book comprehensively brings together the theoretical underpinning and evidence-based practice of REBT. The author sharing ideas from his own applied practice and using quotes and media references throughout the text makes it an engaging and stimulating read.

Dr. Nanaki J. Chadha
Sport & Exercise Psychologist based in India

Martin Turner provides thorough and fascinating insights into the approach of Rational Emotive Behaviour Therapy (REBT) in this practitioner guide. Drawing on his vast wealth of knowledge and practical experiences of REBT in sport, this book is indispensable for anyone looking to fully understand REBT theory, explore technical components of REBT and practically use REBT successfully when working with clients. Everyone who is interested in performance should read it.

Helen Davis
Director and sport psychologist at Think.Believe.Perform, U.K.

Martin Turner is one of the leading figures in REBT, and this book displays exactly why. This book serves as a complete guide for using REBT as a toolkit, and encapsulates the whole process of REBT from beginning to end. This book is fantastically well-written, easy to understand, memorable, and brutally honest in its intentions and in REBT's bounds as a therapeutic framework. This book will be a landmark in the field of sport & performance psychology for many years to come.

Muhammad Saqib Deen
Performance Psychology Consultant

Driven by utilitarianism, Martin Turner draws on over a decade of experience and research to offer populous pearls of REBT wisdom. This belongs on the desk of all practitioners who have a vested interest in facilitating deep solutions for performance issues.

Dr. Faye F. Didymus
Reader in Sport and Performance Psychology
Leeds Beckett University

As an applied practitioner in elite sport and business I have found REBT a hugely valuable and impactful approach when working with high-performing individuals and teams. The principles, frameworks, and language consistently resonate powerfully with those operating in a performance environment who connect to the ideas of working with a more rational mindset. I am extremely excited that Martin has been able to consolidate his learning and experience into this fantastic guide. I thoroughly recommend it as a wonderful companion for anyone looking to learn about and apply REBT in their work.

Dr. Joseph Dixon
Sport & Exercise and Occupational Psychologist

The book provides a forensic and comprehensive examination of the key theory, frameworks, and technical components central to the REBT approach, and an effective guide for those who wish to contribute to the growing application of REBT in sport and performance settings. In my professional lead role as an educator and trainer of Sport and Exercise Psychologists, the book represents an extremely valuable resource for those applied practitioners wishing to develop the knowledge and skills required to effectively use REBT in their service delivery with clients.

Dr. Martin Eubank
LJMU Professional Doctorate Programme Director and
BPS Qualification Lead in Sport and Exercise Psychology

Learning to become a sport psychologist is like picking up shards of a smashed antique jug. As you discuss and grow with others in the field, you slowly piece it together to develop your practice. Learning REBT fully is like being the person who has the vase and uses it to pour out the wine of rational truth for your clients. Dr. Turner's book is of immense value for his robust depth of knowledge on REBT. I would prefer for it to have existed when I began my career providing sport psychology to Olympians and Paralympians. Every day we accept reality and are undisturbed by it. Frequently though, things occur and we become disturbed. In sport we face failure, injury, setbacks, sometimes even death, amidst the harsh existence of life. It is within those most difficult of cases where the most robust and accessible approaches will prevail, and REBT serves these challenges well. In a field that promotes positivity and happiness as the end goal, REBT cuts through the nonsense to leave humans in control of their reality.

Hugh J. Gilmore
Sport Psychologist with British Weightlifting and British Athletics
Podium Psychology

Martin Turner has achieved something special with this book. By combining his sophisticated understanding of REBT and the unique demands coming from the world of sports, he offers great insight and practical solutions that unlock optimal performance. Sport is a microcosm of life. We learn so much from participating in the game. Dr. Turner's *The Rational Practitioner* book helps all of us discover philosophies and applied answers that can help us navigate the complexities of life in addition to sport.

Dr. Scott Goldman
Clinical and Sport Psychologist who has been
embedded with multiple NFL, NBA, MLB, and NCAA teams

Sport culture has for too long propagated a host of incredibly unhelpful attitudes and perspectives around what it means to be an athlete and the inherent value of winning. So few coaches and others in supporting roles are conscious of the perspectives or beliefs that could be dramatically holding back their athletes. REBT is a powerful concept to bring into performance sport because it provides a solid foundational mindset, more closely aligned to the reality of any situation, from which athletes can build on and achieve their potential. Elite sport is crying out for a healthier approach; one that does not break down or burnout its participants so consistently. A more widespread understanding of the theory and practice of REBT would be a vital part of that healthier approach.

Laurence Cassøe Halsted
Director of Mentoring, The True Athlete Project, U.K.

Martin is the go-to person for all things REBT in sport. In this book he unassumingly provides valuable insight for both the REBT novice and expert; a valuable addition to any sport and exercise psychologist's book shelf.

Jennifer Hobson
Sport & Exercise Psychologist

This book provides an invaluable resource for trainee practitioners, experienced consultants, and those with an interest in a particular application of psychology within sport and other high-performance contexts. This book breaks down the REBT approach into meaningful and interconnected components and guides the reader in a clear and coherent manner to encourage effective use of it within applied practice.

Dr. Tim Holder
Senior Lecturer in Sport & Exercise Psychology
University of Winchester

I have found REBT and some of its key tenets to be hugely valuable as I develop as a practitioner. In learning about the theory I have often looked to Martin's writing in the area, and can personally endorse his simple and down to earth way of breaking down key concepts and arming you with actionable tools to take into practice.

Pete Jackson
Trainee Sport & Exercise Psychologist (BPS)

It can be hard to recognise the value of adopting an REBT approach until one is simultaneously fully immersed in its theories and responding to the complex needs of clients who brave high-risk contexts. Until recently a developing sport and performance psychology practitioner may have felt vulnerable relying so heavily on an approach which seemed so un-tested in our context. Dr. Turner's important book, and ever-growing contribution to our understanding of REBT in performance settings, provides practitioners with a much-desired navigation system for applying one of the most efficient and effective approaches to stress and emotion management.

Jenni Jones
Performance Psychologist

The application of REBT in sport and exercise settings is relatively new and rapidly growing. It is the toolkit that practitioners can use to help athletes make sense of their thoughts, actions, and feelings. A great deal of the work stems from Dr. Martin Turner and this book with so many fascinating, insightful, and practically useful chapters will be an asset to practitioners and students alike.

Dr. Andrew Lane
Professor of Sport Psychology
University of Wolverhampton

As applied sport psychologists working within high-performance environments, we are charged with deciding which approaches and frameworks we learn and utilise with clients. In *The Rational Practitioner*, Martin offers a comprehensive account of the REBT approach, and the GABCDE framework found within it, to working in performance settings. Martin links REBT with ideas and techniques common to sport psychology, helping REBT to be seen as a broad approach to working with clients, rather than a niche psychotherapy only for clinical usage. Alongside much theoretical detail, Martin offers many practical ideas and concepts for practitioners to use in their work, making the book useful for applied psychologists working in the real world.

Rebecca Levett
Sport & Exercise Psychologist
Sporting Success, U.K.

This is a very useful and practical book. It is a welcome resource that I enthusiastically recommend. Martin's engaging writing style, suitable demonstration of the effectiveness of REBT as an approach should have a wide appeal to practitioners of all disciplines who support participants involved in sport and high-performance settings. It is an information-packed and thought-provoking read and will no doubt be trusted reference

Andy McCann
Professor of Psychology, Human Performance Practitioner
Manchester Metropolitan University

Dr. Martin Turner's accessible, engaging, and scholarly text about practising Rational Emotive Behaviour Therapy in sport and high-performance instructs as it enlightens. His is the best style of practising guide: it knits its extensive scholarship gracefully into each sentence, it presents concepts and practice in sensible and measured lots, and what sits on these pages permeated from years of exceptional scholarship and practical experience.

Dr. Paul McCarthy
Senior Lecturer in Applied Psychology
Glasgow Caledonian University

REBT can be a useful approach to help performers perceive stressful situations as a challenge. Interestingly, this can be done by reflecting on the beliefs behind the demands, and if these are irrational, REBT can be useful in lowering the weight of the demands, through moving away from the 'musts'. It also helps to draw in the resources to help cope with the demands of the situation, through considering how to work towards healthy emotions. As such, this text is an invaluable resource for practitioners who are working with stress and emotions in athletes.

Dr. Carla Meijen
Senior Lecturer in Applied Sport Psychology
St Mary's University

This book is a much needed delve into the value of REBT in sport. For researchers and practitioners alike, it gives a detailed overview of the key theoretical underpinnings and how to use it in practice. It is a must-read for all those with an interest in working with or using REBT.

Dr. Robert Morris
Lecturer in Sport Psychology
University of Stirling

For those of us researching and consulting in this field, Martin is acknowledged as an academic practitioner who has developed into a World Leading Expert on REBT within the sport setting. I am, therefore, delighted that Martin has translated his knowledge and experience into this accessible text. What follows is a user-friendly guide that will help those involved in sport understand and utilise an evidence-based and flexible approach to emotion management.

Professor Rich Neil
Cardiff Metropolitan University

The Rational Practitioner is a very welcome and timely contribution to the field, providing 14 chapters offering insights and evidence-based discussion. Dr. Martin Turner's new book aims to inform the work of psychologists and is also essential reading for anyone interested in learning more about the field of Rational Emotive Behaviour Therapy in the contexts of sport and performance.

Dr. Siobhain O'Riordan
Chartered Coaching Psychologist

This book is another great contribution by Dr. Martin Turner on the use of REBT in sport. Not only does Martin provide readers with a rich insight into the theory and implementation of REBT within sport settings, but he does so in a witty, engaging, and accessible way. This book is a must-have resource for any practitioner looking to expand their knowledge and practice of REBT.

Erin Prior
Doctoral Researcher and Sport & Exercise Psychologist
Loughborough University

For anyone interested in learning more about the REBT approach, irrespective of their level of practitioner and/or academic and/or research experience, this text is an absolute must. From raising awareness to the theoretical underpinning of REBT, the text comprehensively works through key research contributions and integrates the implications for applied practice. Written in a manner that encourages critical thinking, the text includes many examples that will support reflections and future work using the approach, and perhaps even lead to some new 'Effective beliefs' about the approach.

Dr. Richard Thelwell
Professor of Applied Sport Psychology
University of Portsmouth

The notion that helpful thoughts and actions don't have to be overtly positive is a 'game-changer' to many athletes. This book and its exploration of the use of REBT in sport and performance settings is in many ways a great reflection of the author – rich and deep in knowledge, with tangible simplicity at the fore. The principles of REBT in a wider sense provide a great fit to sporting practice – after all, the things we fear or avoid are all part of life's performance.

Betsy Tuffrey
Chartered Sport & Exercise Psychologist
Seed Psychology Ltd., U.K.

I have been fortunate enough to work with Martin in a business setting and see the benefit of applying REBT to a group going through redundancy. The group benefited enormously to reframe a situation they saw as a 'disaster' into a potential opportunity. As a result, all members of the group were able to move on into new roles with their confidence levels enhanced rather than reduced.

Roy White
Ex Vice President Human Resources, Sony Europe

Introduction

Malcontent.

DOI: 10.4324/9781003200437-1

> Nothing is awful or terrible, it's just a pain in the ass.

For a young person in the 1950s, New York City was brimming with opportunities for romance. But the 19-year-old Albert Ellis wasn't too good when it came to talking to the opposite sex. Numerous adverse past experiences with females had left him with a stifling fear of rejection. Ellis says of his fear, "I was scared shitless of talking to women...this is silly philosophically. What is there to lose or to be ashamed of? If they're going to reject me, are they going to cut my balls off?" (Halasz, 2004).

One day, he decided to do something about his fear, and set himself a task in his break from college. He would go to the Bronx Botanical Gardens every day for one month (August) and talk to every woman sitting alone on a park bench. He would talk to the woman for one minute. This was a huge step for Ellis, he hadn't done anything like this before. To quiet his intense fear, he would use the mantra "If I die, I die. Screw it, so I die". Ellis talked to 130 women that month in the park. Thirty got up and walked away immediately. One hundred women entertained his conversational attempts. Of these women, he made one date...but she didn't show up! Ellis learnt a lot from this experience. He learnt that he could cope with the unpleasant feelings of fear. He learnt that rejection is not fatal. He also learnt to get over his fear of approaching the opposite sex.

Dr. Albert Ellis used this experience and many other personal experiences to inspire the development of a groundbreaking psychological therapy. In the 1950s Ellis conceived Rational Emotive Behaviour Therapy (REBT), then called Rational Therapy (RT). Relating his experience in the park to REBT, Ellis said that

> I prepared myself philosophically, even then, by seeing that nobody took out a stiletto and cut my balls off, nobody vomited and ran away, nobody called the cops...I used techniques I later developed into Rational Emotive Behavior Therapy on myself by thinking philosophically and differently. Nothing is awful or terrible, it's just a pain in the ass. That's all it is...There's no horror in being rejected.
>
> (Ellis, 2006)

Reflect on your experiences working with performers – athletes, artists, businesspeople, or anybody toiling in environments characterised by the requirement for 'performance' (which is most environments). Perhaps you are, as we all are in some capacity, a performer yourself. Swap Ellis sitting on a bench in a park, with an athlete on a bench waiting to come onto the field of play. Swap Ellis for a coach about to give a pre-game speech, a teacher about to take their first class, or a prospective employee about to walk into an interview for that job they have always dreamed about. The performer may succeed, or they may not. If they do not, nobody will die, it won't be awful, there is no true horror in failure. If they succeed, it will not make them more valuable as a person. This is simple truth. This is not intended to make success and failure in sport seem insignificant, trivial, or benign. Failure can lead to intensely unpleasant emotions that can both crush and inspire motivation.

Some may suggest that failure is not bad at all, and is merely 'feedback' about how to improve. The author of this book would prefer to call a spade 'a spade'. Regardless of whether an individual is able to reappraise failure as 'feedback', it is self-evident that failure (i.e., lack of success, not meeting an intended goal) is adverse, and performers had better learn to cope with failure lest they capitulate to the inevitable setbacks that beset the road to development and eventual fulfilment of potential. But when we treat failure as an existentially relevant occurrence that defines who we are as human beings, we inappropriately inflate and aggrandise the importance of success (and/or of avoiding failure), at all costs. Thus, it is no surprise that in my work I meet performers who have paid the price for their extreme and rigid pursuit of success, and/or avoidance of failure; a price paid with their mental and physical health, social and familial utility, and their identity. That is, sporting success is often transacted against health and wellbeing. Of course, for any performer in any domain, failure is just one adversity they will face in their careers and lives. Goal pursuit is usually plagued by rejection, illness, injury, unfairness, poor treatment by others, and the innate human insufficiencies that underpin our fallibility, our humanness. In addition, performers face arbitrary suffering on account of them simply *being*. We are limited as human beings. Thus, we will often fall short of our ideals, and we will often suffer.

Given the unavoidable adversity that decorates the road to goal attainment, this book has essentially one basic guiding principle: *do not make things worse*. To elaborate, do not think, act, and feel in ways that turn adversity into catastrophe. Don't think, act, and feel in ways that facilitate self-destruction and that self-sabotage goal pursuit. Of course, facing adversity may generate unpleasant and unwanted emotion, but don't unnecessarily and foolishly propagate dysfunctional and maladaptive emotions. Things can get bad, really bad. And we have the capacity to make things worse, much worse. So, this book is underpinned, first, by the philosophy of not making things worse by how we think, act, and feel. *Only then* can you try to make things better. This is done by thinking, acting, and feeling in ways that are constructive for goal attainment. *Constructive* does not mean *positive* in valence. This book is not about positive thinking or optimism. Rather, this book is about helping performers to deal with the world as it is, rather than how they would like it to be. Therefore, and crucially, by learning to *not make things worse*, we can *make things better*. Of course, not making things worse and making things better are potentially interrelated or interacting ideas, but they are definitionally different. In this book, I certainly construe REBT as a remedial approach to helping performers deal with adversity, but I also, *and equally*, present REBT as a proactive approach to helping performers fulfil their potential.

What I offer in this book is a flexible approach to emotion management that underpins the pursuit and fulfilment of human potential.

Why REBT for me?

I began my practice as a sport and exercise psychologist working within a non-league soccer club in the United Kingdom. Alongside helping players to deal with the vicissitudes of soccer at this level, the role also involved fetching soccer balls of the roof of the stand, and running down the street to fetch balls that were launched over the stand, by misfiring players. All in a day's work (!). However varied the role was, it was possible to spend significant one-to-one time with players and typically work would start about two hours before training, during training with injured players, and post-training for an hour. This was important because as a neophyte practitioner I was exposed to the complex and idiosyncratic nature of one-to-one work. For many players, I was able to apply psychological skills training (PST) using techniques mainly from the canon of psychological skills (Andersen, 2009). I was surprised at how effective PST work was with players – this was my first role as a sport and exercise psychologist, and I was enthralled by witnessing theory to practice.

As a side note, there is a move in sport and exercise psychology away from PST – we are being encouraged to 'move beyond' the canon, for reasons that are unclear, but are in part no doubt powered by those with a vested interest in seeing the diminishment of PST. I believe that we should not be so quick to abandon PST, and should look to move forward *with* PST, developing new ways of working with the changing population. Those who are having problems with their usage of PST in their practice should look first to the user (themselves!). The ideas nested within PST are incredibly deep. Should we move beyond imagery, the almost miraculous ability to simulate (imagine) the future (which as a form of prediction formulation will have helped our early ancestors to minimise and escape from predation; e.g., Mobbs et al., 2015)? There is a danger that because PST has become so ubiquitous, we forget the depth of the elements that constitute the canon. We should also not ignore the evidence base for the elements of the canon, underpinned by cognitive behavioural theory that exists within and outside of sport and exercise literature. Indeed, in 2021 *The Guardian* ran a piece about what experts suggest sport psychology can teach people about stress and mental health (Usborne, 2021). What did these experts tell us about ways of dealing with pressure? Use effective goal setting, apply positive self-talk, visualise success, come to terms of success and failure, regulate arousal, solve problems, celebrate triumphs, and take time to focus on the task. Sounds like PST to me.

Returning to my case of working as a neophyte practitioner at the non-league football club, there were some issues with my work. First, players would often return with the same issues time and time again – my interventions were superficial and short term. Second, and related to the first point, I was not providing deep solutions to player issues. Not all issues require deep solutions, but some issues do, and I wasn't doing a good job at extracting the roots of their issues. Thus, I could not help them to find the proper solutions. Third, I didn't know what to do with complex existential utterances such as "I'm just a complete loser", and "I must succeed". I could disagree with the former utterance, on the basis of its negativity, but that didn't seem to cut it, and who am I to disagree with them in the first place? With the latter, it was hard for me, at that point, to see why this belief was an issue for the athlete. I had grown up with the same belief concerning sport, and it made total sense to me that an athlete would tell themselves "I must succeed" with great utility. It was surprising to me that an explicit demand to succeed seemed to be causing some issues with the players I worked with. So, I did some research about these demanding utterances and found deep tomes of information about REBT, irrational beliefs, and Albert Ellis. I purchased Ellis and Dryden's 1997 *The Practice of Rational Emotive Behavior Therapy* book and devoured it. I took elements of REBT and started to apply it with players at the club.

My conversations with players became sufficiently deep, as I unlocked beliefs within them that provided solutions to current performance issues. I applied the ABCs (as I understood them at that point) to understand player issues, I began to recognise irrational vs. rational beliefs, and started to become more confident in having disputational conversations. I worked with issues such as performing under pressure (mostly anxiety), anger/aggression (inwards and outwards), self-confidence (a lot!), conflict, injury, retirement, rejection (deselection, and going out on loan), and career transition (some players had jobs too!). All in a single season. All in my first year as a practitioner.

What is important about this rather indulgent tangent is that my introduction to and early usage of REBT was not motivated by the desire to be different or to exploit a marginalised approach to psychology. I was not motivated to piggyback onto a growing trend (the idea that REBT is 'trendy' is genuinely hilarious) or buck a trend in any way. It was pure utilitarianism.

It worked, so I continued to use it and develop my understanding and competence within it. Back then, I didn't understand just how deep and rich REBT was, and I was unaware of how it would influence my work and practice in the years that came.

I do not present REBT as the only way, or as a panacea, for practice, and my role is not to convince you the reader to use REBT, but more sincerely to set out the framework, the evidence base, and utility of REBT in sport and performance for practitioners as comprehensively and lucidly as I can. REBT is not the only approach I use, nonetheless, whether it is a strategy for self-care, a one-to-one approach to helping athletes, or a psychoeducational framework to deliver with coaches, both REBT theory and practice have afforded me a meaningful and comprehensive approach to understanding, explaining, encouraging, and propagating the fulfilment of human potential.

Why should practitioners be interested in a book about REBT?

There are of course many reasons why you should be interested in REBT, but here are three big ones.

1. REBT is foundational to the family of therapies that we know as cognitive behavioural therapies (CBTs). If there is no CBT, then there is no PST. PST is at its core a cognitive-behavioural endeavour, and each element in the canon of psychological skills has its roots in CBTs. So, perhaps you are interested in the foundational ideas that inspired the dominant approaches to sport and performance psychology. If you are, then REBT will be right up your street. (*Wait. I thought the use of psychotherapy in sport was new?! No not quite.*)
2. REBT did not just emerge as a psychotherapy out of the ether, rather, it is steeped in ancient philosophy, and contemporary science. Many of the popular movements in psychology and self-help in recent years, such as Stoicism, and the many books that encourage us to say 'f**k it', have clear links to REBT, even if these links are not made explicit in the works. I call this activity 'cognitive-behavioural intellectualism' in which authors, usually intellectual types, write popular science books that communicate CBT ideas in a digestible manner. So, if you are interested in philosophy, contemporary psychological science, and get a kick from the many CBT-based self-help books on the market, you will probably be interested in REBT.
3. The study and application of REBT in sport is growing a lot. In a recent systematic review of the area by Anna Jordana and colleagues (2020), it was apparent that from 1985 to 2013, little was done in the area. There were a handful of works looking at REBT in sport. Then, from 2013, the work grows. Between 2016 and 2020, 29 studies emerged that examined the use of REBT with athletes. This is in addition to the many studies that examined REBT theory, rather than practice, within athlete populations.

REBT is the toolkit

REBT is not a 'technique' or 'tool' for your 'toolkit'. Rather REBT is an approach to practice, that underpins a vast variety of tools and techniques. In other words, REBT *is* the toolkit, not just a tool. As I will show in this book, REBT can inform a panoply of cognitive-behaviourally derived techniques, such as PST. One maxim that has helped me over the years, and one that I think about more and more as sport psychology becomes flooded by new theories and perspectives, is:

> Beware the person with one gun, for they know how to use it.

What if I learn to use REBT as well as possible, understanding its theoretical and practical depth and breadth? What if I arrive at the scene with only my REBT toolkit? What limits does that place on my work? What opportunities does that give me? My focus has been on deepening my REBT learning and practical competence so that I can use REBT very specifically when I need to, but also flexibly when I need to. I can hold REBT lightly if the context and case require me to, but can also hold REBT tightly if the context and case require me to. What this (almost) singular focus has cost me is the ability to use competently the many (probably hundreds) of alternative approaches to sport psychology. But I wonder, if one trains in everything, how can one make decisions on a case? For, if I were to train in every approach to sport psychology, I think I would suffer from decision-making inertia in the moment, and decision-making reinvestment after the fact. So my approach, which I am not saying is the 'right' approach, is to learn as much about REBT as I can in order to bolster my toolkit as much as possible. If I discover limits to REBT, then I can mitigate them by discovering and becoming competent in alternative approaches.

In this book, I do not latch on to popular themes, all-encompassing meta-theory, or cheesy taglines to superficially garner popular support. I do not use marketing rhetoric or sensationalism to force people to be interested in my ideas, or the ideas of other REBT thinkers, theorists, and practitioners. I do not present my ideas as panaceas or 'game-changers'. I realise that whilst REBT is a broad and encompassing toolkit, it may not contain all the tools we need as practitioners. REBT is not perfect. I openly submit my ideas as contemporary extensions, representations, and articulations, of what has gone before me. I do not claim to be novel or avant-garde. I am simply presenting what I have been using in my practice, which is informed by strong ideas belonging to many influential thinkers. I try to stick to theory as closely as I can, drifting away from theory only when evidence indicates to do so, and where I suggest advancements in theory. I cite the sources I use as often as possible, and whilst there is a preponderance of academic sources, I utilise a variety of media where necessary. I do not try to swallow the entirety of sport psychology within REBT, but try to be as specific as I can when writing about the breadth and depth of REBT.

We are great cherry pickers in sport psychology. We tend to lift ideas from theories outside of sport, legitimately and illegitimately, making use of what works and abandoning what does not. Where we go wrong is when we take theory, stick a new label on it to make it more appealing to a performance audience, and forget where and how the theory originated. It is for this reason in part why Ellis and Beck are rarely cited when PST is discussed, and why it often seems like new theories are just old theories renamed. Theoretical real estate takes prominence over theoretical parsimony and utility. It seems that, in sport psychology, theory and research is sometimes valued on the basis of its memetic qualities, rather than its evidence base and/or practical utility. In this book I make a utilitarian plea to dive deeper into extant theories, specifically REBT, to excavate what can be applied rather than developing new theory for the sake of developing new theory.

Did Ellis not cherry pick from Stoicism and other systems? Yes, for sure. So let us not confound this conceptual selectivity by cherry picking from REBT. Let us fully grasp what REBT has to offer, bringing with us its ancient provenance, making the most of the deep and wide writings of Ellis and those who followed and advanced his works. When I started to explore REBT in performance settings, it was tempting to, instead of making use of what was already within REBT, develop an 'REBT theory for performance', or something like that. But the more I immersed myself into REBT theory and practice, the more I realised that whilst REBT for sure needs to be adapted to fit its surroundings, the fundamental theory of REBT is already suitable for performance settings (and perhaps *any* setting). As I and others complete more research work concerning REBT, then undoubtedly its strengths and limitations will be revealed, and the future of REBT in performance settings might require some theoretical refinement, but not before we have fully examined REBT as it stands, a goal that has not yet been reached. Why not fully explore what is there first, and then figure out what to change second?

Why is REBT especially suitable for sport settings?

> Stress is ubiquitous in human life.
>
> (Turner, 2013)

Stressors pervade all sport and performance settings. Sport, with its mental and physical dangers, appears to be especially conducive to stress. Sport is in part defined by its uncertainty, its requirement for effort, and its capacity to make or unmake one's esteem (Meijen et al., 2020); anybody truly invested in sport risks their ego. Athletes and those working to support athletes, face adversities such as failure, loss, rejection, disapproval, unfair treatment (maltreatment), disrespect, arbitrary suffering and pain, illness, injury, meeting self and others' expectations, the challenge of repeating success, and ultimately, retirement (Turner et al., 2022a); amongst the myriad adversity that besets any human being in life. We are limited and fallible creatures.

Many environments contain these aforementioned demands of course, but not many jobs take on their recruits at age 9, like soccer does, for example. Sport has the additional paradoxical feature that it is 'played' and represents an important pastime, but when it becomes a job, it often does not function or feel like play. In my years working within sport, it never ceases to amaze me just how important sport is to people, often serving as an alter on which many other worthwhile pursuits are sacrificed. The sacrifices made in pursuit of sporting success serve to importantise and aggrandise sport. Bill Shankly said that, "Some people think football is a matter of life and death. I don't like that attitude. I can assure them it is much more serious than that". He also said, "For a player to be good enough to play for Liverpool, he must be prepared to run through a brick wall for me then come out fighting on the other side" and "If you are first you are first. If you are second, you are nothing". I do not mean to belittle or denigrate Shankly, or indeed sport per se; I am merely pointing out the extreme attitudes that pervade sport. I will talk more about how the language of sport is especially revealing and relevant to REBT later in this book, but suffice to say, sport is especially accepting of inappropriate, extreme, and grandiose viewpoints.

I should say something here about my position on sport and the athletic pursuit, because I am sometimes accused of minimising the importance of sport and meaningfulness of an athletic career. As I have said before (Turner, 2020b), I, alongside many, truly appreciate what athletes sacrifice to the pursuit of excellence, in the name of entertainment, patriotism, and the advancement of human potential. I know that many athletes embody the most virtuous of human ideals – voluntarily taking on the unknown in the spirit of human competition, and bearing the heavy burden of the hopes and expectations of their communities (be it local, or national). I know that tirelessly pursuing goals can sometimes consume athletes, and that their passion for constant improvement can sometimes lead to them giving too much of themselves to sport, at the expense of their wellbeing, and at the cost of other potentially worthwhile pursuits (even relationship goals). I also know that, just like all of us, they are not perfect or invincible, and therefore I recognise that they may be suffering, as many of us are. I do not apply REBT to reduce the importance of sport or question the value of athletic pursuit. I apply REBT to help athletes to gain some perspective on what it is to be an athlete, and to take the opportunity to realign or reaffirm their vision of who they are and who they want to become.

> We had better accept what is going on (WIGO) in the world as "reality," even when we don't like it and are trying to change it.
>
> (Ellis, 1996a, p. 26)

Against the sporting backdrop of stress, adversity, and aggrandisement, an approach to psychology that promotes health and function, but is accepting and acknowledging of the demanding and often adverse nature of sport, is valuable. Through REBT, we treat the world as it is, not how we would like it to be. REBT is not for fantasists or blind optimists. In REBT we assume (correctly and self-evidently) that life is difficult and demanding, and that human beings are limited and thus will experience suffering, but have the capacity to cope with life's challenges through volitional choice. William James (considered the father of American psychology) said, "the greatest weapon against stress is our ability to choose one thought over another" and I agree. We have the choice to believe one thing over another, after first engaging critically in what we believe as beings capable of scientific thought and metacognition (thinking about thinking). This idea of thinking about thinking is vital for critical thought, and critical engagement with our environment, and is obviously important in sport. It is also fundamental to the practice of REBT.

So, REBT is especially applicable in sport because it recognises that sport is adverse, and then works to enhance adaptive function under such stressful circumstances. It points the finger *inward* first with regard to emotional control, and *outward* second (or not at all depending on the circumstances). What can *I* do to manage my emotions? *Then*, how could the environment be enhanced in order to help me manage my emotions? If I can manage my thoughts, my emotions, my behaviours, then I might be able to attain some of my goals and forthrightly move towards the fulfilment of my potential.

Why athletes like REBT

Obviously, not all athletes will like REBT (I don't even like it sometimes!). You can please some of the people all of the time, you can please all of the people some of the time, but you can't please all of the people all of the time (attributed to 15th-century monk, John Lydgate). But many of the athletes I have worked with get numerous benefits from REBT, and/or enjoy it, because REBT has its basis in the use of logic and is grounded in reality (as opposed to fantasy). As I have intimated already, athletes feel the full force of reality. They experience physical and emotional suffering. Their mistakes are often felt physically, and the effort they expend has physical consequences, for example, the pain of exhaustion, and on the flip side, muscular and skill development as they progress. In REBT we do not spend time wishing for the world to be different, so that we can feel less pain. Instead, we help athletes to grapple with the world as it is, rather than how it 'should' be, and use inalienable truths to help set them on the straight and narrow. We help athletes to develop reality-based life philosophies, rather than fictional performance narratives. We don't offer delusions. We tether the athlete to the reality they are familiar with, in which negative emotion is inescapable, inevitable, anticipated, and normal, as well as being potentially advantageous, often serving important functions in the pursuit of a meaningful life.

So, athletes like REBT because of its no-nonsense and reality-based approach to the world, and its clearly defined ideas. Whilst REBT has its jargon at a theoretical level, it minimises abstraction as much as possible, and this jargon need not be a part of the work done with athletes – jargon doesn't really serve any purpose in the applied domain. Some abstraction is necessary in order to articulate internal mental states. We could not have psychotherapy if we didn't abstract out our psychological processes into language shared commonly. When we say 'thought' we probably have a broad shared understanding of what we are referring to. But in REBT we try to rest on low abstraction. 'Demands' is about demands – nothing hidden. REBT is very clear and consistent because of its low abstraction, even if it can be a little jargonised in parts. Rationality is defined specifically (but of course, imperfectly). And whilst 'ABC' is simple and clearly abstract, it is one of the most powerful ideas a client can use for effective self-management. We abstract as much as is necessary and no more. This is why the components of REBT theory can be tested, and why the ideas of REBT have continued to propagate. We can train people in REBT because we can break it down clearly and precisely. You can't do this with highly abstract ideas, because of their slippery definitions, aloof rationalisations, their stringing together of disparate constructs – their *over* abstraction. REBT is high-definition and high-resolution, not woolly and non-specific.

Athletes, coaches, and performance directors are also gravitating towards REBT because there is a (seemingly recent) realisation that sport is in fact *not* life or death (for the most part, in most sports) and that sacrificing everything in pursuit of something shiny, or for the promise of happiness, might not be the best approach to life. Some athletes are suffering the mental and physical health consequences of a life defined by the pursuit of sporting excellence. This idea of winning not being everything and athletes (and human beings at large) not being totally defined by their performance is not new. It feels new because new voices are articulating these ideas from new places and perspectives, which is great. But the Stoic philosophers and teachers told us quite clearly about what we should and should not aim for, and Albert Ellis communicated as directly as he could the dangers of applying extreme rigid rules and ideas to our goal pursuits, and to self-definition on the basis of external markers. Since 2013, I have been studying and promoting a rational approach to sport, culminating most notably in the athlete credo (Turner, 2016a), which sets out a more reasoned way for an athlete to view sport – details of which can be found later in this book. Perhaps, as practitioners, we can use this book, amongst other resources, to introduce rational principles into the organisations we work within, aiding athletes, the systems they operate within, and the people who support them.

Therapy?

REBT delivered in sport and performance environments has been called 'Smarter Thinking' (Turner, 2014) and/or REB Coaching (REBC; Breitmeyer & Turner, 2018). This is done in part to reduce the clinical connotations associated with 'therapy'. When I am engaging athletes, or anybody involved in sport, in REBT, I am not doing therapy. I am trained in psychotherapies as a sport and exercise psychologist, but I am not clinically trained. I am using a therapeutic framework to aid athletes as they deal with the ubiquitous vicissitudes and adversity of sport and life. I, as a practitioner, should not shy away from this. Training in psychotherapies, like REBT, furnishes me with incredibly useful frameworks and techniques that can help athletes non-clinically and proactively, not just remedially.

The structure of this book

In the book you are reading, I go hard and heavy on REBT theory in the early parts of the book. I start by outlining what REBT is and cover the work that has been done in sport to date (Chapter 1), before moving on to the core technical components of REBT. This includes the underpinning framework of REBT (Chapters 2 and 3), detailed content around each aspect of the framework (Chapters 5–13), and the key practitioner-client factors to consider for successful REBT (Chapter 4). Within these chapters I also cover assessment and intervention details, but the key intervention content appears when we get to disputation and effective new beliefs (Chapters 12 and 13). Sport and performance settings are unlike many of the environments in which REBT is usually (clinically) applied. Therefore, as I go, I include professional practice guidance for the use of REBT in sport and performance settings.

...and finally

REBT is not insular or niche, and it relates to and draws upon a gamut of ancient philosophies, and psychological theory. Fittingly then, I borrow many ideas in the present book, those chiefly of Albert Ellis, Windy Dryden, Raymond DiGiuseppe, Richard Bennett, Richard Lazarus, James Gross, Michael Bernard, Paul Dubois, Epictetus, Marcus Aurelius, Seneca, Donald Robertson, Joseph Campbell, Mark B. Andersen. But most importantly, I borrow the ideas of the many clients I have worked with; athletes, coaches, performance directors, sport scientists, physiotherapists, medics, parents, and any and all of those I have worked alongside in the day-to-day pursuit of performance excellence – chief of which is Dr. Andrew Wood, who if not for uncontrollable and desperately unfortunate events, would have been my co-author on this book. You will hear echoes of their voices in this book, but you will not read about specific athletes with whom I have worked. I use applied examples throughout this book as illustrations of REBT in use, but I never name or intimate individuals I worked with, and thus, any client names in this book are pseudonyms.

I end this introduction with some words from Paul Dubois. In many ways, alongside Magda Arnold and Karen Horney, Dubois is the progenitor of Ellis (Robertson, 2019b), and whilst his ideas may not be what we would consider contemporary, they offer some utility to the modern practitioner. Here, Dubois speaks of emotional responsibility, education, human fallibility, and the genesis of good and bad ideas – all themes that underpin the current book.

> Yes, we can combat to a certain degree the effects of fatal heredity and escape the noxious influence of exterior agencies. We shall accomplish this by education of ourselves. I have said, without hesitation, the education of ourselves because I esteem this personal culture to be the

most efficacious. But it is necessary to understand it. More or less imperfect from birth, we, mentally, cannot be our own educator in the true sense of the word. It is by intercourse with our kind, by the ideas which they suggest to us, that we can correct our faults and cultivate our good qualities. We have, it is true, the sensation of originating our thoughts, of ourselves deciding the regulating of our conduct. But take care! The mental capital which we attribute to ourselves, from which we draw interest, comes to us from others, from the education which we have received, not only from voluntary education, that of the family, that of the school, that of the priest, but the insensible education which is given by the world and by life. It is sometimes good, sometimes bad, and it is upon this foundation of borrowed ideas that all the scaffolding of our thoughts and our sentiments is built.

(Dubois, 1906, pp. 16–18)

CHAPTER 1
Rational Emotive Behaviour Therapy

A great flood looms.

DOI: 10.4324/9781003200437-2

Nothing is sacred – including RE[B]T!

(Albert Ellis, 1979)

In this chapter I aim to do two things. First, I will introduce Rational Emotive Behaviour Therapy (REBT) to the reader. Second, I will cover the work that has been done to explore REBT practice and theory in the field of sport. I do this to create a foundation and an evidence base from which I can launch into deeper theory and more detailed practical facets.

WHAT IS RATIONAL EMOTIVE BEHAVIOUR THERAPY (REBT)?

In detailing what Rational Emotive Behaviour Therapy (REBT) is, and what REBT is not, there is a lot to unpack. REBT is theoretically and technically rich, and its roots stretch deep into ancient philosophy. I will do my best here to explicate REBT theory as clearly as I can in this first chapter, but of course, I encourage readers to digest Albert Ellis' original works for a truly deep understanding of REBT. What follows in this chapter is a concise introduction to REBT.

REBT was developed by Albert Ellis in the 1950s (it was called RT, then RET, now REBT; Ellis, 1995) and represents the first of the cognitive behavioural therapies (CBTs). REBT is a second-wave CBT that holds a firm place within the CBT family of psychotherapies, predicated on the blending of cognitive- and behaviour-based elements (Bennett & Oliver, 2019). The central goal of REBT is to help clients to improve their functioning by means of introspective identification and direct challenging of the maladaptive beliefs that interfere with their ability to pursue and fulfil their goals (Caserta et al., 2010). In other words, in REBT we help clients to first understand their self-limiting beliefs, and to then address these beliefs forthrightly. Ellis (1988) expressed three main tenets of REBT; "being aware of your dysfunctional and Irrational Beliefs, cognitively-emotionally-behaviorally Disputing them, and arriving at Effective New Philosophies or Rational Coping Philosophies" (p. 10). The same goals could characterise other CBTs, but REBT is distinct from other CBTs (such as cognitive therapy, CT; Beck, 1976, and acceptance and commitment therapy, ACT; Hayes et al., 2013), due to its emphasis on rational (flexible, non-extreme, and logical) and irrational (rigid, extreme, and illogical) beliefs as key cognitive mediators between a situation (or inferences about a situation) and affective and behavioural reactivity (see Turner et al., 2020a for a comparison of CBTs as applied in sport).

It is worth noting at this point, that whilst I clearly focus my attention on REBT for the purposes of the current book, I do not bestow upon REBT any special plaudits. Indeed, comparison studies reveal REBT to be *as effective as* other CBTs (Stefan et al., 2019), and there is little evidence that REBT is superior to other CBTs, but there is clear evidence that REBT is superior to placebo or no treatment controls (e.g., David et al., 2018; Engels et al., 1993). Practitioners need to base their use of any approach on the scientific evidence for that approach within the presenting context. The context within which this book places the reader, is that of a performance sport context, in which the effectiveness of REBT has been suitably demonstrated (I will cover some evidence later in this chapter). Also, whilst REBT is distinguished from other CBTs owing to its specific focus on irrational and rational beliefs, the practice of REBT does not reflect a blinkered obsession with beliefs and on the contrary can incorporate many cognitive, emotive, and behavioural methods found in other CBTs.

The primary form of REBT is known as 'specific', 'preferential', or 'elegant' REBT, in which the client is enabled to weaken their rigid and extreme beliefs and develop and strengthen flexible and non-extreme beliefs. The secondary form of REBT is known as 'general' or 'inelegant' REBT, in which a large variety of cognitive, emotive, and behavioural techniques are applied, and in which belief change is not necessarily the main focus (see Dryden & David, 2008, for a full discussion). Thus, general (inelegant) REBT includes a variety of cognitive-emotive-behavioural methods, not just disputation of irrational beliefs, and as such is synonymous with a broad understanding of what CBT is and does (Ellis, 1977). Indeed, in 1995 Arnold Lazarus pointed out that "the theoretical underpinnings of RE[B]T are so broadly eclectic and so pliable that an extremely wide range of methods and principles can be included. REBT has been described as humanistic, behavioral, insight-oriented, and many things besides" (Lazarus, 1995, p. 99).

Where REBT becomes more distinct from CBT per se is in its specific (elegant) form, where the irrational, deep-seated fundamental, beliefs become more of the focus, alongside a variety of cognitive-emotive-behavioural methods (Ellis, 1977). In other words, general REBT offers a broad cognitive-emotive-behavioural approach which *does not necessarily* address the deep-seated fundamental irrational beliefs, whilst specific REBT can still offer a broad cognitive-emotive-behavioural approach, but it *does necessarily* address the deep-seated fundamental irrational beliefs. So, specific REBT "especially (but never solely) stresses the achievement of a profound cognitive or philosophic change in clients' basic assumptions, especially their absolutistic demanding, musterbatory, irrational ways of viewing themselves, others, and the world" (Ellis, 1977, p. 74). Whilst the main thrust of the current book is specific, elegant, REBT, I recognise and incorporate general, inelegant, REBT in major aspects of this book, because as Ellis recognised himself in 1977, REBT is frequently done inelegantly (i.e., general REBT) and REBT should not be defined monolithically.

REBT's distinctiveness is also achieved by its inclusion of a binary theory of emotional distress (BTED; e.g., Ellis, 1994), in which not all negative (valenced) emotions are considered unhealthy or targets for change (DiGiuseppe et al., 2014). In brief, in the BTED, in response to adversity rational beliefs beget healthy negative emotions (HNEs; e.g., concern [healthy anxiety], sadness, healthy anger), whereas irrational beliefs beget unhealthy negative emotions (UNEs; e.g., anxiety [unhealthy anxiety], depression, unhealthy anger: Dryden, 2008, Ellis, 1994). HNEs are functional and adaptive for goal attainment, and UNEs are dysfunctional and maladaptive (for a fuller critical discussion, see Turner et al., 2018a, 2019a). Therefore, REBT does not explicitly aim to foster positive (valenced) emotion and does not accept mere symptom removal (Ellis, 1977), but works towards healthy emotions and away from unhealthy emotions, more interested in function than valence, *getting* better rather than just *feeling* better (Ellis, 2001).

Unlike CBTs that emerged at a similar time to REBT, such as Beck's (1976) cognitive therapy (CT), REBT is more explicitly informed by ancient philosophy, most notably Ancient Stoicism. The Stoic roots of REBT lay within its emphasis on rationality and reason, on the notion that some things in our world are controllable, and some things are not, and on the cognitively mediated aetiology of emotion and behaviour. The maxim credited to Epictetus "it is not the event that disturbs people, it is the view they take of the event" is central to REBT, and other CBTs, and was repeatedly cited by Ellis in his works. Put simply, in REBT it is posited that our beliefs are central to our emotions and behaviours, and that one can choose to adopt rational beliefs, rather than irrational beliefs, in order to experience HNEs in the face of adversity, rather than UNEs.

Stoic roots and BTED notwithstanding, clearly REBT is most different to other CBTs due to its emphasis on rational and irrational beliefs. There are four core rational beliefs and four core irrational beliefs. Rational beliefs comprise a primary belief known as 'preferences', and three secondary beliefs known as frustration tolerance (FT), anti-awfulizing, and unconditional self/other/world acceptance (USA/UOA/UWA). Irrational beliefs comprise a primary belief known as 'demandingness', and three secondary beliefs known as frustration intolerance (FI), awfulizing, and depreciation (or global evaluation; GE). The veracity of the primary and secondary structure (i.e., REBT-I Model; DiLorenzo et al., 2007) of irrational beliefs has been evidenced in athletes, indicating that the secondary beliefs mediate between the primary beliefs and psychological distress and as such are more proximal to psychological distress (Turner et al., 2019b). In other words, whilst demandingness appears to be part of a primary appraisal process, awfulizing, FI, and depreciation appear to be part of a secondary appraisal process (e.g., David et al., 2002) and as such may be more closely linked to specific emotional outcomes.

Rational beliefs are flexible, non-extreme, logical, and functional, and in contrast, irrational beliefs are rigid, extreme, illogical, and dysfunctional. Unsurprisingly then, given that irrational beliefs are nonsensical and underpin UNEs, one of the chief aims of REBT is to help clients undermine and weaken irrational beliefs, and develop and strengthen rational beliefs, which are sensical and underpin HNEs. REBT is predicated on the axioms that (a) cognitions can be identified and measured, (b) cognitions play a central role in psychological functioning, (c) irrational cognitions can be weakened in favour of rational cognitions, and (d) this irrational-rational transition abets functional emotional, cognitive, and behavioural responses in keeping with personal goals (David et al., 2010a).

The core concepts of REBT, that of rational and irrational beliefs, the BTED, and cognitive mediation, are captured and abstracted within the GABCDE framework (or REBT model), illustrated in Figure 1.1. The GABCDE framework portrays the overarching theory of REBT, illustrates the aetiology of wellbeing and illbeing, and guides client assessment and intervention work. It presents important steps for the practitioner-client work that if not approached properly can undercut the effectiveness of the work. It is also used as a way to teach clients about the relationships between events (and inferences about events), their beliefs, and their emotional and behavioural experiences. If clients present with irrational beliefs (iBs) that, in response to adverse events (A), manifest to block or impede their goals (G), they are likely to experience unhealthy negative emotions (UNEs) as a consequence (C). Thus, clients are encouraged to rigorously dispute (D) and challenge these irrational beliefs (iBs), and then rational beliefs (rBs) are encouraged, challenged, and reinforced (E) to help the client experience healthy emotions and adaptive behaviours (HNEs). The GABCDE framework proposes that irrational beliefs underpin emotional disturbance, and that weakening irrational beliefs and strengthening more adaptive rational beliefs better enables individuals to reach their goals and to live more rewarding lives (Browne et al., 2010).

Importantly, whilst irrational beliefs are at the centre of REBT theory and practice, it is of course recognised that adverse events are important for emotional responding; $A \times B = C$ (Dryden, 2012a; Ellis, 2002a). Indeed, whilst irrational beliefs largely underpin UNEs at C, "REBT theorists are careful to avoid saying that B causes C" (Dryden, 2012a, p. 39) and

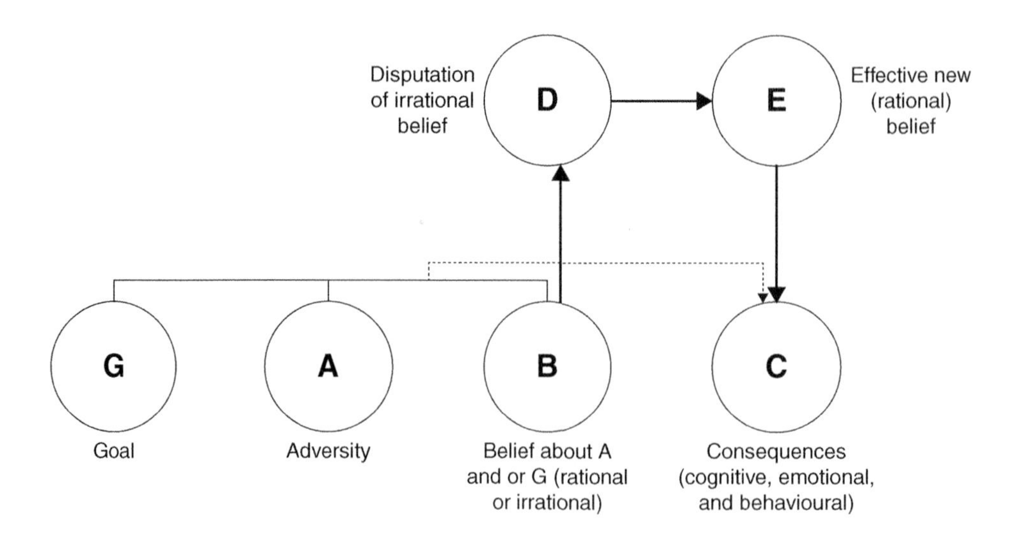

Figure 1.1 The GABCDE framework of REBT.

REBT holds that "cognitions do not by themselves cause emotional disturbance" (Ellis, 1977, p. 75). The present author is not innocent of B–C causation language in his earlier works. It is important to understand that the aetiology of emotion is complex and multifaceted and includes biological and environmental influences. But for REBT, cognition is considered to be the most important source of disturbance in most humans, most of the time (Ellis, 1977).

One of the criticisms of REBT, when compared to cognitive therapy (CT) for instance, is that it is less empirically robust due to its high focus on philosophy and the fact that CT's inception was born out of data-driven research studies (McEachrane, 2009). It is no secret that Ellis was not so much of an active researcher as he was a theorist and psychotherapist, and there is a continuing need to study REBT empirically (Dryden & David, 2008). However, through the 1990s and 2000s various reviews and meta-analyses have been conducted that capture the research that has been undertaken in REBT (David et al., 2018, 2021; Engels et al., 1993; Gonzalez et al., 2004; Jordana et al., 2020; Lyons & Woods, 1991; Trip et al., 2007), both at a practical and theoretical level. Although since the inception of REBT in the 1950s research has grown, particularly from 1980s onwards, we must also consider that Ellis garnered his understanding of the human psyche in large part from his bountiful therapeutic work with clients (e.g., Ellis, 1997). In his 60 years working as a private practitioner, Ellis is estimated to have delivered 180,000 hour-long psychotherapy sessions (Ellis, 2002a). Therefore, the underpinnings of REBT have emerged from philosophy (e.g., Ancient Stoicism), early depth psychology (e.g., Adler, Horney), research data, but importantly from insights gleaned from real work with clients (Matweychuk et al., 2019). So, how can REBT best be captured? I will leave it to Ellis himself to do this:

> When you have discovered some of your unscientific beliefs with which you are creating emotional problems and making yourself act against your own interests, use the scientific method to challenge and dispute them. Ask yourself: Is this belief realistic? Is it opposed to the facts of life? Is this belief logical? Is it contradictory to itself or to my other beliefs? Can I prove this belief? Can I falsify it? Does this belief prove that the universe has a law of deservingness or

undeservingness? If I act well, do I completely deserve a good life, and if I act badly, do I totally deserve a bad existence? If I continue to strongly hold the belief (and to have the feelings and do the acts it often creates), will I perform well, get the results I want to get, and lead a happier life? Or will holding it tend to make me less happy? Persist at using the scientific method of questioning and challenging your irrational Beliefs until you begin to give them up, increase your effectiveness, and enjoy yourself more.

(Albert Ellis, 2019, pp. 43–44)

Studying REBT in sport

The reported use of REBT within sport settings has grown in recent years (see Jordana et al., 2020, for a review). The literature concerning REBT in sport comprises experimental case studies (e.g., Chrysidis et al., 2020), controlled laboratory studies (e.g., Wood et al., 2017) field experiments (e.g., Turner et al., 2019c), practitioner reflections (e.g., Turner, 2019a), hypothetical casework (Turner et al., 2020a) cross-sectional studies (e.g., Chadha et al., 2019), measurement development (e.g., Turner & Allen, 2018), resource development (Turner, 2016a), and explanatory case studies (Turner & Bennett, 2018). One can engage with the strengths, limitations, and implications of the empirical research to date via various review papers (e.g., Turner, 2016b), review chapters (e.g., Turner et al., 2019d), and a systematic review (Jordana et al., 2020). Here, I offer a brief portrayal of the literature to date.

As far as I know, the first article to report the use of REBT with athletes was written by Michael Bernard and was published in 1985. Bernard demonstrated the effectiveness of REBT with Australian Rules Football players, who reported that they were better able to control their thoughts to directly influence performance after receiving REBT education, concentration training, and goal setting (multi-modal; Bernard, 1985). The research examining REBT in sport started with a trickle rather than a flood, as the next article did not emerge until Elko and Ostrow (1991) showed that REBT reduced anxiety and improved performance in a group of gymnasts. Yamauchi and Murakoshi (2001), Larner et al. (2007), and Thomas et al. (2007) continued the REBT in sport research, all reporting positive effects on the management of athlete anxiety. Si and Lee (2008) applied REBT to help an Olympic table tennis athlete to reduce his frustration intolerance (FI) beliefs, finding that the athlete was more able to control frustration, was less perfectionistic, and experienced performance improvements. Marlow (2009) echoed these findings but with a youth ten-pin bowler, finding that REBT enhanced rational beliefs, facilitative emotions, and bowling performance.

In 2013, I began my foray into the examination of REBT in sport settings. In my first study (Turner & Barker, 2013) I found that REBT helped elite youth cricketers reduce their cognitive performance anxiety. I continued this research work by applying Rational Emotive Education (REE; Knaus, 2006) in English soccer academies (Turner et al., 2014, 2015), finding a dose response whereby more REE sessions lead to longer-term reductions in irrational beliefs. Athletes felt that REE helped them to improve their emotional control and performance, but no objective markers of performance were sought. We have since used REE with additional athlete groups (Turner & Davis, 2019; Vertopolous & Turner, 2017; Wood et al., 2018b). Wood et al. (2018b) found that REE with a male blind soccer team led to immediate and maintained reductions in irrational beliefs, increases in facilitative perceptions of performance anxiety, and acute reductions in Systolic Blood Pressure (indicating lower physiological reactivity) measured prior to a penalty shoot-out. Turner and

Davis (2019) and Vertopolous and Turner (2017) incorporated Personal Disclosure Mutual Sharing within the REE intervention, forming Rational Emotive Personal Disclosure Mutual Sharing (REPDMS). Whilst both studies evidenced the positive effects of REE, only Vertopolous and Turner found that REPDMS offered additional effects.

In contrast to the REE studies, much of the research concerning REBT in sport has been done using one-to-one case study work, or via single-case experimental designs (SCED). For example, Cunningham and Turner (2016) found that a three-session REBT intervention reduced self-depreciation beliefs and increased unconditional self-acceptance (USA) beliefs in two of three semi-professional Mixed Martial Arts (MMA) athletes. Wood et al. (2016) used seven one-to-one REBT sessions with a county-level archer who showed long-term (six-month) reductions in irrational beliefs, and increases in self-efficacy, perceptions of control, and archery performance. Wood et al. (2017) also reported the effects of six REBT sessions with a 15-year-old cricketer (batsman), helping the athlete to develop a greater ability to control emotions during challenging moments, an improvement validated by the athlete's father. Deen et al. (2017) used five REBT sessions with five elite Malaysian squash athletes, finding reductions in irrational beliefs and increases in resilient qualities. Five REBT sessions were also used by Wood et al. (2018a) with eight elite Paralympic athletes. Results showed that five of the eight athletes demonstrated reductions in irrational beliefs, matched by enhanced athletic performance, and reductions in resting Systolic Blood Pressure. Wood et al. (2019) also offered a detailed case study of a 42-year-old Paralympic athlete, in which a five-session REBT intervention was met with short-term and maintained reductions in irrational beliefs, enhanced competition concentration and less distraction, and greater emotional control.

Further REBT SCEDs in sport have revealed how REBT is effective in increasing triathletes' self-determined motivation, vitality, and sleep quality (Davis & Turner, 2020), increasing the self-determined motivation and self-efficacy of German American Football athletes (Chrysidis et al., 2020), improving focus under pressure and consistency of performances in a youth tennis athlete (Sille et al., 2020), and reducing social and performance anxiety in golfers who had specific phobias in relation to executing certain golf shots (Turner et al., 2020b). In a further investigation of REBT's effects on self-determined motivation, Wood et al. (2020) presented an idiographic application of one-to-one REBT integrated with Motivational Interviewing (MI; Miller & Rollnick, 2013), with a male archer. MI was used as an identifiable and measurable framework to foster a strong working alliance between the practitioner and client, to increase the athlete's readiness and enhance the effects of REBT. After receiving eight one-to-one REBT sessions, data indicated acute and maintained reductions in irrational beliefs, increases in self-determined motivation, and marked increases in performance.

In a similar study to Turner et al. (2020b), Bowman and Turner (2022) tested an REBT-informed Single-Session Therapy (SST) intervention with five amateur golfers presenting with high golf-specific anxiety. Following Dryden's (2016) framework and guidance for SST, each athlete received one face to face REBT session. Data indicated that all but one athlete reported reduced irrational performance beliefs, golf-specific anxiety, and social anxiety, as well as improvements in their golf performance. Also, in three of these four positively-responding participants, improvements in wellbeing were reported.

In line with the preponderance of one-to-one case study work in the REBT in sport literature, the book *Rational Emotive Behavior Therapy in Sport and Exercise* (Turner & Bennett, 2018) showcased 14 case study chapters reporting the use of REBT across sport and exercise (Outar; O'Connor) settings. Twelve of the chapters report the application of REBT with athletes across a wide range of sports; gymnastics (Huggins), Paralympic soccer (Barker), American football (Breitmeyer & David), MMA (Cunningham), fencing (Vertopoulos), basketball (Artiran), table tennis (Si & Zhang), squash (Deen), rugby union (Morris et al.; Phelps-Naqvi & Katz), tennis (Wood & Woodcock), and karate (Churchman). To discuss each chapter is beyond the scope of the current book, but the range of populations (internationally) and issues covered across the cases reflect the flexibility and applicability of REBT within sport settings.

Of course, it is not only athletes we can work with in sport. Breitmeyer and Turner (2018) present a case study of a Division I West Coast American University basketball coach to help him challenge his irrational beliefs and enhance his rational beliefs. More recently, Maxwell-Keys et al. (2022) applied four one-to-one REBT sessions with elite rugby match officials, a quite specialised and under-investigated population, reporting reductions in irrational beliefs, decreased decision reinvestment, and enhanced match officiating performance (i.e., decision-making and management).

Extant studies have also utilised more didactic and instructive methods to encourage rational beliefs in athletes. Evans et al. (2018) took a between-subjects approach to investigate the use of rational vs. irrational half-time team talks. In an actual soccer match, at half-time team A received a rational team talk (contained the language of rational beliefs), and team B received an irrational team talk (contained the language of irrational beliefs). Results showed that athletes who received the rational team talk reported lower threat appraisal and avoidance goal orientation (more adaptive) concerning their second-half, compared to athletes who received the irrational team talk. In a similar experimental vein, Turner et al. (2019c) examined the effects of rational and irrational self-talk on the pressured putting performance of amateur golfers. Using a repeated-measures (randomised, blind, counterbalanced) design it was found that the golfers' putting accuracy was significantly better when using rational self-talk than when using irrational self-talk.

The applied REBT research will continue to grow as more trainees and post-graduate practitioner-researchers discover REBT and begin to test it in their own practice. In 2023 a special issue in the *Journal of Rational-Emotive and Cognitive-Behavioral Therapy* will bring together studies from across the REBT in sport and performance community. Therefore, our understanding of how REBT can be applied in sport is becoming richer and more nuanced, paving the way for those entering into the field of sport and performance psychology to use REBT in their practice supported by a growing evidence base.

Studying irrational beliefs in sport

The accurate study of irrational beliefs in sport would not be possible without an accurate measure of irrational beliefs for athletes. Therefore, owing to the lack of a suitable psychometric for irrational performance beliefs, we developed the irrational performance beliefs inventory (iPBI; Turner et al., 2018b), and validated a shorter (20-item) version that is perhaps more useful in sport (Turner & Allen, 2018). The iPBI has demonstrated test-retest reliability (Turner et al., 2017), and has been translated into Thai (Chotpitayasunondh & Turner, 2019), German (Chrysidis et al., 2020), Persian (Nejati et al., 2021), and Turkish (Urfa & Asci, 2018). The area of REBT in sport has also yielded bespoke athlete resources such as a Smartphone App (Turner & Wood, 2019a), the athlete rational resilience credo (Turner, 2016a), and an online profiling tool (Turner & Wood, 2019b). Further, in an attempt to capture aspects of the GABCDE framework, we developed the cognitive mediation beliefs questionnaire (CMBQ; Turner et al., 2021) which assesses individuals' proclivity to hold beliefs tantamount to A–C thinking (i.e., emotion is caused only by the situation itself) and B–C thinking (i.e., emotion is caused by what we think about the situation). Early evidence indicates that A–C thinking is associated with poorer emotional outcomes compared to B–C thinking.

Alongside the applied and psychometric work that has been published in this area, there are also a host of papers that concern the testing of REBT theory. Irrational beliefs have been shown to be related to greater threat appraisals (Dixon et al., 2017), greater competitive anxiety and negative affect (Chadha et al., 2019), increased burnout (Turner & Moore, 2016), greater psychological distress (Turner et al., 2019e), greater trait anger (Turner et al., 2019b), and poorer performance under pressure (Mesagno et al., 2020). The extant research in sport also demonstrates that depreciation seems to be particularly pernicious for mental health, with a recent study finding self-depreciation to be significantly positively related to threat and depressive symptoms to a greater extent than the other types of irrational beliefs (Mansell, 2021).

In a recent research paper, we used latent profile analysis (LPA) to identify patterns across irrational beliefs, motivation regulation, and the mental and physical health of student-athletes (Turner et al., 2022b). Data indicated a two-class solution; athletes who report high irrational beliefs, high amotivation, and high controlled motivation regulation (Class 1), and athletes who report low irrational beliefs, low amotivation, and low controlled motivation (Class 2). Importantly, those in Class 1 reported greater anxiety and depression symptoms, and more physical health problems, than those in Class 2. Indeed, data from Turner et al. (2022b), considered alongside applied studies indicating that REBT can increase self-determined motivation, offer some potential conceptual overlap between REBT and self-determination theory (SDT). Practitioners and key stakeholders of athlete wellbeing and performance would be wise to develop and foster a rationally-informed and autonomy-supportive performance environment.

Therefore, whilst irrational beliefs do appear to be an important risk factor for illbeing in athletes, there may be other factors that bolster this association such as motivation regulation (Turner, 2016b). In a recent study of athletes and coaches, Jooste et al. (2022) found that the negative effects of irrational beliefs on mental wellbeing was atemporally mediated by intolerance of uncertainty. Also, Turner et al. (2019e) found that maladaptive schema atemporally mediated the relationship between irrational beliefs and psychological distress in athletes. Chadha et al. (2019) found that indirect relationships between irrational beliefs and outcomes such as competitive anxiety, affect, and the directional interpretations of anxiety, through threat appraisal (and not challenge appraisal). Thus, the negative impact of irrational beliefs upon mental health appears to be exacerbated by various other mental phenomena, such as greater maladaptive schema, intolerance of uncertainty, and threat appraisal, a notion evidenced within and outside of sport (e.g., automatic thoughts: Buschmann et al., 2018; Szentagotai & Freeman, 2007, thought suppression: Szentagotai, 2006).

Summary

It is important to communicate the state of play with REBT research so that readers can understand that (a) REBT is not new, (b) REBT *in sport* is not new, (c) this area is growing and therefore REBT will continue to grow and possibly change beyond the horizon of this book, and (d) there is mounting evidence for REBT theory and practice in sport settings. Are we interested in being evidence-based practitioners? If we are, then are we interested enough to actually engage with the evidence-base? The literature concerning REBT as applied to sport is vibrant and diverse. However, the growth of REBT literature, especially papers that have offered applied developments and innovations, have rendered previous guidelines on how REBT is applied in sport out of date and in need of revision and expansion. Indeed, the earlier works that proposed guidelines for practice were published in 2014 (Turner, 2014; Turner & Barker, 2014a), and since then, numerous papers have helped to refine our practical understanding of how REBT can be used in sport settings. This has included refinements in both technical and procedural aspects of REBT. Therefore, the current book offers a contemporary and detailed account of how REBT can be applied in sport, taking what I have learnt from the emergent research published in the last decade, and from my continual practice of REBT across many performance contexts, with a view to providing a state-of-the-art guide to REBT application in sport and performance settings.

Chapter 2
The GABCDE framework

You, and only you.

DOI: 10.4324/9781003200437-3

> When people have their goals and values (G's) of remaining alive and making themselves happy, and when activating events or activating experiences (A's) block and thwart these goals, they have the choice of making themselves feel healthily or self-helpingly sorry, regretful, frustrated, or disappointed at point C, their emotional consequences; or they can (consciously or unconsciously) choose to make themselves unhealthily or neurotically panicked, depressed, horrified, enraged, self-hating, or self-pitying at C.
>
> (Albert Ellis,1994, p. 17)

This chapter is about the core framework that underpins rational emotive behaviour therapy (REBT) theory and practice. A detailed articulation of the GABCDE framework is necessary if we are to fully explain how REBT is practised, because the framework informs most of what we do in practice (both implicitly and explicitly). Also, this chapter provides the foundation for everything else that follows in this book, since the content of this book is fully aligned with the GABCDE framework. In this chapter I outline the GABCDE framework, cover its Stoic origins, align it with prominent emotion and emotion regulation theory, and detail techniques and strategies that can be used to bring the GABCDE framework to life in practice.

Discovering the GABCDE framework of REBT is like finding a cheat code for a computer game that unlocks all the game levels – it unlocks a way of understanding the human psyche and a way of working as a practitioner. That is, the GABCDE framework (Figure 2.1) describes the aetiology of psychological disturbance, and psychological health, and guides client assessment and intervention work within REBT.

As can be seen in Figure 2.1, G, A, and B coalesce to influence C. In specific (elegant) REBT, D is applied to B, giving rise to E, which influences C. The GABCDE is composed of:

- **G** – Goals
- **A** – Adversity (or Activating Event)

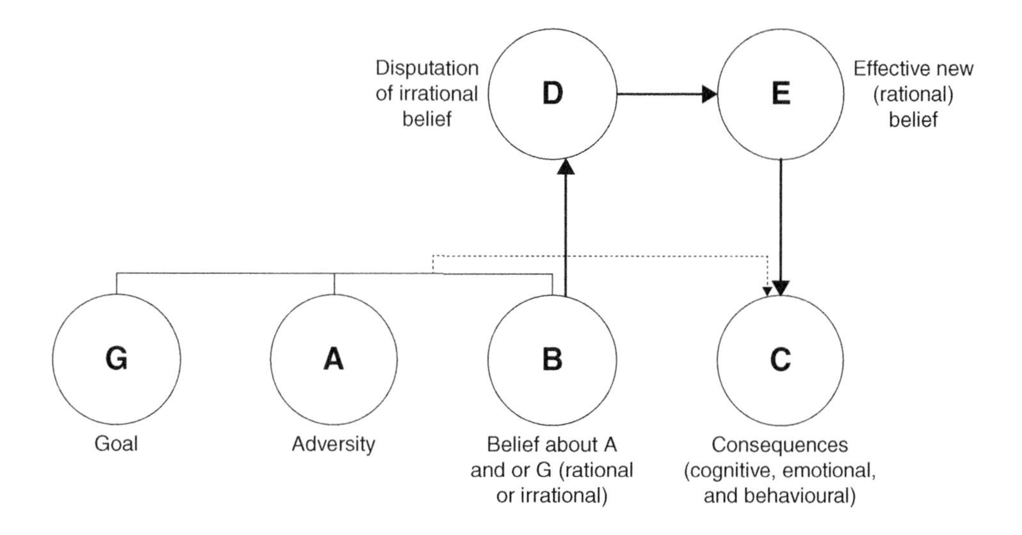

Figure 2.1 Diagrammatic representation of the GABCDE framework. The dotted line between GAB and C reflects pre-REBT and the move to D and E from B reflects the REBT process.

- **B** – Rational and Irrational Beliefs (rBs and iBs)
- **C** – Cognitive, Emotional, and Behavioural Consequences (UNE or HNE)
- **D** – Disputation
- **E** – Effective New Beliefs.

Goals (G)

Preferences and desires to survive, to assuage unnecessary pain, to be fulfilled (fundamental goals; FG), to be satisfied alone, socially, intimately, informationally, educationally, vocationally, economically, and recreationally (primary goals; PG), to be reasonable, logical, and successful in solving and mastering life problems and meaningful tasks, experiencing new and stimulating things, and being stable and secure in work and social life (Ellis, 1994). Importantly, Gs are not 'needs' and rationality should be in the service of these Gs (Nelson-Jones, 2006). Importantly, Gs help contextualise Adversity (A) (Crawford & Ellis, 1989).

Adversity (A)

Unfortunate and undesirable occurrences that interfere with the attainment of Gs (Ellis, 1994; Shea, 2016), and are ubiquitous, copious, and unquantifiable, because As can be concrete or 'real', can be entirely fictional (imagined or fabricated), but are usually inferential, reflecting a perception of something that has happened (or could/will happen). Dryden (2017) defines 'As' as the aspects of the situation that the person focusses on and evaluates. Importantly, by hindering Gs, As help to give rise to negative emotion.

Beliefs (rational and irrational) (B)

Assumptions, attitudes, idea, rules, philosophies, ways of seeing the self, others, and the world, patterns of thinking (schema), that can be rational and/or irrational. Specifically, rational beliefs are "beliefs that are logical, and/or have empirical support, and/or are pragmatic" and irrational beliefs are "beliefs that are illogical, and/or do not have empirical support, and/or are nonpragmatic" (Ellis et al., 2010, p. 3). Rational beliefs comprise a primary belief known as 'preferences', and three secondary beliefs known as frustration tolerance (FT), anti-awfulizing, and unconditional self/other/world acceptance (USA/UOA/UWA). Irrational beliefs comprise a primary belief known as 'demandingness', and three secondary beliefs known as frustration intolerance (FI), awfulizing, and depreciation (or global evaluation; GE). Rational beliefs are usually self-enhancing (Dryden, 2017) and often underpin healthy negative emotions (HNEs) (DiGiuseppe et al., 2014) and thus facilitate (or do not debilitate) goal attainment (Wilson, 2010). In contrast irrational beliefs are usually self-defeating (Dryden, 2017) and often underpin unhealthy negative emotions (UNEs) (DiGiuseppe et al., 2014), and as such are usually unhelpful in pursuing, and inconsistent with accomplishing, one's long-term goals (Maultsby, 1975). As it is the development and enhancement of human functioning that is at the centre of REBT, rational beliefs are encouraged and irrational beliefs are discouraged.

Consequences (C)

The cognitions, emotions, and behaviours arising from the interaction between Gs, As, and Bs. Cs can be healthy (healthy negative emotions; HNEs), whereby they are functional, adaptive, and appropriate, or Cs can be unhealthy (unhealthy negative emotions; UNEs), whereby they are dysfunctional, maladaptive, and inappropriate. Healthy Cs are self-enhancing, leading to constructive behaviour that aids goal (G) attainment, whilst unhealthy Cs are self-defeating, leading to unconstructive behaviour that interferes with goal (G) attainment (Dryden, 2022).

Disputation (D)

A collaborative (client-practitioner) and Socratic argument, or debate, applied systematically and rigorously, focussed on challenging client Bs in order to instigate a philosophic shift from irrationality to rationality. Disputation (D) largely applies logical-empirical methods of science (Dryden & Branch, 2008). Typical arguments include empirical (true or false?), logical (sensical or nonsensical?), and pragmatic (helpful or unhelpful?) questioning, where the veracity, logic, and utility of the Bs is challenged. That is, the practitioner *asks*, not tells. Both irrational and rational beliefs are subject to Disputation (D) so that irrational beliefs can be understood to be false, illogical, and unhelpful, and rational beliefs can be understood to be true, logical, and helpful (for goal attainment). Clients should learn to independently dispute their Bs in the long term, not just dispute the specific Bs relevant to the current client-practitioner work.

Effective new beliefs (E)

The defining, development, strengthening of, and long-term commitment to, rational beliefs. Rational beliefs are encouraged whilst irrational beliefs are discouraged, and cognitive, emotive, and behavioural strategies are meaningfully rehearsed and enacted in service of deepening (strengthen their conviction in) the rational beliefs and applying rationality independently over the life course. The client is supported in integrating the rational beliefs, and the notion of rationality, into their lives via an ongoing commitment to the effective new rational beliefs (E).

Rational vs. irrational GABC

As can be seen in Figure 2.2, if clients hold irrational beliefs (iB) that, in response to adverse events (A) manifest to block or impede their goals (G), they are likely to experience UNEs (C). Then, as can be seen in Figure 2.3, if clients hold rational beliefs (iB) that, in response to adverse events (A) manifest to aid their goals (G), they are likely to experience HNEs (C). Thus, clients are encouraged to rigorously dispute (D) these irrational beliefs (iBs), and rational beliefs (rBs) are then encouraged and reinforced (E) to help the client experience HNEs at C. Simply, irrational beliefs underpin UNEs (e.g., David et al., 2002) and rational beliefs underpin HNEs (e.g., Oltean & David, 2018). At a higher level, the GABCDE framework portrays a cognitive approach to emotion and behaviour, which assumes that consequences (C) are at least in part cognitively penetrable (David et al., 2004). Cognitive penetrability means that emotional and behavioural responses are outcomes of conscious or unconscious cognitive processing, and that change in cognition will induce a change in emotional and behavioural responses (David et al., 2010a). Thus, REBT subscribes to a cognitive model (e.g., Dobson & Dozois, 2010) in which cognitive change is important for treatment.

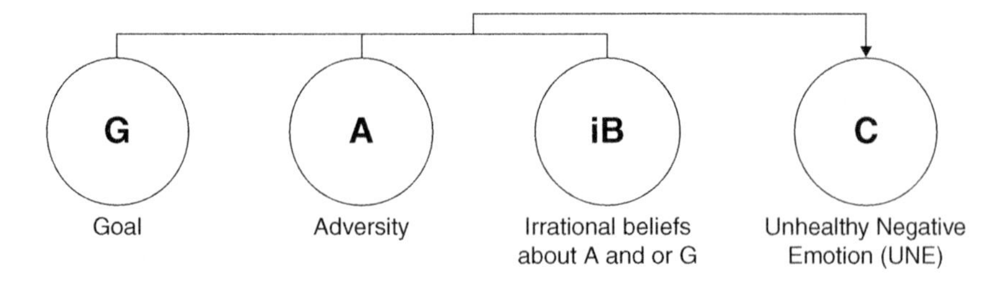

Figure 2.2 Diagrammatic representation of irrational GABC.

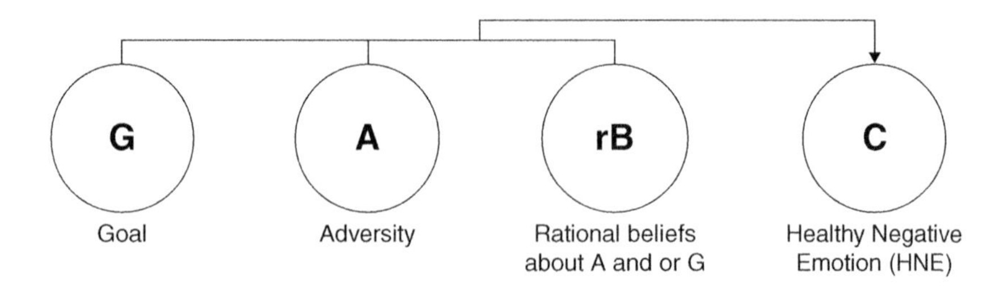

Figure 2.3 Diagrammatic representation of rational GABC.

The Stoic undergirding of the GABCDE framework

> I inducted this principle of the ABCs of emotional disturbance from working with hundreds of clients from 1943 to 1955. But I also took it over from many philosophers I studied from 1929 (when I was 16) onwards. Clearest of all amongst the ancients were the Greek and Roman Stoics, especially Zeno of Citium (the founder of the school), Chrysippus, Panaetius of Rhodes (who introduced Stoicism into Rome), Cicero, Seneca, Epictetus, and Marcus Aurelius.
>
> (Albert Ellis, 1994, p. 64)

Where did the GABCDE framework come from? The GABCDE framework is clearly underpinned in part by Stoic doctrines, particularly the philosophy and teachings of Epictetus. The notion of rationality was extremely important to the Ancient Stoics. The Stoics believed that the distinguishing feature of human beings is our ability to reason, and that human beings and the universe constitute the same rational nature (Murguia & Díaz, 2015). They believed that human nature and nature itself are guided by reason (Logos). For the Stoics, the Logos is the rational principle that governs the organisation of the universe (cosmos), able to be perceived through human reason – some regard the Logos as the articulation of truth in speech – Logos is also the root word for logic, and logic lies at the core of rationality (Pinker, 2021). The Stoics taught that everything operates according to a web of cause and effect, and that the Logos sets the parameters of the human experience. We have internal conditions (biological, including brain structures that allow us to think – the mind must obey the laws of physics) that interact with external conditions (perceived and physical) that determine our actions. We need to develop the correct internal make up to stay in synch with this rationally predetermined order (Frede, 2003).

If we experience passions (dysfunctional emotions), we cannot make decisions that are in keeping with the rational order of things. The human being is responsible for how they interpret and react to environmental factors to maintain wellbeing and stay on the rational course dictated by the Logos. It is up to us to live in accord with the rational principles of the Logos. Because we are helpless in the face of the accidents of life, we become unhappy because we seek to control what we cannot, or as Pierre Hadot (2002) puts it, "people are unhappy, because they passionately seek to acquire things which they cannot obtain and to flee evils which are inevitable" (Hadot & Chase, 2002, p. 127). We can control the will to do good and our conformity with reason; rational discourse reflects self-coherence whereby our rational nature is united with universal reason.

For Epictetus, and the Stoics, there are factors outside of our control that we should accept, whilst our responsibility is to control our internal states in order to move through the rational course of life with the best actions for us and all that is connected to the web of nature. How one chooses to interpret external circumstances, not the circumstances themselves, leads one to enjoy a 'good' life, or suffer from a 'bad' one. The Stoic doctrine speaks to the notion of cognitive mediation, an idea that emerged more formally in the cognitive revolution of the 1950s (Ruggiero et al., 2018). Cognitive mediators are defined as "mental processes or activities that take place between the initial occurrence of a stimulus and the subsequent related response" (Alegria & Cameron, 2020, p. 496). Cognitive mediation is foundational to CBTs as well as to the advancement of emotion regulation science (e.g., Gross, 1998a; Lazarus, 1999).

The immense power, and responsibility, of personal choice was at the heart of the Stoicism of Epictetus, whilst he simultaneously acknowledged that there was much in life which was simply beyond one's control. We can't control events, but we can accept them (i.e., acknowledge that they have happened) and control how we approach events. Deal with the world as it is, not as you want it to be, whilst pursuing self-improvement via wisdom, temperance, justice, and courage (the Stoic cardinal virtues). There are many sayings attributed to Epictetus that succinctly and accurately capture the notion of cognitive mediation, and I offer three such sayings (Epictetus & Dobbin, 2008) that have proved useful in framing cognitive mediation for athletes and coaches:

> It is not events that disturb people, it is their judgements concerning them.
>
> (p. 221)

> Remember, it is not enough to be hit or insulted to be harmed, you must believe that you are being harmed. If someone succeeds in provoking you, realize that your mind is complicit in the provocation.
>
> (p. 225)

> When we are frustrated, angry or unhappy, never hold anyone except ourselves – that is, our judgements – accountable.
>
> (p. 221)

I have also recommended Marcus Aurelius' Meditations to many athletes and coaches, particularly those with a proclivity for leadership, because Aurelius was Roman Emperor from A.D. 161 to 180. Within this work, many beautifully worded representations of cognitive mediation can be found, for example:

> Things as such have not the slightest hold on our soul, nor do they have access to the soul, nor can they alter it or move it; but the soul alone alters and moves itself, and ensures that whatever is submitted to it conforms to the judgements of which it considers itself worthy.
>
> (Meditations 5.19)

> If you suffer distress because of some external cause, it is not the thing itself that troubles you but your judgement about it, and it is within your power to cancel that judgement at any moment.
>
> (Meditations 8.47)

The full implications of Stoicism on psychology and psychotherapy is beyond the scope and aims of the current book (for fuller discussions see Robertson, 2019b; Still & Dryden, 2012). But for the current book, it is sufficient to say that the Stoicism of Epictetus in particular is clearly reflected in the GABCDE framework, and REBT at large. When formally introducing the theory of REBT in 1962, Ellis himself wrote that

> Many of the principles incorporated in the theory of rational-emotive psychotherapy are not new; some of them, in fact, were originally stated several thousand years ago, especially by the Greek and Roman Stoic philosophers (such as Epictetus and Marcus Aurelius).
>
> (Ellis, 1962, p. 35)

Murguia and Díaz (2015) suggest that in REBT Ellis develops two central Stoic ideas, (1) that our beliefs about situations are responsible for our psychological state, and (2) that our belief about our situation is within our control, and as such, we have some agency and volition over how we view our situation. The idea that stimulus interpretation mediates between the external (and internal) environment and ones' emotions (i.e., cognitive mediation) is reflected in the ABC portion of the framework. So most clearly, Ellis progresses the Stoic idea that it is how we think about events that shapes our emotional wellbeing. Pragmatically, if there is something we can reasonably do to disarm the adverse event then we should do it. But, we can also change the way we view the adverse event so that a) the event is perceived as less adverse, or that b) the adverse event is accepted and not transposed into emotional disturbance by applying irrational beliefs to it. Changing the way that we view the event is powerful because it does not exclude actual tangible event change and is obviously useful if there is nothing that can be done about the event. In other words, our approach to disarming the adverse event is best achieved from a position of emotional stability brought about via cognitive change, and if the event is not modifiable, then cognitive change is potentially all we have as a recourse for emotion regulation.

A third Stoic idea that Ellis develops, is that reason is fundamental to being and that a 'good' life is underpinned by the expression of healthy (functional) emotions. Indeed, the Stoic concept of the passions (*apatheia*) is reflective of UNEs and HNEs (at C) whereby some passions are healthy, and some are unhealthy (Robertson & Codd, 2019). Massimo Pigliucci (2019) writing about Marcus Aurelius says that, "the most famous philosopher-king in history was not attempting to suppress emotions (which the Stoics, good psychologists that they were, recognised is both impossible and undesirable), but rather to question them when they take a disruptive form".

Furthermore, the notion of Stoic rationality is of course reflected (but not perfectly) in the rational and irrational beliefs (B) of REBT. But, whilst the sentiment of Stoicism is somewhat captured by REBT (Robertson, 2010), the theory of REBT is not a linear translation of Stoicism. Ellis did not consider himself to be a 'Stoic' (Ellis, 1994), and was clear that REBT does not subscribe to many Stoic ideas (Ellis, 1979). We know a lot more about emotions and emotion regulation than the Stoics could have known (although, sometimes, you would never guess it), so REBT very much has its roots in Stoicism, but is not Stoicism as such. In fact, anybody writing about or applying 'Stoicism' in performance settings will need to reconcile with the fact that they will have to cherry pick from Stoicism the most appropriate elements for the domain they work within. Otherwise, if they wish to utilise Stoicism more completely, they will need to explain how stranger, more esoteric, and metaphysical aspects of Stoicism apply to performance settings. Stoicism does not present a fully integrable system for performance, not least because we don't have a full record of what the Stoics thought, or what Stoicism is in its entirety. Many works have been lost in the sands of time, leaving only 'fragments', and thus, constructing a full picture of Stoicism is not possible. As Donald Robertson (2019a) recognises, the Stoic canon is woefully incomplete and whilst the Stoics were prolific writers, probably less than 1% of their writings survive today.

In my view, in REBT Ellis adopts key Stoic ideas, brings them into the modern age, adapts these ideas and adds to them, to create a therapeutic system that goes beyond a school of philosophy. Throughout this book, I position Stoicism as a foundational philosophy for REBT, which does provide a workable (but still incomplete) system for performance settings. REBT has taken elements of Stoicism, and other schools of philosophy (e.g., Taoism, and Buddhism; Ellis, 1962), that speak to psychological wellbeing. Specifically, Stoic Ethics and Logic and their requisite practical elaborations have a prominent place within REBT, less so the metaphysical components. In this book, I draw out Stoicism to enable the reader to see how Stoic doctrines helped to form REBT. I also use the words of Stoic philosophers to help illuminate important aspects of REBT. Lastly, I refer to Stoic ideas to expand upon Ellis' writings in this area, realising a closer union between REBT and Stoicism, which has been sparsely written about (see the work of Donald Robertson, and Arthur Still and Windy Dryden for glowing exceptions). There is much we can learn from Ancient Stoicism, and through the prism of REBT, we can discover the relevance of Stoic ideas to a modern performance setting.

As a final note for this section about Stoicism, when I use the word 'Stoicism' I am explicitly using a capital 'S' in order to refer to the philosophic school. When readers see small 's' stoicism (e.g., Warwick, 2021), this refers to something different, and is connotated with an unemotional way of coping (Robertson, 2019a). This 'stoicism' is not the same as 'Stoicism' which can lead to confusion especially in the general media (e.g., Jeré Longman's 2021 New York Times article about Simone Biles). Stoicism (capital 'S') is not promotive of emotional suppression and absence, which can of course be harmful and counterproductive, rather, Stoicism is more about modifying underlying assumptions about the world in order to experience healthy emotions, rather than unhealthy emotions (Robertson, 2021a). To be clear, REBT is not promoting of stoicism (small 's') but does adopt and adapt aspects of Stoicism (capital 'S'), some of which are articulated in the current book.

Emotion regulation and the GABCDE framework

> He who is slow to anger is better than the mighty, And he who rules his spirit than he who takes a city.
> Proverbs 16:32 (New King James Bible)

> He that hath no rule over his own spirit is like a city that is broken down, and without walls.
> Proverbs, 25:28 (New King James Bible)

The above Biblical passages from Proverbs in The New Testament speak to the importance of regulating one's emotions, and importantly, assert that it is we who are responsible for this endeavour. Emotion regulation can be defined as, "the set of processes whereby people seek to redirect the spontaneous flow of their emotions" (Koole, 2009, p. 6). A broader definition by Bunford et al. (2015) considers emotion regulation to include modulating the speed of emotion escalation, the intensity of the emotion, and the speed with which the emotion is deescalated in a manner congruent with optimal functioning. Successful emotion regulation supports increased well-being, better social functioning, better coping with stressful life events, and job success (Salovey et al., 2010). The ability to manage, or regulate, emotion is important for psychological health (Kobylińska & Kusev, 2019) and physical health (Sapolsky, 2007). A deficit in emotion regulation is associated with psychological distress and a broad gamut of psychopathological outcomes (Grant et al., 2018) and contributes to major forms of psychopathology (Kring & Werner, 2004). Thus, the capacity to *self*-regulate (e.g., Gross, 1998a) one's emotions is of utmost importance for goal attainment and health. Two useful theories that parallel and help to elucidate the REBT GABCDE framework are Richard Lazarus' cognitive appraisal theory (CAT; Lazarus, 1999) and James Gross' emotion regulation theory (modal model; Gross, 2014). I will cover each, in turn, making important links to REBT as I go.

Cognitive appraisal theory (CAT)

By integrating some of Richard Lazarus' ideas with Ellis' ideas, a more elaborated picture of emotion aetiology can be formed. My motivation for trying to understand the symbiosis between REBT and appraisal theory was singular to begin with – I was confused that the GABCDE framework did not seem to indicate *what* emotion is evinced through G, A, and B. Indeed, the reader may also have noticed that at C in REBT we distinguish between UNEs and HNEs but specific irrational beliefs do not predict specific emotions (although, there is some evidence that FI is specifically conducive to anger, and depreciation is specifically conducive to depression; Bernard, 1998; Turner et al., 2019b). In exploring the REBT literature I came across writings between Albert Ellis and Richard Lazarus which explicated the similarities and differences between their respective theories (Ellis, 1994; Lazarus, 1995). But also, I read the paper by David et al. (2002) which developed appraisal models to predict specific emotions by including both Lazarusian and Ellisian constructs. So, here I have brought REBT and Lazarus' (1999) cognitive appraisal theory (CAT) together, which in my practice has enabled me to understand and be more aware of specific types of emotion (e.g., anxiety, anger, shame, etc.) and their UNE and HNE expressions.

In Lazarus' (1999) cognitive appraisal theory (CAT; also see Lazarus, 1991; Lazarus & Folkman, 1984; Smith & Lazarus, 1993) it is proposed that emotions are the result of a transaction between the goals of the individual and the representation of environmental encounters, characterised by primary and secondary cognitive appraisal. Primary appraisals are concerned with the extent to which the encounter is relevant to one's goals (goal relevance), and whether and to what extent the encounter is congruent or incongruent with one's goals (goal congruence and goal incongruence). Goal relevance is fundamental to whether a transaction is viewed as relevant to one's well-being, and as such, "there is no emotion without there being a goal at stake" (Lazarus, 1999, p. 92). Goal congruence/incongruence concerns whether the conditions of a transaction facilitate or thwart what the person wants, and as such, "if conditions thwart what the person wants, a negatively toned emotion is apt to follow" (Lazarus, 1999, p. 92).

Secondary appraisals concern one's resources and options for coping with the encounter and includes problem-focussed coping potential (evaluations of one's ability to act directly on the situation to bring it in accord with one's goals), and emotion focussed coping potential (evaluations of one's ability to psychologically adjust to the situation by altering one's interpretations, desires, or beliefs; Smith & Lazarus, 1993). Additional appraisal components of accountability (blame or credit), and future expectation are also relevant to the appraisal process and help to determine the shape and intensity of the emotion in a given situation. Lazarus (1999) also posits core relational themes that make it possible to determine the precise emotion generated from a specific constellation of appraisals. For example, anxiety is associated with the core relational theme of uncertain, existential threat (Lazarus, 1991), where primary appraisals of high goal relevance and high goal incongruence combine with secondary appraisals of low emotion focussed coping (Smith & Lazarus, 1993). Dryden (2012a) offers a similar idea of inferential themes which closely aligns with Lazarus' ideas (Dryden suggests that Adversities can *flavour* one's emotions), helping to understand why certain Adversities (As) are associated with certain Consequences (Cs).

Cognitive appraisals are thoroughly couched in, and interconnected with, beliefs as represented in the REBT GABCDE model (Ziegler, 2001). Research indicates that rational and irrational beliefs form part of cognitive appraisal whereby, for example, unhealthy anxiety is best predicted by high goal relevance, high goal incongruence, low emotion focussed coping, and irrational beliefs (David et al., 2002, 2005). In athletes, recent research demonstrates that irrational beliefs interact with cognitive appraisals to elicit pre-competitive affective states such as anxiety and negative mood (Chadha et al., 2019). For example, a basketball athlete has a career goal of winning major trophies (reflecting G in REBT). He is anticipating the tip-off for a play-off final that could lead to him winning his first major trophy as a professional. The game is thus highly relevant to the athlete's goals (reflecting goal relevance in the CAT, and A in REBT), but the athlete has not competed in a final at this level before, is up against the best players in the nation, and is not sure whether he will perform well (reflecting uncertain, existential threat, and high goal incongruence in the CAT, and A in REBT). He doubts his ability to cope (low coping potential in the CAT, and A in REBT), and believes that "I want to and *therefore I must* win a major trophy" and that "failure to win a major trophy on this occasion would show that *I am a complete loser*" (reflecting irrational beliefs [B] in the REBT model; Turner et al., 2019d). Thusly, he experiences unhealthy anxiety and expresses this emotion maladaptively by being unable to focus on his role, avoiding ball possession and withdrawing effort, and therefore performs below what he is usually capable of (reflecting C in REBT; see Figure 2.4). Put differently, the athlete carries the G into the situation, the situation is appraised to be adverse (A) in the sense that he perceives the situation to be goal relevant, goal incongruent, and perceives himself to have low coping potential. This A triggers his irrational beliefs (B) of demandingness and depreciation, which precipitates unhealthy anxiety (C) expressed through maladaptive cognitions and behaviours.

I propose that in light of a particular goal, goal relevance and goal incongruence reflect A in the REBT model; A is 'adverse' to the extent that it is perceived to be an impediment to G. If A is perceived as relevant to and incongruent with G, then the stage is set for negative emotion (C) and the individual can recruit various coping responses to change A or modulate C (e.g., Ellis, 1994). However, if A impedes G, *and* the athlete applies their irrational beliefs to G and/or the A, then UNEs at C are likely to be the result. That is, because the A is rendered highly dangerous (uncertain, existential threat) to his goals (G) and is aggrandised and distorted by the irrational beliefs, the basketball athlete in the example is likely to experience unhealthy anxiety. Thus, the formula $A \times B = C$ becomes $G - A \times B = C$, whereby A is seen as relevant to, and an impediment to, G (A is perceived to thwart G).

Situational characteristics						
My goal is to win major trophies	Tournament final	Novel situation, stiff competition, uncertain performance outcome	Doubts coping ability and potential for success	"I want to and therefore I must win a major trophy" "Failure to win a major trophy on this occasion would show that I am a complete loser"	Unhealthy anxiety	Avoids ball possession, withdraws effort
Alignment with CAT and REBT						
G	A			B	C	
Personal goal	High goal relevance	High goal incongruence	Low coping potential	Irrational beliefs of demandingness and depreciation	Unhealthy negative emotion	Maladaptive emotion expression (action)

Figure 2.4 An example of REBT and CAT integration.

In essence, at A we find the seeds of emotionality, and at B (if irrational) we delineate between the *healthy or unhealthy expressions* of this emotionality. Through a greater understanding of the writings of Ellis and Lazarus, it is clear that G and A are vital parts of emotion per se, but B is prime suspect for emotional *turmoil*. Paul Dubois recognised this in the early 20th century, asserting that:

> We react, first of all, under the influence of our sensibility; it is that which determines the first movement, it is that which makes our blood boil and calls forth a noble rage. But one ought to calm one's emotion and stop to reflect. This does not mean that we are to sink back into indifference, but, with a better knowledge of the mental mechanism of the will, we can get back to a state of calmness. We see the threads which pull the human puppets, and we can consider the only possible plan of useful action – that of cutting off the possibility of any renewal of wrong deeds, and of sheltering those who might suffer from them, and making the future more certain by the uplifting of the wrong-doer.
>
> (Dubois, 1909, p. 56)

Dubois recognises that reactions to events are influenced by what we bring to them, and that cognitive control is the appropriate action for emotional control. The importance of cognitive control is also recognised in emotion regulation science, and it is to emotion regulation theory that I next turn my attention.

Process model of emotion regulation

James Gross' process model of emotion regulation (Gross, 1998a, 2014; Gross & Thompson, 2007) is highly relevant to the GABCDE framework. In the model, a situation-attention-appraisal-response sequence, in which "a person-situation transaction that compels attention,

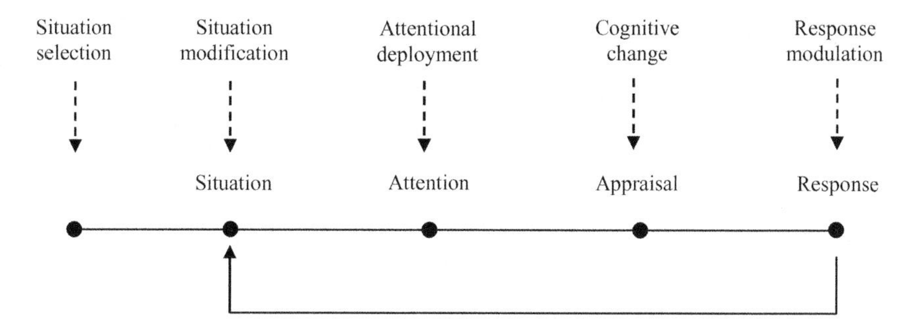

Figure 2.5 Process model of emotion regulation (adapted from Gross & Thompson, 2007).

has particular meaning to an individual, and gives rise to a coordinated yet flexible multi-system response to the ongoing person-situation transaction" (Gross & Thompson, 2007, p. 5) is posited. The sequence begins with a psychologically relevant situation (which can be external or internal to the individual), which is then attended to, and appraised in terms of what it means in light of the individual's currently active goals (Moors et al., 2013), which then generates emotion (Gross, 2015a). From a broader cognitive-behavioural perspective, the process model is consistent with the cognitive model of psychological dysfunction that helps to define (particularly) second-wave psychotherapies such as REBT (e.g., Collard, 2019). This cognitive model, whereby irrational beliefs and/or cognitive distortions are addressed within the context of emotional or behavioural dysfunction, has garnered consistent and copious support across clinical and subclinical populations (see Collard, 2019, for a more protracted discussion).

The process model of emotion regulation also highlights five families of emotion regulation strategies (Gross & Thompson, 2007; see Figure 2.5). The main elements of the process model are: situation selection, situation modification, attentional deployment, cognitive change (which are antecedent-focussed strategies), and response modulation (which is a response-focussed strategy; Gross, 1998b). Situation selection involves taking actions that make it more (or less) likely that one will end up in a situation one expects will give rise to desirable or undesirable emotions. Situation modification involves directly modifying the situation in order to alter its emotional impact. Attentional deployment is about directing one's attention to influencing one's emotional response. Cognitive change (or cognitive reappraisal) involves changing one's appraisal of the situation to alter its emotional significance, in essence by changing how one thinks about the situation. Finally, response modulation refers to directly influencing experiential, behavioural, or physiological components of the emotional response once the emotion is already well developed (see Gross, 2015b, for further strategy details).

All of the strategies posited within the process model are viable strategies within REBT and reflect solutions that are both distal and proximal to the core aims of specific REBT, but fit nicely into the core aims of general REBT. Some strategies are more optimal than others, each having benefits and limitations, when weighed against the goals of REBT. It is possible to take each element of the process model and the GABCDE framework and compare them to appreciate the conceptual overlap (see Figure 2.6). This conceptual overlap provides opportunities for practitioners to help clients to develop and apply a broad range of emotion regulation strategies, whilst remaining theoretically consistent with REBT.

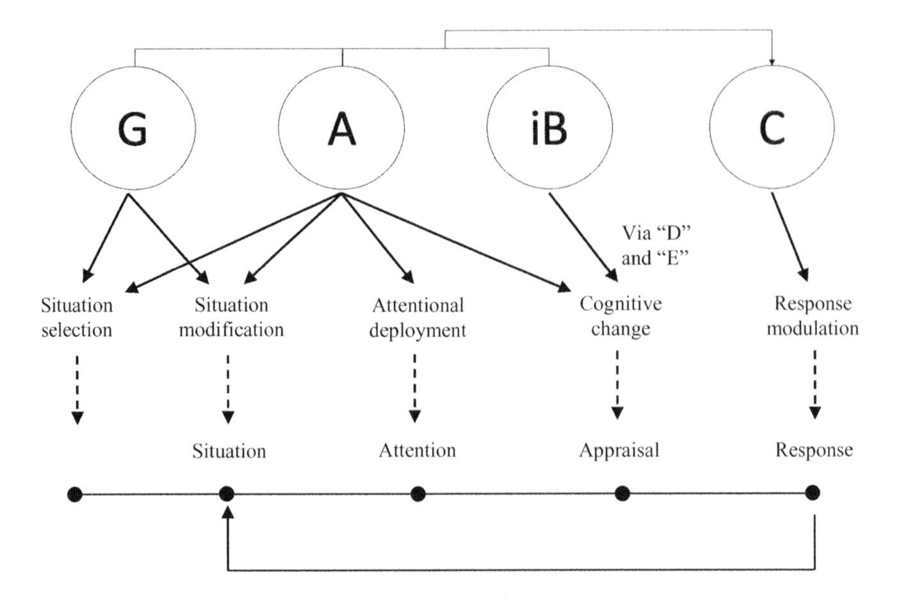

Figure 2.6 The alignment between the REBT GABCDE framework and Gross' process model of emotion regulation (Gross' process model of emotion regulation is adapted from Gross & Thompson, 2007).

The logically consistent overlaps between the GABCDE framework and the process model of emotion regulation can be instructive and provide options for working with clients on specific emotional issues. As can be seen in Figure 2.6, the elements of the GABCDE framework are consistent with the elements of the process model of emotion regulation in terms of emotion regulation strategies. One of the things you may notice is that working with A is very attractive, because it provides many options for emotion regulation. This might help explain why clients would often prefer to change the situation they are in, rather than attempt cognitive change – it seems easier, often involves less cognitive effort, and is demonstrably effective. Indeed, successful cognitive change is usually effortful and requires several potentially taxing cognitive processes, including working memory, task switching, and the ability to override a prepotent response (e.g., Troy et al., 2018). Because of the taxing nature of cognitive change (i.e., decreased self-control resources; Ortner et al., 2016), especially in emotionally intense situations, people are less likely to apply cognitive change within emotionally intense situations (Sheppes et al., 2014).

But it is worth noting that cognitive change is the most well-studied and well-supported emotion regulation strategy (Boehme et al., 2019; McRae et al., 2010), with positive evidence of its effectiveness across psychophysiological (e.g., Ray et al., 2010), and neurological (e.g., Ochsner et al., 2004) outcomes. Cognitive change is preferable to expressive suppression (Cutili, 2014) and distraction (e.g., Hayes et al., 2010). As such, cognitive change is worth the effort. For example, in a recent large-scale study of 21,644 participants from 87 countries/regions (Wang et al., 2021), data indicated that reappraisal consistently reduced negative emotions and increased positive emotions in response to the COVID-19 pandemic.

GABCDE and process model alignment

In aligning the GABCDE framework with the process model of emotion regulation, it is perhaps best to approach this explanation in order of G to E. Focussing on anything other than B in order to regulate emotion is reflective of general REBT, whilst a particular focus on B for emotion regulation epitomises specific REBT (but of course it not off-limits in general REBT). In the below sections, I extend the notion of how the process model of emotion regulation and the GABCDE framework align, and discuss the benefits and limitations of applying change processes to each element.

Goals (G)

Within the process model, G is most relevant to situation selection and situation modification. Since goals in part (alongside A) provide the conditions for emotionality, because there can be no goal relevance and goal incongruence without a goal, then one could avoid situations that give rise to A in the future by redefining, downscaling, or abandoning one's Gs (situation selection). For example, an athlete who never aims for the final, never has to deal with the prospect of losing in the final, and thus would not have to deal with the negative emotions that would surely arise as a result of losing the final. Setting your sights low means that you never have to experience and deal with the emotional turmoil that might be brought about by setting your sights high. That is, by tempering my goals I can assuage some emotional turmoil. One could also stop pursuing a goal that one was working towards, or during a goal relevant situation, one could simply give up pursuing the goal (situation modification).

The benefits of scaling back your goals are that you are clearly less open to disappointment and goal incongruence. The emotional sting of A, and potentially the occurrence of A at all, is removed by removing the goal. There is a big downside to this though. How can you ever fulfil your potential as a human being if you do not explore the limits of your potential? It is the setting and meaningful pursuit of goals, and the perception that you are positively moving towards those goals, that help to generate positive affect and meaning. If we have nothing to aim for, we are by definition 'aimless', and therefore at risk of nihilism, and long-term suffering as a result. Of course, setting and pursuing meaningful goals also sets the scene for negative emotion. Having goals will bring about adversity because meaningful goals are not easily achieved. In sport, you will compete and contend internally (e.g., against teammates for a spot in the team) and externally (e.g., opponents); people won't just let you meet your goals, and if they did, those goals wouldn't be very meaningful. We invite adversity when we pursue meaningful goals, but simultaneously open the door to potential meaning, purpose, and of course glory. So having a goal leads to a gamut of potential positive *and* negative emotions.

But perhaps more realistically and pragmatically, setting your sights towards a more transcendent goal, over and above external markers of attainment or success, may also quell emotion by altering the perceived occurrence and experience of A. A goal based on intrinsically valuable pursuits, such as doing one's best, enjoying the challenge, expressing oneself, or developing one's competence, move our perceptual frameworks away from externally derived markers of attainment which are uncontrollable, uncertain, and ultimately unpredictable, towards internally derived markers of attainment which are self-concordant and bespeak greater self-determination. As such, we are less susceptible to A because it is less likely that environmental vicissitudes will be viewed as relevant to and incongruent with our goals – in some ways, we are protected from A because our goals are less subject to being thwarted by external factors. You are more likely to lose (specific, externally determined goal) a competitive encounter than you are to learn (open, internally determined goal) nothing from a competitive encounter.

As another example, if my goal is "to have a perfect game", then I will constantly be faced with goal incongruence because a perfect game is utopian and fictional. But what if my goal was "to have as good a game as is possible for me"? I will still face some goal incongruence, but nowhere near as much as I would if I had an unrealistically high goal. Also, having a perfect game is not just about my game-relevant behaviours, it also involves my teammates' game-relevant behaviours, which are not under my control. If my goals are oriented towards factors that are external to me, then in goal relevant situations, unwanted and unpleasant emotions are more likely to result. This is because I cannot control those external factors, and this unpredictability will indelibly lead to uncertainty (danger) and goal incongruence, and thus, negative emotion.

In the short term, working with G might be a good strategy for providing rest from constant goal pursuit, making sure the goals set are actually worth aiming for, and that they are not likely to lead to burnout and health issues. In the longer term, it is important not to set goals that solely function to help you avoid negative emotion. By setting goals at all, of course the extent to which negative emotion is experienced is affected, but the setting of goals should not be driven solely by the desire to shape emotion. If you use the logic that having no meaningful goals will bring about no negative emotion, you run the risk of living a life that is characterised by passivity, mediocrity, and low self-expectation, bereft of purpose and meaning. As humans, we are goal-driven beings, and the denial of this would put us into an unnatural state of being, and we would yearn for meaning, and suffer because of this unfulfilled drive. We can perhaps find a place for this innate drive within eudaimonic, rather than hedonic, goal pursuits (more of this in Chapter 8).

So how might we work with G to help clients regulate emotion, whilst avoiding the surrendering of goals altogether? We could help the client to realign or redefine their goals, rather than encourage them to set easier (or no) goals. We can help them to ensure that the goals they set are meaningful and realistic (not perfectionistic), and then of course, we can work with them to orient their lives towards these goals and support them in forthrightly moving towards these goals. We can help athletes to set open and flexible goals that bespeak eudaimonic and humanistic (e.g., self-determined) fulfilment, rather than specific and fixed goals that are hedonistic and focussed on the attainment of external goods. When working with G, we must be careful not to simply encourage clients to make things easier for themselves (although, this may sometimes be relevant) instead of helping them develop the proper nutriments that can fortify them against life's challenges and adversities (As).

Adversity (A)

As can be seen in Figure 2.6, to work with A using the strategies set out in the process model, we have many options: situation selection, situation modification, attentional deployment, and cognitive change. We can help the client to make better (less emotionally provocative) situational choices (situation selection). Paradoxically, as is typical in REBT, we can also help the client to select emotionally provocative situations in order to achieve some stress inoculation. That is, we can encourage the client to avoid or remove themselves from emotive events (situational selection and modification), or paradoxically, help the client to stay in situations they would normally withdraw from to aid the development of frustration and discomfort tolerance. Relatedly, we can encourage clients to imagine negative As in order to help them recruit strategic decision-making and help them develop coping potential in the eventuality that the imagined A occurs. For example, Marcus Aurelius at the beginning of book 2 of his Meditations instructs himself to, "Begin the morning by saying to thyself, I shall meet with the busy-body, the ungrateful, arrogant, deceitful, envious, unsocial".

We can also help the client to distract themselves or avoid attending to a situation that might bring about an unwanted emotion (attention deployment). Paradoxically we can encourage the client to attend to stressors in order to encourage engagement with the situation and possible cognitive reappraisal. Relatedly, we can help the client to adjust their cognitive appraisal of the event to be more positive (cognitive change), or technically, to perceive greater goal congruence and coping potential (in line with Lazarus' theory).

Situation selection and situation modification can be used to change A at the concrete (the physical stimulus) and inferential (the inference made about the stimulus) levels. At a concrete A level, as mentioned, the client could avoid situations in which they think adversity will occur. One could select situations in which goal relevance is low, or where nothing is at stake, such that one's esteem is not in danger. In other words, a client could choose not to enter into goal relevant and goal incongruent situations in which their goals would be potentially at stake or jeopardised. For example, a client who feels unable to socialise with teammates due to fear of rejection, can avoid social interaction with teammates to avoid the risk of negative emotion. Or an athlete who knows that confrontation with an official may give rise to anger and aggression, may choose not to remonstrate with an official if a decision is made against them. For situation modification during adversity, an athlete has limited options, since they usually cannot control the external conditions during a competition, for example, and thus it would be difficult to change the concrete A. But it is possible in some situations, where athletes may attempt to modify situations (and other people's behaviours) in the service of their emotions, or escape from situations that are too emotionally evocative by, for example, benching themselves or in severe cases, feigning injury (e.g., self-handicapping; Prapavessis & Grove, 1998). In other words, *during* adversity performers can *sometimes* modify the situation by influencing others' actions (e.g., defusing a disagreement to avoid confrontation), or removing themselves from a situation they know to be emotionally evocative. This, for the time being, can change or remove a concrete A.

At an inferential level, a client could apply *internal* situation selection and modification (cognitive change). This involves cognitive change at A rather than B – the individual reappraises the meaning of the situation to them, to reduce the personal significance (goal relevance) and or the perception of threat (goal incongruence) of the situation. For example, an athlete could reappraise a tournament final as "just another game" rather than "the most important game of my life" in order to reduce its personal significance, thus reducing anxiety. During an intense competitive situation, an athlete could reappraise a poor refereeing decision as "just part of the game" rather than "a personal attack on my team" to assuage anger, possible aggression, and undoubtedly a caution from said referee. Similarly, the strategy of attentional deployment can be considered an *internal* application of situation selection, where the athlete can apply distraction and concentration to regulate emotion. This again is centred on changing the inferential A, rather than the concrete A. The athlete can choose not to focus on the fact that he has not played in a final at this level before, is up against the best players in the nation, and is not sure whether he will perform well. Instead, the athlete can choose to focus on imagining their first pass of the game, first interception, or first tackle. Below, Marcus Aurelius offers similar advice regarding attentional deployment in the face of adversity:

> You must build up your life action by action, and be content if each one achieves its goal as far as possible – and no one can keep you from this. But there will be some external obstacle! Perhaps, but no obstacle to acting with justice, self-control, and wisdom. But what if some other area of my action is thwarted? Well, gladly accept the obstacle for what it is and shift your attention to what is given, and another action will immediately take its place, one that better fits the life you are building.
>
> Marcus Aurelius (Meditations, 8.32)

The benefits of focussing on A are that you can very quickly help the client to reduce unwanted and unpleasant emotion. Essentially what you are doing here is removing goal relevance and/or goal incongruence to attempt to avoid or extinguish adversity, whether this is physically or inferentially. By avoiding adversity, you avoid negative emotionality in the short term. However, there are some notable shortcomings of this approach. By encouraging the client to modify A, you are communicating that their emotions have arisen through stimulus-response (S-R), whereby emotion is the direct results of the adverse event. Lazarus (1999) suggests that an S-R view of emotion is natural and appealing because:

> We like to explain our disturbed emotional reactions by referring to the fact that we lost our job, failed an important exam, were insulted by someone, injured or placed in harm's way, and so on. To be able to point to harmful external events such as a major loss, justifies our emotional distress, subsequent illness, or dysfunction, ignoring for the moment that, with some exceptions, most such events do not just happen to a passive person, but the victim has probably inadvertently contributed to them in some ways and may be coping with them successfully or unsuccessfully.
>
> (Lazarus, 1999, p. 49–51)

So, endorsing an S-R viewpoint by focussing heavily on A might be counterproductive and does not recognise the role of the client's deeper appraisals in the resultant emotion. Life events do not affect each of us in exactly the same way, so an S-R viewpoint does not account for the (sometimes vast) person-to-person individual differences in emotionality (Smith & Kirby, 2009). In other words, "The existence of substantial individual differences means that a stimulus alone is insufficient to define stress…because it begs the question of what makes a stimulus a stressor" (Lazarus, 1999, p. 54), and therefore, "Putting the person into the equation is the only way to solve the dilemma" (Lazarus, 1999, p. 53). There is little power or volition in emotional responding if we encourage clients to look only for A solutions, and we paradoxically risk emotionally sensitising the client to adversity if we focus on A change. That is, by applying only A solutions, we are communicating to the client, fallaciously, that A is the main or sole cause of emotion. The avoidance that often underpins changing A may bring forth some powerful short-term emotional palliation, because difficult situations can be avoided or ignored, but the emotion is likely to return in the face of a similar situation. Distraction can be considered a maladaptive strategy (Trincas et al., 2016), that is useful in the short term (Ford & Gross, 2018), but can be maladaptive in the longer term (e.g., Sheppes & Gross, 2013).

Changing A does provide some practical regulation options, but is a limited approach to emotion regulation because it is not possible to select or modify the many uncontrollable and unpredictable situations one is likely to encounter. We also cannot reliably predict what and when situations are going to be emotive, so changing A is low resolution and inherently error-prone (e.g., Gilbert et al., 1998). However, and this is very important, there might be very good reasons why a client should be encouraged to remove themselves from situations, particularly if those situations present genuine risks to their wellbeing. Changing A could be useful for emotion regulation because it could encourage sensible active avoidance, or understandable ignorance, of noxious future situations, and/or the removal of oneself from dangerous current situations. I would not encourage an athlete to remain operating in an abusive coaching relationship and to simply work with B. I would help them to leave the situation as safely as possible *and* work with B to ensure the least emotional turmoil as possible. REBT is not at all militantly 'anti A change'.

In sum, when applying REBT, A change offers some powerful emotion regulation strategies that open up a host of interventions and techniques. But A change may not be conducive to optimal functioning since it is based on error-prone assumptions (e.g., misestimation of future situation; e.g., Gilbert et al., 1998), is often not possible (e.g., you cannot always change the situation), and because it encourages avoidance in the interest of short-term gains at the cost of long-term goal attainment. Short-term relief associated with A change may prevent useful exposure to feared stimuli, which could prevent longer term benefits of exposure (Clark, 2001). Often, athletes are thrown into uncontrollable and unpredictable situations and changing the concrete A (situation selection and/or modification), is not achievable. Any change at A could of course help the athlete to manage their emotions, but this is not addressing the core issues of irrational beliefs, and therefore is a short-term and 'general' REBT solution as opposed to a long-term and 'specific' REBT solution.

Beliefs (B)

Cognitive change at B is where the process model is more reflective of the core aims of specific REBT, and is what helps define 'specific' REBT as opposed to 'general' REBT. You can view cognitive change at B in two ways. On the one hand, by only focussing on B, you are limiting the options for emotion regulation. However, on the other hand, this limitation speaks to the elegance of specific REBT. Since B is at the heart of healthy vs. unhealthy emotional and behavioural consequences (HNE and UNEs), and reflects deeply held philosophic core beliefs, then working on B has the potential to influence emotion regulation across many Gs, As, and Cs. I will not dwell on the specifics of B here, because much of the latter parts of this book are dedicated to this. Suffice to say, cognitive change at B, from an REBT perceptive, is not about reframing the event, reappraising the situation, or superficially pasting a positive narrative onto an unfortunate occurrence, it is about deep and philosophic belief change that extends into the future with a view to aiding emotion regulation in the longer term. Of course, changing irrational beliefs to rational beliefs has short-term advantages too. Rational beliefs can be applied more acutely as self-talk, also known as functional reappraisal (FR) in the emotion regulation literature (e.g., David et al., 2020) whereby reappraisal involves the recognition of the negative aspects of the situation whilst being flexible and logical. In performance settings, rational self-talk has been shown to enhance sports (golf) performance under pressure (Turner et al., 2019c; See Turner et al., 2019d, for a full discussion).

As already suggested, cognitive change could include altering the inferential A, but inferential A change does not strike at the core of the issue, and might involve some self-delusion along the way. In order to down-regulate anxiety, an athlete may have to engage in some fantasy that the final match is not important, for example. More 'elegant' or specific REBT (Ellis, 1977) would see the athlete changing her irrational beliefs (B) by disputing them (D), and then utilising rational beliefs (E) concerning the G and the A. In other words, the athlete can deal with the situation (A) as it is, rather than how she wishes it to be, focussing on addressing the underlying faulty irrational beliefs she has about G and A, rather than altering G and A concretely or inferentially, or distracting herself from A. Even if an athlete can select or modify G and/or A, this avoidance might help them to feel better in the short term, but in the longer term it is unlikely that they will be able to always avoid As and it would be potentially disadvantageous to scale down or abandon their Gs. It is potentially more advantageous (for goal attainment) to voluntarily take on meaningful Gs and to face up the As that will undoubtably arise in the pursuit of those Gs.

The benefits of focussing on B for emotion regulation are that beliefs are a key determinant of emotion and so are a worthwhile focus, they are malleable, and individuals can take responsibility for them. The downside of B change is that it is difficult, can be unintuitive, and can be *misconstrued* as victim blaming ("it is the not the situation, but your beliefs that are the problem"). But, anything worth doing is difficult, and when properly learnt it can become intuitive, and is less about blaming clients and more about empowering them to take charge of their internal dialogue. The extant research evidence, and REBT theory, indicates that cognitive change is to be striven for, so long as it is possible within the context that one is working. However, it should be noted that people really do not like to apply cognitive change. That is, it usually isn't their first choice when attempting to regulation their emotions. Research has shown that people prefer to use disengagement strategies with high-intensity negative situations, like situation modification and distraction, and are more likely to use reappraisal in low-intensity negative situations (Sheppes et al., 2014; Van Bockstaele et al., 2019). This might be because reappraisal is more taxing and deliberate compared to distraction, for example.

Given the evidence for the effectiveness of cognitive change, and the importance of B within REBT, we have to work hard with clients to help them develop efficient ways to apply cognitive change at B. One efficient way is to help them adopt a rational philosophy of life that enables rapid rational reappraisal in acutely difficult situations. In other words, rather than focussing the REBT work solely on a specific irrational belief for a specific set of Gs and As, the focus of the work should be on helping the client to develop knowledge and skill in recognising and disputing their own irrational beliefs, and developing and strengthening rational alternatives, thus allowing for effective emotion regulation in the longer term across the many Gs they pursue and the many As they face.

Consequences (C)

Response modulation could be used to influence the already occurring physiological, experiential, or behavioural responses that characterise the emotion. In REBT this represents changing the C, in which the client could use relaxation strategies, for example, or could try to express the emotion in an adaptive, rather than maladaptive way (i.e., UNE vs. HNE), or supress (hide, inhibit) the emotion, which might be socially appropriate in context. It might be the case that there simply is not sufficient will, time, or energy to apply cognitive change, there isn't opportunity to select or modify the goal or the situation, and disengagement would not be fruitful for performance. In these cases, we can apply psychological skills to manage the emotion more directly (i.e., response modulation). We can help clients to learn and apply breathing techniques (e.g., rhythmic diagrammatic breathing), and other relaxation and activation methods, and also to adopt adaptive behaviours (e.g., act confidently, act assertively, act courageously), to more directly modulate C, and/or the expression of C (e.g., Turner & Barker, 2014b).

The benefits of focussing emotion regulation on C is that there are many good options for taking charge of the overtly physical (i.e., somatic) and behavioural aspects of emotion. By applying relaxation techniques, clients feel efficacious in managing an emotion because the application of these techniques helps them to *feel* better quickly. Of course, the downside here is that whilst they might feel better, they have not really addressed the underlying factors that are leading to the emotion. As such, they will probably experience this emotion when they face a similar situation and will have to spend time and energy on the physiologic symptoms of the emotion, rather than dealing with its determinants. Indeed, emotion suppression is demonstrably a poor emotion regulation strategy for the down regulation of negative emotion, deleteriously affecting memory (e.g., Johns et al., 2008), increasing sympathetic nervous system responses (e.g., Demaree et al., 2006) and activation in emotion-generative brain regions (e.g., amygdala; Goldin et al., 2008), and compromising social functioning (e.g., Richards et al., 2003). Furthermore, some research indicates that whilst both irrational beliefs and thought suppression are related to distress, the impact of irrational beliefs on distress is mediated by thought suppression (Szentagotai, 2006), so the suppression of thoughts and emotions may exacerbate the problems associated with holding irrational beliefs.

For the current author, using response modulation to change C strikes me as an inefficient emotion regulation approach that is applied very much after the horse has bolted. In addition, there might not always be time and opportunity to execute a deliberative relaxation or activation routine, and if not applied correctly, the client might enter into a losing battle with their emotions, attempting and reattempting to quell their emotions, rather than focussing on the task at hand. Clients often speak to me about a 'losing battle' with their emotions, where reactive attempts to manage emotion are both time consuming and too often ineffective (and even paradoxical to attempted down-regulation). Also, not all response modulations are conducive to long-term wellbeing. For example, the use of alcohol and other such substances to alter emotion (e.g., Khantzian, 1985), is not a good long-term eudaimonic strategy, but is not uncommon within athlete populations (e.g., Williams et al., 2021).

Disputation (D)

This is applied as part of cognitive change at B, and is a key part of deep belief change in REBT. Not only do we direct the client through disputation for the particular issue/s that have driven them towards seeking our help, but we also teach the client to apply disputation independently to address issues in the future. Thus, cognitive change here is effortful and aimed towards deep philosophic belief change at B, rather than towards situation specific inferences (A). Indeed, in specific REBT we would rarely dispute Gs, As, and Cs, preferring to work with B for a more elegant solution. This is why, in Figure 2.6, D applies only to the connection between iB and cognitive change.

Effective new beliefs (E)

Similar to D, this is applied as part of cognitive change at B, and is crucial for the client moving forward in a rational and healthy manner. It is not enough to weaken irrational beliefs via D, and leave nothing in their place, we need to work hard to instantiate and strengthen rational beliefs that the client can internalise and utilise in the future. The later Chapters 12 and 13 of this book provide much detail concerning both D and E.

Interim summary

What I have tried to achieve in this chapter so far is an alignment of Ellis' GABCDE framework, Lazarus' CAT, and Gross' process model of emotion regulation. The reason I have done this is to a) root REBT theory within well-supported and elaborated scientific literature, b) more fully articulate how it is that a complex constellation of cognitive processes can give rise to emotion, c) articulate the important place that beliefs hold in emotion and emotion regulation, and d) express the breadth and depth of the emotion regulation opportunities that can be subsumed within the GABCDE framework. By aligning REBT with Gross' process model, it is possible to realise that each element of the GABCDE framework can be subject to modulation and modification, with varying degrees of congruence with the core aims of specific REBT.

Clearly, belief (cognitive) change is at the core of REBT and is supported by research evidence, so should be striven for. The strengths associated with cognitive change notwithstanding, there are also limitations to emotion regulation strategies directly aligned with G, A, and C that make B change more appealing. Of course, there are some strengths for G, A, and C modification too. So, the humanistic REBT practitioner should be aware of and sensitive to individual and contextual factors when working with clients, in order to help them to apply the most effective emotion regulation strategies for optimal functioning within that context. This may include applying regulation strategies in one aspect, or all aspects, of the GABCDE framework.

The canon of psychological skills

Considering the relative strengths and limitations of applying emotion regulation strategies across the GABCDE framework, it is pertinent for practitioners (whether or not REBT is your preferred approach) to be able to help clients to develop and nurture their psychological skills. But in specifically approaching REBT work with clients from this broader emotion regulation perceptive, still subscribing to the GABCDE framework of REBT, the practitioner can make full use of the many psychological strategies on offer for clients. In sport and performance psychology, one approach to working with athletes involves psychological skills training (PST) or mental skills training (MST).

Mark B. Andersen (2009) refers to the five most commonly used, and CBT-derived, psychological skills as "the canon of psychological skills" (p. 11), namely, relaxation, self-talk, imagery, goal setting, and concentration. The five skills that make up the canon come directly from CBT but in order to fit the context of sport, have been modified and adapted (see Vealey, 2007). Relaxation refers to the turning down of sympathetic nervous system activation and associated muscle tension (or increasing parasympathetic activation). Self-talk refers to the variety of tactics aimed at countering the negative consequences of disruptive and emotion-producing cognitions. Imagery refers to the deliberate internal creation (or recreation) of experiences in the absence of the real stimulus normally associated with the actual experience (e.g., Morris et al., 2005). Goal setting refers to the explicit setting of goals to direct effort and attention towards goal-related activities and away from irrelevant activities (Healy et al., 2018). Goals in this context are objectives or aims that an athlete is trying to accomplish, usually within a specified time frame (Weinberg, 2013). Finally, concentration refers to the means to the end of productively focussing (i.e., concentrating) on the task at hand (i.e., performance).

In private correspondence with Emily Claspell (2010), Andersen used the analogy of an azalea bush to draw links between the canon and CBT. He remarks on the beauty of the flowers, leaves, branches, main trunk, and root system, and asserts that using PST as a model "is like focussing only on the flowers" (p. 131). The flowers are a part of a broader system of

CBT and Andersen questions whether practitioners working in sport really study the whole plant. I argue that REBT gives us an opportunity to understand the whole plant, from roots to flowers, and by aligning REBT with the broader emotion regulation area, an REBT practitioner can be free to explore deep belief change and/or explore more 'surface level' PST. By surface-level I don't mean to relegate PST, I just mean that PST, like the flowers of an azalea bush, are a valuable part of the whole, but are not the whole.

We can go about aligning the canon of psychological skills with the GABCDE framework of REBT in a similar way as we did with Gross' process model of emotion regulation.

- **Goals**. The main psychological skill useful here is goal setting. In applying the GABCDE framework we are not restricted to using G as an assessment opportunity to help contextualise A and C, in order to eventually examine B. We can help the client to articulate and orient themselves towards appropriate and meaningful goals that will lead to fulfilment. I cover this in detail in a later Chapter 8 so will not dwell on it here, but the setting of proper goals can have important downstream implications on emotion regulation and eudaimonia.
- **Adversity**. There are three main psychological skills that align here, that of concentration, self-talk, and imagery. As previously stated, A is adverse to the extent that it is relevant to and incongruent with G. As such, a client can be encouraged to concentrate on facets of the situation that do not evoke goal incongruence. They could also reappraise the A as less adverse ("I am sure they did not mean to hurt me"), and even positive ("this experience will just make me stronger"), using some self-talk. In addition, they could use imagery to visualise A being how they want it to be, rather than how they *do not* want it to be. For example, an athlete might be better to image successful skill execution, rather than unsuccessful skill execution (depending on the context).
- **Beliefs**. The main psychological skill useful here is self-talk, although imagery is also highly applicable. When assessing the client for the presence of irrational and rational beliefs, it is important for the client to have some access to their internal dialogue. On some level, what we are assessing here is the prevalence of extreme, rigid, and illogical content in their self-talk. But often, irrational beliefs do not present themselves in explicit self-talk, and the practitioner needs to help the client to explore more deeply into their cognitions, their rules and ideas, and philosophies of life. Imagery can be useful for this feat, where we can encourage the client to image the presence of A, or the experience of C, as realistically as they can using all the senses, in order to gain access to deeper Bs.
- **Consequences**. There are two main psychological skills that align here, that of relaxation and concentration. Many performers I have worked with find relaxation techniques very useful as part of their pre, during, and post-performance psychological work. Whether it is to calm down physiologically pre-game, centre oneself in breaks of play, or shut down post-game in order to recharge, techniques such as progressive muscular relaxation and breathing routines are commonly used (Turner & Barker, 2014b). In addition, often when experiencing intense emotion, attention may be drawn to task irrelevant cues. For example, an angry futsal player may spend too long focussing on a poor (in their opinion) refereeing decision, or seeking vengeance on an overly aggressive opponent. The players can refocus their attention on the task at hand by taking charge of their attention in this instance, for example, by using a behavioural cue (e.g., adjusting shin

pads) or focussing on the prospect of the next phase of play (they could even use some self-talk here to trigger this refocus; 'next ball').

- **Disputation**. The main psychological skill that aligns here is self-talk. The extent to which a client is able to direct an internal dialogue towards Socratically questioning their beliefs is an important skill, especially if the client is to successfully utilise REBT independently. It is often useful for clients to clearly internally and externally verbalise their disputation process in order to exercise deliberative control over this Socratic process. Also, self-talk can be used more briefly by the client to instigate critical analysis concerning a thought or belief. For example, having become aware of a potentially self-limiting belief, they could ask themselves "but where is the evidence for this belief?" or simply "is this belief rational?" They could also instruct themselves to think more critically about their belief in the moment (e.g., "just think about this critically for a moment").
- **Effective new beliefs**. Much like with disputation, self-talk is the most relevant here. The rehearsal and repetition of rational affirmations is a very useful approach to internalising rational beliefs. The client, having established their new rational beliefs with the practitioner, can now utilise the rational beliefs as self-talk, or short self-statements (see Turner et al., 2019d). These can be used if the client faces A, or experiences the problematic C, or can just be practised and rehearsed like lines for a play. There is evidence for enhanced athletic performance when utilising rational self-talk (Turner et al., 2019c).

Although I position each element of the GABCDE alongside a specific psychological skill, of course each skill can be used across all elements of the GABCDE framework, and at a meta-level, for the GABCDE framework itself. To the first point, it might be important for a client to envision (imagery) their goals (G), to engage in useful internal dialogue (self-talk) about their goals, and to acutely focus (concentration) on their goals during performance. It might be useful when applying disputation and effective new beliefs in the real world to set goals that aim towards attempting these elements when relevant, and the client may find that accurate D and E are more possible when they are relaxed. Also important for D and E is imagery, and I will cover rational emotive imagery (REI; Maultsby, 1971) later in this book (Chapter 13). To the second point, in as much as the client can use the GABCDE to drive their emotion management, they can affirm their B–C thinking using self-talk ("it is how I am thinking about the situation that is the problem, not the situation alone"), they can use imagery to rehearse using the framework in the real world to manage their emotions, and they can set a goal of understanding the framework enough to apply it independently.

In addition, all psychological skills are linked in a sense that they can be used in combination and can be supportive of each other. It might be important to relax to enable greater focus, for example, and indeed Andersen (2009) argues that for concentration, all skills are relevant. It may also be useful to trigger some specific imagery (e.g., assertive behaviour) with specific self-talk (e.g., 'be strong'). Interestingly, the first formal writing we have on the use of REBT in sport settings was a chapter by Michael Bernard in 1985, in which the effectiveness of REBT was demonstrated with Australian Rules Football players. The athletes received REBT education, concentration training and goal setting. Thus the work, whilst underpinned by REBT, includes mental skills training. So even in the early days of applying REBT to sport, there has been a recognition that it is complementary to broader mental skill development that reflect general, rather than specific, REBT.

The toolkit argument (again!)

As indicated in the convergence of the GABCDE framework and Gross' process model, it is possible, and favourable, to approach using REBT with a pluralistic and eclectic philosophy. As Neenan and Dryden state in 2010, "REBT is a form of theoretically consistent eclecticism, meaning that it advocates the broad use of techniques, from wherever, but to achieve goals in keeping with REBT theory" (p. 17). I take 'to achieve goals in keeping with REBT theory' to be a statement that applies to the whole GABCDE framework, not just B. By adopting REBT as one's approach to working in performance settings, it is possible to utilise a broad range of techniques, and teach clients a large gamut of psychological skills, whilst comfortably remaining consistent with the GABCDE framework of REBT. REBT is not simply a tool in the toolkit of the practitioner, REBT *is* the toolkit, and PST can sit (quite prominently I would argue) within that toolkit alongside many other tools, like the emotion regulation strategies within the process model of emotion regulation (Gross & Thompson, 2007). REBT is eclectic, because people are eclectic.

Specific vs. general REBT

With all the relevant options for helping clients regulate emotions made possible with the alignment of the GABCDE framework with Gross & Thompson's (2007) process model and the canon of psychological skills (Andersen, 2009), the reader might be wondering whether the author has gotten a little far from the main aims of REBT, which is traditionally considered to be cognitive (deep/core belief) change (using cognitive, emotive, and behavioural methods). To be clear, in line with the primacy of cognitive change, the REBT practitioner will usually seek the elegant, specific REBT solution of belief change as a priority, but for various reasons this is not always possible or advantageous. The client may be resistant to belief change, the situation they are in might constitute an emergency or at least involve some sort of temporal limitation or restriction, or despite multiple attempts, the client is unable to comprehend the core tenets of specific REBT and thus is unlikely to engage fully in explicit belief change activities (e.g., Bowman & Turner, 2022). In these cases, the practitioner can compromise (Dryden, 1987) and execute inelegant, general, REBT (e.g., David, 2015; Dryden, 1987; Ellis, 1977), for which Dryden (2019a) presents four options, (a) change their distorted inferences, (b) change their behaviour, (c) learn new skills, and (d) change or leave the situation which provides the context for their problem. In light of the current chapter, it is hoped that the reader can view these four options through the lens of the process model of emotion regulation and canon of psychological skills.

Within inelegant, or 'general' REBT, it is recognised that change can be elicited by applying methods other than the deep belief change that characterise elegant, or 'specific' REBT (Dryden & David, 2008). The REBT practitioner, for example, can help clients to change their distorted inferences (Beck, 1976), to activate themselves behaviourally (Veale & Willson, 2007), and to learn new skills such as assertiveness (Alberti & Emmons, 2001). If we also consider Gross' process model of emotion regulation, we obviously have various other opportunities for helping the client in elegant and inelegant ways, in line with and in addition to Dryden's four very useful options. To be clear, the REBT practitioner can apply elegant (specific) or inelegant (general) REBT and still work within the REBT GABCDE framework. Thus, as Dryden and David (2008) posit,

> there can be a single approach to REBT that details belief change as its preferred target but that incorporates and targets other types of change (e.g., inferential change, behavioral change, and situational change) when belief change is not possible with certain clients or is not acceptable to others.
>
> (p. 197)

There is one REBT, and different paths to take within it (see Figure 2.7). For the purposes of the present book, to describe the path of elegant REBT (characterised by deep belief change), I use the term 'specific REBT' – to describe the inelegant path of REBT (characterised by broader targets for change aside from beliefs), I use the term 'general REBT'.

Furthermore, acceptance-based strategies can be employed in REBT (e.g., Dryden, 2018; 2021a) as antecedent-focussed and/or response-focussed attempts to regulate emotion, with a cognitive shift from judgemental non-acceptance to acceptance taking place, and can be applied to precedent and antecedent cognition (and emotion) (Herbert & Forman, 2013). After all, working on acceptance is change (Collard, 2019) and acceptance strategies can be indirect methods of cognitive restructuring (e.g., David & Hofmann, 2013; Ellis, 2005a). Both Herbert and Forman (2013) and Collard (2019) indicate that acceptance and commitment therapy (ACT) has various similarities to the second-wave CBTs of cognitive therapy (CT) and REBT. Not least, ACT theory does not preclude cognitive causation (Herbert & Forman, 2013), and many of the differences between ACT and REBT appear to be "due to the implicit versus explicit attentional foci of the different models" and "the development of idiosyncratic language by the different authors" (Collard, 2019, p. 126). I agree with Collard when he suggests that there is more to be gained by bringing ACT and REBT together as a broader cognitive-behavioural framework.

Therefore, the astute REBT practitioner will not rigidly and unnecessarily limit themselves to a method or type of intervention or solution for a client, choosing instead to work flexibly with clients to arrive at functional outcomes in contexts where a specific singular type of strategy may not be suited to a particular individual (Collard, 2019). Thus, although in REBT cognitive change could be taken to mean the weakening of irrational beliefs in favour of rational beliefs (i.e., specific REBT), cognitive change of other forms can also take place (e.g., at A). In any case, in REBT we do not promote change in cognition for the sake of it, striving for 'elegance' at the cost of pragmatics. The focus of cognitive change is to enhance functionality across cognitive, emotional and behavioural domains, which can encompass

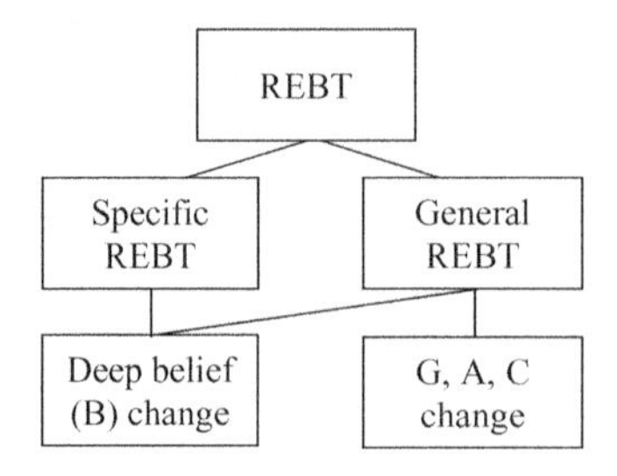

Figure 2.7 Specific REBT vs. general REBT.

'indirect' methods of cognitive change (e.g., flooding, or exposure; e.g., Beck & Haigh, 2014), and of course, direct disputation (D). At a meta-cognitive level, the REBT practitioner also seeks to educate clients concerning a second-order philosophy of scientific empiricism to encourage flexibility and pragmatic evaluation of thoughts, feelings and behaviours. One of the key goals of REBT is to help the client to weaken and decommission the rigid systems through which they are approaching their life (Ellis, 2003a).

Even if specific REBT is successful, it does not preclude working with A and C. Say you have a client who presents with unhealthy anger (UNE), for example. You work with the underlying irrational beliefs and help them to develop and strengthen rational beliefs (i.e., specific REBT), so now the client is able to express healthy anger (HNE). But this anger may still be unpleasant and sub-optimal for performance, so when they face a situation in which they are transgressed by somebody, they can apply some breathing or relaxation techniques, or practise acceptance, to modify C. Going forward, they can learn which situations might lead to anger and can make better choices via problem-solving and situation selection. So, whilst B is the most effective focus for assuaging unhealthy anger, healthy anger can still be acquiesced by addressing A and C (and of course modifying G). These options fit well into the process model of emotion regulation, and within REBT. The goal that drives the work with the client is surely to support them towards more adaptive functioning, and with evidence indicating equivocal differences across CBT modes (e.g., CT, REBT, ACT; Stefan et al., 2019), a practitioner can flexibly, and collaboratively with the client, decide which approach might be the best for the client. REBT, and CBT per se, cannot accurately be reduced to the practice of simply changing 'bad' thoughts to 'good' thoughts (Hofmann et al., 2013).

Critics of REBT often calibrate their concerns against *specific* REBT, and take a rather dogmatic stance over REBT, suggesting that REBT is only about deep belief change. But this is a falsehood, because as early as the 1970s Ellis presented a broader more general REBT that incorporates deep belief change, but does not rely on it exclusively (Ellis, 1977). If we only have a hammer in our toolkit, then we are likely to only see nails in front of us. In other words, if one only adopts a specific REBT approach to working with clients, we will always, and sometimes fallaciously, apply disputation and deep belief change even when it is not needed or warranted. As practitioners, we should aim to be flexible in our approaches, because situations and emotions change dynamically and therefore the ability to respond flexibly to these changes is an essential building block for psychological health (e.g., Blanke et al., 2020).

Practitioners who are REBT fundamentalists and pursue only 'specific' REBT may ascribe to the notion that REBT should *only* be about revealing and disputing irrational beliefs. The current author recognises that practitioners can work with (i.e., assess and intervene) each element of the framework. I subscribe to Dryden's (2010) notions of *specific* REBT in which B (specifically primary irrational beliefs first, then secondary irrational beliefs) is the focus of the work, and *general* REBT in which the practitioner can work with A too. I go a little further in this book, and suggest that we can inelegantly (generally) work with G and C as well as A, or we can elegantly (specifically) work with B; all options fall within the purview of a single REBT (Dryden & David, 2008), but specific REBT is about uncovering and disputing irrational beliefs at B in the service of goal fulfilment. Whether and to what extent the REBT practitioner decides to work with A, for example, instead of or as well as the B, is dependent on the context and the client, and it is important to understand the humanistic notion that people are more important than theories and frameworks.

Context, context, context

One reason why a broader approach to the GABCDE framework is useful for practitioners is because some contexts we work within do not enable a comprehensive exploration into core beliefs. It is practical and pragmatic at times to work with G, A, and C, which still conforms to, and is theoretically consistent with, REBT, but draws upon general REBT principles, rather than specific REBT. Unfortunately, or fortunately depending on your viewpoint, many psychologists working within performance contexts toil in environments which are characterised in part by time, access, and resource limitations. For example, when working within professional football, I had one evening per week (6–10:30pm) in which to work with players. Training would begin at 8pm, and finish at 9:30pm. As such, work with individual athletes was restricted to pre- or post-training, or during training for injured athletes. Match days also created some opportunities for 'light' one-to-one work. Restrictions on time were a result of restrictions in budget – it is common across many sports that the budget for psychological support is dwarfed by various other resource-draining factors. Suffice to say, getting 50-minutes once per week with a client is not particularly common, although it obviously does happen. Therefore, working in ways consistent with the GABCDE framework that can be achieved in brief amounts of time (e.g., Bowman & Turner, 2022), sometimes on an ad hoc basis at short notice, is vital for many practitioners.

Say an athlete approaches you five minutes before a match and reports that "I am absolutely dreading this match, I don't think I can go out there". There is precious little time to execute a full GABC assessment and a protracted meander into D and E is probably out of the question. But say you have worked with this athlete frequently, and as part of your work, REBT has been a focus. Then it might be possible to remind the athlete in that moment with some useful rational reminders, in essence, skipping straight to E. Or you could remind the athlete of the B–C connection, perhaps dissuading A–C thinking. Or, you could even potentially venture into some principles about truth, logic, and pragmatics. However, if you have not worked with this athlete before, and there is no baseline understanding of REBT, then the aforementioned pieces of work are unlikely to be sufficiently comprehended by the athlete, especially in the chaotic storm that often defines the final moments prior to performance.

This is where we can draw more broadly on the GABCDE framework, pursuing some general, rather than specific, REBT goals. We could work with G and help the athlete to clarify and crystallise their match goals. We could work with A and help the athlete to see that there is nothing to dread about the match. We could work with C and help them to relax and centre themselves. Drawing on the process model of emotion regulation, we could help the athlete to deploy their attention towards task relevant information, rather than towards task irrelevant information. We may even do the opposite, if there is a useful focus away from the task that might facilitate some calm. We could utilise some psychological skills such as imagery to encourage the athlete to image successfully executing their first on-pitch actions, or self-talk to encourage some positive affirmations about their ability to perform at this level.

None of this work is designed to facilitate long-term change, philosophic or otherwise. It is designed to help the athlete in the moment. To provide some practical advice or guidance in order to help them into the best possible psychological state prior to competing. Post-match, it is then possible to make arrangements with the athlete to explore their pre-performance experiences in more depth, moving towards longer-term solutions, and a more meaningful exploration of the GABCDE framework, and possibly even specific REBT.

AN ASIDE ABOUT 'CHANGE': IS 'CHANGE' THE RIGHT WORD?

In this chapter I have spent much time covering 'cognitive change' and in this book as a whole, I speak of belief change as a core aspect of REBT. But of course, change is not really the correct terminology at all. You cannot change a belief. You cannot turn the irrational belief into a rational belief. Rather, you weaken the extent to which you endorse irrational beliefs, and strengthen the extent to which you endorse rational beliefs, so that the rational becomes dominant. Even then, it is unlikely that irrational beliefs will be vanquished eternally (e.g., Wills & Sanders, 2013), and the practitioner should prepare the client for continual work to weaken irrational beliefs as they appear and reappear. As Pierson and Hayes (2007) point out, it is less about negative thought replacement and more about following the negative thought with a more balanced thought. In REBT, you will see that rational beliefs usually explicitly negate the irrational beliefs. For example, a preference belief is not just a statement of preference ("I would like..."), it is also a negation of demand ("...but that does not mean I have to"). A variety of cognitions are simultaneously available to us, but the more functional cognitions are more difficult to retrieve especially when experiencing emotional turmoil. Think of rationality and irrationality as two separate dials (Figure 2.8 a,b), like bass and treble on a sound system. Bass and treble are separate, but interact, and can be adjusted independently, just like irrational and rational beliefs. Irrational and rational beliefs are not at opposite ends of the same continuum (Bernard, 2009), they are separate, but interacting.

So, when I speak of belief change in this book, it is the transition away from irrational beliefs and towards rational beliefs that I am referring to, which involves weakening the irrational beliefs, and strengthening the rational beliefs.

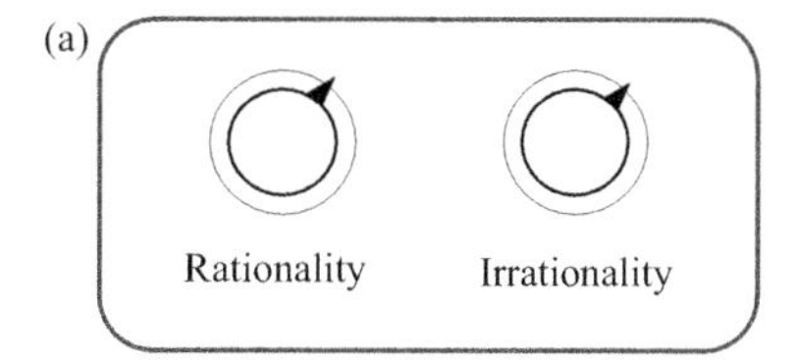

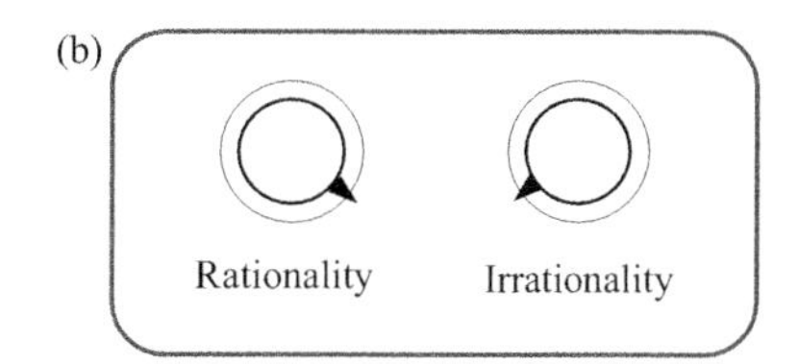

Figure 2.8 (a) Rational/irrational frequency dials. (b) High rationality and low irrationality on the rational/irrational frequency dials.

Anger management: an example

Say we have a client who presents with an issue underpinned by intense anger concerning being slighted by a teammate. After some interactions with the client, it is uncovered that they believe that people must not treat them with disrespect and when they do, they cannot stand it. A specific REBT approach would follow Chapters 5–13 of this book, including disputation (D) of irrational beliefs (i.e., demandingness and frustration intolerance) and the development of rational beliefs (E) (i.e., preferences and frustration tolerance), and the shift from maladaptive or unhealthy anger to adaptive or healthy anger. However, the client may also harbour beliefs such as "they will never respect me", "they always treat me this way", and "they think I'm an idiot". None of these beliefs are irrational in the empirico-logical sense, because they *could be* true. It might actually be the case that the teammate may never respect the client. It might be that the teammate always behaves in this way. The teammate may indeed think the client is an idiot. It is possible for the client to hold these beliefs, and also hold core rational beliefs. So, if a client believes they will never be respected, that the teammate always does this, and that the teammate thinks they are an idiot, but also *rationally* believes "I would prefer it if they did respect me, but they don't have to just because I want it, and it is tough, but I can certainly tolerate them not respecting me" then what do we do as REBTers? Just leave them be? Walk away?

No. We don't need irrational beliefs to be present to work with clients using REBT. We can apply cognitive change to the 'always and never' thinking and the 'mind-reading' (as would be more typical in CT), or we can encourage acceptance (more typical in ACT), or we can help the client to practise functional behaviours when they interact with the teammate (working on C), or we can help the client to avoid interactions with the teammate (working on A), or distract themselves from the negative thoughts that arise, etcetera. We would for sure be helping the client to commit to facing the issues head-on, and anything distraction (or avoidance) based would be short term.

We have many options for helping clients over and above irrational beliefs. Some options are better than others (distraction is usually less than ideal), and each option is to be applied within the context of enabling the fulfilment of potential as a human being. This might mean that some strategies are suitable in a time-restricted situation, whilst other strategies are less suitable. I would rarely recommend deep belief change with a client, five-minutes prior to competition, for example (belief change is taxing). Some strategies might be dependent on a stronger working alliance, compared to other strategies. And of course, all strategies are limited to the extent that we as practitioners are competent enough to apply them. The main point I am making here is that if you adopt an REBT approach to working with clients, be aware that you have many more options than just disputation and core belief change, although you should of course be skilled in these elements to enable specific REBT.

We can apply acceptance-based techniques within REBT (Dryden, 2018, 2021a), in part because this strategy is congruent with the GABCDE framework, and acceptance itself is a cornerstone of REBT (although, there is some disagreement about where that acceptance is directed; Ellis, 2005a). Of course, we can work with clients to redefine their goals (G), to make more advantageous choices concerning the types of situations they enter into (A), and to relax and/or activate in order to make use of a functional physiologic state (C) for competition, for example. We can also help them to challenge core beliefs too (D), learn about the mind through psychoeducation, and develop and reinforce a guiding philosophy of life steeped in rationality (E). REBT is not characterised by a single-minded obsession with cognitive change, but it suits REBT's detractors to paint it as such. In truth, REBT is much broader that is often realised, and in this chapter, I have attempted to illustrate this breadth by showing that the GABCDE framework is congruent with prominent approaches to emotion regulation and sport psychology practice.

Therefore, as a practitioner, I rarely feel the need to venture too far from REBT when working with clients, since the solutions to many client issues can be addressed using the broad and interdependent GABC(DE) framework I propose in this book. This broad and interdependent GABC(DE) framework aligns with prominent emotion regulation and sport psychology literature, and should not be considered to be a peripheral approach to sport psychology work. Without Ellis and REBT, there is no PST. When applying REBT, we are not just engaging in belief change, and sometimes, we *never* (purposely) engage in belief change. In other words, REBT is not shorthand for disputation, and in true REBT fashion, the whole cannot be defined by one part. A humanistic REBTer is sensitive to what the client needs, rather than pursuing specific REBT to the detriment of humanism.

Summary

It would of course have been impossible for the early Stoics to have envisioned the future importance of their ideas or the recapitulation of their philosophy within contemporary psychological theory and research. REBT in many ways flies the flag for Stoicism in this modern age, especially in its GABCDE framework. In this chapter, I introduced the GABCDE framework of REBT, covering its Stoic roots, its reverberations and relations within prominent emotion and emotion regulation theory, aligned REBT with PST, and further delineated specific REBT from general REBT. The blending of Ellis', Lazarus', and Gross' systems of emotion offer a way to manage emotions, that work all the way across the GABCDE framework. The major distinction between Lazarus' and Gross', and Ellis' systems, lay within the emphasis on irrational beliefs in REBT, but also, Ellis developed a coherent therapy alongside his theory of emotion. I hoped to advance the readers' understanding of how the GABCDE framework can be used by aligning it with other models that provide additional tools and techniques for emotion management. It is possible to apply REBT eclectically by making the most of a variety of evidence-based, CBT-derived, psychological techniques, whilst retaining theoretical consistency. In the next chapter, I move the GABCDE framework on further still, by examining the interdependent nature of its constituent elements.

CHAPTER 3
The *interdependent* GABC(DE) framework

We suffer under this burden.

DOI: 10.4324/9781003200437-4

> Ellis has always been clear that beliefs do not cause disturbed or constructive responses to adversity. To make this claim would be tantamount to saying that beliefs are completely separate from feelings, a stance that would violate the principle of psychological interdependence that has been present in REBT theory since its inception.
>
> (Dryden, 2012b, p. 84)

One aspect that is not always fully articulated in REBT works is the interdependent and reciprocal nature of the elements that make up the GABCDE framework. In how I have presented the GABCDE framework thus far, and indeed how it is presented in much REBT literature, it appears as though perception, cognition, and emotion are separated into distinct categories. However, even in his early writings, Ellis was insistent that the elements of the GABCDE framework are *interdependent* and cannot be separated (Still, 2010). The separation of these elements is really a pragmatic approach to understanding and using the framework, rather than a literal and technically accurate portrayal of how the elements relate to each other. As Still (2010) recognises, such separation might be necessary for training and therapeutic purposes, but at a deeper level there is interdependence between the elements of the GABCDE framework. This interdependence not only more accurately reflects how the GABCDE elements function together, but also helps us as practitioners to utilise the framework in practice..

In the current chapter I make the case, or rather recapitulate Ellis' (1962, 1994) assertions, that each element of the GABCDE framework is interconnected and therefore interdependent; each element is dependent on each other element. I introduce and detail the interdependent GABC(DE) framework (D and E are in parentheses to denote them as implicit), which is a representation of the interconnected nature of each element of the GABCDE framework. I cover theoretical justifications for this interdependent GABC(DE) framework, and then discuss its applied implications. To be clear, the author of the current book has not 'invented' the interdependent GABC(DE) framework, but I am articulating it in a way that reedifies or renews the field's appreciation of how interactional the elements are. This is important because the interdependence of the GABC(DE) framework has implications for how REBT can be practised, particularly in light of the specific and general REBT options we have as practitioners, as highlighted in the previous chapter.

Taking what we have covered thus far into consideration, aligning the GABCDE framework with prominent emotion and emotion regulation theory, and recognising specific and general REBT, it is possible to present REBT as a holistic approach to emotion regulation, and more broadly human functioning. I use the philosophical sense of 'holistic' here, in that the individual elements of the GABCDE framework are intimately interconnected only by reference to the whole. To modify, or intervene with, one aspect of the GABCDE framework is to modify, or intervene with, all aspects, such is the interdependent nature of the framework. As such, whether or not an REBT practitioner drives towards specific REBT, each element of the GABCDE framework can be subject to collateral modification in a variety of ways, with a view to helping the client.

Through the alignment of the GABCDE framework with Lazarus' (1999) CAT, Gross' process model of emotion regulation (Gross, 2014), and/or the canon of psychological skills (Andersen, 2009), the management of emotions can be achieved in various ways aside from, and alongside, belief change. You can try to change the situation (selection or modification) to avoid (or reduce) goal relevance and/or goal incongruence (or A); problem-focussed coping. You can choose a different focus of attention in the situation (attention), or deploy cognitive change altering your inferences about the situation (A) or you can modify your beliefs (B) to be less irrational and more rational (via D and E); emotion-focussed coping. And you can modify the emotion after it has been generated (response modulation; C). Lastly, you can downscale your goals (G), making A less noxious, stripping your endeavours of personal meaning and relevance, thus removing the emotion (a nihilistic approach not recommended for those who want to achieve anything worthwhile in a performance setting).

As others have noted, since the inception of REBT in the 1950s, Ellis insisted that each element is interdependent and cannot be separated (Still, 2010). Ellis (1962) clearly states that, "The theoretical foundations of R[EB]T are based on the assumption that human thinking and emotion are *not* two disparate or different processes...they are integrally interrelated and never can be seen wholly apart from each other" (pp. 38–39). He goes on to say that, "...none of the four fundamental life operations – sensing, moving, emoting, and thinking – is experienced in isolation" (p. 39). In line with the Stoics, who considered thinking and emotion to be essentially interdependent, Ellis too stressed the interdependence of thinking and emotion (Still & Dryden, 1999). Dryden (1994, p. 93) refers to this as psychological interactionalism, and has this to say about interrelation in REBT:

> Frequently, people wrongly claim that RE[B]T maintains that cognitions cause emotions. This linear relationship, however, belies the complexity of the cognition-emotion interface, and RE[B]T has never considered it valid. Instead, certain cognitions and emotions are deemed in RE[B]T to overlap and are interrelated in such a complex manner that they become practically indistinguishable from each other.

Although the idea of interrelation of perception, cognitive, emotion, and behaviour was captured within REBT from the early days, the elaboration and systematisation of this interrelation is not always obvious in REBT writing and training. In practice, this interrelation is quite clear, and is self-evident as soon as any meaningful conversation takes place between client and practitioner. Clients usually do not talk about their issues in well-defined and explicit theoretically coherent ways, neatly separating their thoughts from feelings.

In the interdependent GABC(DE) framework, there is no *need* to separate perception, cognition, emotion, and behaviour into distinct categories, although one may *want* to separate the elements because it can be useful for the purposes of research and training. Also, there is no need to view the GABCDE framework as temporally linear. In practice, there is no need for the practitioner to go 'from G to E' in sequential order, so to speak. It is more accurate to consider each element (or letter) of the framework to be highly interactional. Each element affects each other element reciprocally, so that changes in one element are associated with changes in others. For example, irrational beliefs (B) are echoed in our cognitions, which are articulated through language (internally and/or externally) and inform our actions (C). We rehearse these irrational beliefs and thus form habits around them. If I "can't stand" frustration, I will tend to avoid difficult and demanding circumstances and shape my behaviour in service of that avoidance (C). In turn, I will temper my goals (G), since I can't tolerate, and thus choose not to face, the difficult and demanding situations that might be requisite to meaningful goals. My goals change (G), so I am less likely to meet adversity (A) to my goals (since I no longer hold those goals). How will I ever fulfil my potential, if I cannot act towards meaningful goals? Thus, one can begin to see how irrational beliefs can influence each GABC aspect of the framework to undercut fulfilment of potential.

As can be seen in Figure 3.1, each element of the framework is joined with an interaction line to indicate interdependence. It should also be noted that the D and E in the interdependent

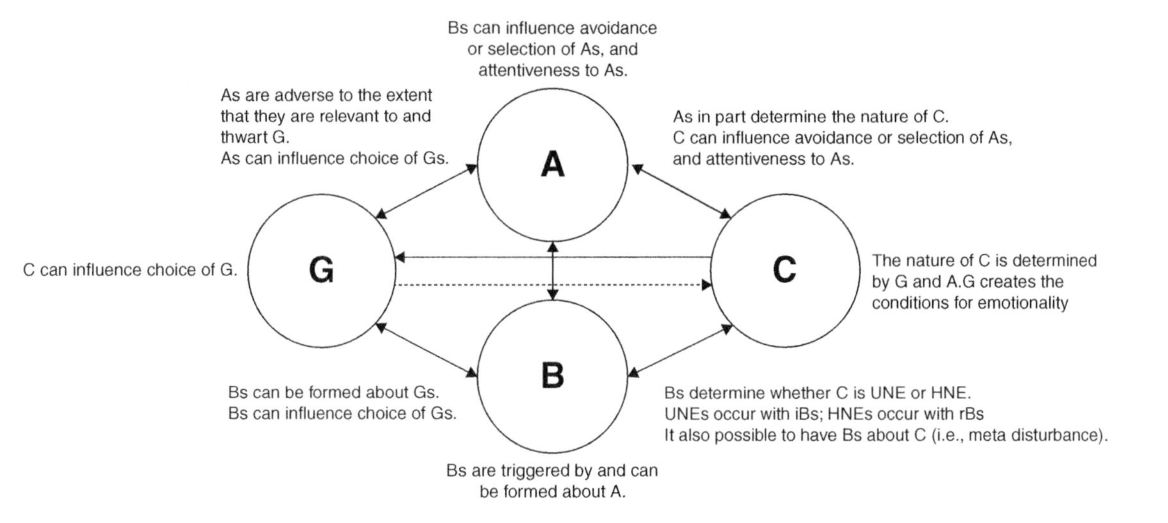

Figure 3.1 A diagrammatic representation of the interdependent GABC(DE) framework. The dotted line between G and C reflects the more distal relationship between these two elements, because it is the relevance and incongruence elicited by A in relation to G that gives rise to negative emotion, not G itself.

GABC(DE) framework are implied and relate only to B, and thus for graphical simplicity, are not displayed in Figure 3.1.

The interconnected way in which the GABCDE framework operates, widely opens the door to broader ways of working, that not only reflect specific and general REBT, but also marry with a whole host of approaches for which REBT (and CBT per se) is the foundation, such as psychological skills training (PST; Claspell, 2010). The interdependence of GABCDE is often lost in practice where the independence and distinctness of each element has served as a convenient (albeit somewhat inaccurate) guide for practical intervention (Still & Dryden, 1999). But we do not move from G, to A, to B, to C, to D, to E. There is no real starting place and stopping place. For example, once we have covered E, we do not down tools and smoke a cigar. The transition from irrational to rational beliefs may bring with it modifications to G, and a whole new set of As, and new Cs. In addition, just because a client transitions from unhealthy to healthy emotions (C), does not mean that the healthy emotion is not in need of regulation. So we work with the client to orient these new experiences towards goal attainment – just because the client is now on the 'right' path to goal attainment, does not mean they do not require or want some guidance in actually walking the path.

Rather than a linear process, it is more accurate to consider the GABCDE framework as an iterative process and guiding schematic for helping clients to regulate emotion (and of course behaviour) with a view to making the fulfilment of potential more likely. In my work with clients the chief aim is to enable greater functioning, which could be in service of healthier being, goal attainment, and more generally, the fulfilment of human potential. To facilitate this chief aim, it is best we do not take a blinkered approach to applying REBT, or be too linear and literal when it comes to using the GABCDE framework. Rather, we should look to each aspect of the GABCDE framework and make use of its interconnectedness with each other aspect, to help the client in whatever ways are most helpful for them – as is the humanistic way – remaining consistent to REBT theory and keeping the context in which we are working at the front of our minds. As discussed earlier, some situations are prohibitive of cognitive change, but are conducive to many other effective emotion regulation strategies.

The GABCDE framework is the broad and holistic framework that Ellis proposed, but this has since been lost in the weeds. It is inaccurate and reductionistic to suggest that REBT is all about disputational belief change, and this inaccuracy is confounded when we as practitioners fail to draw on the many methods, aside from cognitive change, we can use to help clients. As can be seen in the interdependent GABC(DE) framework, because each element is related with each other element, there are multiple points of potential intervention. Perception, cognition, and emotion are inextricably linked, co-occur with, and include, each other (Ellis, 1994).

To B or not to B

Let's say you have an athlete client who is unhealthily anxious (C; constant worry, trouble sleeping, is on edge constantly) about an upcoming important selection trial (A), which is relevant to and incongruent with their goal (G) of becoming a professional athlete. They harbour irrational beliefs (B): "I want to and therefore I must be selected, I can't stand being judged unfavourably, and it would be terrible not to make it into the team"). A core aim of specific REBT is to dispute the irrational belief (D), and to develop and strengthen a new rational belief (E), enabling the client to experience healthy anxiety (C; preparation, approach) about the upcoming selection trial (A). Suitable rational beliefs might be:

> I want to be selected but that does not mean I have to be, being judged unfavourably is tough, but I can tolerate it and its worth it to do so, and it would be bad not to make it into the team, but certainly not terrible.

There is compound interest in investing in a rational belief that can occur due to the independent GABCDE framework. The client is more likely to voluntarily face performance pressure and judgement, putting themselves forward for opportunities that they may not have considered before. They can move towards more meaningful Gs in part because the As they are likely to face are less threatening (i.e., A is likely to be tolerable rather than intolerable). The Cs are not prohibitive of facing As in which judgement is likely, because the rational way in which Gs and As are approached brings about HNEs (i.e., approach) instead of UNEs (i.e., avoidance). Also, the athlete can now take action to try to ensure that they do not face any unnecessary As that could thwart their Gs – they do not need to avoid thinking about or practically dealing with As forthrightly, because the possible occurrence of A is less threatening. The athlete's new proclivity towards approaching As more forthrightly, in the longer term, may also serve to desensitise them to A, so that what was adverse in the past, becomes less adverse in the future. This could reduce the extent to which irrational beliefs are activated in the face of future judgement and evaluation in situations such as trials.

This notion that beliefs can influence the perception of A is similar to DiGiuseppe's (1986) personal paradigm or world-view proposal (influenced by Kelly, 1955), in which beliefs are considered to be schema (conscious and unconscious) rather than just evaluative cognitions. These schema, or self-theories, help to shape our view of the world, and as such, influence our perceptions, inferences, and evaluations about the things we experience. The evaluation process is triggered by the inference, which depends on one's perceptions, which is deduced from one's personal paradigms or schema. In other words, our rational and irrational beliefs

(Bs) about ourselves and the world can influence what we perceive, infer, and evaluate at A. Thus, specific REBT *elegantly* targets and seeks to change these underlying schema or personal paradigms in the form of beliefs. It is the underlying views of the self and the world that we seek to adjust, a task that is not likely to be achieved through the disputation of perceptual or inferential As. By doing this, we collaterally influence the client's perceptions, inferences, and evaluations at A.

So, by instantiating new rational beliefs the client not only experiences healthier emotions at C, but can also manage G and A properly in the service of fulfilling their potential. In addition, by holding rational beliefs, the client is less likely to perceive or form dysfunctional inferences at A (Bond et al., 1999). That is, by approaching situations with a rational philosophy, one is less likely to extract dysfunctional (unhelpful) meanings from potentially emotionally evocative stimuli. If I have the belief that "being embarrassed in public is terrible and I couldn't possibly stand it", then I am henceforth sensitised, or hypervigilant, to stimuli that could bring forth shame, and may even creatively convince myself that I have failed to live up to an ego ideal, even if this is not actually the case. I might see disdain and scorn in my interactions with people, regardless of whether this disdain and scorn is actually and objectively present. This can happen due to the interrelatedness of the GABCDE framework.

In light of the interdependent GABC(DE) framework, one can focus on B specifically (i.e., specific REBT), or one can focus on G, A, and/or C, as part of a holistic approach to client issues and client goal attainment (i.e., general REBT). There is no written rule that in order to apply REBT, one MUST dispute irrational beliefs and instantiate rational beliefs. This type of cognitive change characterises *specific* REBT, but the specific and elegant solution in REBT is only one option; there are many other options. This isn't a novel edification in REBT – Ellis (1977) was quite clear that REBT can be done 'elegantly' (specifically) or 'inelegantly' (generally) as I have already discussed previously in this book. But why the issue about using the GABCDE framework more holistically is important within the context of interdependence is because by focussing on A, for example, we can still instantiate changes in C – a specific focus on B is not always necessary. Of course, if assessment indicates problematic irrational beliefs, and opportunity and will is there to address these irrational beliefs, then specific REBT with an acute focus on D and E is recommended. But the practitioner can be more open to working with G, A, and C safe in the knowledge that changes in the other elements are possible (and highly probable).

In this interdependent view of the GABCDE framework, irrational beliefs of course importantly and significantly contribute to UNEs, but causation is arrived at via a complex transaction between the environment and the individual, involving many interpersonal factors, not just beliefs. To ask "what causes an emotion?" is a very complicated question with more than one answer, and there are volumes of text dedicated to this question (see Barrett, 2018, for a contemporary view on this). In REBT, we recognise this complexity, but notice that irrational beliefs are conducive to maladaptive ways of thinking, feeling, and acting, whilst rational beliefs are conducive to adaptive ways of thinking, feeling, and acting. So, whilst many factors can cause an emotion, in specific REBT, much like in Stoicism, we focus on the factors that can be volitionally and realistically controlled by normal fallible human beings. That is, since beliefs play an important role in underpinning emotional consequences, and since beliefs are malleable, with inclination and dedication, beliefs are a worthy target for helping people to regulate their emotions. We can work with irrational and rational beliefs more reliably and more easily than modifying the many external stimuli that might present as emotionally evocative As. The focus on beliefs in REBT is thus a function of the important role beliefs play in human emotions, and also the pragmatic reality that beliefs can be assessed and modified through a reliable person-centred collaborative process.

To be clear, there is some confusion about the role of B in emotionality. The proper way to view B, based on the evidence, is that it significantly influences the extent to which a healthy or unhealthy emotion arises, and influences the severity (intensity) of negative emotion (and other illbeing markers; Vîslă et al., 2016). Furthermore, the extent to which a belief is causal to a client's emotional issues is arrived at via discursive methods, exploring with the client through Socratic dialogue the extent to which the beliefs they hold are indeed contributing to their disturbance. As pointed out by Dryden and Still (2012), when engaging with a client we are undertaking experimental thinking which includes forming hypotheses, stating them, testing them, forming new hypotheses, and so on. It is not so much that when a client experiences unhealthy anger we just observe the client's self-talk for signs of irrationality. We home in on the causal connection between beliefs and emotional consequences by applying various methods. For example, we can engage the client Socratically in dialogue concerning cognitive differences between instances of healthy vs. unhealthy anger. When they are transgressed by a loved one, what factors dictate their healthy vs. unhealthy response? Also, we can help the client to experiment with different self-talk using imagery, for example (e.g., Dryden, 1990), or out in the real world (Turner et al., 2019d), to test the effects of irrational vs. rational cognition on emotional consequences. The client and practitioner can see whether or not beliefs are playing a causal role in the client's issues, without over relying upon assumptions based on theory, but rather, using theory to guide exploration. Thus, the discourse that takes place between client and practitioner helps to establish causality directly, whilst the copious research data in the REBT literature helps to establish causality indirectly (Dryden & Still, 2012). Both are important, but a discursive approach speaks more to the historical development and practice of REBT.

I do not purport here that B unilaterally *causes* emotion or that only in the presence of irrational beliefs do unwanted and unpleasant emotions arise. Based on the extant research, and commonsensically, G and A (and the incongruence between G and A) are fundamental in creating the conditions for emotionality and in shaping the emotion (and associated action tendencies). Some critics of REBT assume that in REBT, B is the chief causal component for emotion. But taking an interdependent stance on the GABCDE framework, in line with Ellis' (1962, 1994) writings, it is possible to understand that the potential causal role of B is tied to the occurrence of UNEs and HNEs, and/or the exacerbation of negative emotion, rather than the evocation of emotion per se. In other words, it is not 'B = C', but rather, it is more accurate to state that 'G – A × B = C'.

NUTHIN' BUT A G THANG

Goals (G) underpin the desires that formulate preferences, and the extent to which A is relevant to and impedes G plays a significant role in determining the emotion at C, as per Lazarus' (1999) cognitive appraisal theory (CAT). To use the previous example about an athlete whose anxiety stems from facing selection trials, the prospect of not being selected at trials is only problematic and emotive because it is relevant to and might impede a current goal. So, it stands to reason that the more strongly you hold desires at G, the more affecting As will be. In addition, you are more likely to experience UNEs at C when holding irrational beliefs (B). One could reasonably argue that, since Gs underpin our desires, then merely desiring something puts us in danger of emotional suffering. Epictetus (Epictetus & Dobbin, 2008, p. 220) had this to say about desire:

> As for desire, suspend it completely for now. Because if you desire something outside your control, you are bound to be disappointed; and even things we do control, which under other circumstances would be deserving of our desire, are not yet within our power to attain. Restrict yourself to choice and refusal; and exercise them carefully, with discipline and detachment.

The key part for me here is, "if you desire something *outside your control*". Epictetus is warning us against desire, and makes the point that, "strong emotions arise only when we fail in our desires and aversions" (Epictetus, Discourses, 3.2. 1–3a). But he doesn't say that we can never desire – it is more like he is cautioning us against the pursuit of that which we cannot control, which for the most part, means that which is external to us. Donald Robertson (2018) suggests that for the Stoics, it is rational to *prefer* external goods, so long as they are not at the expense of eudaimonia (fulfilment). So when, for example, pursuing a successful career, one should not do so at the cost of one's mental and physical health, and one should consider a eudaimonic goal as one's primary purpose. I will talk about goals in a lot more detail in a dedicated chapter later in this book (Chapter 8). But for the purposes of this section, it is enough to acknowledge that our desires at G pave the way for suffering because we cannot control their procurement, and we are limited and fallible, and thus we are likely to face many As in pursuit of them. In other words, if you have Gs (which all human beings do!), then you should prepare for As, and as a result, Cs. In addition, it is not advisable to apply irrational beliefs to Gs, especially Gs that concern factors outside of our control, else those Cs are likely to present as UNEs.

So, whenever you aim towards a goal, emotional suffering is an indelible part of the goal pursuit, since you will be met with As that epitomise goal relevance and incongruence (key appraisal component for negative emotion). As such, the presence of A implies the existence of G. Therefore, you may as well aim for the highest possible good (reflecting your fundamental humanistic values), and strive to develop and strengthen rational beliefs about yourself, others, and the world, to make this emotional suffering meaningful and to avoid turning this mere emotional suffering into emotional turmoil. Of course, pursuing and perceiving that we are moving towards meaningful goals can also set forth positive emotion too – so as previously stated – the abandonment of goals altogether for reasons of emotion regulation is not a sophisticated strategy.

Practically, in line with the interdependent GABC(DE) framework, modifying G has an impact on what is considered to be adverse (A), and thus, the activation of beliefs (B) and associated consequences (Cs). Carefully selecting Gs is important, but equally, helping clients to reframe or reconsider their Gs so as not to unnecessarily invite As is a useful approach. For example, the athlete's goal of becoming a professional athlete could be modified to a more eudaimonic goal of fulfilling their potential as a human being, or being content that they worked hard and had many enlightening experiences and met lots of interesting people. These goals are not limited to sport endeavours, and are certainly not dependent on being viewed favourably by others (which is uncontrollable). A shift towards a more humanistic goal can reduce the extent to which a trial (i.e., try out) or potential deselection, for example, is seen as adverse (e.g., "deselection might negatively affect my sport career, but I am more than my career, so it can't stop me reaching fulfilment as a human being"), and can thus temper the emotionality of the event. Lastly, a trial is not seen as highly relevant to or a barrier to fulfilment (new G), and thus, the application of irrational beliefs concerning trials becomes less relevant and less disturbing.

Inferential A change

Working to change A does not necessarily mean we need to select or modify an external situation, it can also mean modifying the internal inference we make at A. Inferential change comprises altering one's inferences about one's experiences, rather than working to change deeply held beliefs (B) about these experiences (Dryden, 1994). For example, a client who is deeply hurt by the dismissive actions of a teammate may be encouraged to understand that just because a teammate gave them the cold shoulder, that doesn't mean that the teammate doesn't like them. Perhaps the teammate was having a bad day. A shift from "my teammate does not like me" to "they probably do like me, but maybe they were having a bad day" might enable the client to move quickly past a potential emotive situation simply by disarming the perceived adverseness of the situation. There is much to be gained by assuming or inferring the best.

The interrelatedness of the interdependent GABC(DE) framework means that changing A inferentially makes irrational beliefs inapplicable – if there is no activating event, then there is no activation of B. It is beliefs *about* A (and/or G) that are of import in REBT, so if the nature of A changes, or A is ameliorated completely (i.e., the situation is not adverse), then the relevance of any irrational belief is diminished. Changing the A also means that the client will likely no longer feel hurt (C) since the emotional stimuli is removed.

A valid argument against inferential change is that really what we are engaging clients in here is make-believe. We do not know that the teammate was having a bad day, so we are complicit in helping the client to (potentially) lie to themselves for the purposes of avoiding unwanted and unpleasant emotions. Indeed, if one of the goals of REBT is long-term hedonism, then practitioners should not encourage A change as a primary goal – we cannot sanitise the world – we should prepare the client for the road, not the road for the client (e.g., Lukianoff & Haidt, 2019). In A change, we are doing little to fortify the client against future "cold shoulders" and other slights and transgressions. We are helping the client to *feel* better, but we are not actually encouraging them to deal with life as it is. For these reasons, in part, that in REBT we take the next step, assume the inferential A is true, and ask the client "let's say your teammate does not like you, what would be so hurtful about that?" We can then explore the client's evaluative cognitions more deeply and understand whether irrational beliefs are at the core of the emotional issues seeming to emanate from the perceived transgression.

Although A change is not the primary target of specific REBT (Dryden, 1994), A change can be favourable in many circumstances. As indicated already, A change can be effective, and can be very simple and quick to execute. Inferential change might be a favourable approach in time limited situations with clients, or in situations where deep belief exploration is not possible or suitable. Inferential A change is also a very natural and appealing way to help people regulate their emotion. Think about the last conversation you had with a friend or partner in which they told you about an issue they were having with a colleague, friend, or family member. As a sympathetic friend or partner, your easiest and quickest way to help them feel better may have been to help them to change their inference. Maybe their colleague didn't mean what they said, maybe they misinterpreted their friend's poor behaviour, maybe their sibling was tired from work when they said what they said.

The key facet of this approach, which makes it problematic, is captured in the word 'maybe'. It is suboptimal to base one's emotional wellbeing on 'maybes'. It is more optimal, for longer-term emotional wellbeing, to assume the inference (A) is correct and to understand what it is specifically about the A that is problematic for the client. Is it that they cannot stand (i.e., frustration intolerance) being treated in this way? Is it that this treatment goes against their demand (i.e., demandingness) not to be transgressed? A more powerful solution is to develop rational beliefs concerning teammate transgression, which serve to fortify the client against future instances of perceived teammate transgression.

If you are using inferential A change and/or actual A change (situational selection or modification) as your main modus operandi, then consider what you are teaching your clients. You are teaching them that to control their emotions you need to sanitise the environment by either avoiding adversity, or by creatively constructing a self-serving story about the situation. You are teaching A–C thinking. So, as indicated by the interdependent GABC(DE) framework, whilst A change might be a valid and effective method of ameliorating emotional turmoil at C, and deactivating B, it is often a short-term and surface-level solution.

Premeditatio malorum ("the pre-meditation of evils")

> The wheels are going to come off any minute ... No, no, no. Don't you believe it. Just focus on what you have to do ... What shot do you want to hit here? ... I want to hit a solid drive, a touch of fade ... Fine good that's more like it ... Now, where, exactly, do you want to land it? ... left side of the fairway.
>
> Nick Faldo recalling what he was saying on the 1st tee on the final round of the Masters in 1996

The current author finds particularly useful in service of applying the GABCDE framework an exercise emanating from Stoicism literature. The exercise is called *premeditatio malorum*, and involves premeditation on the adversity and suffering that lies ahead. The practitioner encourages the client to imagine the worst that could happen in order to prepare and plan for known and unknown setbacks (As) that will block their goals (Gs). Seneca (Stoic philosopher and adviser to Emperor Nero died in 65 A.D) intimates towards this technique (Seneca & Campbell, 2004):

> What is quite unlooked for is more crushing in its effect, and unexpectedness adds to the weight of a disaster. This is a reason for ensuring that nothing ever takes us by surprise. We should project our thoughts ahead of us at every turn and have in mind every possible eventuality instead of only the usual course of events...Rehearse them in your mind: exile, torture, war, shipwreck. All the terms of our human lot should be before our eyes.

The idea of premeditating on the potential adversities of the future can also be used at a more acute level, for example, applied to the upcoming day or even the upcoming competition. At the beginning of Chapter 2 of Marcus Aurelius' Meditations, he tells himself that,

> Begin the morning by saying to thyself, I shall meet with the busy-body, the ungrateful, arrogant, deceitful, envious, unsocial...I can neither be injured by any of them, for no one can fix on me what is ugly, nor can I be angry with my kinsman, nor hate him...To act against one another then is contrary to nature; and it is acting against one another to be vexed and to turn away.

Aurelius pre-empts the *possible* adversity he might face, whilst asserting an acceptance of others, and negating A–C thinking.

This technique may seem counter-intuitive to some. Why would we engage the athlete in thoughts of failure and suffering? Because we know that a smooth path to success rarely exists, and *unanticipated* and *unexpected* adversities are more difficult to address when they occur. How can you prepare for something you are not aware of? Clearly, is it impossible to predict the future, but it is possible to use foresight to conceptualise and begin to problem-solve the things that *could reasonably* happen. This may reveal competence deficits in factors that are important for success, and can enable the athlete to plan their development via courses, training, or experiential learning. For the As and Bs that are most likely to combine to underpin UNEs, the athlete can actively or imaginally engage in the As as a form of desensitisation or flooding. The athlete can voluntarily take on that which they are most fearful of, for example. Then, the athlete can optimistically approach their goals safe in the knowledge that they have prepared for some of the adversities, and associated issues, that might befall them.

Behaviour change

Working to change C (directly, rather than through G, A, and B) can involve physiologic regulation such as relaxation and/or activation techniques, to change the somatic experience of the emotion. Wirga et al. (2020) usefully point out that emotional feelings may affect how one thinks about events, and that C may of course serve to change A, or one's perception of A. They use the example of engaging in a new activity (A) and succeeding in it (C), which may help the individual to realise that the activity is not as difficult as they thought. In addition, anger and aggression (C), underpinned by being wronged (A) and a belief that this treatment is "intolerable", may bring about avoidance of A in the future. Where there is no A, there is no C, or as Wirga et al. (2020) put it, "An event that is not perceived is not going to elicit any response" (p. 403). This is in line with Lazarus' (1999) cognitive appraisal theory (CAT), as previously discussed.

So, as well as somatic or physiologic change, we can also consider behavioural change at C. Behavioural change at C can influence G, A, and B, and also emotions at C. Going all the way back to the start of this book, Ellis' park bench escapades are a good example of how behavioural modification helped him to realise more rational ways of approaching the opposite sex and dealing with rejection, which helped him to manage his phobia. In REBT, stress inoculation is frequently recommended, and is often called 'flooding' (Ellis & Dryden, 1997), which is similar to desensitisation. By exhibiting approach behaviour, and intention, it can be learnt that:

1. The A is not *that* adverse after all (e.g., "I have faced A and it wasn't that bad – it didn't kill me or anyone else").
2. My irrational beliefs (B) about A are false (e.g., "I have faced A and therefore it obviously is not intolerable or awful").
3. I can achieve more in sport/work and/or life because I can set more meaningful and challenging goals (G) (e.g., "I can aim high because I no longer need to avoid things").
4. I have greater emotional control and can experience healthy emotions (C) in the face of A (e.g., "When future As present themselves, I have no need to fear them, and can prepare fully and face them head on").
5. Because I am no longer fearful and avoidant of A, my inferences about A are less incongruent with my goals (e.g., "this difficult situation is a surmountable and temporary barrier to my goals").

In brief, by facing that which you fear, goals that were restricted can now be freed, what was adverse is now not so much, or at all, and what was believed to be intolerable and awful is now believed to be merely uncomfortable and inconvenient (and perhaps even enjoyable). At the very least, crippling fear can reside, and healthy anxiety can emerge. Dryden and Ellis (1988) suggest that achieving philosophic change is less likely through inferential and behavioural change, and if B change is the aim of the work, then rigorous D and E are of course the best options. But such is the nature of the interdependent GABC(DE) framework, behavioural change can aid belief change.

When trying to understand the importance of behaviour for G, A, and C, it is worth considering the effects of avoidance. Ultimately, avoidance is no long-term solution to life's vicissitudes, in part because avoidance is only temporary and does not remove the adversity (A), and in part because avoidance reinforces the adverse nature of the event. The event remains, and can become even more, adverse because the client's avoidance behaviour reinforces and strengthens the stimulus. Why would you need to avoid it if it wasn't adverse? Avoidance can also affect the setting and pursuit of goals (G) because one way to avoid A is to modify one's aims so that A becomes an unlikely event. For example, an athlete who has the ability to compete at the highest level, but who fears public scrutiny, may scale back their goals to avoid ever having to deal with the limelight. Indeed, fear of failure per se can be abated by never aiming high, thus never having to deal with the prospect of failure (in theory!). Lastly, avoidance also serves to reinforce irrational beliefs pertaining to A. Because A is being avoided, it then follows that A must be intolerable and awful, or else why would I avoid it? I can continue to hold these irrational beliefs about public scrutiny because they seem legitimate, and I have no evidence that the A is not intolerable and awful since I have successfully avoided this A.

So, whilst avoidance is highly effective in changing C in the short term as a situation selection strategy, it has many drawbacks that make it a poor long-term solution. There is an important caveat though. As I say elsewhere in this book, there are of course situations for which avoidance is the safest and most appropriate option. I would never suggest a client approach or stay in a genuinely dangerous situation, regardless of any hypothetical long-range benefits downstream.

Under pressure: some interdependent solutions

> That's not pressure. Football's not pressure; it's fun. If you want to heap the pressure on, then that's you as an individual. But you play football as a game.
>
> Brad Friedel, USA goalkeeper with 84 caps (McCauley, 2012)

Imagine you are working with a client who freezes in pressure moments, wants to avoid pressure at all costs, and withdraws in training when put under public scrutiny (e.g., complete a drill in front of teammates). Clearly exhibiting unhealthy anxiety, the athlete has various options that we can work towards, that draw on the interdependent GABC(DE) framework. Each option for change here can confer changes to all other aspects of the GABCDE framework. In order of idealness:

1. Apply D and E to challenge and weaken irrational beliefs and develop and strengthen rational beliefs (i.e., philosophic belief [B] change). This option follows a specific REBT path, and works towards healthy anxiety (HNE). Details concerning this path can be found in this book, and is really the main focus of the chapters that proceed the current chapter.

2. Apply behavioural and physiologic techniques to achieve C change. We can help the client to adopt a confident and assertive orientation towards pressure situations, and/or help them to develop a breathing technique (or other relaxation strategy) in order to relax prior to and during pressure events. Alongside coaching staff, we can develop some pressure training drills (e.g., Turner & Jones, 2014, 2018) that allow the athlete to practise their behavioural and physiologic techniques, serving as inoculation against future pressure.
3. Apply situation selection and/or modification, and/or inferential change, to achieve A change. Changing the actual A here is difficult because avoiding pressure is not a good long-term solution for dealing with pressure, and situation selection and modification is not always possible. However, if the athlete is in a situation in which the anxiety is so severe that they may start to panic, then helping the client to have some workable solutions to removing themselves from the situation might be a useful short-term approach. By contrast, inferential change could help the athlete to approach pressure if they can reframe the significance (relevance) and incongruence of the situation. The pressure situation might be anxiety-provoking due to perceptions of judgement and evaluation by people that matter to the athlete, the prospect of letting people down, or the career consequences of failing in pressure moments. So we can achieve A change by scaling back, of redefining, the salience of the situation to their goals. That is, and harking back to the work of Richard Lazarus (1999), one way to reduce the emotionality of the situation is to reduce its personal relevance. The athlete could re-evaluate the importance of the situation to reduce the perceived pressure altogether. Thus, the athlete can change the inferential As by reframing these perceptions (e.g., I am sure people will not be judging me based on this performance, I won't be letting anybody down if I don't perform well, and I will still be able to have a career even if I fail under pressure). However, as mentioned previously, the downsides of this mindreading and clairvoyance, no matter how positively framed, must be considered.
4. The athlete could broaden their goals towards being a well-functioning and healthy human being, rather than just a successful athlete, thus reducing the extent to which the pressure situation is seen as existentially relevant. If there is less of a focus on and drive towards externally determined task success and more focus and drive towards eudaimonic and humanistic goals (enjoyment, learning, freedom, fulfilment), then the situation may be seen as less existentially threatening and actually could be embraced and enjoyed. Carrying the right G into pressure situations may bring forth positive affect, or at least functional negative Cs (HNEs). When approaching the pressure situation, a G might be to enjoy the competition, express oneself, and try to learn and develop, focussing on more self-determined aspects of the situation that are not dependent on external outcomes and markers, and as such, are less susceptible to As. Less As, less triggered Bs, and less UNEs. Also within G change, in the short term the athlete could lower their sights. If we have an easy goal (or no goal), then we cannot face (or are less likely to face) barriers to said goals. As discussed previously, there are some downsides to this, not least the fact that chronic low goals are not conducive to high achievement, and this approach is quite nihilistic. But for some athletes, who are suffering badly due to the constant pressure of performance, taking a step back can be an important moment of reflection and redefinition. Indeed, "I don't want to do this anymore" could reflect withdrawal from A and/or the establishment of a new G.

The main point here is that there are many options for working with a client using REBT that make the most of the interdependent GABC(DE) framework. However, the REBT practitioner will usually explore a specific (elegant) REBT solution first, so long as there are no contraindicators, because philosophic change (B change), applied over a lifetime, can have a continual influence on G, A, and C, and avoids suboptimal or limited solutions at the G, A, and C levels. A focus on G, A, and C can take place alongside, and following, specific REBT. In specific and general REBT, it is prudent for a practitioner to be able to apply multiple strategies across all elements of the GABCDE framework to make the most impact on the client's issues in the most efficient manner.

RECIPROCITY

Because each element of the interdependent GABC(DE) is related to each other element (i.e., the elements are interrelated), in a reciprocal manner, a change in one element can influence all other elements. The reciprocity between the elements of the GABCDE framework is reflective of what we know about how cognition and emotion can fuel one another. For example, trait-anxious individuals, when under stress, are more likely to adopt a threatening interpretation of ambiguous information, leading to the suggestion that anxiety and cognitive distortions have a reciprocal relationship (Mathews & MacLeod, 2002). Much research has demonstrated that anxious individuals display an attentional bias towards threatening stimuli compared with non-anxious individuals (Cisler & Koster, 2010). Indeed, particularly second-wave CBTs capture a bidirectional relationship between cognitions, emotions, and behaviours, whilst allowing for the role of social and biological influences (Beck & Haigh, 2014; Ellis, 1994).

This hypervigilance to threat is no doubt exacerbated by the aggrandisement and inflated perceived consequences of failure, poor treatment, and other such real or inferred adversities, reflected in irrational beliefs. Indeed, listening to anxious automatic thoughts can cause attentional biases towards threat-relevant stimuli (Wenzel, 2006), suggesting that individuals may consciously allocate their attention to threat information (Mobini & Grant, 2007). Thus, being prone to anxiety might sensitise one to more negative cognitive appraisal and greater irrational beliefs, because anxious individuals selectively attend to the threat-related information (Mobini & Grant, 2007).

Cognitive appraisals such as those included within Ellisian and Lazarusian theories of emotion are probably both antecedent and descendant to emotions. As a result, in many clients I have worked with, I have noted positive feedback loops (e.g., Pekrun, 2006) between cognitive appraisal and emotion. For example, negative emotion can bring about negative appraisal, which then leads to subsequent negative emotion, which triggers further negative appraisal, and worsening, more intense, negative emotions, and so on.

The athlete whose anxiety surfaces in reaction to potential deselection by the coach is hypervigilant to any actions displayed by the coach that might indicate the increased likelihood of what they fear actually occurring. Noticing that the coach is not being as jovial as they usually are with me, I then get even more anxious that I might be dropped, which leads to a deeper and darker litany of cognitions that serve to further increase my anxiety, perhaps to the point of UNE, at which point I self-sabotage my performance just to remove myself from the intensifying heat of the self-perpetuated pressure cooker. In cognitive-behavioural approaches to emotion, this is known as the vicious cycle, where appraisal feeds emotion, and emotion then feeds appraisal, which then flows into more intense emotion, and so on. As Hofmann et al. (2013) state, "...the relationship between emotions and cognitions is bi-directional because changes in emotions can also lead to changes in cognitions" (p. 5).

A reciprocal relationship exists between emotional difficulties and seeing events in ways that are exaggerated beyond available evidence (Wills & Sanders, 2013). Similarly, in Bandura's (1989) social cognitive theory, a reciprocal model of causation is posited, in which internal personal factors such as cognitive, affective, and biological events, behavioural patterns, and environmental influences all interact bidirectionally and not necessarily in a simultaneous manner (Bandura, 2006). Further, the idea that emotions can influence cognition is recognised by appraisal theorists (e.g., Frijda et al. 2000), and evidenced within experimental contexts (e.g., Forgas et al., 2009; Niedenthal, 2007). In Memon and Treur's (2010) agent model, it is recognised that emotion can influence beliefs, whereby believing is not fully independent from feeling. They state that, "In a reciprocal manner, the generated feelings may also have a strengthening or weakening effect on the belief" (Memon & Treur, p. 377). Drawing on the work of Damasio (e.g., 1994, 2003), Memon and Treur explain that belief generation does not depend solely on external information, but also on emotional responses that leads to a certain feeling. Further, "A belief usually triggers an emotional response" but "a belief may not only depend on information obtained, but also on this emotional response" (Memon & Treur, 2010, p. 391). In essence, the belief triggers the emotion, and the feeling of that emotion feeds into the belief; a converging feedback loop for the interaction between feeling and belief. The emotion that is felt affects the strength of the belief. For example, the belief that "I must succeed in this upcoming interview, and it would be awful to fail" is generative to, and strengthened by, my felt anxiety. I am so anxious that it is clearly the case that this situation is as desperate and existentially relevant as my beliefs are intimating. Frijda et al. (2000) recognised that whilst beliefs are regarded as one of the major determinants of emotion, "...emotions can awaken, intrude into, and shape beliefs, by creating them, by amplifying or altering them, and by making them resistant to change" (p. 5). The agent model is in line with how Ellis wrote about the belief-emotion interaction.

The reciprocity captured by the interdependent GABC(DE) framework adds some complication to the linear G-E narrative that is usually portrayed in REBT. However, it is a necessary and useful complication because, as I have previously mentioned, specific REBT is not the only option when working with clients. We can also use general REBT, which can have a broader focus than belief change. The GABCDE framework has to be seen as dynamic because at any point in a transaction we can receive new information (from internal and external sources). Thus, each element of the framework is in constant flux, so we had better equip clients with a range of strategies that deal with each element of the GABCDE framework lest we fail to prepare them for the dynamic nature of the world they are interacting with. Indeed, in Daniel David's (2015) contemporary portrayal of REBT, practitioners can help clients to directly address A via practical problem-solving techniques (e.g., assertiveness training, conflict resolution), address C via symptomatic techniques (e.g., relaxation, meditation), without a specific focus on cognitive restructuring at B. Practitioners should keep in mind the options made available to them through both *specific* and *general* REBT modes. The main thrust of this book is specific REBT, that's for sure. But I would be lying if I said that specific REBT constituted 100% of my work with clients. Figure 3.2 offers the interdependent GABC(DE) framework without the elaboration. By taking a holist, pluralistic, approach to REBT, we can help more people in more ways.

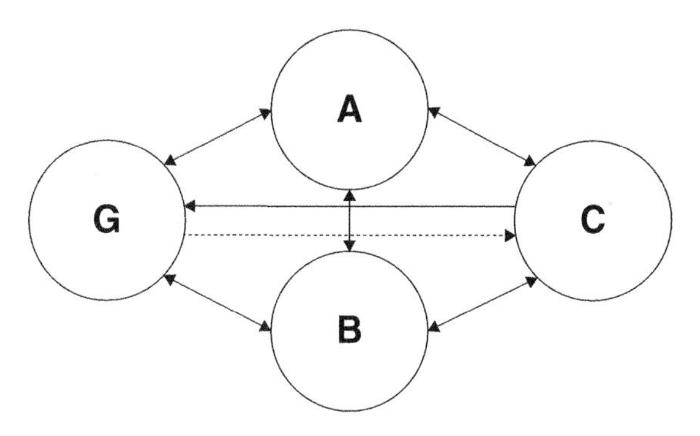

Figure 3.2 Simplified interdependent GABC(DE) framework.

ECLECTICISM IN REBT

In order to practise this broader and more holistic approach to REBT (and emotion regulation per se) I encourage readers to learn and train within many approaches to practising psychology, especially evidence-based formalised psychotherapies, that fit the contexts and issues you are engaging in with your work. Paramount is the development of a deep and broad understanding of REBT including a refined practical skill set. But there is no need to be blinkered and *only* train within REBT. My personal approach has been to learn as much about REBT as is practically possible, whilst developing some knowledge and expertise in a variety of other approaches like acceptance and commitment therapy (ACT) and person-centred therapy (PCT). Indeed, in one paper we offered four potential CBT solutions to an athlete case study (Turner et al., 2020a) including ACT, cognitive therapy (CT), REBT, and schema therapy (ST), and posited the integration of motivational interviewing (MI) with these approaches.

Therefore, whilst one might be highly trained in a particular approach, one can take a pluralistic perspective of one's work. This includes recognising that there is no one best set of therapeutic methods and that different clients are likely to benefit from different therapeutic methods at different points in time (Cooper & McLeod, 2010). Also, one can become skilled in helping clients develop and refine the psychological skills comprising the canon (e.g., Andersen, 2009). In specific REBT, deep belief change is paramount, but work does not need to stop there. REBT is not just about helping clients to solve problems, it is also proactive approach to helping clients to fulfil their potential. As such, even after we have helped the client with B change, we can explore with them how modifications to other aspects of the framework might aid their pursuit of fulfilment (David, 2015).

In sport and exercise psychology, we have for a long time recognised the utility of eclecticism in practice (e.g., Kerr, 1993), and are also cognisant of the pros and cons (see Poczwardowski et al., 2004, for a discussion) of this eclecticism. What I have proposed in the last two chapters is in part about being eclectic, but more about understanding more fully the opportunities that the GABCDE framework provides us with when it comes to supporting clients. There is really no need to don a 'REBT hat' when entering work that includes belief change, and then don a 'PST hat' when entering work that includes teaching imagery and relaxation, for example. The GABCDE framework, due to its interconnectedness, is broad enough to encompass a variety of intervention strategies that sit under the CBT umbrella. If, as a practitioner, your approach to working with clients is underpinned by a cognitive-behavioural philosophy, then your work and the techniques you apply are naturally cognitive, emotive, and behavioural. These three elements are at the core of PST (Andersen, 2009), and of course, are germane to the many CBTs that have emerged since the 1950s.

In REBT, we recognise the importance of eclecticism, but usefully refer to theoretically consistent eclecticism (Dryden, 1986, 2012). Eclecticism in REBT has been considered to emanate from its application of cognitive, emotive, and behavioural methods (Ellis et al., 2010), which can all be used in service of B change of course. David et al. (2010b) refer to practical eclecticism, whereby a practitioner combines interventions from different therapeutic approaches in the hopes of modifying relevant variables. Dryden (2013) refers to this approach as theoretically consistent eclecticism because the practitioner can draw upon methods that originate from outside of REBT. Dryden (2013) also importantly points out that the REBT practitioner is selective in their eclecticism, avoiding methods that are inefficient, mystical, or of dubious validity. In theoretically consistent eclecticism, theory guides technique selection, which is not restricted to the limited number of techniques spawned by REBT itself. For example, there are useful CBT methods within CT and ACT that can aid the client in change across the individual elements of the GABCDE framework. The common taxonomical parent of REBT, CT, and ACT is CBT (Collard, 2019; Turner et al., 2020a), and as such, we can fish in a broad CBT pond for useful techniques whilst remaining theoretically consistent. In contrast, an REBT practitioner would usually not employ psychodynamic methods such as dream analysis or free association. REBT is eclectic at the practical level (not at the theory level) (David, 2015).

What I am proposing here is that the selection of methods for use in the work we do with clients using REBT should be informed by a broad cognitive-behavioural understanding of client issues and potential solutions. Making theoretically consistent decisions concerning the use of techniques within REBT stretches beyond an eclectic approach to belief change. Eclecticism within the interdependent GABC(DE) framework allows a practitioner to draw upon a broad gamut of CBT methods in order to work with any element of the GABCDE framework, knowing that a change in one can instigate a change in all. Whilst I maintain that B change and the development and maintenance of a rational philosophy towards life is paramount, and justifiably central to REBT, I also recognise, as a psychologist working within performance domains, that direct B change is not always possible and as such a *general* REBT solution is often viable and necessary. The contextual limitations I am sometimes faced with often necessitate a focus on the wider GABCDE framework, and the work I complete with 'post-disturbed' clients (e.g., able to experience HNE instead of UNE) benefits from focussed work around G, A, and C.

For example, a tennis athlete experiencing anxiety five-minutes prior stepping on court for a match might not be able or willing to engage in cognitive change (disputation) at B with the practitioner. In this instance, it might be more prudent to help the client practise acceptance or relaxation, image being assertive in their opening exchanges with the opening, or to positively affirm their own abilities. Then, at a later date, I can engage the athlete in a conversation about performance anxiety and ascertain as to whether and what extent core beliefs are hindering or helping their goal attainment.

That is, when using *specific* REBT I would first work at the emotional problem-solving level (B change via D), then move onto practical problem-solving at G and/or A, because a client who is more emotionally stable can better address the problems in their life (e.g., David, 2015). In contrast, when using *general* REBT I can more flexibly work primarily and directly with G, A, and/or C to help the client, and can return to B if there is time, need, and inclination (from the client). Whilst a general REBT solution is not a *poorer* mode of working per se, it is unlikely to address the deeper beliefs that perpetuate disturbance, and therefore, the client may still be vulnerable to UNEs.

Pressure drill: working with a coach

One of the most effective ways to move towards a meaningful goal (G) is to throw yourself against As. How many As could I conquer? How well can I play amidst the worst A I can imagine? We can encourage athletes to practise in volatile conditions, not always perfect conditions. We can infuse training with As to help athletes train under pressure. Imagine you are working within a soccer team and the coach wants your input into a particular training drill she is putting together. The coach wants the drill to test the players under pressure in order to observe their responses to imperative game moments. How can you help the coach to use the GABCDE framework when developing and delivering this drill?

You can set the conditions for pressure by operationalising the G and A elements of the framework (using Lazarus' 1999 theory). We know that emotionality is derived from the incongruence between G and A, and we know that for anxiety, we need to encourage the perception of uncertainty and threat/danger. So, in the drill we can create a meaningful goal (G) for the players to work towards, then we can create barriers, blocks, adversities to that goal, and we can make sure something is at stake (A). The first thing we might do is make sure the drill is competitive – one group of players vs. another group of players. If we have 20 players, we can have four groups of five players, for example. This already ensures some goal incongruence (A) because an opposing team will create blocks, barriers, adversities. A meaningful goal (G) might be a target for the task (scoring x number of goals, not conceding a certain number of goals, making a certain number of passes, retain ball procession for x minutes, etc.) or could be to simply beat the opposing team in the drill. Barriers and blocks (A) might include strict time limits (clock counting down), different starting points for different teams, and can also include incompetent and antagonistic counter-goal decision-making by the referee (played by the assistant coach). So, team A might start 1–0 up and team B have to win the game in two minutes (score at least two goals, maybe more if team A score again), but the referee is penalising team B for every minor incident and thus team A keep getting the ball back from fouls. To make sure something is at stake, create a league table of the wins and losses for each team and assign points so that winning = 1 point, drawing = 0 points, and losing = −3 points. A greater relative negative consequence for loss compared to a smaller relative positive consequence for winning creates risk aversion and presents underperforming as more dangerous. Thus, as a player, the consequences of your team losing are that you come bottom of the league table for all to see – in other words – creating social-evaluative or ego threat.

So, G is created here by the instantiation of meaningful targets and objectives, as well as playing on the internal goals of the players, who no doubt actually desire to be successful in these sorts of drills (not least for bragging rights, but also because selection is always on the line). The A is created via the competitive nature of the task (i.e., the opposing team want to stop you), by the additional task constraints such as time limits and starting scores, and the 'poor' refereeing. Danger is created via the league table and scoring system, and uncertainty is created by changing the time limits and starting scores for each game, and by the referee adopting different decision-making principles for each game (alongside the inherent uncertainty that characterises competition). So, we have helped develop a meaningful and REBT-informed drill in which we are using the core relational theme of anxiety (Lazarus, 1999) and G-A incongruence to foster pressure.

This type of activity tests the players in various ways and can generate a lot of useful data for learning and feedback purposes. Clearly, in terms of the GABCDE framework, our core player observations are related to C. How do they express their emotions before, during, and after the drill? How do they behave under pressure? How do they perform? This last question is not about results per se – not about whether players won more games than lost – it is more about their ability to maintain their standards (physically, psychologically) when under pressure. Can they still execute passes, move intently, make accurate decisions, communicate constructively, and create goal scoring chances, when under pressure? Can they adhere to a game plan?

As well as challenging the players to deliver performances under pressure (which they need to be able to do in real matches), the drill also challenges their responses to unfairness and disrespect (referee behaviour). The players had better keep control of their emotions lest the task will get away from them. For the coach this is an important drill because it can indicate (not perfectly I might add) the extent to which her players can operate under pressure. For the practitioner, the task outcomes serve as useful stimuli for player education and one-to-one work around pressure and emotion management. In addition, if applied regularly in different variations, the task can serve as a pressure inoculation drill, where players become more accustomed to performance pressure and thus performance is less affected. We are not going to get close to the pressure of actual competition, but we can at least practise under some pressure to enable some coping skills to be developed and refined. We as practitioners can lead this skill development, but the drill itself can stimulate some natural adaptation to pressure (e.g., Turner & Jones, 2014, 2018).

> I thrive on pressure now…In the past, maybe, the pressure might have got to me…But now it's more exciting. You want to play in big games. You want to test yourself against the best in the world.
>
> James Anderson (cricketer who has represented England in over 50 Test matches and over 100 One Day Internationals; Brenkley, 2012)

In REBT terms, this drill is clearly a behavioural activity that we could say is akin to desensitisation (e.g., Wolpe, 1973, 1990) or flooding (Dryden & Branch, 2008; Levis, 2009). In sport we have ample opportunity to construct these types of activities in order to animate the GABCDE framework practically and for specific purposes. One of the consequences of the task might be that for some players, irrational beliefs (B) are triggered. This is certainly the case in my experience, and it serves as a useful stimulus for a conversation with a player.

For example, you could venture:

Sport psychologist (SP): I noticed in that drill that you got very irate, and things did not seem to be going your way. Is that accurate?

Athlete: Yeah that's right. I struggled a bit to be honest.

SP: Ok, why do you think that was?

Athlete: I'm not sure really. Things just got away from me and I couldn't bring it back.

SP: What do you mean by 'got away from me'

ATHLETE: I mean, I couldn't pass like normal, my mind was confused, and I didn't feel comfortable at all.
SP: What was it about the drill that led to these experiences?
ATHLETE: I don't know. It was fast, difficult, chaotic.
SP: Do you think the pace, difficulty, and chaos automatically led to your reactions?
ATHLETE: No. I know from our conversations before that my perceptions play a role too.
SP: Yes very good. What role did your perceptions play here in the drill?
ATHLETE: Well as soon as I knew what the drill was, I straight away thought "oh no, I hate these types of drills, I never do well in them, I can't stand them"
SP: That's really insightful. Do you think that way of thinking is helpful for your performance in this drill?
ATHLETE: No its not.
SP: What are some of the issues with what you are saying to yourself about the drill?
ATHLETE: Well it's not constructive.
SP: Yes I agree. Also, is it logical to think in this way?
ATHLETE: No because I obviously can stand it. I got through it in one piece.
SP: Good and what did you learn?
ATHLETE: I need to get ready earlier on in set pieces, and also need to communicate more to the goalkeeper, and could also work on calming down between phases of play.
SP: So, when you think about it, it was worth going through this difficult experience. Look at the learning you have done. Look at the take-away points you can work on.
ATHLETE: Yeah I suppose so. And I also did some really good things too.
SP: Of course! Like…
ATHLETE: I was strong in my challenges, and I didn't let the referee decisions affect me.
SP: This is vital stuff isn't it? You see how facing these tough challenges gives you important feedback? You CAN stand these drills. It is difficult, it is tough, but you can grow from these experiences, right?
ATHLETE: Yes for sure. I can stand them, plus I want to go through these experiences to develop further.
SP: So what might you think next time you go into a drill like this?
ATHLETE: I could say "I am looking forward to this challenge, I can stand it and through standing it I can learn and grow"
SP: Brilliant. Let's see how you do in the next drill like this and compare?
ATHLETE: ok, sure.

As the reader can hopefully see from the above, the practitioner is working around Gs, As, Bs, and Cs here. Whilst there is no clear conversation about 'irrational beliefs' per se, the practitioner is able to address some distorted cognitions and irrational beliefs in a way that is focussed on function and logic. The sentiment of the conversation is about tolerance and the benefits of tolerance, but also about using constructive self-talk for the drill. This 'session' would be a few minutes in duration and yet, the player has something to go away with and work on, and we have managed to help them shift their perceptions of the task. So, in the future their appraisal of this drill may be different. The drill may not be as dangerous. The drill is no longer intolerable. The player may have even developed some coping potential for the next drill. The practitioner here does engage in Socratic dialogue, but is also willing to lead the athlete a little in order to ensure there are some key points to take away for the athlete.

In the drill, as a cherry on top, the coach can also use irrational language in their instructions to players (i.e., Evans et al., 2018), thus adding irrational Bs to the incongruence between Gs and As. The reasons for including this B element are threefold. First, the irrational language can add additional pressure to players. Second, it can enable some acclimatisation to the irrational language that undoubtedly emerges as part of a pressure situation in a real game. Third, it can help coaches to understand the impact of their language when coaching. This can lead to some important reflections for the coach concerning their rhetoric and how they can help shape player emotion and behaviour.

THE PRE-MORTEM: WORKING WITH TEAMS

It is also worth considering the applicability of the GABCDE framework across team-based or group relevant situations. One of my favourite activities to run with teams is the pre-mortem, which was introduced to me by a colleague Professor Andy McCann. Developed by Gary Klein (2014), unlike a post-mortem which happens after the event, in a pre-mortem we project into the future that the "patient" has died, and we ask 'what went wrong?' The team generate plausible reasons for the failure. So, in sport, what we are doing here is asking the team to take their minds to quite a negative space and assume that we, for example, have not qualified for a tournament, or have lost an important competition. We HAVE failed, and are trying to explain WHY. Each member of the group generates their own list of performance limiting factors that led to our (hypothetical future) failure. Then we pool our answers. I usually use this task with multi-disciplinary staff teams. We dedicate a day for this so that we can spend time on it and figure out solutions to the issues raised.

> What is quite unlooked for is more crushing in its effect, and unexpectedness adds to the weight of a disaster. This is a reason for ensuring that nothing ever takes us by surprise. We should project our thoughts ahead of us at every turn and have in mind every possible eventuality instead of only the usual course of events...Rehearse them in your mind: exile, torture, war, shipwreck. All the terms of our human lot should be before our eyes.
>
> Seneca (in Holiday, 2019)

This task, aside from being a group-think version of premeditatio malorum, is a good way to help teams identify possible Gs, As, and Cs. When we have identified key factors that might undercut performance (As) we can work to mitigate and/or eliminate them in order to make attaining Gs more likely. We can do this in a hierarchical fashion by taking the outcomes of the pre-mortem and listing them in order of priority. For example, in one team I worked with, we used a pre-mortem at a pre-tournament phase, and our top factor (most performance-limiting) was "not selecting the right players", so the first thing the coaches did was undertake player selection. Strike whilst the iron is hot. We can also figure out how these As might impact upon Gs and engage in problem-solving to maneuverer around or forthrightly deal directly with As. We can resource certain areas that deal with highly important As. For example, if illness and/or injury of players is on the list (which it always is) then we can plan for the limitation of physical risk closer to the tournament and the medical team can undertake additional risk assessment in terms of hygiene. We can also shape or reshape Gs to account for possible As. We can adjust what we aim for if we believe that the As are immovable and sufficiently limiting to our original goals. For example, in one team a factor that emerged was the fact that "two of the most experienced players are injured" and so we adjusted the game plan for the forthcoming match in light of this set back. New game plan, new targets. We went from a very attacking game plan to a more defensive game plan. In contrast, we might realise that the As we have generated are relatively easy to deal with, and thus the new Gs might be more adventurous than before. We can understand how the team and individual Gs are in some way generative of team and individual As. What factors can we adjust that can retain our pursuit of Gs whilst accounting for or limiting the manifestation of possible As, known and unknown (unpredictable)?

At an inferential A level we can also address distorted thinking concerning the barriers we face. For example, we can try to limit the catastrophic view members of the team can sometimes take of potential problems we face. We can also start to predict possible Cs that will emanate from the interaction (incongruence) between Gs and As. As practitioners we can be prepared to help athletes and staff to arm themselves against the inevitable As we will face as a team in order to prevent team-limiting Cs. We can plan for moments of depressurisation between matches in a tournament, for example. As practitioners we can also start to imagine which irrational beliefs (Bs) might be triggered given the known As. We can prepare educational and support content for players and staff based on what we think might occur. Forearmed is forewarned. Clearly, we cannot plan for everything because there are many unknowns. But we can generate some team confidence in our ability to pursue our Gs by having robust plans to deal with specific As, Bs, and Cs.

SUMMARY

It is unwise, and inaccurate, to view the GABCDE framework as sequential and/or linear. It is more wise, and accurate (and helpful), to view the GABCDE framework as interactive and dynamic, whereby each element influences each other element in a synchronised and reciprocal fashion. Although I have focussed on the interdependence of GABC in this chapter, the DE components will of course influence the occurrence of GABC, in the same way that Gross' emotion regulation strategies in the process model (2014) can be applied prior to, during, or after an emotional episode. That is, if I am entering into a situation with a refined ability to challenge my thinking (D) and I am deeply holding rational beliefs (E), then this will influence the goals I pursue (G), the extent to which adverse events (A) are seen as incongruent with the goals, and of course, the extent to which irrational and rational beliefs (B) shape my emotional experience (UNE vs. HNE).

What I have attempted to achieve thus far in this book is to present REBT as a flexible and pragmatic approach, in line with Ellis' view of REBT, and in line with contemporary theory and practice, not a reductionist view of REBT which is all about cognitive disputation and deep belief change. However, what I present henceforth is more reflective of *specific* REBT applied via a one-to-one mode of practice. That is, the following content focusses on the theory and application of REBT aimed towards deep philosophic change in order to make clear the distinguishing features of REBT as a framework for practice.

CHAPTER 4 The practitioner and the client

Yours, and only yours.

DOI: 10.4324/9781003200437-5

The author now turns to the important practitioner and client characteristics that should be considered by anybody wishing to apply REBT in performance settings.

The practitioner

The nature of the practitioner-client relationship is characterised by humanistic appreciation for the client, a strong working alliance, and a collaborative goal-directed pursuit of long-term hedonism. The REBT practitioner takes a "human first, athlete second" (Turner, 2016b) or a "human>performer" (Turner, 2016c) stance whereby the athlete is viewed chiefly as a human being, rather than viewed only in line with the vocation they pursue. As well as being factually the case, viewing the athlete as a human being first and foremost enables the REBT practitioner to help the athlete to move towards long-term (or long-range) hedonism, rather than short-term hedonism. Short-term hedonism is characterised by seeking momentary pleasures only, immediate gratification (whatever the cost or danger), and striving for ease or comfort (Ellis, 1976). The REBT practitioner should be helping the client to get better (long-term human development) rather than to feel better (short-term remediation). That is, the REBT practitioner is concerned with the long game and whilst vocational, relationship, and academic (for example) goals are within the purview of REBT work, these goals are superseded by the mental and physical health of the human being. To serve this long game, the REBT practitioner teaches and encourages emotional responsibility; the notion that you can disturb, and therefore can un-disturb yourself, via your beliefs (Dryden, 2022).

One of the questions fellow practitioners often ask me is "to what extent is REBT humanistic?" Indeed, some trainees and neophyte practitioners reading this book may have been (incorrectly) challenged by peers when they have described REBT as 'humanistic'. This error is not new (e.g., Finley, 1979), and Ellis noted in 1973 that REBT was often incorrectly viewed as anti-humanistic in part because people mistakenly viewed it as overintellectualised, mechanistic, and manipulative. Ellis rebuts these assumptions and makes it clear that by stressing cognitive control over emotions, REBT is one of the most humanistic approaches there is (he outlines ten ways in which REBT is indeed humanistic). Ellis positioned REBT squarely as a humanistic psychotherapy (1973, 1979, 1996b). In his book *Humanistic Psychotherapy*, Ellis (1973) states that "the essence of humanism, in both psychological and ethical areas, is that man is fully acknowledged to be human – that is, limited and fallible – and that in no way whatever is he superhuman or subhuman" (p. 2).

Tying humanism to REBT more directly, he goes on to say that humanistic psychology is the "study of the whole individual, by logico-empirical means that are distinctly human, for the purpose of helping him live a happier, more self-actualizing, and more creative existence" (p. 3). Ellis recognises humans as limited, self-directed, goal-directed beings, important in their own right just because they are alive, and have the right to exist and fulfil themselves. Ellis continually references the 'humanness' of man and developed REBT to describe, and to function within, this humanness. For example, he considers thinking about thinking (i.e., metacognition) to be a distinctly human quality, and as such, the practice of REBT is highly metacognitive and requires clients to engage in and develop this ability. Ellis defined REBT as "a revolutionary humanistic approach to psychotherapy" (p. 4), and places cognitive psychotherapists (e.g., himself, Aaron T. Beck, George Kelly, etc.) alongside humanists such as Carl Rogers and Abraham Maslow. Therefore, the REBT practitioner holds a humanistic philosophy exercised in a cognitive-emotive-behavioural manner, placing the client at the centre of their world as an autonomous and sentient human being.

The REBT practitioner helps the athlete to apply what is effective, rather than what is expedient, and focusses on the person rather than the symptom (Trower & Jones, 2001). Albert Ellis said that whilst Sigmund Freud had a gene for inefficiency, Ellis himself has a gene for efficiency, but this should not be confused as a call for haste. Rather, REBT *can be* a very brief approach to working with athletes (Bowman & Turner, 2022), but this brevity is not achieved at the expense of deep and meaningful change. In the volumes of research that report REBT work with athletes (Jordana et al., 2020), one can be forgiven for assuming that REBT is easy to apply because the effects of REBT on target variables are often positive, and usually very little detail is provided as to how this was achieved (largely due to page limits in peer-reviewed journals, see Wood et al., 2020, for an exception). REBT is simple, not easy, and even if the work is brief, deep belief change is a very difficult process for client and practitioner alike. Therefore, the REBT practitioner should be prepared to engage in, often, difficult conversations that address deeply entrenched beliefs that athletes are not always willing to easily relinquish. Within these challenging conversations, specific REBT can be executed, whereby individuals are encouraged to address the deeper roots of their emotions, rather than the superficial correlates or symptoms of emotions. The REBT practitioner challenges ideas, not people, and applies Socratic dialogue as the main discursive tool. The practitioner and the client are scientists in cahoots, applying the principles of proof, logic, and function, collaboratively (e.g., Bond, 2002) to the client's beliefs (ideas). I encourage practitioners to make sure they do the basics of counselling well in their REBT work, or 'Brilliant Basics' as I call them (I stole this phrase from my ex-gaffer at England Futsal). In brief, this means don't abandon good counselling skills for the sake of expediency or arrogant problem-solving, don't underestimate the importance of Socratic dialogue, and don't forget that you are helping the client to find *their* solutions, not adopt *your* solutions. Listen actively and carefully, use your paraphrasing, reflecting, and summarising skills judiciously, and help the client to piece their thoughts and words together in ways that move them forward towards some solutions. If we listen well, ask the right questions in the right way, and enable the client to arrive at their own solutions, then REBT is more likely to be effective, and the client is more likely to commit to the new beliefs that they have instantiated. How can we know what clients think if we do not let them speak? How do clients know what *they* think if they do not get the opportunity to talk?

The REBT practitioner *can be* active-directive in their work with athletes in order to keep the work focussed and goal-directed, and in order to facilitate often challenging conversations. This allows the practitioner to educate the athlete about the GABCDE framework, for example, and enables a focus on the present, rather than on the past. Psychoeducation is a hallmark of REBT (Turner & Barker, 2014a), and the active-directive style allows for the use of a didactic approach to *some* elements of the work. One of the goals of REBT is to furnish the client with the knowledge and skills to apply REBT independently in their lives after the work has ceased (Dryden et al., 2010), and therefore the practitioner should be redundancy-seeking and should not become a crutch for the client. This active-directive style is not to be read as 'harsh' and 'cutting' (David, 2015), and just because Albert Ellis was at times blunt in his public demonstrations of REBT, the effectiveness of REBT does not rest on the practitioner's mimicry of Ellis. Importantly, the active-directive consulting style should not be applied unilaterally to all athletes in all contexts, and should not be adopted at the expense of the working alliance or client-practitioner rapport. Lastly, the REBT practitioner should strive to demonstrate unconditional acceptance of their clients, but should also teach clients that they can unconditionally accept themselves regardless of the perceived approval (or lack thereof) of others (including the practitioner!).

The client

REBT has been applied across a variety of ages, cross-culturally, across many sports, and across various competitive levels (Jordana et al., 2020; Turner & Bennett, 2018). It is difficult to imagine for whom REBT would *not* be applicable, but there are some factors that could influence if and how REBT is applied. In sport, there is little evidence of REBT's effectiveness with very young (pre-teen) athletes. The author's own experiences indicate that when applying REBT with pre-teen athletes one should take one's time and adopt a more educational style. We should not underestimate the complex mental processing at play during REBT, where the client is required to introspect deeply, and exercise volition over their abstract inner vocalisations. Indeed, metacognitive ability has been shown to improve significantly with age during adolescence (Weil et al., 2013), so younger athletes should be given more time to grasp the notion of cognitive mediation and cognitive change. Relatedly, regardless of age, if a client is not able or willing to introspect, share their thoughts, situational, emotional, and behavioural experiences, and/or is resistant to conversation in general, then the REBT practitioner must work harder to form a strong connection with the client to 'grease the wheels' so to speak. It is not enough to give up on a client or blame them for their disengagement.

However, when working with younger athletes, beliefs are usually not highly ingrained and as such, it is possible to help them develop, commit to, and ingrain, rational philosophies that can serve them well as their athletic career develops. In my experience, it is the parents of the young athlete who are in more need of REBT than the child themselves. One client I worked with (aged 11) was a promising cricketer. His parents had erected a full-size batting practice net in the back garden and were employing a private coach and a psychologist to supplement his club and county training. The child was told that he had to choose between pursuing cricket or medicine, and that if cricket was the choice, then the child had better commit 100% to it, due to the financial investment the parents were making in this pursuit. Much of my work with this client was done with and through the parents, teaching them about REBT and the importance of using more flexible and non-extreme language in communicating with their child.

Much literature in sport reports the usage of REBT within settings where engagement is not to be assumed (e.g., soccer academy) because the work is delivered in a group format to all athletes in a team (e.g., Turner et al., 2014), rather than one-to-one, in which interest in REBT (and sport psychology per se) will be variable. As REBT practitioners we are at pains to engage clients in as many ways as possible, given the importance of imbuing the client with the wisdom (sometimes ancient) held within REBT. It is of course possible that client reluctance is underpinned by irrational beliefs (e.g., "I can't stand uncomfortable conversations", "It is awful to share how I really feel"), therefore early work with a client might be concerned with helping them to express themselves and to develop strong client-practitioner rapport.

One key factor about the client that the practitioner must understand is the extent to which the client *wants* to be in the session. Does the client want to solve a problem? Or are they just looking for an empathetic ear? Figure out which it is because if the client does not want to solve their issues, REBT is not for them. REBT is not about dragging somebody unwillingly to safety, they have to partake in the process, by first expressing a desire to change. In some performance settings, such as youth sport, it is sometimes the case that the athlete has been told to, or coerced into, seeing the psychologist. This is a difficult situation to be in, because even if the client would benefit from working with you (the practitioner), they may not engage in the work because they do not perceive themselves to be requiring of psychology support. I worked with such a client (non-league soccer athlete) who was highly ambivalent about psychology and really did not want to be in session, but had been coerced by the head coach. So, I took it slow, developed strong rapport with the athlete, and over a period of two months got the relationship to the point where the athlete began to open up about their issues. Then, tentative advice was offered to the athlete only at moments where the interaction was conducive to my input. The approach here was "since we are here together, why don't we make use of the time by having a chat?" rather than "right, I know you don't want to be here, but there is this thing called REBT…".

The client can be aided greatly by the practitioner leaving their own irrational beliefs, such as "I can't tolerate the work not going smoothly" or "if the work does not go well, I am a failure", at the door. Physician heal thyself (Luke, 4:23). Indeed, DiGiuseppe et al. (2014) offer a wonderful piece of advice for practitioners: "relax" they say (p. 73) – you do not need to solve the client's problems immediately, so take time to properly get to know the client and their issues. Spending time here will enable you to develop a strong working alliance.

The working alliance

When trying to ascertain the significant factors that determine the effectiveness of applied psychology (e.g., psychotherapy), the importance of the therapeutic relationship is chief and extends across the many approaches and 'therapies' (e.g., Sprenkle & Blow, 2004), including CBTs (Raue & Goldfried, 1994). Regardless of theoretical orientation or client presenting issues, the development of a strong working alliance is important to the therapeutic relationship (Woody & Adessky, 2002), because it is the working alliance that makes core aspects of any approach viable. Without a client-practitioner relationship underpinned by a strong working alliance, inviable are core aspects of REBT such as setting therapeutic goals, deep excavation of thoughts and beliefs, Socratic dialogue, disputation, and adherence to therapeutic tasks. The working alliance provides the context through which counselling strategies work (e.g., Horvath & Greenberg, 1989), and as such, a good working alliance is considered to be vital for CBT success (e.g., Dobson & Shaw, 1988). One of the most robust findings within counselling psychology is the importance of a strong working alliance between the client and psychologist for successful therapeutic outcomes (Watson et al., 2018).

In REBT, like in other CBTs, the development and continual strengthening of a strong working alliance is important (Bernard & Dryden, 2019). There is of course recognition and application of the core conditions of empathy, unconditional acceptance, and genuineness, but whilst these conditions are seen as desirable, they are not seen as sufficient for therapeutic change (Dryden, 2017). The key change mechanisms and levers upon which the practitioner and client must apply pressure are covered in detail later in this book. But I wanted to be clear here that good REBT is associated with the development and maintenance of a strong client-practitioner working alliance (Bordin, 1979). This is underpinned by a solid bond, openness, clear aims for the work, and the forthright effort expenditure towards those agreed aims (e.g., Dryden, 2009a; Dryden & David, 2008).

A full guide to developing a strong working alliance is beyond the scope of the present book, but Horvath and Greenberg's (1989) Working Alliance Inventory (WAI) offers a useful insight into what constitutes the working alliance and provides a tool to measure this important facet of therapy or coaching. For example, the WAI subscales assess agreement about goals of therapy, agreement about the tasks of the therapy, and the bond between the client and therapist. The focus on these factors is justified because, according to Raue and Goldfried (1994), successful CBT is less likely to occur unless there is a good working alliance underpinned by a good therapeutic bond, and a mutual agreement on goals and therapeutic methods (also see Castonguay et al., 2010).

I first trained in person-centred counselling prior to undertaking REBT training, which was useful in providing some grounding in working alliance development via Carl Rogers' (1957) core conditions (see Irving & Dickson, 2006, for a more contemporary conceptualisation). In addition, many REBT practitioners (notably Andrew Wood, and Hugh Gilmore) have undertaken training in Motivational Interviewing (MI; Miller & Rollnick, 2013), which "offers a structured communication and relational framework that actively promotes the working alliance and facilitates the action orientated process of REBT" (Wood et al., 2020). In a research study, Wood et al. (2020) found that this MI-REBT integrated approach yielded reductions in irrational beliefs, and increases in self-determined motivation, in an elite archer.

I do not want to overstate the importance of the working alliance here, and there are some critics of the importance of working alliance in predicting outcomes. In the executive coaching literature, de Hann et al. (2020) found that working alliance between client and coach was not strongly related to coaching effectiveness. De Hann and colleagues suggest a range of client factors that might better affect coaching outcomes, such as clients' propensity to relate, and their trait personality (particularly openness), resilience, hope, and self-efficacy. So, whether or not you hold much stock in the 'working alliance' as a vital active ingredient for REBT effectiveness, the client certainly brings with them some personal factors that might in part determine the effectiveness of the work. You as the practitioner also bring some important factors to the party – not least – your own competence in applying REBT and your experience in doing so across a range of clients. This, of course, begins with training in REBT. In a review of 37 CBT training programmes Rakovshik and McManus (2010) concluded that extensive programmes lead to higher therapist competence, which, in turn, correlates with better client outcome. This training should include reading, attending lectures/talks, role-play, self-experiential work, and reflective practice (Bennett-Levy et al., 2009). For REBT, we have a REBT Competency Scale (Dryden et al., 2010) which has 22 steps, which can be scored so as to assess practitioner performance. But even this tool is calibrated somewhat against client 'difficulty' (easy, average, difficult/resistant), and one of the steps is 'establishing an appropriate bond with the client'. So, even in REBT, where the working alliance alone is not considered sufficient to achieve change (Dryden, 2019b; Ellis, 2004), particular importance is placed on establishing and maintaining an appropriate bond with the client (Dryden et al., 2010).

The aims of the work

It is important not to assume the reasons for the client wanting to engage in the work with you. Many people suffer emotionally, but a small proportion actually seek help. To illustrate, reportedly 75% of adolescents with mental health problems are not in contact with mental health services, primarily due to a reluctance in seeking help (Aguirre Velasco et al., 2020). So, understanding what has led the client to seeking help is important, as it can help to frame the work and ensure that the work delivers on what the client wants to get from it, so long as they have reasonable expectations for course (!). As stated previously, as part of developing a strong working alliance, the goals of REBT are negotiated and agreed upon by client and practitioner. This often includes the practitioner asking the client if they have undertaken psychology work in the past, and whether this work bears any relation to REBT. This information is useful to ascertain the degree to which the client already understands core ideas such as B–C thinking and cognitive mediation per se, for example. But regardless of whether the client has undertaken previous and similar psychology work, it is usually for the practitioner to explain to the client what REBT (or 'Smarter Thinking'; Turner, 2014) is and how the work between client and practitioner might be executed. We can then address any concerns the client may have, and correct any misconceptions they have about performance psychology in general.

It is important that the client understands the autonomy they have in the work. That is, the practitioner should explain to the client that whilst much can be achieve in one-to-one sessions, the bulk of the work is undertaken by the client independently. Furthermore, the work taking place is for them, and thus they are able to dictate the direction of the work. The client can make use of many options during REBT – it is not a formulaic and rigid process. Everything that takes place between client and practitioner is agreed upon – consented to by the client. Indeed, there is an ethical responsibility for the practitioner to obtain informed consent from the client about the work that will take place should the client wish to engage (Dryden, 2021b). Thus, we can explain to the client about what REBT is and the likely activities we will undertake as a working partnership.

REBT is often described as persuasive and active-directive (DiGiuseppe et al., 2014) which it can be, and perhaps it usually is, but this style of working is not necessary for successful REBT. As I stated previously, not all clients will appreciate this active-directive style, so we must meet the client's needs as much as possible. This is especially important in performance settings where time with clients is often limited and so anyway that we can be in tune with the client's preferred way of working is beneficial to the working alliance and the REBT work that takes place. Thus, the communicative style between client and practitioner is dynamic, so long as the aims of the work are being worked towards effectively.

But what are the aims of the work in REBT? DiGiuseppe and colleagues (2014) suggest the goals of REBT are to minimise distress, maximise the length of life, and enhance joy in the process of living (i.e., responsible hedonism). Of course, specific aims are particular to each client, and Dryden (2021b) suggests developing a problem list and then figuring out what the client would rather think, feel, and do in response to adversity (A). This information then becomes the goals of the work in the short term, with longer term goals that are more developmental also emanating from the work. Bearing all this in mind, and taking into consideration that the goals of the work are negotiated and agreed upon by client and practitioner, I propose that the broad aim of REBT work is to:

Support the client to develop and strengthen their rational engagement with life, in service of long-term wellbeing, biopsychosocial functioning, and goal fulfilment (eudaimonia).

It might be useful to visualise the above aim as a Venn diagram comprising beliefs and reality (Figure 4.1a,b). The darker space between the two circles of 'beliefs' and 'reality' should

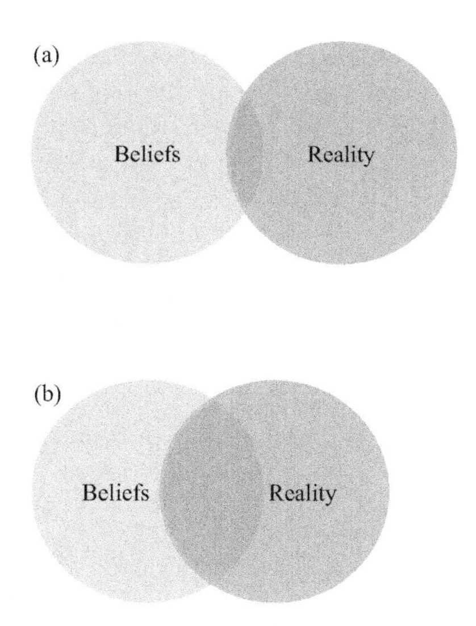

Figure 4.1 (a) Lower self-integration with rationality. (b) Greater self-integration with rationality.

become bigger through engaging with REBT, recognising that a full eclipse might never be possible (or even desirable). The alignment of beliefs with reality reflects the client integrating themselves with rationality, able to view the world through a rational lens.

To achieve this broad aim, I will help the client to understand that they can exert some control over their thoughts, emotions, and behaviours. I will teach the client that they can re-evaluate some of the ways that they see themselves, other people, and the world. I will encourage the client to take a critical, scientific, stance with matters of the mind. Using this scientific stance, I will enable the client to develop beliefs that meet stringent criteria of truth, logic, and function. I will do all of this by interacting with the client openly, Socratically, and forthrightly, teaching them skills and ideas that contribute to, rather than detract from, their life. This teaching may involve the client undertaking homework assignments, reading, watching, and listening to relevant material, and undertaking practical tasks in and out of sessions. Most importantly, to achieve the broad aim, the client will be actively involved in the work, not just as a passive participant, but as an active collaborator in every aspect. The client does the work – the practitioner supports the client in their undertaking. Ultimately, at the end of the work between client and practitioner, the client should go out into the world able to apply REBT independently. The practitioner's goal should be to make themselves redundant in the client's life. In other words, we should encourage the client to become their own therapist (Dryden et al., 2010).

The REBT 'process'

In the next chapter, I move on to the core 'process' of REBT. I am careful with my use of the word 'process' because the GABCDE framework is not to be followed in a linear or mechanical way. REBT is structured, logical, educational, directive, present-centred, future oriented, and skills focussed (e.g., Dryden, 2021b). But REBT is not inflexible, because we tailor the content and delivery to the client. We are not machines, but a framework is useful and helps to ensure accurate REBT. As you will see, in the next chapter I start at C because this is often what is presented to me by the client, so I assess it first. If a client presents with A, then I can assess C later, without any real consequences for REBT effectiveness. So, the henceforth order of the chapters is instructive but not inflexibly so, and is roughly based on Dryden et al.'s (2010) REBT Competency Scale. I will use the ordering of the chapters to communicate the main stages of REBT as applied in performance settings. But in brief, the stages are:

1. Develop and strengthen the working alliance.
2. Establish the aims of the work, agree on a target problem, and a way forward.
3. Assess C – establish the existence of UNEs and HNEs concerning the target problem.
4. Assess A – establish the inference/s concerning the target problem that is/are triggering irrational beliefs (B).
5. Assess G – establish how and to what extent A impedes G in the target problem. Also, support and encourage eudaimonic goals.
6. Teach the B–C connection – educate the athlete in the idea of cognitive mediation.
7. Assess B – establish the existence and nature of irrational beliefs (iB) and rational beliefs (rB).
8. Teach the athlete about iBs and rBs, and how to distinguish between them.
9. Ensure client is able to see the connection between their Gs, As, Bs, and Cs.
10. Disputation (D) – challenge and weaken irrational beliefs.
11. Effective New Belief (E) – develop, challenge, strengthen, and commit to rational beliefs.
12. Ensuring redundancy – client becomes their own 'practitioner'.

As an idea of the structure, in Figure 4.2 I have included a completed GABCDE assessment sheet. This sheet doubles up as a record of the main outcomes for each stage of REBT with a particular athlete. I worked with an elite skeet shooter who was having some trouble performing to his potential when competing at larger, more prestigious, events. The client arrived with this issue, and so the direction of the work was quite clear early on. Of course, some clients will not arrive with a clear issue, but the example is illustrative rather than prescriptive. I do not provide this example to demonstrate perfect REBT (if such a thing even exists) but to illustrate the GABCDE with a real athlete.

HOMEWORK

A full exploration and guide to homework is beyond the scope of this text, and really could be the subject of entire other text, however it is commonly recognised that REBT is more effective when clients are engaging in some meaningful between-session activities germane to the work being undertaken (Kazantzis et al., 2010). Homework is relevant all the way through the REBT process. That is, for each of the 12 stages I highlight above, a homework task can be negotiated to further the work in the client's own time. I would generally not use the term "homework" with the clients I work with due to its connotations with school (nobody wants to be reminded of school, surely!). The reader can call it what they like in keeping with the context they are working within, but I tend to call it "between-session training" and help the client to undertake "mental training activities" or "mental training tasks" (Turner & Barker, 2014a). The homework is to be negotiated between client and practitioner, not 'set' by the practitioner. This is important for three main reasons. First, it is the client who will be carrying out the task and thus is more likely to commit to a mutually agreed upon activity rather than one that is forced on them. Second, we must be sure that the client feels confident and competent enough to complete the task – we can only garner this by discussing the task thoroughly. Third, the client must see the purpose of the task which is more likely if they have been party to the creation and particulars of the task (Dryden, 2019c).

C – *unwanted and unpleasant thoughts, emotions, and behaviours*
Think: distracted, mind wandering, overthinking, competitors will beat me. **Feel:** anxiety, shaking, weak, uncomfortable, poor control of body, sweating. **Behave:** fidgety, felt and acted differently to normal, isolated myself, underperformed, skill breakdown.

What thoughts, emotions, and behaviours would be more desirable?
Think: focussed, clear-minded, things just clicking, auto-polit, confident. **Feel:** nervous but relaxed, ready, strong and prepared. **Behave:** chatting, interacting with people, fluid skills, perform to, or close to, potential.

A – *in what situation did you feel the negative emotions and behaviours*
I had a major event that was very a prestigious competition. There were elite opponents, and also international scouts were watching. This was a great chance to show how good I am to the scouts, so underperformance here would ruin my changes.

G – *your career and life goals*
To be the best I can be in my sport To be content with my contribution to the world

How is A stopping you from attaining G?
If I don't perform well at this event, then it might ruin my selection chances. If I underperform at events like this, then I will not be able to reach my potential.

B – *your beliefs about A that led to C*
1. "If I underperform, I'm a loser, failure, worthless" 2. "I want to be, and so I must be, thought of as one of the best, or else I'm nothing" 3. "I can't stand failing when it matters"

Figure 4.2 Example GABCDE assessment sheet from working with a skeet shooter. (Continued)

D – *Disputing your irrational B's*
Evidence Q: Where is the evidence for these beliefs? Are they true? **A: There is no evidence. No rules, nothing written at all. I know I can stand failing because I have come back from defeat many times. It is not true that failing makes me a loser – failing just means I have failed, that's it.** Logic Q: Are these beliefs logical? **A: No, they are not. They are not consistent with reality. Just because I want something, does not mean I must have it. The world doesn't owe me anything.** Helpfulness Q: Are these beliefs helping your performance? Are these beliefs moving you towards your goals? **A: No – they are actually harming my performance and reducing my chances of reaching my goals.**

E – *Replacing your irrational B's with rational B's*
1. "If I underperform, I'm a loser, failure, worthless" **If I underperform, it does not mean I am a loser, it just means I failed, which I am allowed to do as a human being.** 2. "I want to be, and so I must be, thought of as one of the best, or else I'm nothing" **I would like to be, but I don't have to be, thought of as one of the best. If this doesn't happen though, I can accept myself and am certainly not 'nothing'** 3. "I can't stand underperforming when it matters" **Failing is really tough, but I can stand it. Although I don't like it, underperforming will not end me, and it is worth tolerating it so I can learn and improve.**

Figure 4.2 (Continued) Example GABCDE assessment sheet from working with a skeet shooter.

Sufficient time should be spent negotiating the specifics of the task (when will they do it and how?) and this element of the session is not to be tagged onto the end of a session when time is running out. Tasks need to be purposefully discussed and set so that the client has all the details needed to complete it. The practitioner should provide a strong rationale for homework and help the client to understand its importance for the work they are doing. It should also be highlighted to the client that it is important for the homework to be challenging (but not stressful) so that it can stretch them and really test their REBT learning. After all, we want the client to actually complete the task, so it makes no sense to negotiate an activity that is too difficult or stressful for them to complete.

One of the ways we can express the importance of the homework is to review its completion in each session as a meaningful part of the session. Did the client complete the task? Did they execute the task as discussed, or change it? When was it done? How many times? How did it go? What feedback did they get externally (reactions of others) and internally (emotions, thoughts)? Was it worth doing? What did they learn? These questions plus others that are more specific to the particular task can be discussed to bring meaning to the homework and to ensure proper reflection. Clients that do not complete homework should not be admonished – rather – we need to get to the bottom of *why* they failed to complete the task. Their avoidance of the task might indicate some faulty inference and/or irrational beliefs about the task that can be addressed in session. Also, perhaps we did not set the right task.

Homework tasks tend to fit into three main categories of cognitive, emotive, and behavioural, and we would try to include all categories of homework in our work. Cognitive activities could include the client reading some relevant material, listening to podcasts, or engaging in psychoeducational content. Tasks could also include noting down their Gs, As, Bs, and Cs in the early parts of the work (on a blank version of Figure 4.2), and practising D and E in mid- to later parts. They could use the Smarter Thinking App (Turner & Wood, 2019a), for example. Also, I tend to use psychometrics as cognitive assignments too. I would use the Smarter Thinking Profile (Turner & Wood, 2019b) or the irrational performance beliefs inventory (Turner et al., 2018b) to measure irrational beliefs, and use specific questionnaires that monitor emotional and behavioural issues germane to the client's issue/s. Emotive tasks could include imagery in which the client might picture themselves in their mind's eye facing A and practising a healthy response (via rational belief usage). Behavioural tasks could include risk-taking exercises, which involves the client forthrightly facing the A that they fear and/or have been avoiding. This can show that the A is not unbearable or awful, for example. An athlete with disapproval irrational beliefs ("I cannot bear being disapproved of") could assertively speak up in a team session. An athlete afraid of failure, with failure irrational beliefs ("I must not fail and failure is awful"), could do or try new things in training – force the failure in order to realise that it is not fatal! Behavioural exercisers are not just about facing A, they could include practising relaxation, for example.

A 'TYPICAL' SESSION

Being organised as a practitioner is an important part of applying REBT, not least because the client probably will not want to engage in an unstructured amble with no apparent beginning or end. But also, we can be very systematic in REBT in our assessment and intervention, and this depends on knowing where you are with a client in any given session and across any given programme of work. DiGiuseppe et al. (2014) suggest a working session outline, which I have adapted, that includes:

First 10 minutes

- Ice-breaker/rapport building (yes, in every session).
- Old business from the previous session.
- New business: any major life changes.
- Check on homework.
- Setting the agenda for the session.

Middle 30 minutes

- Work time, in which the aims of the work are pursued.

Last 10 minutes

- Summary of work done in the session.
- Negotiation of homework and identification of barriers to completion.
- Closing questions.

But in sport and performance settings, is there a 'typical' session? In my experience, the answer is 'yes and no'. If you have the opportunity to work week to week for 45–60 minutes, then the 'typical' session above can be executed regularly. Also, if you are imbedded within a team and you are on camp, so to speak, and get some good chunks of time for one-to-one meetings, again the 'typical' session can be attempted. But a lot of the time when working in sport and performance settings we do not get 45–60 minutes and often our one-to-one sessions are ad hoc, unplanned, sprung upon us. We have to be flexible with the way we use REBT because we are not always going to get the structure and time needed for a 'typical' session. Indeed, REBT can be applied very briefly, and effective sessions (or conversations) can be achieved in as little as 15 minutes (see Dryden, 2018). So, imagine crunching the 'typical' session down to 15 minutes, what elements would remain? For me, it tends to look like this:

First 3 minutes

- Ice-breaker/rapport building (e.g., "How have things been?" "How was training earlier?" "Did you see the game last night?").
- Setting the agenda for the session (e.g., "What do you want to talk about today?") "What can we get done?" "What shall we do with our time?").

Middle 10 minutes

- Work time, in which the aims of the work are pursued.

Last 2 minutes

- Summary of work done in the session ("To wrap things up…" "so, going forward you say you are going to…" "so let's try x today/over the next week/in your next training session, and see how things go".
- Closing questions (e.g., "is there anything else you wanted to talk to me about?" "Do you have any questions regarding what we talked about today?").

Notice that formal homework setting does not appear here, and this is because often these ad hoc sessions do not happen in the context of consistent and ongoing work with the client, and may be the first and last time we see the client. A solution-focussed approach is appropriate in contexts where time is very limited, and the reader may wish to consult Dryden (2016, 2020) for guidance on very brief REBT.

We have to be realistic about what is achievable in very brief sessions, but ultimately, we are trying to help the athlete to solve an issue or problem, or we are helping them develop in some way or other, so we can (a) be very targeted in our work, (b) be guided by what the athlete wants, and (c) make use of the interdependent GABC(DE) framework. This last point is important because remember we can apply general REBT or specific REBT and still work within an REBT framework. It might be that the brief session highlights a useless old G that can be abandoned and a new G that can be instantiated and worked towards, an A that can be changed (concretely or inferentially), or a C that can be modulated. It is also possible to do some 'B' work of course, but forget trying to execute a full elaboration and disputation (D) of an irrational belief. It is more achievable to do some 'quick and dirty' B disputation in a more didactic and direct way, and offer up some alternative rational beliefs (E) for discussion and potential commitment towards. Whilst we can still be very Socratic in our interaction with the athlete, a more direct approach is often needed to make the most of the short time and give the athlete something to work with and apply. Usually, if what you came up with together works for the athlete, they will tell you when you next see them, and if it did not work, most athletes will not be unforthcoming (!). They want solutions that work, but they often do not have the time for deep dives into their psyche. This is of course a bit of a catch 22 because we know that a more meaningful programme of work with longer and more sessions might help the athlete over the long term. But we have to be pragmatic and help as much as we can within the contextual constraints we are faced with, if we are to work effectively in sport and performance settings.

How about a five-minute session? What elements would remain? For me, it tends to look like this:

First 1 minute

- Setting the agenda for the session (e.g., "What do you want to talk about today?" "What can we get done?" "What shall we do with our time?").

Middle 4 minutes

- Work time, in which the aims of the work are pursued.

Last 1 minute

- Summary of work done in the session ("To wrap things up…" "so, going forward you are going to…" "so let's try x today/over the next week/in your next training session, and see how things go".

No time for ice breaking, no time for closing questions here. We cut to the chase and prioritise forming a solution to a very well-defined issue. These interactions typically take place in a competition venue prior to a game, walking with an athlete between training sessions, encounters court/pitch side before/during/after training, on the bus on the way to training/competitions, at dinner cuing up for food (!). You may need to sacrifice some Socratic dialogue here and offer some things for the athlete to try based on your reading of the issue. But again, there is little need to stray from the GABCDE framework here. Say an athlete approaches you pre-game and says "I am really nervous, I am not sure I can do this!" We can try some inferential A change ("maybe how you are seeing the match is not as helpful as it could be" "perhaps you could focus on and visualise what you know you can do well in the game"), some C change ("let's take some nice rhythmic breaths here and restore some control" "let's look at your heartrate monitor and see if we can lower your heart rate a bit"), or some B change ("remember, this is not life or death here, don't let your 'want' become a 'must'"). The reader can of course be creative here, but the point is that even in brief exchanges with athletes, we can still apply REBT.

A 'TYPICAL' REBT PROGRAMME

In the previous section, we asked "is there a 'typical' session?" and here we ask "is there a 'typical' programme?" Again, the answer is yes and no. In light of the flexible way that we often have to work in sport and performance settings, we may never actually formulate a programme of work with an athlete. Some athletes interact with the practitioner transiently and therefore the formal articulation of a programme may not be possible, relevant, or needed. When working in this way, my focus is more on the goals of the broader athletic psychological development programme for which I am (partly) responsible. Whilst I can be reactive to the individual athlete's needs, I am also guided by the strategic aims and objectives of the organisation within which I am working. For example, when I began my work with England Futsal my main remit was to help the team to optimise their performance under pressure. As such, much of my work on an educational and one-to-one level was guided towards helping players to develop skills and techniques (including REBT) to enable them to execute their skills in pressured situations.

But when working privately, and outside the confines of an organisation, there is a greater capacity to develop and follow a programme of work, because we can be more planned with the time we have and we are more likely to get dedicated and sufficient time with the athlete in which to implement said programme. So, what might an REBT programme look like? The previously covered 12 steps are a good guide, but see Figure 4.3 for a client-friendly version that is an imperfect *example* of what we might offer the client. Each programme will be different for each client, but for this particular client, the below is what was offered. You can see distinctly REBT elements, and PST elements too.

As you can see in Figure 4.3, I have planned for ten one-to-one sessions in the programme, but again, this depends on the client's issues, context, and nature of the work. The programme is also subject to change as we learn more about the client, their issues, and their goals. Often, the actual work that takes place looks very different to the proposed programme. In our applied research we often use very few sessions (one to four sessions of one-to-one, one to three sessions of group education) that focus on very specific issues or themes. For example, in one paper we applied a single-session REBT approach (Bowman & Turner, 2022), in another we used three sessions (Turner & Barker, 2013), and in another we used five sessions (Davis & Turner, 2020). When you look across the extant research, four to five sessions is the norm in sport (Jordana et al., 2020), although more sessions have been used too (eight sessions; Wood et al., 2020). In the research we see session length range between 20 and 60 minutes, but as indicated previously, I would often have 5- and 15-minute sessions. However, it is useful to approach work in sport and performance settings with a 'single-session' mindset whereby it could be the only meaningful client-practitioner encounter. As such, time had better be used purposefully (Bowman & Turner, 2022). This approach can be referred to as One-At-A-Time (OAAT) therapy (Hoyt, 2011), whereby 'one-at-a-time' does not necessarily

Session Outline	Background to Session
1. Deeper exploration.	We will have an in-depth discussion about your particular performance experience and start to uncover where areas of psychological improvement can be made.
2. The GABCs of spot psychology	Introduce you to the GABC framework as a way to understand how the mind and body work for performance. This framework will help guide us in the development of new psychological skills. This includes dealing with setbacks, negativity, and over analysis.
3. Focusing on the 'B'	We take a look at a specific part of the GABC framework, the 'thoughts' and start to challenge any thoughts that are not helping. You will start to develop skills that help you to deal with these thoughts effectively.
4. Routine	Once we have a good handle on dealing with unhelpful thoughts, we move onto developing useful thoughts and attitudes for performance. This includes developing a specific routine (or number of routines) that get your head where it needs to be for performance.
5. Strengthening	We reflect on the routines we have put in place and look to change and then strengthen the helpful routines. These routines include ways of thinking and behaving prior to, during, and after performance and training.
6. Goal Setting	After developing and refining the routines, we focus here on what you wish to achieve in your career, and what it might take to get there from a mental perspective. Here we focus on what processes you can put in place to be the best you can be. Any gaps in your knowledge of the mental side of the sport are uncovered.
7. Skills training	I introduce a suite of psychological skills, tailored to your needs based on goal setting we completed.
8. Refinement	We refine your psychological skills and challenge your ability to get into the right mind-set for performance.
9. Reflection	In this session we reflect on what we have done, and what we may have missed. Any additional issues will be addressed, and we will decide on the best way forward for your paychological skills development.
10. Debrief	We tie up any loose ends here and make sure that you are confident and able to progress with your new skills. We look back across how you have developed. A clear plan will be formed for the future.

Figure 4.3 An example of a client-facing REBT-based psychology programme.

mean 'one time'. "It is knowing that more help is possible that enables the client to relax and get the most from the first and often only therapeutic encounter" (Dryden, 2020, p. 27).

So, I might plan for ten sessions as the best-case scenario and if we have *properly* completed our work in less than ten sessions, then great! The flow of the sessions is dictated in part by the aforementioned 12 steps but really is determined by the client. That is, the specifics of the work are dictated by the nature of the issues, the goals of the client, and the progress the client makes. But having a plan means at least we are not going into the work blind to the possible direction and flow of the work. Realistically, the plan will change because people, situations, emotions, change. So again, be flexible and do not just stick to the plan for the sake of it and sacrifice the ability to be sensitive and reactive to a changing context. The context of sport is uncontrollable, ever changing, and unpredictable. We cannot compensate for these contextual challenges by being rigid in our approach to work, but we can at least initially offer a plan to the client to provide some much-needed structure, and we can attempt to stay on track, flexibly making changes if needed.

Summary

In this chapter I have covered the major client, practitioner, and logistic considerations when applying REBT in sport and exercise settings. What I stress here in particular is the development and fostering of a strong working alliance, some procedural consistency in applying REBT regardless of context or mode, and practitioner flexibility. Whilst I offer some guidance on programme and session structure, flow, and content, this is all dependent on the client, their issues and goals, and the context in which we are working. Regardless of the specifics of the work, we can comfortably apply the GABCDE framework of REBT.

Next I move onto the specific procedural components of REBT. I structure the remaining chapters using the order by which I would *typically* work *through* the GABCDE framework, and is geared to towards specific REBT. Clearly, every client is different, and REBT is flexible in its proposed application of the GABCDE framework, but I am hopeful that the chapter order hence forth is informative, rather than prescriptive. In what follows, I present each element of the framework in the order in which the element is *typically* addressed in my REBT practice. Therefore, I first cover C, then A, then G, followed by B, before moving onto D and E. Regardless of the precise ordering, GABC should be fully assessed before moving to D and E, and for the purposes of this book, I believe the reader is furnished with sufficient detail for each element to be able to reorder the process if the situation warrant it.

Chapter 5
Consequences (C)

Mine, and only mine.

DOI: 10.4324/9781003200437-6

What have you come to see me about? What seems to be troubling you at the moment? What can I help you with today? Perhaps you could tell me what has brought you to see me?

All of the above questions are formulated to elicit from the client the first pieces of information that will help the practitioner to get some insight into the nature of the client's issues. Quite often, the answers to these questions contain emotional material. Often, the reason prospective clients approach me to undertake some psychology support, is that they are experiencing, or have experienced, an unwanted and unpleasant emotion. This emotion is usually associated with, or perceived to be, a hinderance to goal attainment and/or wellbeing by the client. As such, they wish to ameliorate the emotion and its behavioural concomitants which are often performance limiting. They wish to do this in part because the emotion is unpleasant and unwanted – in other words, they are suffering and are motivated to ameliorate this suffering now and to avoid this suffering in the future. But they also wish to do this because the emotion is limiting their ability to fulfil their potential.

Healthy vs. unhealthy negative emotions

The core work undertaken here for the client and practitioner is to determine whether the emotions being experienced are unhealthy negative emotions (UNEs) or healthy negative emotions (HNEs). In other words, although the client is experiencing a negatively valenced, and thus often unpleasant, emotion, does not mean to say that this emotion is maladaptive to their wellbeing or goal attainment. In line with Stoicism, REBT does not promote the absence or eradication of emotion, rather, it promotes adaptive emotions (Robertson, 2019b). In REBT we do not delude ourselves into thinking that we can help clients remove negative emotion completely, and we do not believe that this would be advantageous. Whether an emotion is unhealthy (UNE) or healthy (HNE) is a crucial focus of REBT theory, predicated on the fact that not all 'negative' emotions are disturbed or appropriate targets for change (DiGiuseppe et al., 2014). Emotions evolved to help us solve problems like overcoming goal obstruction (anger), avoiding pathogens (disgust), and adjusting to loss (sadness; Tooby et al., 2008). Indeed, as Kashdan and Biswas-Diener (2014) point out, negative emotion can be very useful (functional) as sources of information concerning our progress, interactions, environment, and actions. If we try to suppress negative emotion, we miss out on valuable information that could help us to assuage harm, stand up for ourselves, and correct ourselves when we miss the mark in our life pursuits (be it work, relationships, hobbies, etc.).

> Society is missing out on something right now to think that anger and hostility are things that are in the violent realm of emotions, that they're all completely 100% bad and should be avoided at all costs, I don't think that's true at all. Those emotions are very much relevant.
>
> Jack White III, musician (Team Coco, 2013)

Thus, negative emotions are not always dysfunctional, and can be adaptive (e.g., Franken, 1994; Kashdan & Biswas-Diener, 2014), and so REBT theory does not imply that negative emotions are *desirable* but holds that they are an essential part of both adaptation and coping in the face of activating events (Turner et al., 2018a, 2019a). This discussion about the utility of negative emotion is an important subject to broach with clients, because by understanding that negative emotion is not the enemy, they can learn to utilise negative emotion in the pursuit of their goals. Clients might be motived to eradicate negative emotion because by definition negative emotions are unpleasant – they don't feel good (!). Also, negative emotions represent things not going to plan, conditions not being optimal, or a perceived loss of personal control (Kashdan & Biswas-Diener, 2014). It is possible that the client has received feedback from their external environment that their expression of negative emotion is alienating to others. So, it is understandable why clients might be driven to wanting to extinguish negative emotion, or avoid negative emotion in the future. But most of the downsides of negative emotion are not necessarily to do with the negative emotion itself – it is more to do with the intensity, frequency, and expression of the emotion, and how the emotion is regulated (or not, as the case may be). In other words, it is not the mere experience of anxiety that is problematic, but how intense, pervasive, and ultimately, disruptive the emotion is. In REBT emotions are targets for change when they are unhealthy (UNEs), not when they are negative. It is the function of the emotion that is important in REBT, not the valence. When emotions are too intense, too frequent, or inappropriate, they can interfere with goal attainment and health (Kring, 2008), and as such, UNEs are justifiable targets for change within REBT. The concepts of HNEs and UNEs are captured in the REBT-derived Binary Theory of Emotional Distress (BTED; Ellis & DiGiuseppe, 1993). For a critical discussion see Turner et al. (2018a, 2019a), and a more detailed description of UNEs and HNEs can be found in Chapter 5.

In brief, HNEs are associated with adaptive behaviours or action tendencies (actual and/or intended) and healthy physiological responses, whereas UNEs are associated with maladaptive behaviours or action tendencies (actual and/or intended) and unhealthy physiological responses (e.g., David & Cramer, 2010). The distinction between HNEs and UNEs concerns function, adaptiveness, appropriateness, and health. HNEs are functional, adaptive, appropriate, and healthy, whilst UNEs are dysfunctional, maladaptive, inappropriate, and unhealthy. HNEs are self-enhancing, whilst UNEs are self-defeating. HNEs lead to constructive behaviour and aid goal attainment, whilst UNEs lead to unconstructive behaviour and interfere with goal attainment (Dryden, 2021b).

The reader might wonder, "maladaptive or adaptive for what?" The reader should bear in mind what the present author said regarding a "human first, athlete second" stance, and consider the implications of long-term hedonism. Adaptivity should be in the service of the long-term health and wellbeing of the human being, and therefore, the practitioner may experience situations in which an athlete perceives that a UNE is helping them to achieve a short-term goal, but this is at the expense of long-term wellbeing. For example, an athlete who has withdrawn from all social engagements and obsessively thinks about their flaws might attribute their goal attainment to these sacrificial and life-limiting actions. The practitioner must wrestle with the dilemma, "what if the athlete is right?" and decide whether they should focus on (a) athlete wellbeing in the long term, or (b) athlete performance in the short term. The author of the current book strongly sits in the former camp (a), and believes that post hoc rationalisation of unhealthy 'athletic' behaviours cannot be equal to the wellbeing of the human being. Performance attainment should come as a *consequence of and coexist with* wellbeing. So the question we must ask when determining the UNE or HNE status of an emotion is; is the emotion functional, adaptive, and appropriate for the attainment of *long-term eudaimonia*?

Whether or not the client is attaining their short-term performance-related goals should not distract from the proper focus on long-term hedonism and eudaimonia. As practitioners our efforts should be in the service of the whole human being, not just the 'performer'. Of course, it is possible for the practitioner to help the client attain their short-term goals, so long as this work is clearly not antithetical to the client's long-term functioning. Some readers could make an argument that if one is successful in sport, wellbeing will come with financial comfort and self-esteem. I do not share this view for three main reasons. First, there is no guarantee that short-term goal attainment, no matter how great, will bestow long-lasting benefits. To this point, more and more we are realising that athletes are suffering long term in part as a consequence of their drive for short-term accolades (e.g., Park, 2021). Second, often the attainment of short-term external goals is met with relief, anxiety about the future, and guilt, rather than the short- or long-term joy (positive affect) that one might hope for. The emotion that is evoked in response to goal attainment is subject to cognitive appraisal (e.g., Kreibig et al., 2010), just like any other stimulus, and thus individual differences are inevitable. Lastly, I follow the Stoic viewpoint that external attainment cannot define the internal being. I agree with Epictetus when he says:

> These reasonings have no logical connection: "I am richer than you; therefore I am your superior." "I am more eloquent than you; therefore I am your superior." The true logical connection is rather this: "I am richer than you; therefore my possessions must exceed yours." "I am more eloquent than you; therefore my style must surpass yours." But you, after all, consist in neither property nor in style.

In other words, the attainment of short-term external goals (e.g., titles, trophies, medals, accolades) are pursued alongside the development, maintenance, and strengthening, of wellbeing including psychological and physical health, in the interest of long-range hedonism (i.e., eudaimonia). Human first, performer second (Human>Performer; Turner, 2016b).

It is not that the client must present with a UNE in order for the practitioner to apply REBT. As I have previously stated, using the GABCDE holistically we can apply *general* REBT with clients who wish to down-regulate an emotion, even if the emotion does not qualify as a UNE. Thus, even if the client presents with *healthy* anxiety, they may still wish to exercise more control over the anxiety, and can thus apply the various emotion regulation strategies we have covered previously in the present book. We can help the athlete to express the emotion in as functional way as possible, help them to quell the emotion, and we can also help them to weaken irrational beliefs and strengthen rational beliefs. But most importantly, we can educate the athlete in the idea that negative emotions per se are not the enemy of performance and wellbeing.

One of the ways we can help the client to understand the functionality or dysfunctionality of C, and motivate them towards working against the UNE and towards the HNE is to foster some cognitive dissonance. We can ask the client to think about an area of their life in which they experience and express HNEs, and to compare that functional experience with the dysfunctional experience they are reporting in relation to their main issue. The idea that they do experience HNEs, and therefore can move towards HNEs in this instance (and in any instance) can help the client to realise that their current way of being is not serving them and can strengthen their will to change – to bring about HNEs and ameliorate UNEs.

Assessing C

Whether or not C is a HNE or UNE can be ascertained by carefully clarifying whether the emotion helps or hinders the client's goal attainment and/or long-term health and wellbeing. The practitioner is being steered here by what the client reports in terms of how the emotion is limiting or detracting from a contented or fulfilled life. The practitioner is assessing the healthiness (HNE vs. UNE) of the client's emotions by gaining information on the cognitive, physiologic (somatic), and behavioural (actual or overt, intention or impulse) aspects of the emotion. The behavioural components of the emotion are perhaps most important because they illustrate how the emotion is expressed, which can have clear implications on how the client engages with their environment. So, to identify whether the client is experiencing a UNE or a HNE, we need to assess their reported concomitant behaviours (overt) or action tendencies (impulses, intentions) when they are experiencing the emotion (Dryden, 2012a). The extent to which UNEs are dysfunctional, and HNEs are functional, is determined largely by the intended or actual expression of maladaptive or adaptive behaviours. UNEs involve maladaptive (destructive, self-defeating) behaviours that do not enable the client to modify or adapt to As, or successfully pursue Gs. HNEs involve adaptive (constructive, self-enhancing) behaviours that do enable the client to modify or adapt to As, and successfully pursue Gs (Dryden & Branch, 2008). In other words, is the emotion and its associated cognitive, physiologic (somatic), and behavioural components, *appropriate* (HNE) or inappropriate (UNE) for the pursuit of goal attainment, fulfilment, eudaimonia?

We can undertake C assessment by developing a conversation with the client concerning the specific details of their emotional experience. The practitioner asks a variety of open questions in order to understand what the client was thinking, doing (or intending to do), and feeling, when they were experiencing the emotion, or when in the specific situation. When doing this, it is important to avoid questions that reinforce or suggest an A–C connection (Dryden & Branch, 2008). That is, the REBT practitioner avoids questions such as, "how did that make you feel?", "did that make you angry?", or "what emotion did that cause within you?". Rather, the REBT practitioner would ask questions like, "when that happened, how did you feel?", "what feelings did you experience in that situation?", or "how did you feel *about* that?" (Dryden & Branch, 2008). This can be applied to questions pertaining to the thoughts and behaviours of the client too (e.g., "when that happened, how did you act or want/intend to act?" or "what were you thinking in that situation?").

Based on the client's responses, the practitioner and the client can start to determine the precise emotion in question, and whether what they were thinking, doing, and feeling are healthy (i.e., in service of the client's goals and wellbeing), or unhealthy (i.e., counter to the client's goals and wellbeing). For example, if a client responds to the question "when that happened, how did you feel?" with the answer "down", then we do not know precisely what they are experiencing, and have no details about the cognitive or behavioural aspects of this feeling. So, we need to dig a bit deeper here in order to clarify the client's emotion, and then whether the emotion is a UNE or HNE. Encourage the client to report what they *feel* or what *emotion* they experienced, because clients can often be vague or report inferences, rather than emotions. Just be patient and if needed, explain to the client the differences between thoughts and emotions in order to help them supply the information you seek.

As a way to orient the particular methods of client questioning around C, we can ask the client to recall a recent and concrete situation in which the emotion was experienced so that they can better detail how they felt, thought, and behaved (or wanted to behave). If a recent event is not apparent, then the client can use a particularly powerful memory they have of the emotion being experienced, or they can give an account of how the emotion typically plays out in relevant situations. From my experience, the more recent and concrete, the better, because detail is paramount. We can also utilise imagery to help the client to take themselves, in their mind's eye, to a situation in which the emotion is evinced. If done successfully, with realistic imagery, the client can report on the cognitive and behavioural information emanating from how they are presently feeling (in the room, as it were). In addition, the practitioner can engage the client in role-play, in which the adversity (A) is played-out and information about C emerges. This is particularly useful if the main characteristic of the situation in which the emotion emerges for the client is one of social interaction or interpersonal conflict. The practitioner can assume the role of the perceived antagonist, whilst the client tries to engage with the situation to the extent that their emotions are evoked. The client can observe and report on their emotional experience.

One other method of C assessment that is useful in practice is to ask the client more directly about what is going wrong for them currently, and if things were going right, how it would look and feel. In other words, we can help them to lay out the ways in which their current C is hindering goal attainment and the ways in which an alternate C might aid their goal attainment. Once we have painted a realistic (not utopic) picture of how they would like to function (think, feel, behave), we can help animate the client towards realising that picture. We can do this Socratically by having the client conceptualise a C that would best help them, or we can provide some potential alternate Cs to help the client conceptualise healthy negative emotion. For example, a client who is unhealthy anxious about an upcoming selection trial can be Socratically encouraged to formulate a more functional C (e.g., "how would you like to think, feel, and behave when approaching this event?"), or they can be directed towards healthy anxiety (e.g., "perhaps it is possible to feel anxious, but in a helpful way?"). Either way, we are communicating to the client that there is a different way to think, feel, and behave that might serve them, rather than hamper them.

Cognitive specificity

The adaptive and maladaptive cognitive and behavioural concomitants of various UNEs and HNEs can be found in Figure 5.1. This can help practitioners to assess the presence of UNEs and HNEs in what the athlete is experiencing. By thoroughly and accurately assessing C, we can also begin to understand the precise nature of A, following Lazarus' (1999) core relational themes. For example, if the assessment shows that the client is experiencing unhealthy anger, then following Smith and Lazarus' (1993) taxonomy for anger, we can surmise that the client may have perceived "a demeaning offence against me and mine" and may have appraised high goal relevance, high goal incongruence, and high self or other-accountability (self or other-blame) . Indeed, Dryden (2012a) suggests that inferential themes (similar to the core relational themes) at A determine the "flavour of an emotion" (p. 7), whilst the rational/irrational beliefs determine whether the emotion is expressed as a UNE or a HNE. Whether and to what extent this anger is unhealthy or healthy must be determined by the practitioner, based on an assessment of the specific characteristics of the emotion, in terms of behavioural, physiologic, and cognitive expression. But what I am proposing here is similar to the notion of cognitive specificity (e.g., Kendall & Ingram, 1989), in which there are a range of cognitive processes that appear to be specific to an emotion. This is in line with Lazarus' (1991) thinking in terms of the role of particular patterns of cognitive appraisal in emotion.

G-A		B	C		
Appraisal	**Core Relational Theme**	**Belief**	**Healthy or Unhealthy**	**Example Cognitive Consequences***	**Example Action Tendencies (actual or intended)***
High Goal Relevance High Goal Incongruence Low/uncertain (emotion - focused) coping potential	Threat/Danger Facing uncertainty and existential threat	Irrational	Unhealthy Anxiety	• Overestimate probability and or magnitude of threat. • Has more task -irrelevant thoughts.	• Withdraw physically and or mentally from the threat (avoidance). • Ward off the threat (e.g., superstitious behaviour). • Seek reassurance and or protection. • Perform below potential. • Tranquilise feelings. • Over preparation. • Risk aversion. • Hide or distract self from threat. • Keep checking on status of threat. • Hypervigilance to threat.
		Rational	Healthy Anxiety	• Realistic about the probability and or magnitude of threat. • More task relevant thoughts.	• Face up to threat (approach). • Deal with the threat constructively. • Take constructive action to reduce/minimise the risk or danger. • Perform to potential.
					• Appropriate preparation. • Take calculated risks. • Seek support to help self to face threat. • Appropriate awareness of threat.
High Goal Relevance High Goal Incongruence Low (problem-focused) coping potential Low/negative future-expectancy	Irrevocable loss or failure (with implications for the future) Helplessness about harm or loss Undeserved plight	Irrational	Unhealthy Sadness (non-clinical depression)	• See only negative aspects of the loss or failure. • Think of other losses and failures that one has experienced. • Think one is unable to self-help (helplessness) • Hopelessness.	• Withdraw into oneself. • Create an environment consistent with feelings. • Attempt to terminate feelings in self-destructive ways. • Over-dependence on others. • Push people away. • Bemoan one's fate.
		Rational	Healthy Sadness	• Able to recognize both negative and positive aspects of the loss or failure. • Able to self-help. • Able to look to the future with hope.	• Express feelings about the loss or failure (e.g., talk about these to significant others). • Seek out reinforcements after a period of mourning. • Allow self to be comforted. • Create environment inconsistent with feelings.
High Goal Relevance High Goal Incongruence	Self- or other-blame for goal obstruction, threat	Irrational	Unhealthy Anger	• Overestimate the extent to which the other person acted deliberately.	• Attack the self/other physically. • Attack the self/other

*Examples are not exhaustive, in part, because people are idiosyncratic in their C expression and thus these examples are rules of thumb, not gospel.

Figure 5.1 The articulated GABC framework incorporating Ellisian and Lazarusian concepts (in part adapted from David et al., 2002, 2005; Dryden, 2012a, 2018; Dryden & Branch, 2008; Smith & Lazarus, 1993). (Continued)

Other/world-accountability Self-accountability	to self-esteem, or transgression of personal rule A demeaning offense against me and mine Frustration Other shames or ridicules me			• See malicious intent in the motives of others. • See self as definitely right; other(s) seen as definitely wrong. • Unable to see the other person's point of view. • Plot revenge.	verbally. • Attack the self/other passive-aggressively. • Displace attack onto another person, animal or object. • Alienate others. • Withdraw aggressively. • Recruit allies against perceived transgressor.
		Rational	Healthy Anger	• Do not overestimate the extent to which the other person acted deliberately. • Do not see malicious intent in the motives of the other(s). • Do not see self as definitely right and the other(s) as definitely wrong. • Able to see the other's point of view. • Do not plot revenge.	• Assert self with the other. • Request, but not demand, behavioural change from the other. • Non-aggressively step-away from an unsatisfactory situation after attempting to deal with it.
High Goal Relevance High Goal Incongruence Self-accountability	Hurt the feelings of significant others Having transgressed a moral imperative,	Irrational	Unhealthy Guilt	• Assume that one has definitely committed the sin. • Assume more personal responsibility than is warranted.	• Look for ways to escape from the guilt in self-defeating ways. • Beg forgiveness from the person wronged and or reject offers of
	code, or rule (i.e., act immorally, unethically) Self-blame			• Assign less responsibility to others than is warranted. • Do not put behaviour into overall context. • Think that one deserve s and will get retribution.	forgiveness. • Promise unrealistically that they will not 'sin' again. • Disclaim responsibility for wrongdoing. • Punish self physically or by depreciation. • Make excuses for behaviour.
		Rational	Healthy Guilt	• Consider behaviour in context when making judgements concerning the 'sin'. • Assume appropriate level of personal responsibility to self and others. • Take into account mitigating factors. • Put behaviour into overall context. • Do not think they deserve or will get retribution.	• Face up to the healthy pain that accompanies the sin. • Ask, but not beg, for forgiveness. • Understand reasons for wrongdoing. • Atone for the sin by taking a penalty. • Make appropriate amends. • No tendency to make excuses for one's behaviour or display defensive behaviour. • Accept offers of forgiveness.
High Goal Relevance High Goal Incongruence	Being looked down on by others (i.e., others' negative judgement)	Irrational	Unhealthy Shame	• Overestimate the 'shamefulness' of the information revealed. • Overestimate the	• Remove self from the 'gaze' of others. • Isolate self from others. • Save face by attacking

Figure 5.1 The articulated GABC framework incorporating Ellisian and Lazarusian concepts (in part adapted from David et al., 2002, 2005; Dryden, 2012a, 2018; Dryden & Branch, 2008; Smith & Lazarus, 1993). (Continued)

Self-accountability	Having failed to live up to (i.e., falling short of) an ego-ideal Actions reflected badly on social ingroup			likelihood that the judging group will notice or be interested in the information. • Overestimate the degree of disapproval self (or reference group) will receive. • Overestimate the length of time any disapproval will last.	other(s) who have 'shamed' self. • Defend threatened self-esteem. • Ignore attempts by others to help.
		Rational	Healthy Shame	• Sees information revealed in a compassionate self-accepting way. • Is realistic about the likelihood that the judging group will notice or be interested in the information. • Is realistic about the degree of disapproval. • Is realistic about the length of time the disapproval will last.	• Continue to participate actively in social interaction. • Respond to attempts of others to restore social equilibrium.

Figure 5.1 (Continued) The articulated GABC framework incorporating Ellisian and Lazarusian concepts (in part adapted from David et al., 2002, 2005; Dryden, 2012a, 2018; Dryden & Branch, 2008; Smith & Lazarus, 1993).

Overt behaviour vs. action tendencies

The REBT practitioner in their assessment of C is trying to understand whether the behavioural and cognitive characteristics of the emotion are adaptive or maladaptive for the client's goal attainment and wellbeing. It is important to distinguish between overt behaviour and action tendencies. Action tendencies reflect impulses to act in a certain manner, which could be suppressed by the athlete, so the behaviour is not enacted (Dryden, 2012a). The reader could consider action tendencies to be behavioural *intentions* aligned with the emotion. There might be contextual restrictions that do not permit a client to literally avoid an anxiety provoking situation, but all the same, they *want* to avoid the situation and believe that only by avoiding the situation can they control their anxiety. This would be evidence of a UNE (e.g., unhealthy anxiety) because it is evidence of an *intention* to avoid (they would avoid, if they could). The client may not always act in a way that aligns with their UNE (Dryden & Branch, 2008).

Does the emotion 'label' matter?

On assessing C, of course it helps to understand what emotion is being expressed as this can indicate the nature of the goal and adversity from which the emotion partly emanates. But ultimately, I argue that labelling and naming the emotion matters little, in so much as the type of emotion does not necessarily influence the work. That is, whilst the practitioner may be aware of the type of emotion and the technical terminology, it is more advantageous for the practitioner to accept whatever label the client wishes to put onto the emotions they experience. More importantly for the work we are doing with the client is the extent to which the consequences being expressed and portrayed are maladaptive (vs. adaptative) and are not leading to (vs. leading to) goal fulfilment. The labels are just abstractions and cannot perfectly reflect the precise emotion being experienced anyway. In contrast, in some cases it may be helpful for the client to be able to label the emotion accurately and technically. It can be comforting for clients to be able to label their emotions, bringing their complex experiences into a singular concept that is common across human beings. Clients are not different or special for their emotional experiences, an idea that can help normalise their experiences somewhat.

A HNE example: I felt like I wanted to prove him wrong

SP: So, when your coach told you that you were underperforming, what feelings did you experience?
Chris: I got angry.
SP: Angry?
Chris: Yes, very.
SP: And tell me Chris, when experiencing this anger, were there any actions that went along with this?
Chris: No not really. I just came away from the situation because my teammates were present.
SP: Well, if you could have done something, if your teammates were not present, what would you have done?
Chris: I would have told him that I don't agree with him, but that he is entitled to his opinion. But I don't agree with him!
SP: OK, how would approach this?
Chris: I would just be upfront and honest, not aggressive or anything. Just stern, and sure.

In the above example, the SP elicits from the client some information about the behaviours and action tendencies that were aligned with the client's anger. The client indicates an appropriate intention to act in an assertive way here, and thus, it would appear that the anger experienced by the client is healthy (HNE). Of course the client would be angry – they feel that they have been transgressed in a way that obstructs their goals. But the client is able to incorporate useful and appropriate behavioural intentions.

A UNE example: I felt like I wanted to hurt him

SP: So, when your coach told you that you were underperforming, what feelings did you experience?
Chris: I got angry.
SP: Angry?
Chris: Yes, very.
SP: And tell me Chris, when experiencing this anger, were there any actions that went along with this?
Chris: I ran up to him and went to grab him. My teammates had to pull me away from the situation to be honest.
SP: I see. If they had not pulled you away, what would you have done?
Chris: I would have told him that he's an idiot and that he doesn't know what he is talking about. There is no way I am underperforming.

SP: OK, anything else?
CHRIS: I'd have probably punched him to be honest. I was this close (client gestures with thumb and forefinger) to hitting him.
SP: So things would have got physical?
CHRIS: Yes. I can't let him get away with this, and to hell with teammates who disagree with me.

In the above example, the SP elicits from the client some information about the behaviours and action tendencies that were aligned with the client's anger. The client indicates an inappropriate intention to act in an aggressive way here, and thus, it would appear that the anger experienced by the client is unhealthy (UNE). So, whilst the client's anger is understandable, the client is wanting to and attempting to incorporate destructive and inappropriate behavioural intentions. As such, our work here would be to steadfastly attenuate this UNE (unhealthy anger) via REBT, and move towards HNE (healthy anger). The issue here is not whether or not the client should be angry, but rather, the extent to which the anger is healthy or unhealthy.

How about underperformance?

It is often the case that underperformance, when compared to a client's envisioned potential capabilities, is the chief reason why the client has sought my help. Dryden (2018) notes that, in his demonstrations (with volunteers) of very brief therapeutic conversations, performance anxiety is the most common issue raised. The threat, and negative consequences, of underperformance live large in the minds of many performers I have worked with. Underperformance can be a behavioural C, or it can be an adversity (A). This is the case for any C really – emotions or behaviours at C can become new As, because the client can observe their Cs and disturb themselves about what they see (meta-disturbance; e.g., DiGiuseppe et al., 2014). If an athlete has been driven to seek my support due to underperformance, prior to working towards ameliorating underperformance, it is first important to understand whether the client is experiencing any Cs in response to underperforming. In response to underperformance, clients can experience a range of UNEs across the broad gamut of emotions. It is important to work towards helping them remove UNEs concerning this A, before we move onto helping work towards stopping underperforming itself. Thus, I would treat underperformance as the A in the first instance, working to understand the activated Bs and Cs that the client might be struggling with. One might suggest working to ameliorate underperformance is the more efficient strategy here – if there is no A then there is no C. This could be correct. However, underperformance will occur at many points in a performer's career, so in my view it is best to teach the client how to deal appropriately with this occurrence so that it is not such a tumultuous experience each time they do not perform as they would like. For example:

- **G** – To obtain a professional contract
- **A** – I underperformed in a very important match with scouts spectating (making judgments and decisions on me).

Core relational theme – failure (with implications for the future)

- **B** – I 5.5want to and therefore I must be evaluated positively by the scouts, and it would show I am a useless failure if I was not

Irrational beliefs of demandingness and depreciation

- **C** – unhealthy sadness, hopelessness, withdraw into oneself.

One can also see how this chain of events can precipitate a downward spiral. The athlete's unhealthy sadness could lead to disengagement in training and coaching, thus bringing about further declinations in performance, and further emotional turmoil.

In contrast, if underperformance is treated as a C, then we can help the client to examine the situational (external) and psychological factors that are contributing to this behavioural consequence of underperforming. Oftentimes, As centre around evaluation or judgement, which present danger to the clients' goals (G), to which they can apply rational or irrational beliefs. For example, the case might be:

- **G** – To obtain a professional contract.
- **A** – I have a very important match with scouts spectating (making judgments and decisions on me).

Core relational theme – threat/danger

- **B** – I want to and therefore I must be evaluated positively by the scouts, and it would show I am a useless failure if I was not

Irrational beliefs of demandingness and depreciation

- **C** – unhealthy anxiety, focus on task irrelevant cues, underperformance.

In sum, it is important, if underperformance is the presenting issue that has driven the client to seek help, to fully explore this issue first for meta-disturbance (i.e., underperformance as A). If a meta-disturbance is present, help the athlete to take a more rational view of the underperformance in order to ameliorate the disturbance. Then, we can focus on helping the athlete to perform to their potential in the future, safe in the knowledge that WHEN underperformance does occur, they can think, act, and feel in ways that are self-enhancing rather than self-defeating. If meta-disturbance is not present, then we can go ahead and forthrightly help the client to think, act, and feel in ways that prevent underperformance and/or enhance performance.

Summary

In this chapter I discussed the C element of the GABCDE framework. I distinguished between HNEs and UNEs and explained some of the main ways a practitioner can assess C. I also discussed underperformance as a presenting issue, and how this can be viewed as an A or as a C. Thus, meta-disturbance should be considered when assessing C. The C assessment involves exploring the emotion in detail with the client and taking a largely person-centred approach to the conversation. The job here is to non-judgementally help the athlete to communicate the nature of the emotional experience as accurately as possible in as many ways as it takes for you to grasp whether a UNE or HNE is being experienced. If the details are not forthcoming, then the practitioner can move to the assessment of A, which can help to bring C information to light.

CHAPTER 6
Adversity or activating event (A)

Protect, do not avoid.

DOI: 10.4324/9781003200437-7

> Emotionally mature individuals accept the fact that, as far as has yet been discovered, we live in a world of probability and chance, where there are not, nor probably ever will be, absolute necessities nor complete certainties. Living in such a world is not only tolerable, but in terms of adventure, learning, and striving, can even be very exciting and pleasurable.
>
> (Ellis, 1983, p. 3)

> A gem cannot be polished without friction, nor a [person] perfected without trials.
>
> Seneca

In REBT, people have basic goals (G; more on this in Chapter 8) and at times (inevitably) unfortunate and undesirable occurrences, known as adversities or activating events (A), interfere with the attainment of these goals (Ellis, 1994; Shea, 2016). Importantly, as both Ellis and Seneca intimate above, trials are not only the norm, but can actually be advantageous for human development and fulfilment. It is in this spirit of acknowledgement and acceptance (rather than ignorance and denial) that we approach As in REBT. As has been posited in this book, G and A are related; A is adverse to the extent that it is relevant to and represents an impediment to (or is incongruent with) G. An integrative approach to emotion views emotions as reactions to action outcomes in relation to an individual's goals (Carver & Scheier, 1998), and the goal construct is invoked both as reason to act and as leading to emotions when obstructed or facilitated (Frijda, 1986; Kreibig et al., 2010).

Pursuing meaningful Gs can bring about positive emotions if we receive feedback that we are making positive progress towards the goal. But meaningful Gs can also bring about negative emotions because you are limited, and by pursuing these goals you will undoubtedly face challenges, barriers, and setbacks – the world, and the people you engage with and contend with, are not predictable, controllable, or wholly benign. You will fail, be rejected, be treated unfairly, and suffer in pursuit of meaningful goals. Even if you achieve your meaningful goals, this attainment will set forth new challenges, new As. 'Life' will generate As in pursuit of your Gs because humans (you!) are limited and unmachine-like. Your fallibility mixed with the volatility of existence makes the occurrence of As a certainty, confounded by our natural goal-driven disposition. Indeed, the experience of A implies G, because A is adverse to the extent that it is perceived to thwart G. For example, an A such as "I failed in an important task" implies a G of succeeding (or not failing) in the task, or implies a less proximal G for which this particular A is seen as incongruent (e.g., being seen as perfect).

So, we should expect to face As in our lives (just like Marcus Aurelius does at the beginning of Chapter 2 of his 'Meditations') and thus we can anticipate some As, acknowledge and accept As, so long as we have some strategies to take perspective on and cope with As. But, what are As? What types of adversities am I referring to? The As can be differentiated amongst confirmable, perceived, and inferential reality (DiGiuseppe et al., 2014). Confirmable reality signifies a social consensus by a group of observers to have witnessed the same event and describe it in an identical manner (e.g., "I did not score"). Perceived reality signifies clients' subjective description as to what happened (e.g., "My parents and coach criticized me, when I did not score"). Inferential reality signifies the conclusions clients' make about what happened based upon their own perceptions (e.g., "I am not a good soccer player because I did not score"). The inferential occurrence may or may not be true, but since it stimulates emotional disturbances amongst clients, it is considered to be an actual event.

I could provide a full list of As for reference, but this would take up the entire book (and then some), because As are ubiquitous, copious, and unquantifiable. This is in part because As are definitionally idiosyncratic within the individual – one client's adversity may not be adverse at all to a different client, partly because people's Gs are idiosyncratic – and also in part because we can, as human beings, creatively invent our own As seemingly out of nowhere (see Mahoney, 1974, for a protracted and critical discussion on symbolic self-stimulation), sometimes out of satiated monotony. Of course, there are As that are typically and *almost* universally considered to be 'adverse'. Data collected using the Holmes and Rahe (1967) Social Readjustment Rating Scale (SRRS), which identifies major stressful life events, reveals that the top five are: death of spouse, divorce, marital separation, personal injury or illness, and jail term, which is equal to marriage (Scully et al., 2000). So, there is commonality across our subjective interpretations of reality, but whether and to what extent a stimulus is viewed as adverse is highly variable due to the individual differences in perception and cognitive appraisal.

In short though, *A is the aspect of the situation that the person focuses on and evaluates* (Dryden, 2017). Dryden (2021b) helpfully provides themes that clients' As typically fall into: failure, rejection, disapproval, uncertainty, lack of control, betrayal, unfairness, illness, frustration, and criticism. In athletic populations, injury could be added here alongside illness, and I would argue that 'success' can be an A. In addition, to help understand the most pertinent As in performers, it might be useful to use the content areas in which irrational beliefs (Bs) are measured, as a guide. For example, when we developed the irrational performance beliefs inventory (iPBI; Turner et al., 2018b) and later the Smarter Thinking Profile (online profiling tool; Turner & Wood, 2019b), we nested the irrational beliefs within ten content areas, or performance domains, which are akin to the broad As that individuals may face in a performance setting. The content areas can be seen in Figure 6.1, and in Figure 6.2 the

Figure 6.1 The performance content areas (A themes) and their descriptions.

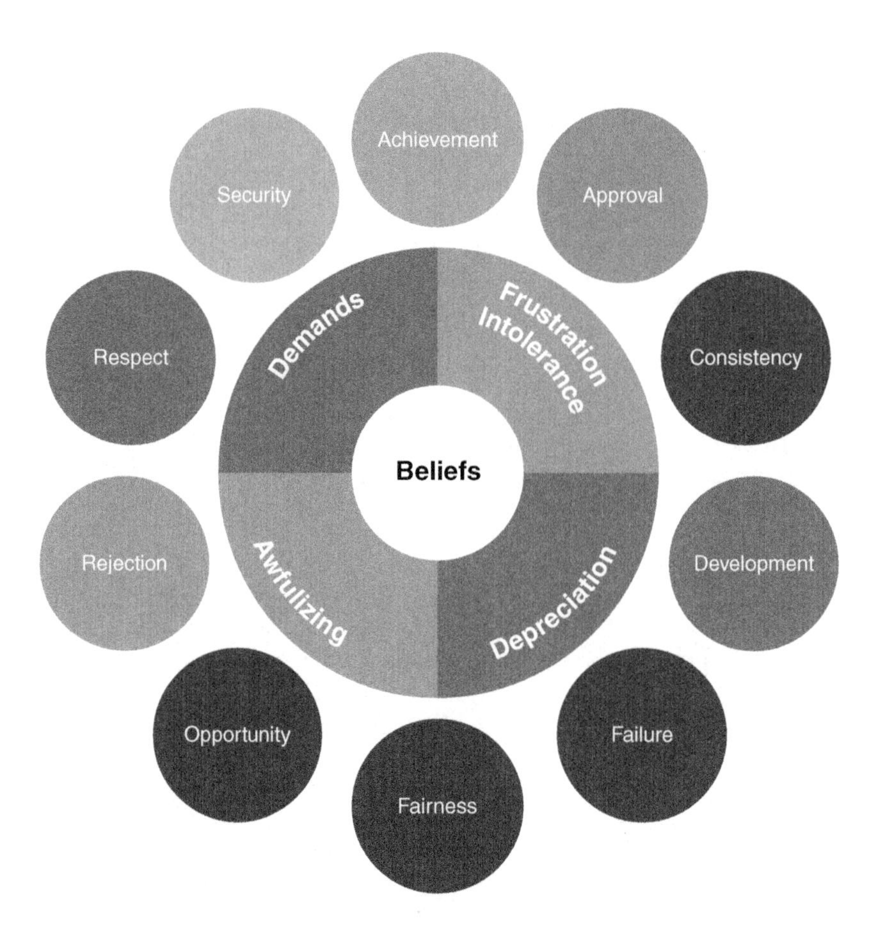

Figure 6.2 The performance content areas (A themes) and four core irrational beliefs.

reader can see the performance content areas oriented around the four core irrational beliefs to indicate that one's irrational beliefs can be nested within any of the content areas.

So, a typical A could be 'not achieving what one sets out to achieve', or 'not being respected by people that matter to me', or 'being treated unfairly by one's peers', or 'being rejected by somebody important to me'...you get the picture. I would also add to this list, as an even broader category of A, the notion of 'control'. Control does appear in the content areas for some measures of irrational beliefs (e.g., DiGiuseppe et al., 1988; Hyland et al., 2014), alongside achievement, approval, comfort, and justice, and a great many of the irrational beliefs captured by REBT relate to features of the world that are not within our control. In this way, REBT demonstrates its roots in Stoicism, whereby the recognition that some things in this world are under one's control (internal states), whereas other things are not (the external environment), is stressed. For example, look at the content areas in Figure 6.1. They all reflect aspects of life that are not within our control, and therefore go some way to explaining why the performance domain is rife with As. So, not only do individuals desire what cannot be controlled, they also apply rigid and extreme rules to those desires (G), and to the thwarting of those desires (A). In sum, we cannot go into our work with clients assuming to know what As will be presented or revealed, and we cannot help them to deal with every A in their world. So, part of utilising A in REBT is about boiling the many representations of A down to the most potent and salient A.

THE CRITICAL 'A'

Trying to understand with the client which precise A is proving to be so troublesome is not necessarily an easy task. In any meaningful conversation between client and practitioner, especially in the early stages where you are both trying to figure out what is going on, many As will emerge. But there is little utility in treating every A as the main protagonist (or activator) of the irrational or rational beliefs. Therefore, the REBT practitioner attempts to uncover the critical A (Dryden, 1995, 2009a), which is the A that the client is most disturbed about and is most proximal to the irrational belief/s. This is vital because not all As activate irrational beliefs, so the practitioner had better help the client to find the critical A or else the work may become tangential and fruitless, and will not address the unhealthy negative emotion (UNE) at C. It is important to understand that the A is usually inferential, reflecting a perception or an evaluation of something that has happened (or will happen), but could be completely internal (i.e., no external event has taken place). As previously discussed, the A in its capacity to hinder G, gives rise to negative emotions on the basis of its core relational theme (e.g., Lazarus, 1999), so by accurately defining the critical A we can be sure that we are dealing with the root of the emotion being experienced by the client at C. If the practitioner's assessment at C reveals anger, then it is more likely that the critical A will reflect self or other-blame, for example.

But we do not need to assume the critical A on the basis of C. The REBT practitioner can use various strategies to dig a little deeper into the presenting As to understand which As are 'non-critical', and which A is 'critical'. For example, the author most frequently uses inference chaining, a good example of which can be found in Palmer (2009). Inference chaining was introduced by Moore (1983), but has been refined, developed, and extended over the years (Dryden, 1995, 1989; Neenan & Dryden, 1996, 1999a). Inference chaining is a technique that "combines speed with depth in rapidly taking clients from the periphery to the centre of their emotional disturbance" (Neenan & Dryden, 1996, p. 231) and links the client's personally significant inferences about an activating event (A) in order to find the one (sometimes called the critical A) which triggers her irrational belief (B) which then, in turn, directly leads to her emotional reactions at C (Neenan & Dryden, 1999a, pp. 95–96).

The links are created by 'Let's assume' … 'then what?'… 'so what?' questions, starting with the UNE, and/or can use the UNE in the questioning (e.g., "what is so shame-provoking about x"?). For a simplified example, a soccer athlete (Kelly) presents with shame (UNE) in response to "missing an open goal" (assumed A). The sport psychologist (SP) enquires:

SP: Tell me Kelly, what is shame-provoking in your mind about missing an open goal?
KELLY: Well, everybody saw me miss. It was mortifying!
SP: Would you have been as ashamed if nobody saw you miss?
KELLY: No because nobody would have known! But its more the fact that certain people saw me miss…
SP: Certain people?
KELLY: Well, my coach, teammates, friends, family saw it.

SP: Why would that bring about shame?
KELLY: Well, they probably judged me. They probably questioned my ability.
SP: Let's assume that is the case. What if they did judge you and questioned your ability?
KELLY: It would mean that I've let them all down.
SP: Ok let's assume that you have let them all down. What would be shame-provoking about that?
KELLY: They've given up and sacrificed so much for me to succeed, and then I go and let them all down. What a thing to do!
SP: What do you mean by 'what a thing to do'?
KELLY: Letting them all down like that. That's the worst thing in the world to me. It would be awful.
SP: When you say 'it' would be awful. What are you referring to here as being awful?
KELLY: Letting people who are important to me down.
SP: So, are you ashamed of letting these people down because you think it would be awful?
KELLY: Yes. It IS awful. For me, there is nothing worse in life.

In the above, it is possible to see how the non-critical A of missing on open goal is not challenged for its validity. Rather, it is assumed to be true so that we can dig a little deeper to uncover the critical A (Neenan & Dryden, 1996), which is the prospect of letting significant others down. This closely ties to the irrational belief of awfulizing ("It would be awful to let people down"), which we would take further into the assessment of B to instantiate a full irrational belief (primary and secondary) derived from a preference (potentially: "I want to and therefore I must have the approval of others, and it would be awful to let people down"), before we dispute it at D. What if we had stopped at "missing an open goal" and taken this as the critical A? We are no nearer to the centre of Kelly's shame if we do this because she is not ashamed about the missed penalty per se, it is specifically the *inferred* social-evaluative features ("letting people down") of that event that is leading to this shame, alongside her irrational beliefs about letting people down. We cannot assume the client holds irrational beliefs about the first A they present to us, else we construct the client's issue inaccurately and thus form inaccurate solutions by misspecifying B. It should also be noted that in the above example with Kelly, we already 'know' (from previous C assessment) what the UNE is so we can start there. But if we don't know the UNE, or we start the assessment at A rather than C, it is more appropriate to start the inference chain at "So you missed an open goal, why is this difficult for you at the moment?" (instead of referring to shame). A good example of inference chaining can also be found in Ellis & Dryden (1997) on p. 35.

Finally, what is also apparent in the dialogue with Kelly is that some potential As are concrete (i.e., reflecting confirmable reality), some are perceptions of reality (i.e., presumed to be the case) and some are inferential (i.e., conclusions about what has been perceived; DiGiuseppe et al., 2014). Concrete As could be "missing an open goal" and "my coach, teammates, friends, family saw it", perceived As could be "everybody saw me miss" and "They've given up and sacrificed so much for me to succeed", and inferential As could be "they probably judged me. They probably questioned my ability" and "I've let them all down". In REBT, whether these As are *actually* true or not, the client reacts to them emotionally so the practitioner considers them to be true (DiGiuseppe et al., 2014). As such, we would not dispute these As before we have disputed the Bs (or at all, depending on the case).

In conversing with the client, you will uncover these A layers (concrete As, perceived As, inferential As) and will have to distinguish which As are germane to the client issues and are triggering of Bs. In any situation there are many facets that can be attended to, few of which are perceived, and even fewer of which lead to inferences (e.g., Wessler & Wessler, 1980). But one of these inferences will be particularly important because it triggers B – this inference, the critical A, is the aspect of the situation that the client then applies their irrational beliefs to, taking a 'bad' event to an 'awful' event, for example.

Say I am working with an athlete who says he will not speak up in front of his teammates in team meetings. I ask him why, and he says that there are too many dominant voices in the team. I ask him what it is about these dominant voices that make it so he can't speak up. He said that they would probably judge him and ignore what he had to say anyway. I ask what would happen if they did judge him and disregard his words like this. He said he would look foolish. I could go further here (!) but hopefully the reader can see what is happening – I am going beyond the concrete (e.g., he will not speak up), and the perceptual (e.g., too many dominant voices), to the inferential (e.g., they would judge him, ignore him, he would look foolish). By doing this I am more likely to locate the critical A that is triggering B, and as such, I am more likely to locate B accurately.

Another complimentary strategy for assessing A and finding the critical A is to present the client with the As that have been discussed, and to ask them which A they are most disturbed (e.g., anxious, angry, ashamed) about. So, in the Kelly example the practitioner could ask, "Are you most ashamed of missing the open goal, being judged, or letting people down?" In the author's experience, as you take the client deeper into the As, getting closer to the critical A and the irrational beliefs, often the athlete will experience, or begin to experience, the relevant emotion in the session. For example, Kelly might start to avoid eye contact with the practitioner and may become visibly withdrawn (e.g., closed body language, slumped shoulders), and may be slow to respond to questions. The perceptive practitioner will treat this rise in emotionality as a sign that they are on the right track, but caution must be applied. Haphazardly facilitating a journey into disturbance could damage the working alliance, and may instigate some distrust. The practitioner should tread carefully, but still pursue this line of enquiry with a view to helping the client to address the UNE through REBT work.

Assume A is true

As mentioned, an important stance to take as an REBT practitioner is to assume A is true (Dryden, 2009a), which is also reflected in the inference chain. For example, an athlete might say "the coach ignored me in practice yesterday" which might be an accurate representation of events, or it could be a perception (inaccurate or accurate). Taking the stance that 'what the client says at A is true' is more likely to help us with a specific REBT solution whereby B becomes the focus of the disputation, rather than A. In the above example, the practitioner could spend lots of precious session time questioning the veracity of the perception that the coach ignored the athlete. Maybe she did, but was having a bad day so can be excused. Maybe she didn't and the client is laying some bias over the situation. It might be a mixture of both of these potential occurrences, it might be neither, but why speculate? Why not just respect the client's perspective on this A and treat what they say as true? If we challenge every A, then the work will go nowhere, the client will incorrectly assume that As are the root of their UNEs, and they may even go on the defensive because their perceptions are constantly being challenged (Neenan & Dryden, 1996). The client feels better in the short-term thinking that they have not been treated poorly, but this is no long-term solution for the irrational beliefs at the root of the UNE, and will not fortify them against future transgressions (perceived or actual). In REBT we can encourage the client to assume the worst and feel healthy, adaptive, but still negative, emotions even if the concrete, perceived, and inferential As were true (DiGiuseppe et al., 2014). So, for REBT it is more fruitful and efficient to assume A to be true and to work towards understanding what the source of the UNE is; specifically the irrational belief/s. Fruitful because we can address what is underpinning the UNE, and efficient because we won't be challenging and addressing every non-critical A. We know that A is contributing to the emotion, but that it is unlikely to be the source of the UNE alone, and importantly, once undisturbed, the client can address the A if necessary, but from a place of rationality.

Assuming A is true also necessitates acceptance of A at least for the time being. It is self-evident that amongst other things, life is adverse. If we accept this as a part of our being, and work to function as well as we possibly can, implementing reason and wisdom, we can ensure that being can be tolerated and even enjoyed. Once we have put ourselves together properly, we can go out into the world and address A if necessary. What can we do other than to accept adversity as part the human experience? Deny this is the case? In REBT, we encourage clients not to lie to or delude themselves.

For other useful techniques for finding the critical A, the reader could consult Dryden's work on the subject (1989, 2009b, 2019b, 2022), and for a detailed discussion and examples of inference chaining, the reader should consult Neenan and Dryden (1996). Further reading and training is important because some critical As can be arrived at quite simply, whilst others require some dedicated teasing out.

Emily's As, Bs, and Cs

In order to further illustrate the potential locality of As, I have provided a narrative of an athlete case study below. The reader is tasked, if they so wish, to read the narrative and identify particularly salient features. When reading this narrative there are four features that are relevant to client assessment pertaining to REBT.

1. Concrete As – As that are verifiable observations about what happened (Ac).
2. Inferential As – As that go beyond the data and reflect perceptions about what happened, or bestow meaning upon what happened (Ai).
3. Irrational beliefs – utterances that reflect the four core irrational beliefs (iB).
4. Emotional and behavioural consequences – feelings and actions in relation to the event (C).

> Emily is an accomplished soccer player who has played and captained her country at international level for 8 years, accruing a total of 51 caps. Emily is the most senior player within the team and has always been held in high regard by her fans, club, and country. During international camps Emily plays a pivotal leadership role, working alongside the manager and players equally. For key international fixtures Emily always features in the starting line-up and her performances have largely supported her selection. Although collectively the national team underperforms at major championships, her performances have received little criticism, and she has been one of the better players within the team.

Emily has recently experienced a dip in form, certainly not playing to the standard that she and others are accustomed to. As a result this has cast doubt over her position in the starting line-up for club and country in the mind of her coach, who has expressed this view to her. She thinks, "Maybe I have passed my best" and "it's only downhill from here" and feels extremely anxious about her future within soccer. She tells herself that "I must play better and meet the standards I and others expect of me, I must regain my form, otherwise it would be terrible". Not only has she been dropped from the starting line-up she has also lost her captaincy to a younger and rising star within the team, inferring that she has lost the respect of her fellow teammates. Emily feels extremely sad and tells herself that she is a complete failure. Emily has begun to isolate herself during training camps, and her low levels of effort in training have been recognized by the coaching staff.

Whilst her teammates and manager appear to be supportive, the media have been critical of her recent form, and as a result the fans have also started to boo her during international fixtures. At home with her family she vents to her partner "how dare they boo me, do they not remember all my past performances, do they not know what I have sacrificed to represent the nation?". Emily, starts to resent the fans and the media for being portrayed in this manner. At a press conference a journalist asks her "how committed are you towards the national team?" Emily infers that they are portraying her as a de-motivated and lazy and responds angrily, swears (curses), and storms out of the conference. Emily demands that she should be treated fairly and cannot stand being disrespected by others. She tells herself "that journalist was an idiot, a completely bad person".

My brief A, B, C 'analysis', as it were, of the narrative can be seen in Figure 6.3.

The narrative case of Emily and my analysis are provided for illustration purposes only. Of course, *in the real world* we would obtain lots more information about Emily and the situation

Ac	Ai	iB	C
Dip in form	I have passed my best	I must play better and meet the standards I and others expect of me	Extremely anxious
Not playing to the usual standard	Only downhill from here	I must regain my form, otherwise it would be terrible	Extremely sad
Coach doubts her position in the starting line-up	Lost the respect of her fellow teammates	I am "a complete failure"	Isolating herself during training camps
Dropped from the starting line-up		I should be treated fairly	Offering low levels of effort in training
Lost her captaincy		I cannot stand being disrespected by others	Resentment
Media critical of her form		Journalist was an idiot, a completely bad person	Mistreatment of others
Fans boo her during fixtures			Anger and avoidance (press conference)

Figure 6.3 A brief analysis of Emily.

to aid an accurate analysis. From this brief information I would try to figure out with Emily which of the As, if any, are Emily's critical As, and if none of them are, I would forthrightly pursue a line of enquiry which would arrive at the critical A.

SUMMARY

In this chapter I discussed the A element of the GABCDE framework. I defined what As are and nested potential As in themes that could guide assessment. I also covered inference chaining, the importance of locating and establishing the critical A, and finally introduced an athlete case in order to help illustrate some A assessment. Given that we now have an understanding of A and C, next I will move onto a fundamental concern in REBT – the notion of A–C vs. B–C thinking.

CHAPTER 7
A–C connection vs. B–C connection

Into the wilderness.

DOI: 10.4324/9781003200437-8

> It is really not the situations that you experience that are affecting, but how you internally experience those situations…how you accept them…how you live through them.
>
> I just told myself before the match I am going to try to switch off as much as I can from what is happening all around us and just be there, be present.
>
> At times you just try to ignore it, which is quite hard, I like to transmutate it in a way. So when the crowd is chanting 'Roger', I hear 'Novak'. It sounds silly, but it is like that.
>
> Novak Djokovic speaking to the media after his win against Roger Federer at Wimbledon in 2019 (Falkingham, 2019)

What Djokovic is referring to above, whether he knows it or not, is cognitive mediation. But, as far as many athletes are aware, the emotional consequences (Cs) they are experiencing are a sole result of something that has happened to them, is happening to them, or could happen to them (actual and inferred adversities [As]). In other words, often they (as we all do) draw a direct connection between A and C, and in REBT, we call this 'A–C thinking' or the 'A–C connection' (in some literature it is also known as a stimulus-response belief; Turner et al., 2021). That is, A–C thinking reflects the idea that another person or a life event can directly cause your emotions and behaviours (Dryden, 2003). You will hear A–C thinking in the way people often talk about their emotions and the situations in which those emotions arose, and you will probably hear it from the athletes and coaches you work with. For example, "they made me so angry", "the competition is making me nervous", "missing the shot made me so ashamed", "what they said to me made me feel so hurt". Or the A–C connection can be directed from inside out, such as "I made them feel so bad". This way of thinking gives ownership and responsibility to external factors, leaving us with few *viable* and achievable solutions for our unhealthy negative emotions (UNEs). It also pompously suggests that we have the power to make others experience UNEs with what we do and say. Importantly, clients are unlikely to attempt to change something that their language implies is not in their control (DiGiuseppe et al., 2014).

If you believe that the event directly causes your emotions, then you *have to* control the external environment in order to control the emotion – it is your only option for emotion regulation. So, you tyrannically try (and fail) to put the world around you into *your* order, controlling all that you can. When you do achieve emotion down-regulation by changing the situation, it reinforces your view that external events are indeed solely to blame for your emotions. People around you may fall into line for a while in service of your emotional reactivity, but they will tire of a life governed by your emotions. We have all met people who are "highly strung" for whom everybody around the person needs to adapt their behaviour so as not to trigger them into flying off the handle.

> Any person capable of angering you becomes your master; he can anger you only when you permit yourself to be disturbed by him.
>
> Epictetus

Thinking critically about some of the practices that are taking place in our society at present, it is possible to see the hallmarks of A–C thinking at a large scale. At first sight, trigger warnings, safe spaces, cancel culture, and de-platforming (Lizza, 2020) protect people from provocation, under the auspices of enhancing emotional wellbeing by making the environment less emotionally provocative (Lukianoff & Haidt, 2017). Sanitising the world from stressors offers short-term gains (e.g., feeling better in the moment), but much is to be lost. We risk sensitising people to difficult emotions, rather than protecting them (Bruce et al.,

2021; Lukianoff & Haidt, 2019). By focussing on external stimuli, we lose focus on the key ingredient for human emotion; the conscious human mind. It is the meaning we ascribe to events that shape emotion, not events alone, and it is the beliefs we have about our emotions that shape that meaning (Faustino & Vasco, 2021).

> I am more and more convinced that our happiness or our unhappiness depends far more on the way we meet the events of life than on the nature of those events themselves.
>
> Wilhelm Von Humboldt

Back to Lazarus

For Richard Lazarus, this A–C connection reflected a stimulus-response (S-R) view of emotion reactivity. Lazarus (1999) suggests that the S-R viewpoint has proliferated because it is a natural and appealing way to think about emotions, as it encourages people to attribute their unwanted emotions to external causes and helps them to justify their emotional distress. In addition, as I will discuss later, people don't always have conscious access to their deeply held beliefs and appraisals (DiGiuseppe et al., 2014), so the true underpinnings for their emotional reactivity are obscured from them, so an external A (stimulus) seems to be the most obvious root of emotion. But there are many disadvantages to an A–C viewpoint, and it is flawed in various ways. For example, if an athlete believes that A directly causes C, then there is little justification for attempting cognitive change by way recognising and disputing irrational beliefs. The task of cognitive change is a non-starter, because in the athlete's mind there is no justification for it. Also, As do not affect everybody in the same way, and therefore the A–C viewpoint cannot account for the (sometimes vast) person to person individual differences in emotional responding to similar circumstances (Smith & Kirby, 2009). "Putting the person into the equation is the only way to solve the dilemma" (Lazarus, 1999, p. 53). By removing the person from the equation, as is achieved by taking an A–C viewpoint, the athlete has little power or volition in their emotional responding, and they lay their emotions at the feat of circumstance.

Neenan (2009) provides a useful example, which I will adapt to fit a sporting situation. Think of an athlete joining a new club and going to the weights room for the first time. They try lifting a weight and stumble, and their new teammates laugh at them (concrete A). The athlete may experience shame (C), and one might say "who wouldn't be ashamed if they were laughed at?", which in Neenan's view "allows for no individual variation to the same event; the laughter itself makes you upset even if you didn't want to feel upset the laughter wouldn't allow you to have any other reaction" (p. 22). So, the A–C viewpoint is problematic for emotion regulation because it supports the assumption that we are passive recipients of whatever happens to us in life, likely to keep us in a state of helplessness as we believe we can only feel differently once events (which are often uncontrollable) change in our favour. Lastly, an endorsement of the A–C connection would have the athlete entering into the aforementioned event only with situation selection (e.g., do not attend the new club again) and modification (e.g., tell others to stop laughing) emotion regulation strategies (Gross & Thompson, 2007). As discussed, whilst these approaches can be powerful strategies for emotion regulation, they are prone to error, encourage avoidance, and depend on the reliability of foresight and influence.

Instead, the REBT practitioner helps the client to understand the B–C connection (Dryden, 2009b), which reflects the cognitive mediation viewpoint that underpins many CBTs, and emotion theory (e.g., Gross & Thompson, 2007; Lazarus, 1999). The B–C connection puts the athlete at the centre of emotion regulation and encourages emotional responsibility; a far more powerful viewpoint for the purposes of emotion regulation. Taking a B–C view enables the client to understand the importance of their inferential As and irrational beliefs (B) in their experience of UNEs, thus helping them to take charge of their emotions by disputing irrational beliefs, for example. As Epictetus said, "Another person will not hurt you without your cooperation; you are hurt the moment you believe yourself to be".

To be clear, the B–C viewpoint does not endorse or reflect 'victim blaming'. It does not mean that it is all the athlete's fault for the ills that befall them. That is, emotional responsibility does not by proxy discharge the responsibility of others and legitimise nefarious behaviour, and acceptance of emotional responsibility is not akin to resignation and/or complacency to the circumstances in which we find ourselves (Neenan & Dryden, 2015). I do not want the message here to be that "well if athletes are responsible for their emotions, then I can just do and say what I want to them and around them". No! Individual emotional responsibility does not discharge societal ethics or virtue. Also, excluding G for the moment, the equation is $A \times B = C$, not $A = C$ or $B = C$, therefore A and B inform emotional reactivity not just A, not just B. In other words, nested within the GABCDE framework is the idea that the nature of A is important for the generation of emotion, so if your behaviour as a coach seems to be leading to negative emotionality in athletes, then you cannot put the blame solely on the athlete. Athletes should take their portion of the responsibility (to align their inferences and beliefs with reality as much as they can) and similarly, coaches should take their own portion (not doing things to actively instantiate goal incongruence and core relational themes conducive to negative affect – unless in a controlled environment where the purpose of a drill is to trigger negative affect, i.e., pressure training).

I also argue that cultural awareness of the B–C viewpoint can actually reduce victimisation rather than increase it. As a potential perpetrator of interpersonal transgression, if I am armed with the knowledge that my actions do not automatically trigger the emotions of those around me, then it can serve to delegitimise my attempts to hurt others. If my goal is to hurt somebody with my words and actions, then I am in part disarmed by the knowledge that it is not really my actions that entirely cause the hurt of others. I cannot control others' feelings because A does not equal C. What is the point in sacrificing my virtue with vindictiveness if my actions will not lead to the consequences I malevolently desire? So, culturally we can strip aggressors of their power over our emotions by holding and spreading the B–C philosophy. But for this to happen we have to fully endorse the notion of cognitive mediation.

The current author takes the stance similar to Roseman and Smith (2001) that, "most emotions are reactions to events, and reactions that are dependent on the way the situation is perceived and evaluated by a particular person" (p. 16). Further, as we come to understand more about emotion aetiology and expression, a constructionist view of emotion has taken shape. Lisa Feldman-Barrett is a prominent voice in this theory of constructed emotion, and states that "emotions are not built-in but made from more basic parts…They are not triggered; you create them" (location 92) and "Emotions are not reactions to the world. You are not a passive receiver of sensory input but an active constructor of your emotions. From sensory input and past experience, your brain constructs meaning and prescribes action" (p. 31). These views are consistent with the constructionist position taken in REBT (Ellis, 2003a). That is, REBT has a constructionistic rather than associationistic view of human thought and functioning – humans form constructs to understand their world and therefore will inevitably produce various incorrect constructs (DiGiuseppe, 1986) – we create our emotions rather than the emotion being conferred onto us by an external stimulus.

> The mind is its own place, and in itself can make a heaven of hell, a hell of heaven.
> (John Milton, 1746, Paradise Lost, Book I, Lines 254–255)

> It is he himself who creates, or at least exaggerates, the suffering.
> (Dubois, 1906, pp. 20–21)

STRESSOR + APPRAISAL

A note of caution. I am not saying that the situation cannot and should not be changed in light of emotional suffering, but I am saying that the idea that the situation is 100% responsible for emotional responses is not accurate or helpful for the athlete. So, the B–C viewpoint can help people to understand that they can take responsibility for their emotions by applying cognitive change/restructuring (Clark, 2014), as is evidenced in many research studies (see Mahoney, 1974, for an in-depth discussion, and see Roseman & Smith, 2001, for a review).

Some useful illustrations of the B–C viewpoint can be found in Monroe and Kelley's (1997) chapter in an edited volume concerning stress measurement, which I have adapted. In Figure 7.1, the stimulus is in part responsible for perceived stress, but the layers of cognitive baggage we add to the stimulus exacerbate this stress.

In Figure 7.2, you can see that some stimuli drive greater stress than other stimuli, and stress can be comprised of a varying mixture of stimuli and appraisal. Athlete A's stress level is being driven mostly by the stimulus because the stimulus is so severe, whereas athlete D's

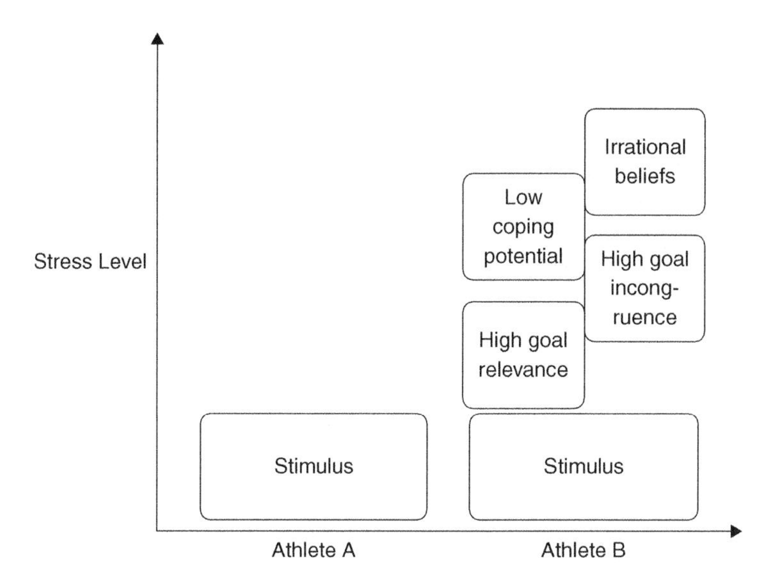

Figure 7.1 Stress level caused by stimulus vs. stimulus plus cognitive appraisals and irrational beliefs (adapted from Monroe & Kelley, 1997).

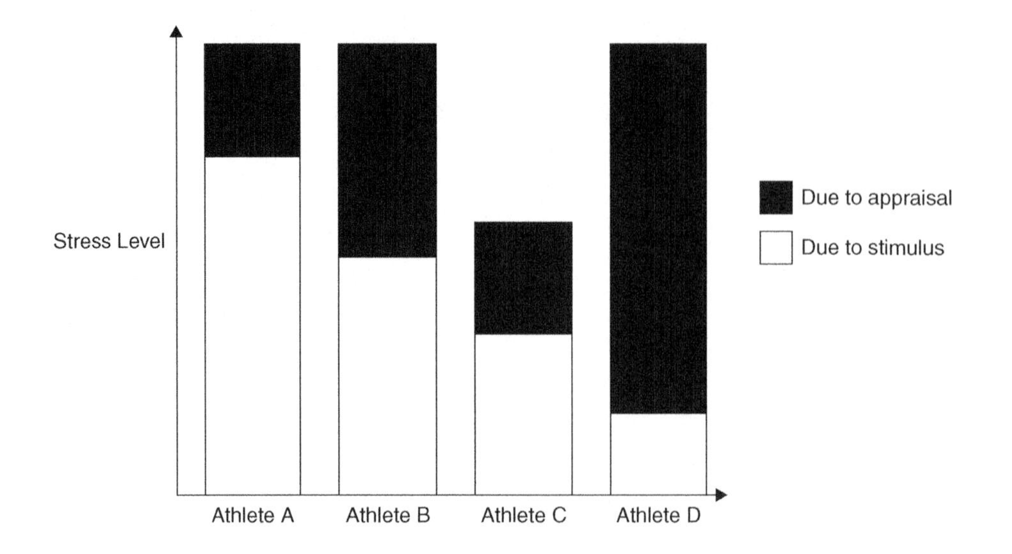

Figure 7.2 Four athletes with different stimulus-appraisal patterns underpinning stress.

stress level is driven mostly by their appraisal concerning a less severe stimulus. Practitioners should recognise that whilst emotional responsibility is a noble aim, not all stimuli are equal, and some events are considered (within Western culture) to be universally highly stress provoking (e.g., death of a spouse; Scully et al., 2000).

> Human freedom involves our capacity to pause between stimulus and response and, in that pause, to choose the one response toward which we wish to throw our weight.
>
> (May, 1975, p. 100)

Emotional responsibility

The emotional responsibility garnered through the endorsement of the B–C viewpoint also encourages the athlete to first look within themselves when experiencing negative emotion. Before they try to address whatever external stimulus may have led to the emotion, they are encouraged to first introspect on whether and what extent irrational beliefs about some facet of the stimulus might be contributing to how they feel. Indeed, Matthew 7:3–7:5 (New Testament) has us consider,

> why do you look at the speck in your brother's eye, but do not consider the plank in your own eye? Or how can you say to your brother, 'Let me remove the speck from your eye'; and look, a plank is in your own eye? Hypocrite! First remove the plank from your own eye, and then you will see clearly to remove the speck from your brother's eye.

In other words, take responsibility for your part in the emotion you experience, before you address what is external to you. Do not be too eager to change the world around you, *if* there is a solution within. When you have addressed that which is within, you will be able to more clearly understand whether and what extent you can address that which is without. It is no use remonstrating with a wrongdoer when you are enraged – indeed, "*He who is* slow to wrath has great understanding, But *he who is* impulsive exalts folly [foolish action]" (Proverbs 14:29, New King James Bible).

Helping the athlete to understand and endorse the B–C connection requires some education work concerning cognitive mediation, obviously using terminology and examples relevant to the client. In the present author's experience, a strategy that lands well with athletes is the individual differences argument, which reflects the above arguments against A–C, or S-R, by Lazarus. Here, the practitioner makes the point to the athlete that if A directly causes C, then there would be no individual differences in how people respond at C to the same A. The practitioner can ask for an example of a time when the client faced a shared adversity with a teammate or friend, and recall the differences in how each individual responded, for example. A dentist's waiting room is also a good example of individuals in a similar situation, but emotionally reacting idiosyncratically based on their appraisals.

The practitioner can also present the athlete with an 'A–C solution' and a 'B–C solution' and appeal to the athlete's logic and common-sense (Dryden, 2009b). For example, the practitioner could say

> there are two potential reasons for your unhealthy anxiety. One says that the important competition is *making* you anxious. The other says that it is your beliefs *about* the important competition that is making you anxious. Which one sounds right?

Figure 7.3 Client B–C thinking.

The athlete's confirmation that the latter is the case helps to move into determining the precise B at play, because it is more possible to have a direct conversation about B since the athlete understands that it is the B that is underpinning the UNE. The practitioner could say, "Great, since we know that it is your beliefs about the competition that is the problem here, lets figure out what that belief actually is. Does this sound like a good plan?" Or with a particularly perceptive athlete the practitioner could ask, "Given that we know that it is your beliefs about the competition that is the problem here, what would you say should be our next step?" It may be the case that the athlete suggests identifying the belief is the next logical step, which would be ideal, but if this does not happen, the practitioner could ensure that this is the next step following the active-directive style typical in REBT. Additional ways in which the B–C connection can be made are found in Dryden's more recent work (2019b, 2021b).

Teaching the B-C connection

Based on what we know about the importance of the B–C connection, we usually need to educate the client in this viewpoint. As stated earlier in this chapter, an A–C viewpoint of emotion is attractive and it is not unlikely that the client endorses this perspective. So, we need to make a case for the B–C connection. We can do this diagrammatically using the ABC aspects of the GABCDE framework, and/or we can use 'real life' or hypothetical examples to illustrate the fallaciousness of A–C and the obvious veracity of B–C. For example, we can use sport examples such as:

> Let's say two athletes from the same nation, working under the same coach, have made it to the final of a 100m competition. In qualifying rounds both have set personal bests and their finishing times are comparable. Athlete A is anxious, but focussed and prepared for the race – they can't wait to get off the blocks. Athlete B is also anxious, but is dreading the race and just wants the race to be over with. Given that the two athletes are going into the same situation objectively, how could you explain the differences in their approach to the race?
>
> Imagine that two soccer players go for the ball in a 50/50 challenge. Both miss the ball and a collision occurs which sends the players rolling around in pain. Both players were legitimately going for the ball. The referee runs over to the situation and both players stand up to engage with the referee. Both players receive a yellow card. Player A pleads with the referee, but ultimately walks away annoyed, and switches back onto the game and gets back into position. Player B pleads with the referee and gets extremely angry that they have been booked. The player shouts and screams at the referee and teammates have to restrain them from assaulting the referee. Given that the two athletes are innocent and have received the same punishment, how could you explain their differing reactions?

What we are trying to do in using the above examples, from which the reader can of course construct their own stories, is to help the client to see how individual differences can explain the emotional approach or reaction to the event. Situational differences cannot fully explain the response differences. Then we can discuss what it is within the individuals that might distinguish between the two opposing reactions to the same event. Many proposals can be made by the client – personality, experience, sensitivity – but ultimately the differing reactions are determined by the individual and idiosyncratic differences between the two athletes. One of these important differences is how each athlete perceives the situation, and the personal meaning that each athlete ascribes to the situation. It is not that the situation is automatically causing the reactions (A–C), otherwise the athletes would have reacted in the same way. It is more likely that personal factors, such as how they viewed the situation (B–C), had an important role in creating the differences in responses. We are trying to help the client to connect with the idea that there would be little variance in emotional responding across people if their idiosyncratic viewpoints about the world were not influential for emotional reactivity (e.g., Dryden, 2006)

To further illustrate this point, you can encourage the client to think about times where they have been in sport situations with teammates or in social situations with friends, where their own emotions and behaviours were different to those around them, despite the situation being equal for all. Of course, one of the points we are trying to make with the client here is that there is no 'equal' situation because each person brings their own meaning to an event. But from an REBT perspective, we are really driving towards the important role that irrational and rational beliefs might play in both the inference and reaction to events.

Regardless of how you choose to accomplish teaching the client about the B–C connection, it is an important part of REBT because a client who does not understand or endorse a B–C viewpoint is less likely to achieve cognitive change, since there is no perceived veracity in altering beliefs if the client does not consider beliefs to be central to their emotional reactivity (Crum, 2018; Turner et al., 2021). We try to establish the B–C connection in part to legitimise the focus on irrational belief detection, and ultimately, irrational belief change. Helping the client to appreciate the B–C connection has important downstream consequences in REBT for disputation (D) – the D process is impeded from the outset if the client cannot or will not see the veracity and utility of the B–C connection (Crum, 2018). In our research, we have found that those who endorse a B–C view vs. an A–C view of emotion report greater thought control abilities, and greater tendencies to regulate emotions via cognitive change, alongside less sensitive, intense, and persistent emotional reactivity (Turner et al., 2021).

> If you can't control your own emotions, then you have to end up controlling other people's behaviour.
>
> John Cleese (actor and comedian; Tuning In, 2021)

CHAPTER 8
Goals (G)

The danger and opportunity of the unknown.

DOI: 10.4324/9781003200437-9

> According to REBT Theory, humans are happiest when they establish important life goals and purposes and actively strive to attain these.
>
> (Ellis & Dryden, 1997, p. 4)

We are probably the most adaptable mammal that has ever evolved on earth, in part because we seek out novel places to explore (according to Rick Potts, in Neimark, 2012) – we are driven to exploring (perhaps genetically; Campbell & Barone, 2012) and are adept in taking on and conquering the unknown. Ellis considered human beings to be, biologically and by social learning, goal-seeking animals, and in REBT goals are fundamental to being (Ellis, 1994). Goal pursuit "constrains a person's information processing and behaviors in order to increase the likelihood that he or she will successfully attain that goal's end-state" (Huang & Bargh, 2014, p. 122), and thus, it appears that goal pursuit has human survival and adaptation implications, thought to be neuropsychologically regulated by dopamine (Bromberg-Martin et al., 2010; Salamone & Correa, 2012).

Put simply, we humans are mobile creatures with a deep proclivity for exploration – but we need to know which direction we should travel in. The manifestation and pursuit of goals helps to constrain our actions (alongside social and physical affordances and limitations) and give us direction. How do we know where we are going if we don't have some aims to orient ourselves towards? The manifestation of goals in part emanates from our values – some things are worth aiming for because we value them. As we move towards that which we value, we focus our attention and expend resources on this pursuit, so the goal had better be worth pursuing lest we waste finite time, attention, and energy. Shallow and trivial aims will not sustain us through the inevitable adversity and suffering that accompanies our lives, so we should make use of meaningful and noble aims. Perceiving that we are moving towards our goals can bring about positive affect, just as perceiving that our progress is thwarted can bring about negative affect. So, goals have a big influence on human health and fulfilment.

Given that we are goal-seeking animals, it begs the questions: what should our goals be? What should we be aiming for? What goals can limit, and make tolerable and worthwhile, the suffering of being? In this chapter I start by covering the importance of goals in REBT, and then move onto making the case for particular types of goals.

Goals (G) in the GABCDE framework

Every aspect of the GABCDE framework is relevant to the goals of the client, in keeping with the interdependent nature of the framework. When I speak of goals here, I do not mean the goals of the work we are doing together in the sessions (i.e., therapy goals or aims). This is commonly used by other authors, which is fine. But here I refer to goals in a similar way to how Ellis (1994) referred to goals, whereby humans have fundamental goals (FGs; to survive, to assuage unnecessary pain, to be fulfilled), and primary/sub-goals (PGs; to be satisfied; alone, socially [including intimately with some], informationally/educationally, vocationally, economically, and recreationally). Explicit in REBT are the broad human goals of living this life with as much enjoyment as possible, living peacefully within our chosen group, and relating intimately with certain people of our choosing (DiGiuseppe et al., 2014). Ellis (1994) added human goals of reason and logic, success in solving and mastering life problems and meaningful tasks, experiencing new and stimulating things, and stability/security in work and social life. These broad goals "provide a context that affects how people perceive their activating events and how they evaluate the world" (Crawford & Ellis, 1989, p. 3). Importantly, these goals are preferences and desires, not needs or necessities, and rationality should be in service of these short- and long-term goals (Nelson-Jones, 2006).

The goals (G) posited by Ellis have been carried forward into more contemporary conceptualisations of REBT (e.g., DiGiuseppe et al., 2014), but also align with more expansive notions of human goals. For example, FGs could be considered 'superordinate goals' which sit at the highest level of a goal hierarchy as posited by Carver and Scheier (2001), and are very similar to values (Höchli et al., 2018). Superordinate goals refer to idealised conceptualisations of one's self and reflect what is (not) important to a person (Boekaerts et al., 2006). Importantly, superordinate goals inform intermediate level goals (e.g., PGs from an REBT perspective), and subsequently, intermediate goals determine subordinate goals (precisely what to do and how to do it). This goal hierarchy is analogous to the FGs and PGs of REBT but add a concrete and tangible level of goals at the lowest point of abstraction (subordinate goals). We can work with clients to articulate exactly what needs to be done to attain the PGs that underpin and serve their FGs.

Further, in Austin and Vancouver's (1996) Taxonomy of Human Goals, they include within-person goals such as affective (e.g., physical well-being), cognitive (e.g., understanding), and subjective organisation (e.g., unity), as well as person-environment goals such as self-assertive social relationship (e.g., self-determination), integrative social relationship (e.g., belongingness), and task (e.g., mastery). Furthermore, Chulef et al. (2001) offer a Hierarchical Taxonomy of Human Goals which includes 135 goals, developed through a review of the literature and deliberation amongst a team of researchers. A cohort of participants were asked to sort the 135 goals into groups that represented common themes or topics. Goals fell into three broad clusters: (a) Family, Marriage, Sex, and Romance goals; (b) Interpersonal goals (e.g., physical, belonging, approval, respect, helping others); and (c) Intrapersonal goals (e.g., freedom, personal growth, well-being, achievement, self-determination, career, education). Whether we take Ellis' (1994) FGs and PGs, Carver and Scheier's (2001) superordinate, intermediate, and subordinate goals, or the taxonomies offered by Austin and Vancouver (1996) and Chulef et al. (2001), there is a sense that human beings structure their goals within hierarchies in order to correctly orient themselves, and organise their behaviour, towards that which they value most. We have to decide how to act in the world, and we form goal hierarchies in order to inform these decisions.

In the almost ubiquitous self-determination theory (SDT; Deci & Ryan, 2000), the fulfilment of three basic psychological needs of autonomy (the need to experience ownership of one's own actions and choices), competence (the need to feel competent in doing optimally challenging activities and to achieve desired outcomes), and relatedness (the need to have sense of belonging and mutual respect) are considered to be a sign that the individual has created a life that is yielding the nutrients most required by human nature (Deci & Ryan, 2000). Fulfilling these three basic needs is conducive to positive experience, including more stable senses of vitality and thriving (Ryan & Martela, 2016). For example, the extant empirical evidence suggests that the satisfaction of the three basic psychological needs brings about higher levels of overall psychological well-being in athletes (e.g., Mack et al., 2011; Reinboth & Duda, 2006). Thus, whilst the taxonomies of Carver and Scheier (2001), Austin and Vancouver (1996), and Chulef et al. (2001), offer insights into the many goals human beings pursue, perhaps the three basic needs (echoes of which can be seen in the taxonomies, and in Ellis' FGs and PGs) represent the human nutriments that are to be pursued in the interest of living a healthy and fulfilled life.

The reader may wish to consult the taxonomies mentioned above to gain a fuller understanding of the myriad goal pursuits human beings engage in, but fundamentally people are goal-driven consciously and unconsciously, and therefore will run into adversities (As) that impede and threaten their goals, such is the human condition (fallible, limited) and such is life (uncontrollable, unpredictable, uncertain). As is clear in the discussion about goals thus far, there is a depth and complexity to people's goal pursuits, and multiple goals may be implicated during specific adversities, and therefore, a diversity of emotions can arise (David & Cramer, 2010). Perceived or anticipated goal attainment usually leads to positive emotion, and perceived or anticipated threats to goal attainment usually lead to negative emotions (e.g., Frijda, 1986, 1988).

Because people are goal-driven, at times (inevitably) unfortunate and undesirable occurrences (As) will interfere with the attainment of these goals (Ellis, 1994; Shea, 2016), because we are limited and fallible beings, and our environment is unpredictable, uncertain, and (largely) uncontrollable. As such, G and A are related in REBT, because A is adverse to the extent that it is incongruent with G. Because emotions are reactions to action outcomes (obstructed or facilitated) in relation to an individual's goals (Carver & Scheier, 1998; Frijda, 1986; Kreibig et al., 2010), G and A create the conditions for emotional consequences (C). The pursuit of meaningful Gs can bring about negative emotions because by pursuing these goals one will undoubtedly face challenges, barriers, and setbacks because the world, and the people you engage with and contend with, are not predictable, controllable, or wholly benign. Your humanness, limited and imperfect, means that your pursuit of meaningful Gs will be met with some challenges to overcome, some pain, some suffering. Also, positive emotions emanating from progress towards an important goal are more likely to occur under conditions where some obstacle had to be overcome (e.g., Kreibig et al., 2010).

To bring all this into line with Lazarus' (1999) ideas of cognitive appraisal as previously discussed, when people evaluate A as congruent with or helpful towards their goals (G), they generally experience positively valenced emotions at C. But when people evaluate A as incongruent with or sabotaging their goals (G), they generally experience negatively valenced emotions at C. If these people then make a choice, consciously or unconsciously, to apply *irrational* beliefs to this G-A incongruence, then unhealthy negative emotions (UNEs) are likely, If, however, these people make a choice to apply *rational* beliefs to the G-A incongruence, then healthy negative emotions (HNEs) are likely.

When people experience or infer A, whether and to what extent A impedes or is inimical to G, and the nature of this impediment, plays a significant role in determining the emotion at C, with the application of rational or irrational beliefs (B) to G and/or A establishing either HNEs or UNEs. Goals (G) underpin the desires that formulate preferences (or 'wants'), which people can then apply demandingness (or 'musts') to. People can have preferential desires (primary rational beliefs), or demanding desires (primary irrational beliefs; Ellis et al., 2010). The more strongly you hold desires at G, the more affecting As will be, and the more likely you are to experience UNEs when holding irrational beliefs (B).

For example, an athlete wants to achieve a full and illustrious career (G), but sustains a career-shortening injury (non-critical A). This A could clearly generate many additional As and the practitioner would work with the athlete to identify the critical A, as outlined in Chapter 6. But say the critical A is, "I have spent my entire life pursuing this career, for nothing". The athlete can choose to rationally believe that "I want to, but I don't have to, have a full and illustrious career, and even though my life's pursuit has now ended, it does not mean that I am a complete failure". Or they can choose to irrationally believe that "I want to, and therefore I must, have a full and illustrious career, and because my life's pursuit has now ended, I am a complete and utter failure". The rational belief is likely to underpin sadness (HNE), whereas the irrational belief is likely to underpin depression (non-clinical; UNE). We can make this assumption about the nature of C based on the information in Figure 5.1 where the Ellisian meets the Lazarusian, but of course we would undertake a detailed discursive C assessment with the athlete to fully understand the precise C related to the apparent G-A incongruence.

People covertly and overtly sneak musts into their Gs, As, Bs (and Cs), and they importantise their Gs (Ellis, 1994) which appears to justify their musts ("Because G is so very important, then I simply must achieve it"). It is important to state that the client's Gs maybe explicit or implicit in the work that you do with them, but As are problematic to the extent that they are perceived to impede the client's Gs. In other words, the presence of A implies the existence of G. The perceived impediment at A does not necessarily mean that the client will not achieve those goals. But the application of irrational beliefs and the likely experience of UNEs will not help, and will probably hinder and undermine, the client's efforts to achieve those goals (Browne et al., 2010).

For example, as previously mentioned, in SDT (Deci & Ryan, 2000) it is asserted that three particular basic psychological needs are vital for human fulfilment. But as fundamental and foundational to human fulfilment as these basic needs are, *demanding* competence, autonomy, and relatedness, is associated with psychopathology (e.g., Artiran et al., 2020; Devey et al., 2022). Evaluating a lack of these needs as awful, believing that you cannot stand not having these needs fulfilled, and basing your self-worth on these needs being fulfilled, is related to markers of psychopathology in adolescents in the general population (Artiran et al., 2020) and in athletes (Devey et al., 2022). So, even fundamental human nutriments such as the basic needs are best approached as *preferences*, rather than *demands*. Indeed, "unlike the law of gravity, or the first law of thermodynamics, there is no universal law of nature which stipulates that everyone must treat us well and that our environment must always be agreeable to us" (Murguia & Díaz, 2015, p. 43).

So what?

How can this information about goals be used by the practitioner? Clients often come with problems at A or at C, and we can gain greater insight into just how problematic A and C are, by understanding G. In other words, we can figure out precisely what A and C are prohibiting the client from achieving. We can better understand the nature of the client's problems against the backdrop of their goals, and particularly, how these goals are being, or will be, thwarted by A. This allows greater specificity when seeking and articulating client irrational beliefs, because we can be mindful of both G and A and the incongruence that specific As present to specific Gs. So, a thorough A and G assessment is ideal in order to gain a full picture of the client's issues. Also, understanding G allows us to put A in context, and helps the client figure out which Cs would be useful in fulfilling G. That is, we can help the client formulate and articulate the HNEs that would serve their G attainment in light of the As they will face. So, establishing G is important in situations where the client is seeking our help with an A or C (which is usually the case). If we want to help clients to achieve their goals, then we *and they* need to know what those goals are. This could be considered a remedial approach to REBT, in the sense that we are helping the client to solve a problem (the problem being a thwarted G). But I also take a proactive approach to REBT in which goals have particular importance, which I turn to next.

Proactive GABCDE

Thus far, I have illustrated how the GABCDE framework applies to issues and problems that the client is experiencing or presents with (i.e., remedially), both with regard to A and C. But the GABCDE framework can be used *proactively* to help athletes understand what their goals are, what they *should* be, and how to forthrightly and meaningfully move towards those goals with a keen awareness of the As, Bs, and Cs that might need to be addressed to facilitate a functional path to success. As the athlete moves towards their goals, to what extent can they problem-solve at A, dispute (D) their irrational beliefs (B), and utilise rational beliefs (E), and manage their emotional symptoms at C, in order to stay on the right path to success? This will undoubtedly include work to influence A, B, and C directly and indirectly (due to interdependence), drawing on both specific and general REBT and keeping the interdependent GABC(DE) framework in mind. The REBT practitioner can help the athlete to voluntarily take on the adversity that decorates the path to attaining meaningful goals, helping them to proactively experience functional rather than dysfunctional cognitions, emotions, and behaviours through the utilisation of rationality.

For if we take the athlete who experiences a career-shortening injury, for example, once we have helped the athlete with their current issue (remedially, if you will), we can apply proactive GABCDE:

- **FG** – To be fulfilled in life. To fulfil one's potential as a human being.
- **PG** – Develop a new and fruitful career in coaching that sustains me vocationally and economically
- **Potential As** – Transition, failure, sacrifice (time, effort, and money), judgement, uncertainty, rejection, unfairness.
- **Potential UNEs** – Unhealthy anxiety, unhealthy anger, shame.
- **Potential iBs** – I really want to and therefore I must have a fruitful coaching career, and I cannot stand barriers to this goal, impediments would be terrible, and if I don't achieve this it would make me a complete failure.
- **D^1** – Where is the evidence for these beliefs? Are they consistent with reality? What function do these beliefs serve? (see Chapter 12 for detailed disputation [D] arguments).
- **Potential rB** – I really want to have a fruitful coaching career, but I do not have to. When barriers to this goal emerge, it will be tough but I can stand it, impediments would be inconvenient but certainly not terrible, and if I don't achieve this, it just shows that I am a fallible human being and can accept myself fully as that.
- **D^2** – Where is the evidence for these beliefs? Are they consistent with reality? What function do these beliefs serve?
- **Potential HNEs** – Healthy anxiety, healthy anger, disappointment.

In the above example, we have moved beyond the athlete's career-shortening injury, towards a new career path with the articulation of new goals (Gs), and thus, new potential As, Bs, and Cs. Importantly for the FGs and PGs, we need to encourage the client to be specific about the details of these goals. We can ask, "what does a fulfilled life look like to you?", "how will you know you have fulfilled your human potential?" (FGs), and "what exactly would a fruitful and sustaining coaching career look like", "how will you know you have attained a fruitful and sustaining coaching career?" (PGs). We can encourage the client to envision the future them, having attained these FGs and PGs, so that we can gain some important specifics regarding these goals. It is important to bring some reality to the goals lest we facilitate the conceptualisation of goals that are too loosely defined and too abstract. To be clear, our job here is to be humanistic in helping the client to define their goals. Clients can decide what FGs and PGs will be most ennobling and worthy of their time, attention, energy (resource) sacrifices. We can guide the client and play the part of critical friend as a scientist in cahoots with them, but it is not up to us as practitioners to dictate a client's goals. It is the client who must decide on the proper telos (goal, or end; Sedley, 1998), and we can listen and guide.

Proactive GABCDE is about helping clients to establish and pursue meaningful and superordinate FGs whilst understanding, avoiding, and also voluntarily taking on, adversity in pursuit of their goals. Proactive GABCDE is about helping the client to prepare for the inevitable suffering of a meaningful life, fortifying themselves against adversity through rationality. Proactive GABCDE is about enabling the expression of healthy negative emotions (HNEs) rather than unhealthy negative emotions (UNEs) and also making possible the experience of positive affect through the movement towards eudaimonic FGs. In proactive GABCDE we ask; what G's are worth aiming for? what As can we anticipate and disarm? what Bs can be used in order to assuage disturbance when As do occur? what Cs could serve to be adaptive for goal striving and how could we make more likely their expression?

THE PROPER TELOS

> High performance when I was younger was about outcomes...it was all about whether the ball went through the post...whether you hit the mark...whether the guy was tackled...whether he went backwards all of these things were running up on the stat sheet and that defined who you are and whether you're successful...I look at it now as like...what would be a great life lived?
>
> Jonny Wilkinson (speaking on The High Performance Podcast, Humphrey & Hughes, 2020)

Using the GABCDE framework proactively, we can help clients to consider the appropriate FGs and PGs that will in part direct the course of their lives, and as a result, influence their experience of As, Bs, and Cs. That is, the client's goals will in part influence the As they face (and how they are interpreted), the Bs they develop and apply to their Gs and As, and the Cs they experience in the face of As. Pursuing any goal involves discrimination and sacrifice; one discriminates between a range of potential life paths, and sacrifices effort, time, and resources in the service of the chosen path. The bigger the goal, the bigger the sacrifice, and the more potentially noxious As become, and the more intense the negative emotions potentially are at C – but of course, the bigger the potential pay-off. Even though As become potentially more noxious, it is possible that by making suitable sacrifices in the pursuit of the proper goal that clients can reduce the likelihood of facing As. For example, a client who thoughtfully sacrifices time, effort, and resources (e.g., money), to the development of practical resources (e.g., skills, knowledge, competence) in the pursuit of the proper goal, will be able to organise their lives in a way that can minimise adversity. We face As in part because we are limited and fallible, and thus by working to become a bit less limited and a bit less fallible, we can assuage some foreseeable As (and some unforeseeable As too). So, the client had better be careful in identifying their goals, or else they will suffer pointlessly, in part by forgoing short-term pleasures, and by pursuing a goal not worthy of their sacrifices. This suffering can be confounded by attaching irrational beliefs to the Gs, A, and Cs, underpinning UNEs rather than HNEs. As time goes by in the pursuit of said goal, sacrifices build up and As seem more and more threatening and irrational beliefs become highly salient (e.g., "I have sacrificed so much thus far, I couldn't bear any setbacks at this point, and failure at this point would be terrible"). Therefore, helping the client to identify their goal/s is of utmost importance, because we create our world via what we strive towards and the aims we set (Ellis et al., 2010).

Given what I have said about Gs inevitably creating the conditions (alongside A) for negative emotion, then it is important that we have Gs that are worth the suffering we will face in pursuit of Gs. So it is important to encourage athletes to develop as meaningful and enriching goals as they can for their lives, in order to sustain them amidst the adversities that life will throw at them. Shallow, trivial pleasures do not sustain us. An idealist goal of "fulfilling my human potential" (FG) might not be possible, but aiming for this is worthwhile because on the way to it I will learn and achieve many things. I may or may not attain the fulfilment of my potential, but by driving towards this goal I am sustained through adversity and suffering. One could consider FGs to be self-concordant goals that speak to deep values, permitting continual growth and expansion (Sheldon, 2002; Sheldon & Elliot, 1999). If I am smart and can avoid and/or deal with the many As that impede me, and remain rational in how I view my pursuit and the challenges that I face, I can pursue this FG whilst being healthy, functional, and I may even experience some positive emotion. Eudaimonia is an idealistic aspiration – it is ok to not get there – the pursuit of it is more important than eudaimonia itself. I can develop myself and be around (because I am healthy, functional, not burned-out and spent) to help others pursue their PGs and FGs and pass on any wisdom I have accumulated in pursuit of my own PGs and FGs.

Ellis (1991) indicated that "to make a stable habit of full functioning, one had better consciously choose the goal or purpose of becoming fully functioning" (p. 187). So, what goals should clients choose? What should clients be aiming for? As discussed earlier, human beings strive for many goals, which can be dependent on stage of life (Chulef et al., 2001), so, far be it for us to tell athletes what they *should* and *should not* work towards. Indeed, it is not possible or appropriate for the practitioner to specify a goal *for* a client, particularly the FG, as it should reflect their personal values. However, we can help clients to ask themselves the right questions concerning their goals (e.g., Ellis, 1991), such as:

- What do I really like and dislike?
- What do I want and not want?
- How can I experiment and discover what I truly like and dislike?
- Which of my likes and dislikes will probably harm me in the long-term?
- What am I likely to prefer and abhor in the future?
- What do I want to move towards?
- What do I want to move away from?

- What do I do to enhance my likes and decrease my dislikes?
- How can I align my options more closely to the data of my experiences?
- How can I align my short-term goals with my longer-term goals?
- How can I align my PGs with my FGs?

But no matter what the specific goal is, ensuring that the goal is eudaimonic seems to be a fine idea. For the Ancient Greek philosophers, *Telos* was that for the sake of which everything is done, whilst it is not itself done for the sake of any further thing (Sedley, 1998; Brennan, 2002). The Stoics believed that the correct goal (or *telos*) for human beings, or the ideal state of the human mind, is rational fulfilment of potential, or *eudaimonia* (Robertson, 2019b). This is not short-term happiness or self-esteem (unhealthy goals), but is more closely aligned with inner potential and living in accord with our core values (Robertson, 2019a). The Stoic concept of *eudaimonia* is an aspiration towards an ideal (Ierodiakonou, 2015), and like any ideal, the idea is to hold it aloft and aim towards it, knowing full well that its attainment is unlikely (few people will ever achieve perfect reason).

By 'fulfilment of potential', I do not speak of fulfilment of potential as an *athlete*. Rather, I speak of fulfilment of potential as a *human being*. In my use of 'fulfilment of potential' I align myself with the notion that it consists of,

> carrying to fruition one's deepest desires or one's worthiest capacities. It is a bringing of oneself to flourishing completion, an unfolding of what is strongest or best in oneself, so that it represents the successful culmination of one's aspirations or potentialities.
>
> (Gewirth, 2009)

Fulfilment of potential betokens a life well lived, one that is deeply satisfying, fruitful, and worthwhile (Gewirth, 2009). In order to live a good life, Rogers (1961) offers that one must voluntarily "launch oneself fully into the stream of life" (p. 196) in order to stretch and grow towards the becoming of one's potentialities. As humanistic practitioners applying REBT, the whole person should be considered not just the role-related expression of the person (i.e., 'Athlete', 'Coach', etc.). Eudaimonia is not a feeling, but is more accurately a way of life that can be evaluated as a life that is good and fulfilling (Ryan & Martela, 2016), deriving from rational activity in accord with psychological virtues, and as such, is autonomous, self-generated – it comes from within (Robertson, 2019b). The Stoics believed that although we human beings are not the strongest or fastest in the animal kingdom, our capacity for reason sets us apart from other animals. The Stoics stressed that in order to attain eudaimonia we should live in agreement with (or according to) nature, in essence suggesting that we live in agreement with our unique endowment of reason and rationality (Stephen, n.d.).

In order to pursue eudaimonia, human beings need to cultivate their wisdom beyond all else; the everyday pursuit of wisdom is defined as the highest human purpose. Wisdom incorporates rationally grasping the knowledge of what is good or bad in life (Robertson, 2021b), understanding what is and is not within our control, and being honest with oneself. It captures the ability to know what practically helps us to fulfil our potential in life, and thus the pursuit of wisdom is vital for eudaimonia (Robertson, 2021c). Thus, we can encourage clients to carefully consider whether their goals will help them to develop, and act out, this wisdom, and help them to apply this wisdom as they move towards their goals. Whatever the specific FG, ensure that it necessitates movement towards eudaimonia via wisdom and reason. REBT has always been about helping the person as a whole, not just confined aspects of who they are (e.g., job roles).

This all sounds quite lofty and complex, and may seem tangential to the work we are doing with clients, but at ground level it simply means that, as practitioners, we help the client to gain some clarity on (a) the composition of their core values, (b) what they believe their inner potential is, and (c) what fulfilment or eudaimonia would look like to *them*. Although generally we would not challenge a client's preferences and desires, it is useful to do so if it is clear for client and practitioner that these preferences and desires might be introjected (taken from others without consideration) or false (Dryden, 2012c). Sometimes, the goals an athlete holds have been transacted onto them by people around them, and these goals do not speak to what they *actually* want from life or will lead to their fulfilment. So, we can help clients to work towards eudaimonic FGs via the development and enactment of wisdom, rather than unwisely working towards superficial, facile, introjected goals such as fortune and fame, momentary happiness and short-term pleasure. Indeed,

> short range hedonism – eat, drink, and be merry, for tomorrow you may die! – has its distinct limitations, for tomorrow you will probably be alive with the hangover!...immediate gratification had often better be avoided and long-range hedonism sought out and abetted.
>
> (Ellis, 1991, p. 193)

As Robertson (2019b) points out, Ellis derived the notion of short-term vs. long-term hedonism from Stoicism. Ellis, like the Stoics, did not promote enjoyment at the expense of deeper goals, and encourages us to not do things the easy way but to do things the rewarding way.

A meaningful conversation with an athlete directed at revealing FGs will undoubtedly uncover a hierarchy of goals, atop of which will likely be a goal that is reflective of a meaningful and humanistic drive for the fulfilment of potential (i.e., a life well lived). We just have to help them explore deeply enough to be able to identify these FGs. So, the difficult question we can pose to clients are, "what does you fulfilling your human potential look like?", "what is your fundamental goal in life?", and "what could you work towards that would help you to look back on your life and think, 'that was a good life?'" Obviously, this line of questioning is not to be rushed, and it might be the first time the client has ever been asked to think about and articulate their FGs in this way.

By identifying a proper FG (or telos), we can encourage clients to consider the bigger picture, and look beyond what they desire as part of their PGs, to what they would like to move towards as an FG. It is the moving towards eudaimonia that makes the sacrifice, suffering, and adversity, worth it, and as a by-product may even increase momentary happiness. Fulfilment comes from the seeking of and pursuit towards *eudaimonia*, not from the attainment of wishes and wants. The PGs are more likely to be imbued with meaning and purpose if they are in service of the FG. Therefore, we can ask the athlete, 'Is the PG in service of the FG?' In other words, does the PG help the athlete move towards eudaimonia? Instead of asking the athlete 'what do you desire?', we can ask 'what do you want to move towards?' and 'what PGs in life would help you move towards your FG?' By pursuing proper FGs, developing and putting into action wisdom, clients are more likely to attain their meaningful PGs, and if they do not attain their PGs, at least they have not sacrificed their health in pursuit of them.

It is the current author's view, also echoed in Ellis' (1994) view of FGs and PGs, that a PG such as vocational satisfaction (e.g., athletic achievement), should not be confused for an FG. In other words, vocational success (PG) should not be the underpinning fundamental goal (FG) for human beings, but should be in service of the broader and grander FG that transcends work, sport, economics – i.e., is eudaimonic and reflects core values. This is not to denigrate the endeavours that constitute PGs, but human beings are more than the roles they play at work or in sport, and are certainly more than their bank balance. This PG and FG distinction is important, in part, because the attainment of PGs are dependent on external factors; the Stoics warn against overvaluing external things, because they are outside of our control. Sporting success, for example, is dependent on various internal *and* external factors, thus evading our total volition. For example, whilst is it nice to be approved of, yearning for approval and making it our FG in life is dangerous especially if we unwisely sneak demands for approval into this desire. We can't control it, and we certainly don't 'need' it, so why would we make it an FG? Nobody can bestow our FG upon us; eudaimonia is self-generated, it comes from within, and come from truth, reason, integrity, and wisdom, is autonomous – it depends only on itself (Robertson, 2019a). So, clients are encouraged to pursue PGs but not at the cost of FGs, which are primary and paramount.

To be clear, it is not that I am saying that clients should not seek success in sport, whatever that looks like for them. I issue a caution against overvaluing goals that are not within the client's control, confusing PGs for FGs, and more importantly, warn against attaching irrational beliefs to goal pursuits. "I know I don't have to win a World Cup, but I would really like to, so let me see if I can make that more likely to happen". Approaching goals with rationality in service of the fulfilment of our potential does not preclude clients being competitive, aiming high (e.g., personal bests), and enjoying the spoils of victory, or seeking the things that they desire. A rational approach to goals removes the irrational notion that clients *must* have what they *desire*, and that failure to get what they desire is awful, intolerable, and self-defining.

Too much importance placed on PGs can lead to a fusing of the self with the endeavour, making it dangerous to fail or face setbacks. In other words, self-worth becomes conditional on the achievement of said goal. I cover this idea in more detail in Chapter 10, but suffice it to say that as a result, you (the self) become trapped in your endeavour and will find it more difficult to stand up to wrongdoing or step away from it when necessary. This is because you do not want to jeopardise the goal you have placed as your FG, which you have attached your self-worth to – 'If I withdraw from sport, who am I?'. Never let your goals trap you. If we consider FGs as eudaimonic, then PGs should be in the service of FGs. When a PG is erroneously placed as an FG, the genuine eudaimonic FG is less likely to be attained because it has been overshadowed by the PG, and thus the pursuit of the proper FG has been neglected. In short, dissuade clients from staking their self-worth as a human being on their goal pursuits.

> I had an unhealthy relationship with snooker. A lot of my self worth and value is built around the game. If I do well at snooker I'm ok as a person.
>
> Ronnie O'Sullivan (Mundie, 2022)

The greater focus on goals that is proposed in my proactive GABCDE is somewhat in line with Hutchinson and Chapman's (2005) integration of REBT with Viktor Frankl's (2000) Logotherapy. Hutchinson and Chapman "argue for a philosophical, existential system of psychotherapy that increases rational thinking in the context of a broader, unique purpose and philosophy of life" (pp.147–148). They assert that people suffer not only from irrational beliefs, but also from a lack of meaning or life goals; both of which will impair the appraisal process related to life, the behaviours of others, and one's own phenomenal experience. They also point out that in both REBT and Logotherapy, people are not seen as responsible for uncontrollable situations (e.g., unfair treatment, biological states), but are responsible for their attitudes towards the situations. In applying Logotherapy alongside REBT, it is possible to help clients through a process of *discovering* life meaning and purpose, whilst simultaneously developing self-enhancing, *rational* codes, underpinned by personal *responsibility* and personal *agency* (Hutchinson & Chapman, 2005). We can use the methods of Socratic questioning to (a) prompt the discovery of life purpose and meaning, aiding the articulation of FGs and PGs, and to (b) help clients challenge and reformulate their beliefs to aid the healthy and functional pursuit of these goals. In articulating and pursuing FGs and PGs, the client must be fortified against the As they will inevitably face, by holding and applying rationality.

THE PURSUIT OF HAPPINESS

The reader might notice that 'happiness' does not feature in my conception of fundamental goals (FG) and primary goals (PG). For the present author, it doesn't seem that happiness is a suitable goal for human beings. Evidently, this is not what life is about. If happiness was a core goal for human beings, we have failed catastrophically in achieving it. It is more accurate to take The Buddha's stance on life, that life contains inevitable, unavoidable suffering, and that happy *moments* are just that – momentary. In Gordon W. Allport's forward to Viktor Frankl's masterpiece *Man's Search for Meaning*, he addresses existentialism, noting that, "to live is to suffer, to survive is to find meaning in the suffering" (p. 9). Thus, a proper goal is that which makes this ubiquitous suffering worthwhile and meaningful. Arthur Schopenhauer (German philosopher, 1788–1860) believed that suffering gave meaning to life, stating that "If the immediate and direct purpose of our life is not suffering then our existence is the most ill-adapted to its purpose in the world…misfortune in general is the rule" (Schopenhauer, 1850, location 626). In his essay 'On the Suffering of the World' Schopenhauer suggests that our lives are punctuated by constant struggle both metaphorically and actually, because we live in conflict with ourselves and others.

This might seem pessimistic, which Schopenhauer certainly was, but optimistically our capacity to acknowledge suffering as a matter of existence helps us to embrace our imperfections and shortcomings, enabling us to marvel at our achievements and recognise that our failures are a reflection of our nature – we are fallible human beings – as is recognised in REBT. Schopenhauer advises us to order our expectations of life "according to the nature of things" and to "no longer regard the calamities, sufferings, torments and miseries of life as something irregular and not to be expected" (Schopenhauer, 1850, location 765). Expect to suffer, and recognise not only that suffering is part of life, but that suffering is necessary for a meaningful life. Amidst the axiom 'to live is to suffer', the pursuit of happiness seems rather insipid and facile.

In REBT, helping people to reduce emotional turmoil leaves the door open for happiness. For example, Michael Bernard and colleagues (2010) point out that, "when a person does not face an adversity at 'A', then he is free, theoretically at least, to engage fully in meaningful activities and, thus, experience happiness when thus engaged" (p. 309). They go on to say that when an A *is* faced, so long as one has rational beliefs and subsequent HNEs, one can experience *some* happiness through meaningful activity. This links nicely to the integration of Richard Lazarus' work and the GABCDE framework discussed earlier, whereby if A does not represent goal incongruence (i.e., the situation is not perceived as 'adverse'), then negative emotion is unlikely to be evinced. But it is difficult to conceptualise the movement towards a meaningful goal that is not beset by adversity – the meaningfulness of the goal is in part defined by the challenge undertaken in order to achieve it. Avoiding *all* challenge is unlikely to engender proper adaptation and unlikely to facilitate eudaimonia. Bruce Lee (martial artist, actor) famously said, "Do not pray for an easy life, pray for the strength to endure a difficult one".

In a study by Baumeister and colleagues (2013), it was found that whilst happiness and meaningfulness are related, they are distinct. Happiness is about getting what one wants and needs, whereas meaningfulness is about doing things that express and reflect the self (e.g., doing positive things for others). Meaningfulness can beget stress and anxiety, and whilst happiness is focussed on feeling good in the present, meaningfulness integrates past, present, and future, and can mean feeling bad. Baumeister et al. state that, "...happiness without meaning characterizes a relatively shallow, self-absorbed or even selfish life, in which things go well, needs and desire are easily satisfied, and difficult or taxing entanglements are avoided" (Baumeister et al., 2013, p. 515). Therefore, coming back to Bernard et al.'s (2010) point that happiness comes about when we do not face an adversity, meaningful goal pursuit will be taxing and difficult, As cannot be completely avoided (because we are limited, and the world unpredictable, uncontrollable and often volatile), so happiness is a potentially fallacious goal.

Relatedly, Marcus Aurelius, aforementioned Roman Emperor between 161 and 180 BC and espouser of Stoicism, wrote that "to expect a bad person not to harm others is like expecting fig trees not to secrete juice, babies not to cry, horses not to neigh – the inevitable not to happen" (Meditations, 12.16). In other words, there is no utility in expecting the world to be less noxious (or wishing for no As), and it is more useful to develop ways in which you can cope with the noxiousness of the world so that you can minimise suffering. If we revert REBT back to its Stoic ideals, happiness seems ill fitted to life, and the concept of eudaimonia seems more appropriate. If you experience happiness, it is often fleeting and unpredictable. For example, you might imagine that, when you achieve something that you have worked for a long time to achieve, you would be happy. But this rarely the case. Just talk to graduates and athletes about this – they will tell you that after reaching their goals, they might be relieved, authentically proud, perhaps even anxious about what is next – but happiness often doesn't quite cut it.

So, it seems to me that structuring one's goals in the service of a transient unpredictable emotional state such as happiness is not very meaningful, but being fulfilled might be a more appropriate goal. As Daniel Kahneman puts it,

> I don't think that people maximize happiness in that sense...this doesn't seem to be what people want to do. They actually want to maximize their satisfaction with themselves and with their lives. And that leads in completely different directions than the maximization of happiness.
>
> (Livni, 2018)

Happiness and satisfaction are distinct. Whilst happiness is a momentary, fleeting, and spontaneous experience, satisfaction is a long-term experience built over time, based on achieving goals and building the kind of life you admire. This, to me, seems to capture the types of goals that would offer meaning enough to justify the sacrifices in its pursuit. Now, you may experience happiness on the way to your goals as a consequence of making positive steps forward, but happiness should not be the *reason* to strive for those goals. In Stoicism, joy is experienced by someone who has attained genuine personal fulfilment (eudaimonia), and the Stoics viewed joy as a by-product of successfully pursuing wisdom (Robertson, 2019a). Joy emerges as we head in the right direction and pursuing joy directly at the expense of wisdom might lead us down the wrong path (Robertson, 2019a).

Allied to this last point, there is a developing body of evidence which suggests that valuing happiness impairs emotion regulation, paradoxically decreases happiness and well-being, and is associated with a range of psychopathologies (see Mahmoodi Kahriz et al., 2019). Indeed, it appears that extreme valuing of happiness may contribute to the development and maintenance of disorders such as depression (Mauss et al., 2011). Viktor Frankl is credited with saying, "It is the very pursuit of happiness that thwarts happiness", and in the preface to the 1992 edition of *Man's Search for Meaning* he says, "happiness, cannot be pursued; it must ensue, and it only does so as the unintended side-effect of one's dedication to a cause greater than oneself" (p. 12). He goes on to say that "a human being is not one in pursuit of happiness but rather in search of a reason to become happy" (p. 140).

Therefore, when working with clients it is important to explore what a meaningful goal might be for them, and encourage them to aim for the highest possible good in the service of fulfilment, rather than seek short-term pleasure. They will suffer anyway, as this is the human condition, so they could pick a goal that justifies this suffering, which could be a eudaimonic goal. As Baumeister and colleagues (2013) conclude, "Clearly happiness is not all that people seek, and indeed, the meaningful but unhappy life is in some ways more admirable than the happy but meaningless one" (p. 516). Indeed, in order to maximise fulfilment, Ellis (1991) suggests we throw ourselves into long-term vital and absorbing interests, placing significance in what is intrinsically valuable.

In all, we can't tell clients what their 'meaning of life' is or should be, because we don't know. Even if we did think we knew, we wouldn't presume to enforce this on clients; the client needs to discover that for themselves. But we do know that eudaimonia is as good a life purpose as any, and the fulfilment of potential it represents is a worthwhile thing to move towards. It goes deeper than medals, money, adulation, and adoration. It is more likely to uphold and support mental health if pursued on rational terms, and as a *by-product* may even produce moments of genuine happiness. REBT holds that,

> People who use rational thinking will take proper responsibility for their lives and emotions, accept uncertainty and themselves, and practice tolerance…will make reasonable compromises, take risks, and have higher levels of frustration tolerance, and sacrifice immediate pleasures for long-term benefits.
>
> (Hutchinson & Chapman, 2005, p. 147)

Using REBT, we can help clients to, as Jordan Peterson asserts, "Pursue what is meaningful not what is expedient" (Peterson et al., 2018, p. 201).

An iterative process

Once the goals have been articulated, then the practitioner can help the athlete to orient their life towards the goals, employing problem-solving concerning As, Bs, and Cs. As the athlete strives towards the goal, and more information and clarity comes to light concerning the ABCs, we can help the athlete to reformulate their solutions flexibly, holding the belief that

> it would be nice if I was able to achieve my goals without any hiccups, but that doesn't mean that I have to, and whilst it is tough, I can certainly tolerate the many barriers and setbacks that might come my way on the way to my goals.

Proactive GABCDE should be seen as an iterative process, rather than a one-stop shop. In addition, as the client meets PGs and shorter-term goals, this will influence their conceptualisation of future PGs. I have seen it so often with the people I work with. The client at one time believes that in achieving a particular short-term goal that they will be satisfied, only to find that meeting that goal opens up a range of other possible goals. In this chapter, I have argued that, regardless of specific PGs and short-term goals, the continuous forward movement towards eudaimonia (FG) is a life-long endeavour. As Bob Dylan famously said,

> An artist has got to be careful never really to arrive at a place where he thinks he's at somewhere...you're constantly in a state of becoming. As long as you can stay in that realm, you'll sort of be alright.
>
> (Bob Dylan, in Madden, 2015)

Summary

Ellis highlights that REBT has an existential focus, stating that to function well humans require meaning and purpose in life and that it advocates that people create and work on building purpose and meaning (Ellis, 2003a, 2005a). In line with this, he strongly advocated for disputation to promote individuals to develop a healthy philosophy towards life that encourages self-fulfilment and self-actualisation (Collard, 2019). In REBT, we consider human beings to be goal-driven, and we can help clients to pursue many personal and professional goals ('PGs'), underpinned by eudaimonic (long-term life fulfilment) and meaning-laden goals ('FGs'). Because of the chaotic and unpredictable world clients inhabit, they will face many adversities (A) in pursuit of their goals, and will necessarily suffer as a result, especially emotionally (C). Clients who pursue their goals through the development and application of wisdom and rationality, are more likely to experience HNEs rather than UNEs in the face of adversity (A). Thus, clients able to check and challenge their perceptions of the world, understand what is and is not with their control, and hone their rational beliefs, can fortify themselves against the adversities that will occur as a result of their pursuit towards meaningful goals. In other words, rationality can help clients to pursue what is meaningful, readying them to forthrightly face the inevitable vicissitudes of life, without sacrificing their mental and physical health as they do so.

As part of proactive GABCDE, we can help the client to (a) articulate and orient themselves towards G, (b) problem-solve at A, (c) address potential irrational beliefs that could bring about UNEs, (d) bolster potential rational beliefs that could bring about HNEs, and (e) use the GABCDE framework and the 'rules' of REBT, including how to use disputation on their own rigid and extreme beliefs. Again, the author defers to Seneca (Seneca & Campbell, 2004) who said that,

> Everyone faces up more bravely to a thing for which he has long prepared himself, sufferings, even, being withstood if they have been trained for in advance. Those who are unprepared, on the other hand, are panic-stricken by the most insignificant happenings.

As such, by using the proactive GABCDE framework we can help clients to prepare and train for the arduous endeavour of goal pursuit. In the interest of life eudaimonia, or any goal attainment, it is advantageous to not be panic-stricken. Thus, by learning how to use the GABCDE framework the client gains some autonomy over their goal pursuit, including the emotion regulation that will surely have to take place as they pursue this goal. As Ellis (1991) notes, "with self-actualization: Only by working at planning, plotting, scheming and steadily acting at it are you likely to become a fully-functioning person" (p. 193).

CHAPTER 9
The nature of beliefs (B)

In the darkness, we face our fears.

DOI: 10.4324/9781003200437-10

> There are many things that I want in life, and because I want them so very much, then I simply must have them. If I don't get what I want, then I would not be able to bear it, and it would not just be bad, it would be terrible. My not getting what I want would go to illustrate that I am a useless idiot, and that the world is a rotten place, and so are the people in it.

The above piece captures the four core irrational beliefs of REBT, and you may recognise some of this language from the clients you work with, people you surround yourself with, and indeed, from your own internal dialogue and speech. These four core irrational beliefs will be covered in detail in Chapter 10, but in this current chapter, I detail and explain the concept of rationality at the heart of REBT, discuss the notion of belief, and offer some thoughts on why human beings have and hold irrational beliefs.

THE 'RATIONAL' ANIMAL

Modern human beings have selected the name Homosapien for our species. Homo is Latin for 'human', and Sapien is Latin for 'wise', 'astute', or 'judicious', and human beings are classically considered to be 'the rational animal' (Aristotle Metaphysics; Ritter, 1930). However, despite this favourable nomenclature, human beings can of course demonstrably operate unwisely, non-astutely, injudiciously, and irrationally. Oscar Wilde (1891) writes in his book *The Picture of Dorian Gray* that "Man is many things, but he is not rational" and Bertrand Russell (1950) noted that, "[I]t has been said that man is a rational animal. All my life I have been searching for evidence which could support this". Lisa Feldman Barrett (2017) points out that "A brain did not evolve for rationality" (p. 3). Clearly, human beings frequently and ubiquitously think and act in ways that are irrational, and Albert Ellis (1976) makes a point of listing 259 examples of human irrationality, which is not exhaustive (!). Human beings are capable of rationality, in part because they are capable of irrationality, unlike other animals who can only be arational (De Sousa, 2007). But despite our rational capabilities, the deployment of our rationality is not a fixed matter and is not to be assumed. Rationality is not a power that one either does or does not have (Pinker, 2021). It is perhaps more accurate to suggest that, as John McDowell (2010) asserts, we possess a potentiality for rationality which does not imply actuality. Society plays an important role in our rationality (Ellis, 1976) and to move from potential rationality to actual rationality, we must engage in a process of initiation into a social practice, such as education (Kern, 2020).

In this chapter, and in REBT per se, rationality is more closely aligned with what Keith Stanovich (2012) calls the "stronger sense" (p. 344) of rationality. Specifically, "Rationality (and irrationality) comes in degrees defined by the distance of the thought or behaviour from the optimum defined by a normative model" (p. 344). Stanovich, whose contribution to the study and understanding of rationality is substantial, describes two types of rationality; Epistemic (evidential, theoretical) rationality which concerns how well beliefs map onto the actual structure of the world, and instrumental rationality which concerns behaving in the world so that you get exactly what you most want, given the resources (physical and mental) available to you. These types of rationality are clearly within the remit of rationality as held in REBT, with a congruence in characteristics of empirical, logical, and functional elements to rationality. Stanovich (2018) suggests that, "Somewhat more technically, we could characterize instrumental rationality as the optimization of the individual's goal fulfilment"

(p. 345), aligning REBT even more closely with Stanovich's representation of rationality. REBT constrains its definitions of 'rational' and 'irrational' by suggesting that rationality is explicitly counter to irrationality. This is why, for example, rational preferences include the negation of demands.

Recently, Stephen Pinker (2021) wrote a book on rationality: *Rationality: What It Is, Why It Seems Scarce, Why It Matters*. In the book, Pinker offers that rationality "is a kit of cognitive tools that can attain particular goals in particular worlds" (p. 7), is "the ability to use knowledge to attain goals" (p. 36), and suggest we "ground our beliefs in truth" (p. 37). True to what we have discussed thus far in this book, a rational agent must have a goal – if you want things, rationality is what allows you to get those things. Pinker's ideas align with Stanovich's (2018) thoughts on epistemic and instrumental rationality, and both are in congruence with REBT's view of rationality. But it is important to stress that whilst perfect rationality should be striven for, it is an aspiration that no mortal human can attain (Pinker, 2021). What we try to do in REBT is help clients develop this 'rational kit of cognitive tools' (i.e., beliefs) in service of their goals, all the while knowing and understanding that people will not and cannot *always* think and act rationally.

Beliefs

There are multiple viewpoints on what beliefs are. Schwitzgebel (2010) suggests that belief is the mental acceptance or conviction in the truth or actuality of some idea. A belief has a specific meaning that can be expressed in the form of a sentence; as an attitude, it involves a mental stance on the validity of a proposition. Connors and Halligan (2015) posit that beliefs are "enduring, unquestioned ontological representations of the world and comprise primary convictions about events, causes, agency, and objects that subjects use and accept as veridical" (p. 2). Halligan (2006) indicates that because beliefs provide the basis for us to understand the world and act within it, they are perhaps better considered as mental scaffolding for appraising one's environment and constructing a shared meaning of the world (Halligan, 2007). Because beliefs facilitate the appraisal of ongoing experiences, they can have emotional consequences, and can inform our goals and actions (Harris, 2006; Tullett et al., 2013). Thus, it makes sense that beliefs which are wayward and dysfunctional are subject to extinction and/or change in various CBTs, including REBT. Unlike memory, beliefs can be held about the present and the future, and unlike knowledge, beliefs are regarded as true and have a large self-referential element (Connors & Halligan, 2015).

Another school of thought holds that beliefs can be considered as probabilistic neural representations that include perception and subjective valuation of signals in the environment via re-interative, bottom-up and top-down processes (Seitz & Angel, 2020). They are a subjective assumption concerning environmental information to which we are exposed which have a neural basis in the brain (Seitz et al., 2016). They are the "neuropsychic product of neural processes allowing individuals to develop a personal affective stance concerning the signals in their environment" (Seitz & Angel, 2020, p. 4). In other words, beliefs are thought to be the product of fundamental neural processes (Boyer, 2003), in that belief formation results from perceptive and affective information processing that takes place in the brain (e.g., Sachs & Hirsch, 2008). Importantly, beliefs can manifest below the level of awareness (Bar et al., 2006; Smith, 2011) and include processes that attempt to link past events to future events – in this sense beliefs are probabilistic (Friston, 2010; Taves & Asprem, 2016). Beliefs reflect the meaning we ascribe to past and future interactions with the environment and therefore guide behaviour (spontaneous and contextualised) and decision-making (Seitz & Angel, 2020).

When taken together, there is a sense that beliefs are propositions that help shape our perceptions of the world and are guiding principles that provide direction and meaning in life (Sathyanarayana Rao et al., 2009). They can offer a consistent representation of the world, provide an explanatory framework for interpreting the world and processing incoming information, configure and calibrate perception, language, memory, and attention, and inform how we navigate social relationships and interpret other people's motivations (Connors & Halligan, 2015). The purpose of forming such beliefs is to increase the efficiency of brain mechanisms involved in problem-solving, decision-making, goals setting, and manoeuvring in the environment (Garcés & Finkel, 2019). Indeed, the processes underlying beliefs take place in the order of milliseconds (Seitz et al., 2018). As such, beliefs that more accurately reflect reality are likely to maximise survival (McKay & Dennett, 2009) because they can more functionally guide our behaviour. Therefore, beliefs can serve as heuristic tools that enable us to act or react to our physical and social environment as fast and adequately as possible, in theory, thus enhancing our chances of survival. Beliefs are an important building block of intelligent behaviour (Elliott et al., 1995; Howlett & Paulus, 2015). So, beliefs are really fundamental to how we make sense of our environment, our place within it, and how we act within it. Therefore, beliefs that are faulty or do not represent reality sufficiently will lead to skewed perceptions of our world, and ourselves, and help create inappropriate and maladaptive contextual behaviours. Sam Harris (2006) sees beliefs as an adaptive outgrowth of the human capacity for action because by believing various propositions about the world we are able to orient our behaviours in light of our predictions and projected consequences of our actions. Harris states that beliefs "are processes by which our understanding (and misunderstanding) of the world is represented and made available to guide our behaviour" (p. 52).

There is a sense that because some beliefs are conceptual and language-based, that the acquisition of beliefs is culturally informed, such that the narratives that permeate our cultural milieu can shape what we believe (Seitz & Angel, 2020). Many beliefs are not likely to be conscious or reportable, but instead simply taken as granted without reflection or awareness (Connors & Halligan, 2015). But when beliefs *are* articulated verbally in language, humans can provide accounts of their beliefs and share their beliefs with others, who are subject to holding the same beliefs if they consider it to be of value (true, useful). This ability to articulate, together with the idea that beliefs are not fixed or static (i.e., they reflect neural processes), means that beliefs can be updated and changed (Seitz & Angel, 2020). That is, beliefs can be reinforced and further ingrained, or altered and updated, through learning. Although beliefs can be considered to be enduring (Connors & Halligan, 2015), this does not mean that they are fixed and unchangeable. Beliefs are flexible and subject to modification via new information, in line with the principles of brain plasticity (Angel & Seitz, 2017; Merzenich & Sameshima, 1993), and there is variability in the level of conviction or degree of confidence people have in a belief (Connors & Halligan, 2015). If we challenge beliefs by contradicting them, or cut them off from the stimuli that make us think about them, then they will weaken. If this weakening is then combined with very strong reinforcement of new beliefs, then you're going to get a shift in emphasis from one to the other (Kathleen Taylor, neuroscientist at Oxford University; in Jha, 2018). This is good news for REBT practitioners, because the focus of our work is prominently on the weakening of irrational beliefs, and the strengthening of rational beliefs.

Beliefs in REBT

In REBT, in line with what was proffered in the previous section, beliefs are deeply held (tacit) propositions, assumptions, rules, ideas, attitudes, sets of expectations, ways of seeing the world that have cognitive, emotional and behavioural concomitants and consequences. They are considered to be enduring, contextual (they are often *about* something), and can exist as tacit-like schemata and/or as deliberative evaluations, but are subject to change through rigorous discursive and experiential means. But specifically, in REBT, the notion of beliefs is contextualised within the ideas of rationality and irrationality. There is certainly a sense that Stoic reason and rationality provided some of the seeds for Ellisian reason and rationality. For the Stoics, reason was fundamental for human well-being because human nature is characterised by our ability to reason – an ability through which we make sense of our environment and act accordingly. As such, if our decisions reflect this rational ability, then we are functioning optimally as human beings (Murguia & Díaz, 2015). But rationality in modern REBT is quite a precise idea based around particular core beliefs that are conceptualised rather specifically with explicit boundaries and borders. Rational beliefs are propositions, assumptions, rules, ideas, attitudes, ways of seeing the world, that are scientifically warranted, flexible, non-extreme, and usually underpin human survival and fulfilment, at least more so than irrational beliefs which are unscientific, rigid, and absolutistic, and undercut human survival and wellbeing (Ellis, 1987a; Ellis & MacLaren, 1998; Robb, 2003). In other words, in REBT rational means self-helping and irrational means self-defeating, and as such the chief aims of REBT is to help people weaken their irrational beliefs and strengthen their rational beliefs (Ellis & Dryden, 1997).

DiGiuseppe et al. (2014, p. 33) perhaps offer the clearest definition of rational and irrational beliefs in REBT. They state that irrational beliefs have the characteristics of: being absolute, dichotomous, rigid, and unbending; illogical; inconsistent with reality; not helpful to achieve one's goal; lead to unhealthy/dysfunctional emotions. In contrast, rational beliefs have the characteristics of being: flexible; logical; consistent with reality; helpful in pursuing one's goal; lead to healthy/functional emotions, even when the person is facing negative events. More broadly, irrational beliefs are cognitive expressions of the unwillingness to accept an unwanted outcome related to one's striving to achieve something positive or to block something negative. This can be reflected in demands on reality (i.e., "musts" and "shoulds"). In contrast, rational beliefs are cognitive expressions of the basic willingness to accept an unwanted outcome of reality related to one's striving to achieve something positive or to block something negative, regardless of how much it deviates from what one wants and independent of how strong one's desire is (DiGiuseppe et al., 2014).

In REBT, irrational beliefs underpin unhealthy negative emotions (UNEs), and rational beliefs underpin healthy negative emotions (HNEs). Having helped the client to establish what their UNE is at C, and what their critical A is, and perhaps what their G is, it is now vital that the correct and full irrational belief is located and articulated. Previous examples of A assessment are helpful here, such as inference chaining, which will get the client close to their B. But there are additional techniques that can be used to uncover the B, or cluster of Bs (a 'B hive', if you will). It is important not to assume the presence or type of irrational beliefs the client may hold. If the client is experiencing or reporting UNEs, then of course irrational precursors are likely to be present, and as practitioners we may have a sense of what type of irrational beliefs might be present. But we do not know precisely the type of irrational belief being harboured, its depth, or its pervasiveness. So, we must undertake a full assessment of B in order to be precise in our formulation of the problem. But before I share some methods of B assessment (Chapter 11), it is first important to understand what rational and irrational beliefs are, and importantly, delineate the differences between rational and irrational beliefs in detail, since the concepts of rational beliefs and irrational beliefs are central to REBT.

In REBT, rational beliefs refer to "beliefs that are logical, and/or have empirical support, and/or are pragmatic" and irrational beliefs are "beliefs that are illogical, and/or do not have empirical support, and/or are nonpragmatic" (Ellis et al., 2010, p. 3). As can be seen by the use of 'and/or', a belief need not fit all three criteria to be rational, but it is necessary that a belief meet at least one criterion, or a combination of criteria (Ellis et al., 2010). As such, rational beliefs in part are defined in line with scientific and intellectual thought, in that they are logically consistent and supported by empirical evidence. But importantly, rational beliefs also enable people to achieve their goals (Wilson, 2010). It is therefore useful to consider rational and irrational beliefs to be defined psychologically rather than philosophically (Ellis et al., 2010), because after all, it is the development and enhancement of human functioning that is at the centre of REBT, not just logic for logic's sake. Indeed, rational beliefs are usually self-enhancing (Dryden, 2017), and often underpin HNEs (DiGiuseppe et al., 2014), whilst in contrast irrational beliefs are usually unhelpful in pursuing, and inconsistent with accomplishing, one's long-term goals (i.e., they are self-defeating; Dryden, 2017; Maultsby, 1975), and often underpin UNEs (DiGiuseppe et al., 2014). The three ideas of logic, truth, and pragmatics help to drive the disputation (D) of rational and irrational beliefs. As Albert Ellis puts it, "beliefs that are scientifically warranted are usually rational in the sense that they normally lead to human survival and happiness – or at least do so more often than do unscientific, absolutistic beliefs" (Ellis, 1987a, p. 137). As such, absolutistic, dogmatic, extreme thinking is irrational in part because it often leads to poor emotional and behavioural results and therefore tends to sabotage happiness and survival. In addition, irrational beliefs are unscientific in part because they offer many propositions that are unfalsifiable (Still, 2010) and inconsistent with reality.

Taking beliefs seriously

In REBT, we take some beliefs seriously, because we recognise that beliefs can be the determining factor in the expression of UNEs and HNEs. Whilst some CBT approaches might suggest that we should not take beliefs seriously at all, REBT suggests that we should take seriously beliefs that can stand up to truth, logic, and functionality (pragmatics). In REBT, it is more sensible and adaptive to align our beliefs with reality, and therefore, to not take seriously those beliefs that are not aligned with reality, such as extreme, rigid, illogical, and empirically false, beliefs.

But what about our clients – do they take their beliefs seriously? This is an important question because if a client has a fleeting thought that "I am such a massive loser" but does not take this seriously, by which I mean to say, does not give this belief credence, then it is highly likely that the thought will not be problematic for the client. Not all irrational utterances or thoughts are suitable targets for change. Indeed, Dryden and Neenan (2020) talk about time-limited irrationalities, whereby despite having an irrational thought, some clients may be able to stand back and cope with the adversity, and thus do not consider the irrationality to be a problem. They also state that some clients do disturb themselves about an event but are able to engage in rationality fairly quickly. So, many people can apply irrational beliefs to their adversities and suffer acutely, but then return to a 'normal' (undisturbed) state quite quickly, realising their irrationality and addressing it. But if suffering continues and irrationality contributes to perpetual unhealthy emotion, and/or the client is stuck with their irrational beliefs (Dryden & Neenan, 2020), then we can target irrationality for intervention. Not all irrationality will underpin disturbance, and all disturbance is not underpinned by irrationality.

Thus, as practitioners it is important that we do not 'jump on' every 'irrational' utterance within hearing distance – we are not the rationality police (nee-naw). On this issue, Robb and Ciarrochi (2005) suggest that "trouble comes when certain kinds of private, or public, language is not only prevalent but also 'believed'" (p. 170). They suggest that when we 'believe' something, it means that we 'take it seriously' such that the belief in some way determines our behaviour. This goes beyond mere flippant utterances that seem to have a flavour of irrationality. Does the client really believe what they are saying or thinking? If not, then their irrationality could be just a cathartic expression of their frustration ("you idiot! What a terrible shot!"), for example. However, if the client does really believe what are saying or thinking, then their irrationality might be a true and accurate reflection of a deeply held and potentially pernicious philosophy that they hold on to and which helps determine their emotional and behavioural reactivity to adverse events.

Therefore, perhaps the issue lays not within the demand for fair treatment, for example, but in my conviction in the belief that I must be treated fairly. The more strongly I believe that I must be treated fairly, the more likely I am to evince dysfunctional emotions and behaviours. The thought "I must be treated fairly" may appear in my mind's eye fleetingly, and I do not take it seriously. But if I do take it seriously, then I risk problematic consequences. The level of belief in a dysfunctional cognition may influence the level of consequent dysfunction (e.g., Beck, 2015). Indeed, Beck and Freeman (1990) note that it is the intensity to which a dysfunctional belief is held that influences the level of dysfunction it will promote. Collard (2022) also points out that if a person views a dysfunctional cognition as just a spurious and fleeting event, it would be less likely to drive dysfunction. For example, an irrational, potentially depreciating, thought like "I am such an idiot" could be held lightly and humorously, not held tightly or truthfully, and thus would not be pathological. In REBT, we encourage clients to not take seriously, and actively work against, beliefs that are irrational, and to take seriously and actively strengthen, beliefs that are rational.

Practical rationality

In the defining features of rational and irrational beliefs, we are not trying to brainwash the client (or the reader!) into thinking irrational beliefs are the route to all human misery on account of absent truth and faulty logic. I agree with Julian Baggini's (2019) assertions that human beings do have a sense that truth is not just an abstract construct but is in some manner essential to living well. Indeed, if your life turns out to have been built on nothing but lies, it is as though it has not been real (Baggini, 2019), so truth, which is in part embodied by empiricism and logic, is of course an important attribute of Ellisian rationality. However, the notion of something being 'true' can also mean that it is 'straight' or is fitted, formed, or functions accurately. Thus, alongside the evidence and logic of a belief, we also consider the function of the belief in determining its rationality – what Wilson (2010) calls 'practical rationality'. It is important not to be too dogmatic regarding evidence and logic of a belief, and to recognise that unless the belief is currently undercutting, or is likely to undercut in the future, the client's goal pursuit, then we should question whether it should be disputed. We can help clients to strive towards disbelieving what they know to be false, using dysfunction as a key barometer. Also, in terms of 'truth' it is more useful to approach rational and irrational beliefs with the question of whether the belief *could* be true (i.e., falsifiability), rather than whether *it is* true or not. This offers a more objective view of truth and avoids irrational beliefs being endorsed merely because they are "true for me". For example, the demandingness belief of "I would like people to respect me, and therefore they absolutely must", *could not be* true. Indeed, one of the chief characteristics of irrational beliefs is that they *cannot* be true because they violate empiricism and logic. A demand ("I must") cannot legitimately, logically, follow ("and therefore") a preference ("I want"). As Pinker (2021) writes, "if anything lies at the core of rationality, it must be logic" (p. 12).

Readers who are not interested in the debate of what is and what is not 'rational' can be forgiven for looking away now, because the next section wades in to weeds of what could be meant by 'rational' and 'irrational' in REBT. I appreciate that this may be a bit of an indulgence, and as such, the casual reader could simply take as writ the distinctions offered by Ellis et al. (2010, p. 3) offered earlier in this chapter:

- **Rational beliefs**: Beliefs that are logical, and/or have empirical support, and/or are pragmatic
- **Irrational beliefs**: Beliefs that are illogical, and/or do not have empirical support, and/or are nonpragmatic

FUNCTIONALLY IRRATIONAL

So, are rational beliefs 'rational' because they meet logical-empirical standards, or are they 'rational' because they are self-helpful? And similarly, are irrational beliefs 'irrational' because they do not meet logical-empirical standards, or are they 'irrational' because they are self-defeating? It is of course possible for beliefs that are not consistent with reality to be functional, and beliefs that are consistent with reality to be dysfunctional. So how do we decide what is and is not rational when working with clients? I draw heavily on James Collard's brilliant 2019 article in the *International Journal of Cognitive Therapy* in what follows.

It seems for Ellis (and Beck) that logical empiricism (rational consideration of evidence) is important when considering the functionality of beliefs. But both also endorse a pragmatic truth criterion whereby "rational means self-helping and irrational means self-defeating" (Ellis & MacLaren, 1998, pp. 19–20). Beck offers a balanced approach whereby thought functionality can be assessed for both "its validity and/or utility" (Beck, 1995, p. 108). So, in the spirit of the "and/or" used in Ellis et al.'s (2010, p. 3) definition of rationality/irrationality, this of course means it is possible that thoughts that do not stand up to empirical and logical standards, can still be functional, and thus rational. As Collard (2019) puts it "while thoughts may be functional in many situations, they are not inherently considered to be functional under all conditions and at all times" (p. 129).

This stimulates some important implications about what we choose to challenge in our clients. If functionality is paramount, then disputing a belief because of its lack of empirical grounding or logic *alone* is potentially not the correct approach. In contrast, again if functionality is paramount, then a belief that has good empirical grounding and logic can be challenged if it is dysfunctional (self-defeating). If part of what makes a rational belief 'rational' is that it helps one function and healthily attain one's goals, then does this mean that non-empirically based and illogical beliefs should be promoted so long as they are healthy and helpful? The position I take is a balanced one that applies what the research evidence tells me about the downsides of irrational beliefs and the upsides of rational beliefs. The evidence that irrational beliefs are *unhelpful* for goal attainment and wellbeing, and that rational beliefs are *helpful* for goal attainment and wellbeing is copious (Turner, 2016b).

So, I end up in a position reflective of Robb and Ciarrochi's (2005) perspective, whereby I ask, "what can be believed?" and answer "Verbal things that actually help one accomplish one's goals" (p. 172), which excludes verbal things "which are contrary to empirical fact" (p. 172), because they are *unlikely* to help. To Robb and Ciarrochi's (2005) answer, I add the notion of temporality and health: *Verbal things that actually help one accomplish one's long-term goals whilst maintaining one's health.* I add temporality ('long-term') and health because one could justifiably use a fleeting self-statement such as "It would be terrible if I did not reach the finish line" that could inspire the necessary expending of additional effort at the end of 10k race, but not truly *believe* this statement or *take it seriously* outside of the race context. For me, beliefs are more stable, not fleeting, and are carried into and across many goal-relevant situations. I add health because goal attainment that sacrifices health reflects a poor (non-eudaimonic) goal to begin with and a rational belief should be in service of both, but health should take precedence...because it is precedent to human fulfilment. When I say human fulfilment, I do not mean success, money, trophies – I mean eudaimonia (see Chapter 8).

To elaborate on the above, perhaps a belief that is contrary to empirical fact is helpful for goal attainment, but emotional turmoil is experienced in pursuit of the goal. In contrast, perhaps a belief that aligns with empirical fact is unhelpful for goal attainment, but emotional turmoil is *not* experienced in pursuit of the goal. Which criteria do we use to distinguish rationality here? It cannot be function or emotionality, because goal attainment and emotionality suggest opposing valences (i.e., goal attained, but disturbed emotion vs. goal unattained, but non-disturbed emotion). Even though emotional turmoil is experienced, the goal is still attained, so is the belief functional?

So I pose these questions:

- Why would I promote a belief that is extreme, inflexible, false, and based on faulty logic?
- Even if an irrational belief is assumed by the client to be leading to goal attainment, why would I encourage them to entertain beliefs that are clearly out of synch with reality (as I and the client understand it)?
- By 'allowing' a client to hold beliefs that are demonstrably false, what down the line longer-term emotional issues and discontent might I be party to?

These questions are especially pertinent in sport, because clearly, goal pursuit and goal attainment are paramount, often at the cost of mental and physical health, as is becoming clear in the extant literature (Wolanin & Marks, 2019) and in the media (e.g., Thomas, 2021). As practitioners we have to ask ourselves, is it ok to encourage, or at least not dispute, a belief that is contrary to empirical fact or logic, even it appears to be helping the athlete to attain athletic goals, knowing that the belief could be problematic for health? The data are in – the weight of evidence indicates that irrational beliefs are deleterious (Turner & Moore, 2016), or at least concurrent (e.g., Turner, 2016b; Vîslă et al., 2016), to mental ill-health. Even if the irrational belief does appear to offer some momentary functional advantages, we should be very cautious and highly judicious in our decision not to dispute the irrational belief. Also, I believe I can help the client to 'get there' without the irrational belief. That is, we can help athletes in their performance and goal attainment with a huge panoply of cognitions, ideas, beliefs, psychological skills, that can be applied on a momentary basis, without turning a blind eye to irrational beliefs just because they appear to be helpful in some circumstances.

> It is undesirable to believe a proposition when there is no ground whatever for supposing it true. I must, of course, admit that if such an opinion became common it would completely transform our social life and our political system.
>
> Bertrand Russell

Contextual irrationality

My stance is that, unless the athlete has a sophisticated understanding of how beliefs can be used and abandoned contextually, then irrational beliefs *should not* be endorsed or left to run riot. That is, some athletes are capable of 'doublethink', which I cover in detail in Chapter 13, whereby they can hold and endorse two contradictory beliefs. Whilst they understand at a deep level that they do not "have to succeed" and that their performance "does not define their self-worth", they can use demandingness and depreciation in the service of performance acutely – rapidly and effectively abandoning that belief when they are outside of the competitive situation. These athletes can pick and choose their beliefs based on demonstrable situational utility, and some athletes report to me that the intensity and power of irrational beliefs make them useful in particular performance situations. As practitioners we have to tread carefully here, and make sure that athletes do not apply irrational performance beliefs to their lives *in general*, or take these irrational beliefs *too seriously*. I believe that some ideas are irrational regardless of who believes them. In other words, I agree with Wessler (1996) when he states that in REBT beliefs "are not divided into the categories of rational and irrational based on their relationships to empirical outcomes in an individual's life, i.e., according to their utility for the individual" (p. 46). I see utility in treating the irrational/rational beliefs of REBT as nomothetic, because I believe little can be gained long term from holding beliefs that are false, inconsistent with reality, rigid, and extreme. In cases where athletes are able to execute doublethink, my work with them is to try to get them into a position where irrational beliefs can be abandoned. No belief should be relied upon to produce a performance – in my experience, the best athletes are those who can find a way to attain their goals regardless of their internal dialogue.

But let me be balanced here and repeat Ellis' assertion, "beliefs that are scientifically warranted are *usually rational* in the sense that they *normally* lead to human survival and happiness – or at least *do so more often* than do unscientific, absolutistic beliefs" (Ellis, 1987a, p. 137). The italicised elements illustrate that it is not the case that *all* scientifically unwarranted beliefs are dysfunctional for goal attainment. This is clear by reading the REBT research literature, where although it is clear that stronger irrational beliefs (operationalised as false and illogical in most psychometrics) are robustly related to psychological distress, this association can be considered moderate ($r = 0.38$; Vîslă et al., 2016), and thus, irrational beliefs are not *always* deleterious psychopathologically. So, it is vital that we discursively ascertain with clients the extent to which their beliefs are harmful and unhelpful for their goals, hence the salience of pragmatic arguments in disputation (see Chapter 12), and Hank Robb's (2003) assertion that pragmatism is the "thoroughgoing, unambiguous 'truth test' for REBT" (p. 43). Robb (2003) adds, "Does it lead to your fulfilment? If not, it is irrational. If so, it is rational" (p. 43). It is also important to understand that in our C assessment, we are trying to ascertain the presence of UNEs or HNEs, and if a UNE is present, we can invite the client to unearth the roots of this UNE, opening the door to likely irrational beliefs. If a HNE is present, there is no case to answer, from a specific REBT point of view. So even at the assessment stage, function (and dysfunction) is central to the work we do.

Where do we land?

When one cuts through the debate concerning logical empiricism vs. pragmatism/functionality, I rest on this position: some beliefs encourage the healthy (undisturbed) pursuit and attainment of long-term goals – 'rational beliefs'; some beliefs encourage the unhealthy (disturbed) pursuit and attainment of goals – 'irrational beliefs'. Whilst it is possible that irrational beliefs in some cases offer some short-term advantages in acute performance situations, the potential longer-term costs of holding such beliefs outweighs the potential benefits. In REBT we try to help clients develop, strengthen, and implement rational beliefs, whilst challenging, weakening, and decommissioning irrational beliefs, in pursuit of their meaningful life goals. REBT, like second-wave CBTs per se, holds that mental health in part relies upon there being an interaction between a person's thoughts and an objective reality (Dobson, 2013). If we endorse *only* functionality as *the* marker for rationality, we potentially open clients up to believing all sorts of wacky and wonderful ideas that do not align them with the world as it is. But if we lose sight of or ignore the importance of functionality, we may miss opportunities to help clients utilise a vast range of cognitions for the healthy pursuit of their goals. I believe this diplomatic position offers the most options for helping clients, whilst remaining consistent and congruent with the GABCDE framework.

What are the rational and irrational beliefs of REBT?

In REBT, there are four core rational beliefs and four core irrational beliefs (see Ellis et al., 2010, for in-depth discussions). The rational beliefs are full preferences, anti-awfulizing, frustration tolerance (FT), and unconditional acceptance (self; USA, other; UOA, life/world; UWA). The irrational beliefs are demandingness, awfulizing, frustration intolerance (FI), and self, other, life/world depreciation/global evaluation (GE). The organisation of irrational beliefs has been subject to debate and enquiry. Ellis and Dryden (1997), and research both with non-athlete (DiLorenzo et al., 2007) and athlete (Turner et al., 2019b) samples, indicate that the secondary beliefs (awfulizing, FI, and depreciation) are derived from the primary (demand) belief. This is known as the "REBT-I Model" (DiLorenzo et al., 2007, p. 767) or as "Ellis' Model" (DiGiuseppe et al., 2014, p. 37). See Figure 9.1a,b for a diagrammatic representation of REBT-I Model. In essence, whilst demands contribute in important ways to emotional disturbance, they do so through secondary irrational beliefs which are more proximal to the disturbance. This REBT-I Model is also valid for relationships between rational beliefs and psychological health (Oltean & David, 2018). However, in line with many practitioners, the present author subscribes to the idea that all beliefs can underpin emotional disturbance and REBT can still be effectives even if the REBT-I Model is not adhered to

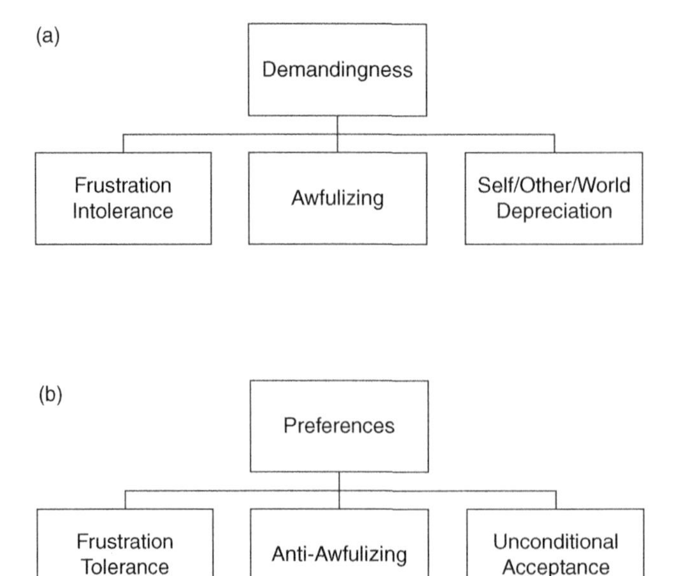

Figure 9.1 REBT-I model – (a) irrational beliefs and (b) rational beliefs.

(Şoflău & David, 2016). Treating the irrational beliefs as independent is known as "DiGiuseppe's Model" (DiGiuseppe et al., 2014, p. 38), and the practitioner should stick to theory as closely as they can, but recognise that both models might be useful and could depend on the client, and the context.

The way that I see the structure of rational and irrational beliefs in REBT is through a superordinate, subordinate, and basic system. *Superordinate* (high level, highly abstract) are the categories of "irrational" and "rational". *Subordinate* to each superordinate category are the core beliefs namely preferences, anti-awfulizing, frustration tolerance (FT), and USA, UOA, UWA (subordinate to "rational"), and demandingness, awfulizing, frustration intolerance (FI), and self, other, life/world depreciation/GE (subordinate to "irrational"). Then, at the basic level (low abstraction) are the specific articulated beliefs held by the client which are particular to either their Gs and/or As (e.g., "I want to, and therefore I must, play professional football", "being mistreated by my coach is not just bad, it is awful").

Prevalence of Irrational Beliefs

Why are beliefs important? Perhaps Mahatma Gandhi said it best:

> Your beliefs become your thoughts,
> Your thoughts become your words,
> Your words become your actions,
> Your actions become your habits,
> Your habits become your values,
> Your values become your destiny.

So, beliefs can shape your destiny, so we had better ensure that we adopt rational, functional, and healthy beliefs, if we want our destinies to be functional and healthy. But it is not just a smattering of people who hold irrational beliefs. Irrational beliefs, as presented in REBT, have been assessed and identified in many cultures (e.g., Columbia, Costa Rica, El Salvador, Spain, and the United States; Lega & Ellis, 2001, Germany; Michel-Kröhler & Turner, 2022, Hungary; Tóth et al., 2022, India; Chadha et al., 2019, Malaysia; Deen et al., 2017, Nigeria; Eseadi et al., 2019, Iran; Nejati et al., 2022, Ireland; Turner & Moore, 2016, Romania; David et al., 2002, Thailand; Chotpitayasunondh & Turner, 2019, Turkey; Artiran et al., 2019). In our own research in sport, we have found that irrational beliefs are prevalent across different sports and athlete levels (e.g., Turner et al., 2019b), even at the elite level. Thus, it cannot be the case that irrational beliefs *alone* preclude progression in sport – if this was the case, we would not see a prevalence of irrational beliefs in elite athletes. As is hopefully clear in this book, I am not evangelical about REBT or irrational/rational beliefs – I realise that predicting and supporting performance and health goes beyond REBT.

I developed an online profiling tool with Andrew Wood for the measurement and reporting of irrational beliefs, and hundreds of individuals across the globe have completed the profile (Turner & Wood, 2019b). Between September 2019 and January 2022, almost 700 people completed the 80-item profile, and data demonstrate (for the most part) a normative distribution indicating that most people report moderate agreement with irrational belief statements (scored on a 1–5 agreement scale) across demandingness, frustration intolerance, and awfulizing (see Figure 9.2). However, as you can see in the figure for depreciation, people score lower on average and thus data are skewed to the left (see Figures 9.3–9.6, for graphed data). This is consistent with data in research studies (e.g., Turner et al., 2019b), and perhaps indicates the extremeness of depreciation beliefs, such that generally people score quite low on it. Indeed, based on the data in Figure 9.2, the mode score is 1, indicating that most people "strongly disagree" with statements of depreciation. The population low score in depreciation does not make it any less pernicious though – most research in sport reports strong associations with psychological distress (e.g., Mansell, 2021).

	Demandingness	Frustration intolerance	Awfulizing	Depreciation
Mean (SD)	3.14 (0.64)	3.10 (0.71)	3.16 (.071)	2.44 (0.84)
Median score	3.19	3.15	3.22	2.42
Mode score	2.99	3.18	3.15	1.00
Minimum score	1.00	1.00	1.01	1.00
Maximum score	4.89	5.00	5.00	5.00

Figure 9.2 Descriptive statistics for profile data across the four core irrational beliefs.

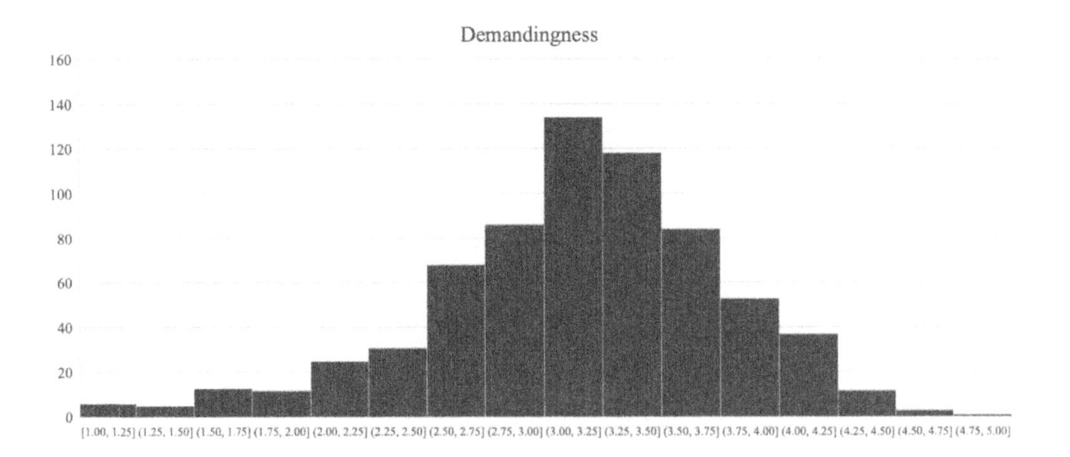

Figure 9.3 Demandingness profile data.

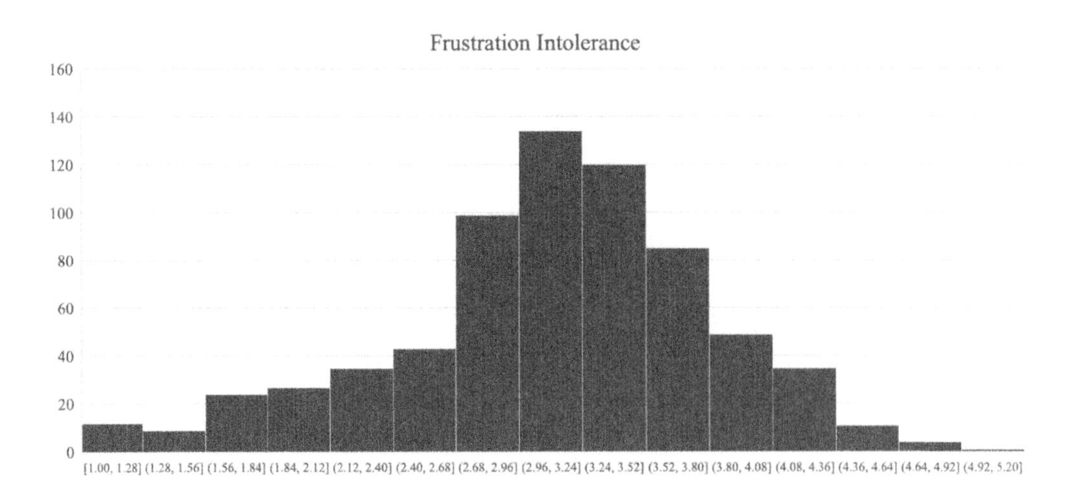

Figure 9.4 Frustration intolerance profile data.

Thus, if the question is 'do people have irrational beliefs?' then the answer 'yes', and data from across the field indicate that greater irrational beliefs are associated with, in particular, greater psychological distress (e.g., Vîslă et al., 2016). However, a far more interesting question is '*why* do people have irrational beliefs?'

> Some neurotic adults in our society are, in many ways, like the unsafe child in their desire for safety, although in the former it takes on a somewhat special appearance. Their reaction is often to unknown psychological dangers in a world that is perceived to be hostile, overwhelming and threatening. Such a person behaves as if a great catastrophe were almost always impending i.e., he is usually responding as if to an emergency. His safety needs often find specific expression in a search for a protector, or a stronger person on whom he may depend.
>
> (Maslow, 1943, p. 16)

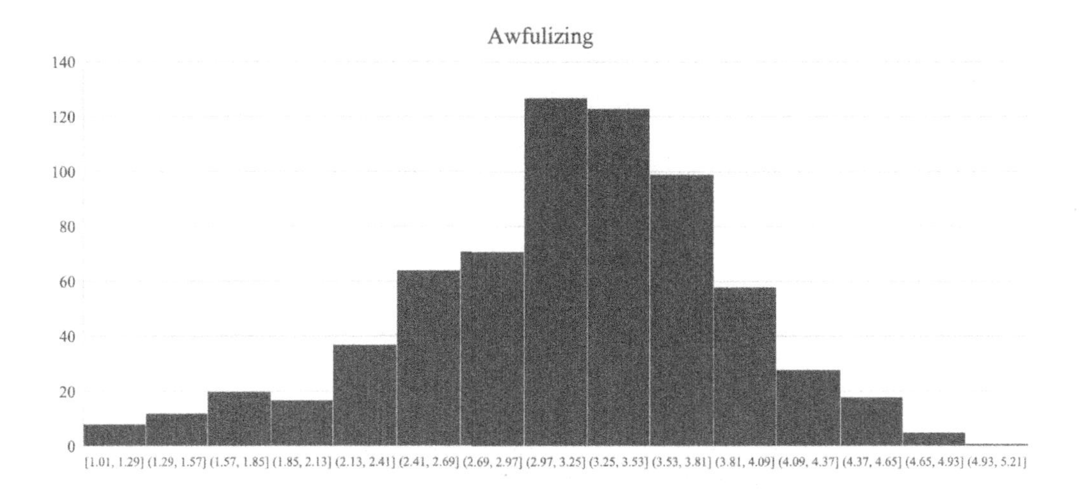

Figure 9.5 Awfulizing profile data.

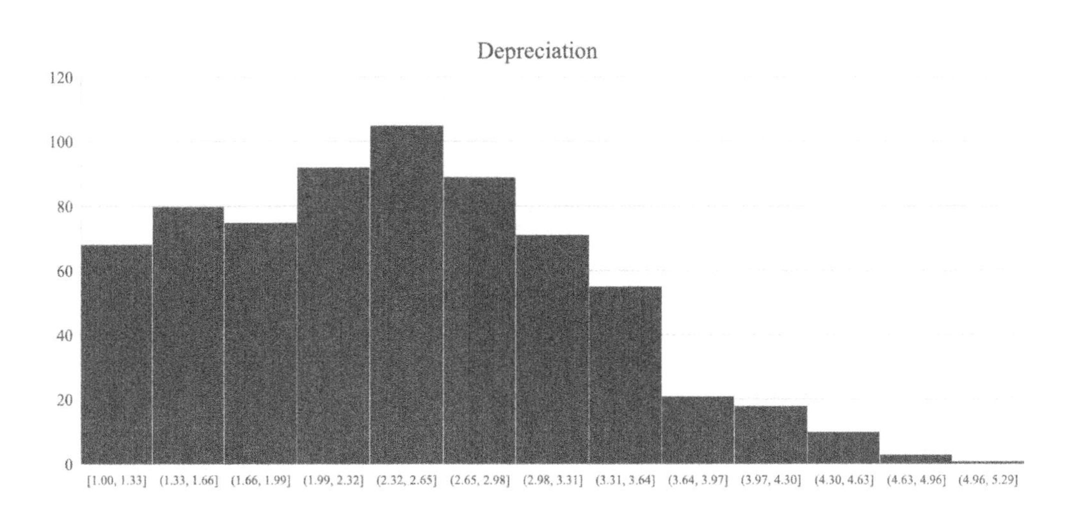

Figure 9.6 Depreciation profile data.

Why do we have irrational beliefs?

The statement from Abraham Maslow above indicates that irrational beliefs are in some sense particular to the 'neurotic adult', but Ellis believed that irrational beliefs (and rational beliefs) are universal across all human beings. Ellis (1976) believed that there was a biological basis (i.e., a genetic predisposition; Ruth, 1992) for human irrationality, evidenced by the myriad ways in which all humans think and act irrationally in their lives. He thought that most of these irrational beliefs are shaped by society (e.g., adverse conditioning and harmful upbringing), and that we hang on to them because we are biological predisposed to do so. Society plays an important role in encouraging and discouraging irrationality, with Ellis (1976) stating that,

> a good many of our main irrationalities have an important cultural component – or at least get significantly encouraged and exacerbated by the social group with which you reside. But a good many seem minimally taught; and many others get severely discouraged. They still ubiquitously flourish!
>
> (p. 32)

Ellis' core argument is that all humans at some point believe, think, and act in ways that are self-destructive, reflecting the illogicality of holding such beliefs, thoughts, and behaviours (Sharf, 1996). In other words, irrationality is endemic, innate, to the human experience, nurtured by societal influences, such as educational experiences, parenting, and engagement with media. Ruth (1992) offers an enlightening paper on Ellis' proposal that irrationality is innate. In the paper, Ruth makes it clear that for Ellis, irrational characteristics are quite easy to acquire and develop, but are difficult to modify or extinguish, and that irrationality is primarily innate, as opposed to primarily learnt. It is also clear that Ellis (1987b) believed that human beings needlessly disturb themselves and are *predisposed* to prolong their own mental dysfunctioning and resist giving up their irrationality.

> [there appears to be] inherent biological limitations of the human organism to think straight, and especially to think clearly and logically about his own behavior, for any consistent length of time.
>
> (Ellis, 1962, p. 378)

Society

Speaking to this previous point concerning the media, a day does not go by without the language of irrational beliefs being inappropriately injected into the reporting of world events by the media (if we believe what we read, the world is ending every week!) and it is especially noticeable in sport reporting. For example, Louis van Gaal (Manchester United Football Club manager) described a Boxing Day match against Stoke City Football Club as a "must-win" stating that "When you have lost three times in a row you need to win". He remarked "We have to focus on that match and we have to win that match". Manchester United lost 2–0, which apparently was a "must-win" (Sheen, 2015). We consume this media and unconsciously digest this language, shaping the way we view the world (e.g., Entman, 1989; Macey et al., 2014). The use of sensational language is more prevalent today that it was in the past, in part because of the competition for the readership of media consumers who engage with media in a transient and fleeting manner (e.g., Hendriks Vettehen & Kleemans, 2017). Hence, clickbait. Stories really need to grab our attention in a media market drenched in content, most of which is free to access and unsolicited by consumers (e.g., Twitter, Facebook). Indeed, sensationalism can be defined as content that is capable of provoking the senses, and eliciting attention and arousal responses in viewers (e.g., Grabe et al., 2001). Negative content is especially conducive to grabbing our attention (Lang et al., 1996; Soroka & McAdams, 2015). Indeed, distorted cognitions can orient or bias people's attention towards threat-relevant stimuli (Mobini & Grant, 2007; Wenzel, 2006). Therefore, one can summarise that sensational and irrationality-inflected media content would be particularly attention grabbing. This may go some way to explaining why irrational beliefs are also highly communicable, memetic, and consequently, scalable.

More broadly, societally, individuals operating within an environment in which irrational beliefs are prevalent are more likely to develop irrational beliefs (David & DiGiuseppe, 2010). Irrational beliefs are exacerbated by those around us to whom we look for guidance on how to live our lives (Sharf, 1996). I have proposed that sport propagates irrationality and A–C thinking (Turner, 2019a). Sport is a perfect environment for spreading and becoming entrenched in irrationality for at least five reasons:

1. Athletes are often recruited into clubs, and/or engage with organised sport, at a very young age. As such, their minds are very mouldable to irrational ideas, in part because they undoubtedly lack the critical thinking required to discern the irrational from the rational.
2. The sport environment is littered with adversity (A) because it is unpredictable, dangerous (psychologically and physically), and uncontrollable, and we as humans are limited and vulnerable. As such, sport is conducive to the triggering of irrational beliefs.
3. The importantising and aggrandising of goals (Gs) is commonplace, because there is a persistent belief that by presenting Gs (such as optimal performance) as 'do or die' or 'life and death', there is a greater chance of success (perhaps via the maximal expending of attention and effort).
4. Irrational language is memetic, and as such, is easily spread via coaches, parents, athletes themselves, and anyone else involved in the sport climate. Thus, an 'irrational climate' is likely to be created, maintained, and strengthened. To confound this, irrational language and ideas are often not challenged, rather, they are encouraged.
5. Sport can encourage the fusing of the self with one's athletic pursuits, such that a committed participant in sport can exclusively define their whole self as "an athlete" (i.e., strong athletic identity; Brewer et al., 1991). This makes them susceptible to global evaluation beliefs, which are underpinned by the definition of the whole self by one (or few) part ("I failed, so I am a complete failure").

Many sporting institutions appear to have an ethic of 'win at all costs', 'do or die', 'must-win', and 'devastating defeats'. Also, athletes, particularly young athletes, look to leaders in their sport (i.e., coaches, sport scientists, famous athletes) and outside their sport (i.e., peers, parents, teachers) to help guide them in their careers and lives (Knight et al., 2018) – if these leaders interact with these athletes in ways that are expressing of irrationality, then these athletes are more likely to develop similar irrationalities. For example, children with parents who report high levels of psychopathology and irrational beliefs report higher levels of irrational beliefs (Barlow et al., 2003). Learning irrationality through modelling those around us seems to be a feasible explanation for such irrational belief transaction (e.g., social learning theory; Bandura, 1977). See the work of Ailish King and colleagues (2022) for more discussion on the sociocultural impact of sport on athlete irrational beliefs.

Consider the below vignette, for example:

> Thomas is on his way to practice and is riding in the backseat of Dad's car. Suddenly, another motorist speeds past the car, takes over, and narrowly misses the front bumper. Dad explodes in rage "you complete idiot! What a bloody stupid idiot! You could have killed us!" he screams, as he honks the horn violently and manically.

What has Thomas potentially learnt from this incident? First, the other motorist caused his Dad's anger and aggression (A–C thinking). Second, that this encounter was unbearable for his Dad (hence the outburst). Third, people can be 'complete idiots' (other depreciation).

Forth, perhaps, cars are dangerous (which is not true – it's the people in them that cause the problems!) – but who knows whether this experience will colour Thomas' future car-based experiences – perhaps he will fear car travel. I don't want to make too much of this singular event, but imagine this happens in dozens of other situations where Dad is transgressed in some way. The repeated communication to Thomas that this emotional reactivity is appropriate will inform Thomas' views of the world (i.e., his beliefs) and his behaviour.

Alternatively, imagine a youth soccer coach on the side-line reacting to a poor decision (i.e., against what the coach wants!) made by the referee. The coach is running up and down the pitch maniacally yelling at the referee and kicking inanimate objects (e.g., water bottles) as she charges around the side-line. Onlookers, including the young athletes who are under her charge, can only presume that the referee's decision *made* the coach angry – that the actions of the referee *caused* the coach's emotions. This unnuanced A–C view of the world is easily transferred to young athletes because of the clarity and overtness of the A (referee decision) and the C (coach anger). The nuance of cognitive mediation (B–C) is not explicit in this event – the coach's cognitions cannot be seen by the athletes. It is through the language and behaviour of role models (e.g., parents, coaches) that young athletes learn how to view and interact with the world (including their performance environment). Coaches do not need to necessarily sit down with athletes and explicitly instruct them on how to think and believe – they can illustrate appropriate views of the world with their behaviour. By exercising behavioural control in emotionally provocative situations, coaches can illustrate and model to athletes that the situation does not necessarily automatically lead to or cause one's emotional reactivity. Rather, one can choose one's response. What a great lesson for a young athlete to learn. Coaches can model healthy negative emotions (HNEs) to A.

In simple terms, being around people with whom you relate can confer upon you their beliefs, ideas, and behaviours – thus – if you surround yourself with irrational believers who express this irrationality in speech and behaviour then you are more likely to develop and endorse irrational beliefs. In contrast, if you surround yourself with *rational* believers who express this *rationality* in speech and behaviour then you are more likely to develop and endorse *rational* beliefs.

It is in part because of the possible irrational socialisation that I, and others (Lukianoff & Haidt, 2019), are perturbed and concerned about some of the polices making their way into intellectual and occupational settings, such as trigger warnings, safe spaces, cancel culture, and de-platforming (e.g., Lizza, 2020). These practices seem so antithetical to the CBT philosophy – they teach people, who as human beings are already naturally predisposed to threat detection, that the world is dangerous and the way to avoid negative emotion amidst this danger is to remove threats rather than learn to cope with them. These practices also increase the threatening nature of adverse events by teaching that they must be avoided or stopped – why would one need to avoid or stop something if it was not dangerous? In one paper with trauma survivors Jones et al. (2020) found that trigger warnings (i.e., alerts about potentially disturbing forthcoming content) counter-therapeutically reinforced survivors' view of their trauma as central to their identity and that trigger warnings had no meaningful effect, and even a small increasing effect, on anxiety, which is in line with other research findings (e.g., Bellet et al., 2018, 2020). From an REBT perspective these findings make sense. They teach the A–C connection (the situation alone *causes* emotions), reduce emotional regulation options (one has to change A), and aggrandise the threatening nature of adverse events – all of which serve to increase emotional reactivity. In REBT we teach the opposite. We teach the B–C connection, rather than the A–C connection, expand emotional regulation options (see GABCDE framework), and seek to reduce the threatening nature of adverse events.

> Athletes, for example, navigate a complex social world of coaches, teammates, support staff, opponents, supporters (and non-supporters), the media, and of course friends and family. From these sources, athletes gather information about how to develop an athletic career through formal and informal communication and interaction, and since people are influenced by language used in communication with others and oneself, when imprecise language is used (such as the verbal expression of rigid, extreme, and illogical beliefs) this can augment imprecise thinking.
>
> (Turner, 2019a, p. 320)

Evolution

> During the course of human evolution, it appears quite possible that the process of natural selection might have operated on individuals who possessed certain cognitive tendencies, particularly tendencies to think both rationally and irrationally, because of the specific adaptive, reproductive, and survival advantages which these mechanisms facilitated.
>
> (Ruth, 1992, p. 9)

The above statement by Ruth (1992), who I lean upon in this section heavily, indicates that during the course of human development there might be something adaptive about rational and indeed *irrational* beliefs. Adaptive information, such as specific tendencies, are inherited by offspring through the transmission of genetically coded material. Organisms with adaptive traits were able to pass on their genes, and such, these tendencies proliferated in future generations. To be clear, neither Ellis nor Ruth suggest that specific irrational beliefs are genetically based, rather, that the *capacity* to develop and hold on to such beliefs may have a genetic basis, which are then strengthened and/or weakened through environmental (e.g., societal) exposure. From an evolutionary perspective, it might be that certain types of irrationality were beneficial, leading to adaptive reproduction and survival outcomes. In other words, it might be that irrational beliefs may have facilitated adaptive emotions and behaviours, helping to fulfil critical evolutionary goals (Ruth, 1992). Irrational beliefs may have, or would have once had, some adaptive value (David & DiGiuseppe, 2010). Although for our ancestors perhaps this irrationality may still have underpinned non-lethal conditions (e.g., anxiety or depression), humans may have nonetheless benefited from this evolutionary inheritance (Ellis, 1989; in Ruth, 1992). Also, even if anxiety and depression proved to be life limiting, the genetic material predisposing us to the capacity for irrationality would have been passed on before deleterious effects materialised.

The capacity for specific irrational beliefs in REBT might also have evolutionary roots that underpin the biological and cultural basis for irrationality. Irrational beliefs reflect a low-resolution over-simplification of the world that, it could be argued, make interacting with the world simpler and more efficient. This may have been especially the case in early humans where the instantiation of explicit dogmatic rules would have served us well in our fight for survival. For example, there was a time in our distant past when human existence was beset by great dangers and genuine and frequent existential threats to survival. We were preyed upon by bigger and stronger animals, had to fight for dominance with other early humans, and had to overcome great environmental shifts and diseases. We competed and fought (often literally) tooth and nail for status, resources, and reproductive opportunities (Alexander, 1987). Low resolution rules and ideas, leading to overt emotions that directed approach (i.e., aggression) and avoidance (i.e., retreat) behaviours may have been particularly important in the truly existentially relevant situations that would have been part of early human existence. As such, irrational beliefs may have evolved by design (Pelusi, 2003; Ruth, 1992, 1993) because the emotional and behavioural responses invoked as a result (e.g., anger, rage) may have been advantageous in solving existential problems for our early ancestors (David & DiGiuseppe, 2010; Gould, 2002).

In modern times, most danger is that which threatens the ego, rather than our existence, which is clearly a near miraculous happening, as life for human beings continues to improve. Life expectancy was 29 years old in 1800, and 71 in 2019, and poverty continues to decline (World Data Lab, 2022). Irrational beliefs appear more and more distinct from reason and logic, as the developments in human civilisation move us further from the need for dogmatic rules in order to ensure our survival. In other words, as we move away from our earlier primitive origins, our irrationality appears more so irrational within the modern context of relative safety and plenty.

One can imagine how important 'musts' would have been as a clear and simple warning to engage, or not engage, in an activity that may have had life threatening or life sustaining consequences. In the face of a big cat, snake, or bird, early humans will have been better off with the rule of "I must run away or else this will end in terrible disaster" rather than "I would like to run away, but if I don't it's not the end of the world". (Note: Of course, it is unlikely that early humans would have internally articulated these thoughts in precisely the manner expressed in the language of irrational beliefs, and I am taking some artistic licence here to get my point across concisely). This is life a death stuff. One can imagine that, "I must catch that antelope, or I will starve, and that would be unbearable" would have served us quite well. Or if our status were challenged by a rival, our demanding that the challenge must not occur (expressed inwardly or outwardly), and consequent forceful and aggressive action this may have recruited, could have helped to ensure that this status threat was eliminated (e.g., David & DiGiuseppe, 2010).

As discussed earlier, practical (or instrumental) rationality would have trumped epistemic (or factual) rationality (see Wilson, 2010 and Kelly, 2003, for a discussion), not least because factual rationality requires an enormous amount of information processing at an individual level, and an elaborate infrastructure associated with education and science at the societal level. These feats can flourish under conditions of high existential security, but they cannot survive otherwise, and thus the environment of early humans may not have been conducive to the pursuit and proliferation of factual rationality. As Wilson (2010) puts is, "It is unreasonable to expect people to invest their personal and collective resources on such activities when they feel, often for the best of reasons, that their very lives are at stake" (p. 70). Of course, evolution proceeds to increase the reproductive fitness of genes, not to increase human rationality (Stanovich, 2004), and thus, beliefs do not always track the world with maximum accuracy in order for fitness to increase (Stich, 1990). As Stanovich (2012) points out, evolution might not select out epistemic mechanisms of high accuracy if they are costly for organismic resources (e.g., attention, energy), echoing Wilson's (2010) above views. In other words, rationality might not have been a necessary a requisite of evolution, and "Mother nature is concerned with our survival, not with the emotional quality of our life" (Ellis, 2004, p. 12).

Ellis (1994) suggests that

> Tens of thousands of years ago humans who strongly believed and felt that they *had to* perform well, eat well, have sex, avoid pain, and kill off their human and animal enemies may have survived better in those rough days and borne more progeny than there more wishy-washy neighbours and relatives. If so, this would make them prone to black and white thinking.
>
> (p. 14)

Performance was not about medals and accolades; it was about survival (e.g., hunting, evasion) and reproduction. If you could not wield a weapon or tool effectively, or out-manoeuvre adversaries (animal and otherwise), your chances of survival were reduced. Socially too, being a social outcast was existentially relevant, since co-operation and resource sharing was important for survival. 'Billy no mates' would have become 'Billy no life' very quickly. Establishing and maintaining relationships with others would have been one of the most crucial tasks faced by our evolutionary ancestors (Leary & Cottrell, 2013). Thus, demanding beliefs relevant to social interaction ("I must be accepted by my group") were not based on a mere hedonistic preference or desire to fit in – it was a survival imperative. As such, *demanding* rather than just *preferring* probably had its evolutionary advantages (Ellis, 2002a). In a similar interpersonal context, one can imagine how the other-depreciation ("they are useless, evil, idiots") of potentially threatening members of an outgroup may have fostered ingroup bonding and helped to compete against those outgroup members for resources. We have a violent past, and the proclivity to demonise and then aggress against rivals would surely have been an important factor in our survival. The small group contexts in which our ancestors lived means that they were frequently in conflict with other groups, and as such, it was functional for them to view members of other groups as potentially dangerous (e.g., Brewer & Caporael, 2006; Navarrete et al., 2004). Indeed, social psychologists have found that people act more prosocially towards members of their own group (in-group) relative to those outside their group (out-group) (Abbink & Harris, 2019; Everett et al., 2015). This can include the expression of negative social preferences and derogation for outgroups (Hewstone et al., 2002), expressed through spite, and social preferences for negative outcomes for the out-group (e.g., Anderson & Putterman, 2006).

Of course, this hypothesising concerning irrationality is mostly speculative, and was recognised as such by Ellis (1994). But irrational beliefs and various other errors in thinking (e.g., black and white thinking, overgeneralising, discounting the positive) may have served adaptive functions. It is safer to think the worst ("it would be terrible, intolerable!"), because even if the situation turns out to be not as bad as one thought, you get to preserve your life and propagate your genes, despite the thinking errors. But if you do *not* assume the worst ("it would be bad but not terrible, and I could tolerate it"), then evasive or protective action is not taken with the energy and urgency called for by the existentially threatening event, and injury or death could befall you. It was better to believe in dogmatic and extreme ways, and live (despite some emotional suffering), rather than hold non-dogmatic and non-extreme beliefs, and die. Stich (1990) writes that,

> a very cautious, risk-aversive inferential strategy – one that leaps to the conclusion that danger is present on very slight evidence – will typically lead to false beliefs more often, and true ones less often, than a less hair-trigger one that waits for more evidence before rendering a judgment. Nonetheless, the unreliable, error-prone, risk-aversive strategy may well be favored by natural selection. For natural selection does not care about truth; it cares only about reproductive success.
>
> (p. 62)

Assumably, it would have been a good idea to not only think in this risk-aversive and 'quick and dirty' way, but also to pass this thinking onto those around you for whose welfare you cared about (and depended upon). Even before this thinking was articulated in language, observing the behaviour of those around you would have intimated dogmatic and extreme rules. Observing the desperation of a kinsman or kinwoman being attacked by a rival tribe, or predatory animal, would have surely been enough to imbed behavioural rules about survival. In the interest of simplifying the environment, "I must not be caught off guard by a big cat" or "I must always have a weapon with me when foraging, hunting, or scavenging" could have been proliferated through behaviour, demonstration, and possibly instruction. We can connect with this idea quite easily – if you have ever witnessed a fellow human being in a life-threatening situation, it takes very little to create a dogmatic rule that might help you to avoid the same fate.

> If an individual believes that one "must" and "should" mate, that one absolutely "needs" to address this urge, and that one "deserves" and is "entitled" to complete fulfillment, then this individual would probably feel more compelled and lustful, and engage in sexually related behaviors and strategies more readily, than another individual who did not believe, or believed less, in such ideas.
> (Ruth, 1992, p. 13)

If the commandments of the Old Testament (Deuteronomy 5:6–21) portray anything about the development of civilisation, which they might do, then it is difficult not to notice that eight of them are characterised by 'shalt nots' (or 'absolutely should nots'). For example, prohibiting murder, theft, adultery, and lying, would have been vital rules in our volatile past. In the modern age, we see these commandments as moral dictates, but it is easy to imagine how, in early humans, rules like this would have been necessary to maintain the integrity of a group – with dissolution of the group implicating survival. These rules must have been important for early humans, lest they would not have been canonised in such a way that communicates their primacy – they were written in stone (Exodus 34:1)! The author is not a practising Christian, but does recognise the formative importance of biblical works, and the potential that these works are to some extent a literary articulation of human societal development.

Irrational beliefs are problematic in the modern age in part because they are applied to contexts in which the ego is at stake, rather than one's actual existence. Therefore, although irrational belief tendencies may have been adaptive for early humans, they might not be so adaptive for most humans in contemporary society (Ellis, 1989; in Ruth, 1992). It is the incongruence between the extremeness of the belief and the non-extremeness of daily events that make irrational beliefs so harmful. It is the conversion of our preferences into demands that is troublesome, because in the modern age there are very few genuine musts, and life's 'must haves' and 'must dos' are not in jeopardy for most of us (e.g., air, water, food). Thus, it is possible that irrational beliefs are a vestige of our relatively pre-civilised past in which daily existence was beset by threats to procreation and survival. When these irrational beliefs are applied to the modern condition of our existence, they are out of synch and inappropriate, and when used in this context, make existential threats out of non-existentially threatening stimuli.

Of course, Ellis' biopsychosocial arguments apply to irrationality *and* rationality, in that both have a biological basis (e.g., genetic) and both are subject to socialisation. The advantages of rationality are perhaps more intuitive and obvious given that as a society we do value rationality more than irrationality. But our early ancestors may have benefitted from rationality both in terms of environmental problem-solving and interpersonal connection. Whilst being aggressive and vigilant to threat will have been important for survival, so will have been the capacity to step back and calmly analyse and plan. Those able to demonstrate logic and pragmatics will have been invaluable in assuaging potential harm, and those able to use collected knowledge (i.e., empiricism) to shape future action will have been able to solve many existential issues for themselves and their kin. A group member with world-acceptance may have been better able to acknowledge the existential reality to allow for problem-solving and planning – not burying their head in sand. Indeed, Samar et al. (2013) found that greater rationality and lower irrationality was related to greater conscientiousness and openness. In other words, it may have been useful for a group to have somebody around that is dutiful and hardworking, who one can trust to execute certain tasks, and also imaginative and curious, who one can seek out and utilise important information. It seems that greater rationality is conducive to these two characteristics. If we view personality as a set of evolved psychological mechanisms developed in reaction to the problems faced by our ancestors (e.g., Michalski & Shackelford, 2010), then associations between rationality and personality might be enlightening with regard to what psychological factors may have increased the survival and procreation of our ancestors.

Also, individual survival will have been determined in part by one's ability to bond with members of one's ingroup. It is likely that a group member who is emotionally stable, can solve problems, and is more balanced in their approach to interpersonal communication would have offered great value to a group and would have been more accepted as part of that group. The most consistent associations between irrational beliefs and personality indicates that great irrationality is related to poorer emotional stability (Blau & Fuller, 2006; Davies, 2006; Sava, 2009) and less agreeableness (Samar et al., 2013; Sava, 2009; Spörrle et al., 2010). Having individuals within the group that are willing and able to cooperate and conform to group norms would be advantageous for group affiliation, organisation, and coordination. Furthermore, a group member who demonstrates other-acceptance (in-group) may have been better able to foster relationships. Indeed, whilst human beings possess adaptations to seek acceptance, we also have adaptations to reject individuals who are judged to be poor relational partners and group members (Leary & Cottrell, 2013). Your individual survival may have depended on your ability to act as a group member.

Ultimately, the duality of rationality and irrationality, the fact that they are not orthogonal, means that when we are thinking about the function of rational/irrational beliefs we need to consider the 'functional for what?' question. Both no doubt will have had their utility – and even today, there are of course times where irrational beliefs are helpful, for example, in a genuine life or death situation (where acute survival behaviours need to be recruited rapidly). Ellis (1994) is certainly aware of the fact that irrationality is not harmful for all people under all conditions. This is why in assessing clients we must try to determine the extent to which irrational beliefs are self-defeating for the client before we charge in and dispute. In REBT, we are not on a blind mission to eradicate all irrationality.

The idea that both rational and irrational beliefs may have had utility to our early ancestors expresses the importance of population individual differences (if we were all the same, we would not be adaptive as a species), but also the importance of the individual (and/or group) being able to express and enact both rationality and irrationality, depending on the context. Linking again to personality, there are costs and benefits to dispositions characterised by the five-factor model of personality (McCrae & Costa, 1987), and therefore interindividual variation may have been advantageous thus explaining the ubiquity of variation (Nettle, 2006). Human evolutionary development notwithstanding, the weight of evidence in modern times indicates that if you are interested in being healthy whilst attaining your goals, rational beliefs are more supportive of this endeavour compared to irrational beliefs.

Here and now

Ultimately, Ellis did not believe that irrational beliefs are formed in a vacuum, absent of social influences, but he did believe that irrationality transcends environmental and cultural differences (Ellis, 1962, 1976, 1980a, 1987b). In a candid exchange with a client, Ellis (1962, pp. 176–177) recognised the social genesis of the client's irrational beliefs:

AE: By telling yourself these catastrophizing, utterly false sentences at point B, you bring about, yes, literally bring about results at point C.
CLIENT: Doesn't my early upbringing have anything to do with this at all?
AE: Yes it has something to do with what you're telling yourself at point B, because obviously you weren't born thinking this nonsense at B, and you must have learned it somewhere.

Then Ellis, in a true REBT manner, rests the responsibility (not the blame) onto the client:

AE: The main and much more important thing is that you continued for the last 15 years or so to tell yourself the same kind of false statements that you were originally taught to say and it is your reiteration of those statements that now keeps them alive and perpetuates the illogical things you are telling yourself at point B.

So, regardless of where a client's particular beliefs came from, or how they came to believe in ways that are self-defeating, it is their tendency to reinforce, rehearse, and preciously hold onto these beliefs that is problematic in the present (and possibly for the future). Thus, whilst in REBT we recognise the influence of the past on client issues, we focus our solutions on the present by encouraging clients to take responsibly for holding onto their false beliefs, and choosing to abandon them (or not).

WHY DO HUMAN BEINGS HOLD ON TO IRRATIONAL BELIEFS?

Ellis (1994) noticed that we hold onto irrational beliefs even though they are harmful, and he used this logic as partial evidence for the innateness of irrational beliefs. But aside from a possible evolutionary biological hangover, if irrational beliefs are so bad for humans in the modern age (e.g., deleterious for health and fulfilment), why do they continue to proliferate? Also, once we have irrational beliefs, why do we not just ditch them instantly owing to their fallacious and harmful properties? Well, not only are there biological and broader societal aetiologies for holding irrational beliefs, there are more tangible and practical reasons too. That is, there might be self-serving and pragmatic motives (conscious and unconscious) that make holding onto and expressing irrational beliefs resilient to challenge and extinction.

For example, it is often the case that we get swift and positive feedback for expressing irrational beliefs out loud, either to ourselves or to people around us. When we vociferously and enthusiastically express that "I can't stand it when this happens", "this is worst thing ever", or "I'm such a stupid idiot for doing that" we experience a cathartic release from the expression of what could have been suppressed. This catharsis should not be confused with the extinguishing of the emotion however, for which catharsis seems not to be an effective strategy (e.g., Scheff, 2007). But it does undoubtably feel good in the moment to 'let it all out'. In social settings, with friends and family, for example, the expression of irrational beliefs can garner sympathetic behavioural reactions from those in ear shot of our extreme utterances. When we describe our day as "awful" or engage those around us in a tale from work about an "evil" boss or "unbearable" situation, we may elicit attention from those around us (DiGiuseppe et al., 2014), who may offer emotional support by way of an arm around the shoulder or a kind word such as "it will be ok". They may also side with us against the "evil" boss as a display of unity. In this way, by using the language of irrational beliefs around friends and family, we can (knowingly and unknowingly) manipulate and control them. This feels good – people listen to me. I have the power to elicit attention, sympathy, and allegiance merely by expressing my irrationality. By using such evocative, sensational, and exciting language, I can almost guarantee their attention – what kind of person does not jump to their friend's aid when they have experienced something "terrible"? I could get used to this attention, so I continue to express myself in this irrational way, as a conditioned response to hardship.

In contrast, it could be the case that our irrational utterances and verbalisations are met with challenges and disputes from people around us who are astute enough to recognise the falseness of our inferences. Close friends and peers might perhaps be less likely to challenge and dispute, opting for pacification by agreeing with you whilst lending a shoulder to cry on. But teachers, coaches, psychologists (!) might be able to intervene with the utterance sensitively, strategically and helpfully, encouraging you to try to think more rationally, and to step back from your inferences and asses them for their accuracy and utility. In REBT terms, those around us could instigate inferential A change and B change informally as it were (one can dream…!). Depending on who they are, they may also be able to inspire and support actual A change, if you are in a situation in which physical danger is likely, for example. So, if we take a balanced perspective, it is possible to see that there are many reasons for why irrational beliefs *expression* might be self-serving in a social context.

As well as other-manipulation, irrational beliefs also facilitate self-manipulation. If I can convince myself that not only is the interview important, not only do I want to perform well, but I *must* perform well and not doing so would be the *end of the world*, I force myself to perform well through the expression of great attention and effort. Theoretically, that is. If I demand that what I want must be so, I constrain the possibilities and engage in a delusion of increased odds. If it must happen, then there is zero chance that it won't happen. Also, by considering the consequences of failure as "awful" and "unbearable" and tethering the outcome to my self-worth ("I would be a failure if I failed") then I force myself to care about the performance to the point where it is existentially relevant – which it almost never is, of course. In other words, by applying dogmatic and extreme rules to our pursuits, we desperately try to force the self and the world to comply with our desires, which *might* bear fruit from time to time. One could also make the opposite argument, that holding the belief that you are "worthless" or "useless", you could justify withdrawal of effort in achieving your goal(s) (Backx, 2012) – as a form of learned helplessness – what is the point in trying, when I will only fail on account of me being a failure?

Ellis (1994) also offers some pragmatic reasons as to why we may endorse, or at least not abandon, our irrationality. Take other-depreciation, for example ("because they acted badly, they are a completely bad person"). Although condemning people leads to much human harm, the anger and rage that it might inspire no doubt can motivate a fight against incompetence and injustice. Whether or not this approach to righting the wrongs of the world is the correct (or most effective) way to go about change notwithstanding, this incensed rage adds excitement to our lives and may provide all-consuming meaning and purpose. This can help us to feel good and noble and can successfully distract us from our own inadequacies. Regardless of the potential palliative benefits though, and whilst rage may have been important for our early ancestors, in modern times other-depreciation and the rage it often underpins can be recruited for malevolent purposes which could actually lead to human annihilation. The social consequences of out-group other-depreciation ("they are evil, bad people!"), for example, could lead to extreme polarisation and fallacious and disadvantageous out-group rejection and violence.

In terms of frustration intolerance (FI), Ellis notes that although this belief underpins much human misery, "it also comforts and pleasures" (p. 133). By believing that there are things you cannot bear, you may actually intelligently, creatively, and energetically work to eliminate those things from yours and your loved ones' lives. Your intolerance of frustration may help you to push yourself to create a better and more enjoyable means of surviving, a task that you may find challenging, engaging, enjoyable, and rewarding. Thus, you may continue to perpetuate FI because you see it as a necessary motivator for life change and betterment. There are of course many reasons as to why irrational beliefs are less than beneficial in the *modern age* – they are life limiting and potentially pathological – but we cannot discount that sometimes for some people this irrationality could have some benefits.

As another example of a potential benefit, irrational beliefs reflect an oversimplification of the world that could help us to process the vast amounts of information that confronts us on a day-to-day basis. Because irrational beliefs lack the nuances of rational beliefs, they provide an easy and efficient way to make sense of the world, and direct behaviour. Because irrational beliefs are clear, narrow, and dogmatic, they are not easily confused and indeed are rather explicit in there meaning. Let's face it – the language of demandingness is perfect for rulemaking as the word 'must' leaves nothing to the imagination. The problem is, as easy as irrational beliefs are to understand and assert, they are also not reflective of how the world actually works. Applying musts to the world does not ensure compliance, unless enforceable conditions are attached to the demand. For example, although most societies have a law against theft, people still steal. But no law would propagate a dictate of "we would prefer you not to steal". In law, the rule that you must not steal is not based on a preference of not stealing – it is a conditional must; an explicit rule; a socially conscious moral imperative. Your freedom and moral integrity is conditional on you not committing theft (I cover conditional musts in the next chapter). Unlike the law of gravity, or the first law of thermodynamics, there is no universal law of nature which stipulates that everyone must treat us well and that our environment must always be agreeable to us (Murguia & Díaz, 2015).

So irrational beliefs offer a clear and concise way to interact with the world. Michael Shermer (2011) suggests that once beliefs are formed, we look for confirmatory information to support the beliefs, which when found, reinforces the beliefs. Thus, we enter the beliefs into a positive feedback loop. For example, on approach to an athletic performance, when we apply "I must succeed in the upcoming competition" and succeed in the match, we fortify the belief with the 'evidence' that when we believe in this way, we succeed. But we ignore and forget all those times when "I must succeed" was applied and we did *not* succeed. Shermer (2011) states that, "Facts of the world are filtered by our brains through the coloured lenses of world view, paradigms, theories, biases etc, we have accumulated through living. Then we select those that confirm what we believe and ignore those that contradict our beliefs" (p. 43). This is in part why belief systems are powerfully pervasive and enduring, because they shape (or bias) the way we perceive the world and evaluate what happens to us. Thus, as has been discovered by many REBT practitioners, including Ellis, "The majority of our most deeply held beliefs are immune to attack by direct educational tools, especially those who are not ready to hear contradictory evidence" (Shermer, 2011, p. 5).

In sum, clients who deeply hold irrational beliefs are committed to their ipsedixitisms for a variety of reasons; in part biological, in part evolutionary, in part societal, in part habit, in part hedonistic and self-serving. As such, working to reveal the irrationality of these beliefs to the client, and then extricating them from this way of thinking, is not an easy task, and I cover disputation (D) in detail in Chapter 12.

Belief as behaviour

> We don't believe something by merely saying we believe it, or even when we believe that we believe it. We believe something when we act as if it were true.
>
> (Dallas Willard, 2021)

It is important to recognise that so far in this chapter irrational beliefs have mostly been conceptualised as lexiconic, as language articulated in speech and/or thought. But beliefs can also be expressed through behaviour, and Ellis was keen not to separate out beliefs, emotions, and behaviours, and the interdependent GABC(DE) framework speaks to this interconnectedness. So in working with clients, we can ascertain the prevalence of irrational beliefs in how the client expresses their beliefs when we work to reveal them, but we can also asses their behaviour as a clue to their irrationality. In other words, whether or not the client reveals and articulates irrational beliefs, we can ask 'does the client act irrationally?' and/or 'does the client's behaviour indicate irrationality?' We can gather useful information to this end when we are assessing C – if UNEs are present then there is a likelihood that irrational beliefs are also present.

In addition, we have to be cognisant of the client's typical way of being, by that I mean their action tendencies, in the face of As. When thwarted, does the client cower, avoid, withdraw? When transgressed do they aggress, attack, hit out? Does the client operate within a very strict way of being? Do they appear to live by very rigid sets of principles? Do they have a tendency to act out suddenly in extreme ways? The information collected from these questions all give *clues* to some underlying irrationality within client. These clues can steer further enquiry about deeply held beliefs. We might take this approach when a client is not forthcoming, or has not become aware of their irrational beliefs. Perhaps they are unable or unwilling to articulate their irrational beliefs. That is, we are not assuming irrationality based on reactivity to As or expression of Cs, but are using this information to engage the client in further enquiries as to their beliefs and philosophies.

We can challenge the client a little too, in order to reveal beliefs that the client has perhaps not realised or engaged with declaratively. For example, "so you *say* you *can* tolerate failure, but you *act* as if you *cannot* tolerate failure. Why might this be?" Or, "you are *telling* me that the situation is *not awful*, but you are *behaving* in a way that would suggest that it is. What do you think about this contradiction?" I am not trying to catch the client out here, I am merely assessing the client more fully by employing logic and Socratic questioning. To be clear, I do not *want* to reveal irrational beliefs in the client, but I am going to assess whether irrational beliefs are present and salient to the client's problems as rigorously as possible.

One of my favourite examples of belief-behaviour incongruence assessment comes from Robb (2003, p. 38):

> ...if I were to ask a client how to get out of my consultation room and they pointed to the door and said, 'Through the door', but then attempted to actually leave by walking through the wall, I could explain that their behaviour showed they did not actually believe what they had said.

So, behaviour can betray self-reported beliefs. But also, we can act in ways that do not align with our beliefs due to contextual and social factors. I might believe that "I cannot stand it when the coach is disrespectful to me" but when I suffer disrespect from the coach in a team setting my behavioural reaction is one of passive acceptance. Just because I decide not to behave in an intolerant manner, does not mean that I actually accept this disrespect, but it does mean, from a therapeutic perspective, that as a practitioner we can use such instances to demonstrate to clients how their experiences are often not in-line with their irrational beliefs. It is not every time that a person with frustration intolerance beliefs acts intolerantly to the adversity that triggers their frustration intolerance. So, whilst beliefs and behaviours are related, there are many reasons as to why we cannot assume a client is reporting either of these factors as accurately as we would like. In other words, we cannot always infer the belief from the behaviour, and vice versa. So when working with clients, it is important to not assume that just because they are tolerating adversity that they automatically have frustration tolerance beliefs. Also, frustration intolerance might manifest in behaviour temporally disassociated with the triggering adverse event. For example, an individual might be mistreated at work but direct their intolerant actions (e.g., aggressiveness or distemper) at home towards loved ones even though the loved ones had nothing to do with the triggering event.

What irrational beliefs are *not*

Some thoughts and beliefs are for sure negative and potentially unhelpful for goal attainment, but do not qualify as irrational by REBT standards. For example, in my view thoughts like "I will never succeed" and "They will always hate me" are not irrational because they are unfalsifiable and untestable – it is not possible for me to know whether or not you will succeed or whether or not you will always be hated. These two examples do not fulfil the criteria for the four core irrational beliefs, and are better considered as cognitive distortions (they could also be As), that whilst are not irrational beliefs (in part because they could be true), are usually unhelpful in the service of the athlete's goals (e.g., "I'll never play for my country because I am just not a good enough player"). Whilst cognitive distortions are a key part of Beck's cognitive therapy (CT) rather than REBT, research has demonstrated that irrational beliefs represent core and intermediary beliefs that lead to specific automatic thoughts (cognitive distortions; Buschmann et al., 2018; Şoflău & David, 2016). In practice, I would work with the deeper irrational beliefs underpinning these cognitive distortions first, and then address (e.g., cognitively restructure) these cognitive distortions if needed. Or if applying general REBT, I could address these cognitive distortions forthrightly if irrational beliefs were not present or relevant, or if time was of the essence.

It is important to understand that negative thoughts can serve an adaptive function, as well as a maladaptive function, and thus we cannot apply rigid standards like "I must not think negatively". Rather, when it comes to negative thoughts such as "I will never succeed", I help the client to understand whether and to what extent the thought is helpful in their goal attainment, but not before we address underpinning irrational beliefs about success. For example, perhaps the thought "I will never succeed" will inspire some dedicated strategic planning on the athlete's part in order to ensure that this premonition does not become reality. Therefore, it is within the remit of REBT to address negative non-irrational thoughts, which can be underpinned by irrational beliefs. In REBT we do not invalidate negative thoughts per se, but we do devalue them if they present as barriers to psychological health (Beck & Haigh, 2014; Ellis 1994). In REBT we teach acceptance of negative internal events and apply scientific and utilitarian standards to those internal events to ensure that thoughts, ideas, beliefs, are consistent with provable reality, and above all, functional in pursuit of eudaimonia.

A FINAL WORD ON INTELLIGENCE

> Practically all the irrationalities...hold true not only for ignorant, stupid, and severely disturbed individuals but also, for highly intelligent, educated, and relatively little disturbed persons.
>
> (Ellis, 1976, p. 30)

An important point to make before I move onto looking at each of the rational and irrational beliefs in the next chapter, is that rationality is not a proxy for intelligence. There are many examples of intelligent people thinking and acting irrationally, just like there are examples of unintelligent people being rational (e.g., Dysrationalia). This is confounded by, as Michael Shermer (2011) notes, the fact that, "Smart people believe weird things because they are skilled at defending beliefs they arrived at for non-smart reasons" (p. 43). Ellis and Harper (1975) state that REBT is

> showing reason, not foolish or silly, sensible, leading to efficient results for human happiness, producing desired effects with a minimum of expense, waste, unnecessary effort, or unpleasant side effects; helping to achieve the individual and social goals that you strive for.

Intelligence is not explicitly implicated here – and nor should it be. Indeed, there is some evidence that intelligence does not predict CBT outcomes (e.g., Doubleday et al., 2002; Haaga et al., 1991). Thus, practitioners should not let the presumed or apparent intelligence, or lack thereof, of their clients dictate whether they decide to apply REBT with a client or not, but rather, should adapt their REBT approach for the idiographic characteristics (including intelligence) of the client (Dryden, 2009a).

SUMMARY

In the current chapter I have tried to communicate the nature of beliefs in REBT, including the background for rationality as codified by Ellis. I also discussed the presence and proliferation of irrational beliefs, and the potential evolutionary and societal development of rational and irrational beliefs. I suggest that we have rational and irrational beliefs due to evolutionary and societal factors, and may hold onto irrational beliefs for self-serving reasons and because we have a tendency to defend our beliefs (no matter how faulty). Beliefs are more than their articulation in speech and thought, and a behavioural view of belief is encouraged. With the background of beliefs and rationality considered, I now move on to detailing the specific rational and irrational beliefs of REBT.

CHAPTER 10
The rational and irrational beliefs (B)

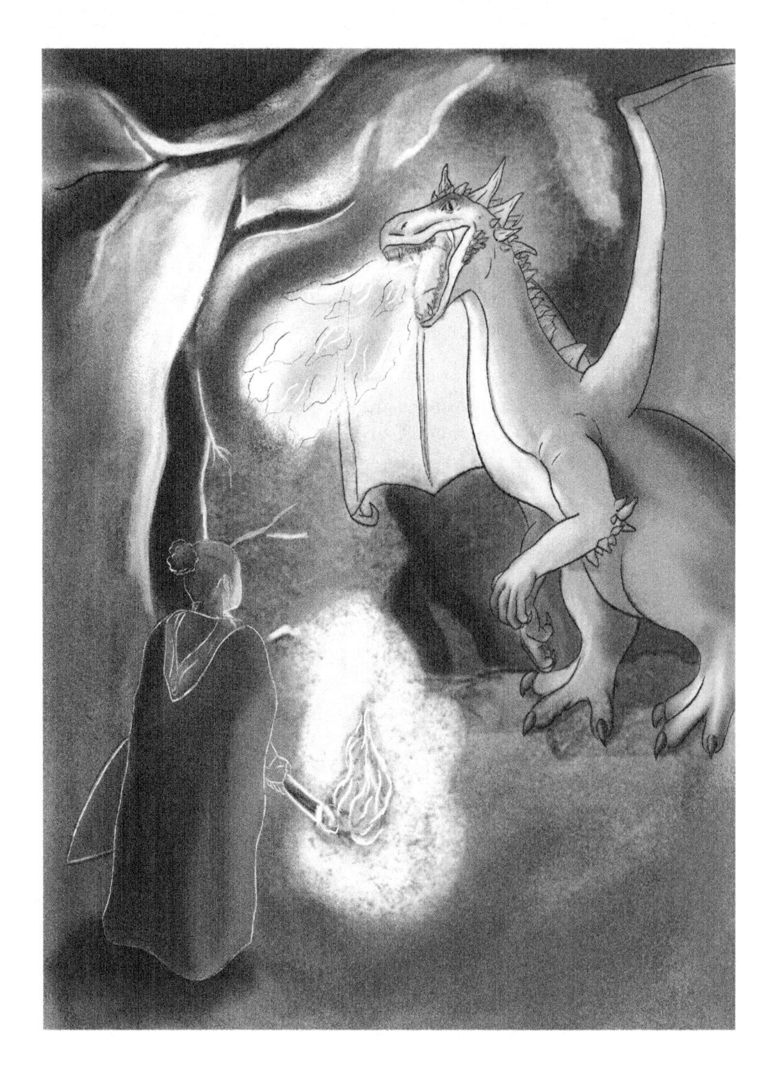

Who dares?

DOI: 10.4324/9781003200437-11

My aim in this chapter is simply to introduce and detail the four core irrational/rational beliefs of REBT (see Figure 10.1 for some brief examples). I move through each belief pairing thusly:

- Demandingness (e.g., "I want to achieve my goals, and therefore I absolutely must") vs. preferences (e.g., "I want to achieve my goals, but that does not mean that I must").
- Frustration intolerance (e.g., "I cannot tolerate being treated unfairly") vs. frustration tolerance (e.g., "Being treated unfairly is difficult to tolerate, but I can certainly tolerate it, and it is worth it to do so").
- Awfulizing (e.g., "underperforming is not just bad, it is truly awful") vs. anti-awfulizing (e.g., "underperformance is bad, but certainly not *awful*").
- Depreciation (global evaluation) (e.g., "because I have been deselected from the team, it shows that I am a completely worthless person") vs. unconditional acceptance (e.g., "being deselected from the team is not ideal, but it does not make me a worthless person – it just shows that I am a fallible human being, just like all other human beings").

Figure 10.1 Client irrational beliefs.

DEMANDINGNESS VS. PREFERENCES

> In Brazil, we always have to win, everybody knows that. It's too much pressure.
>
> Júlio César (goalkeeper, 87 caps for Brazil)

In light of individual goals, people's desires first include partial preferences (e.g., DiGiuseppe et al., 2014; Dryden, 2009a; Ellis et al., 2010) such as "I want to perform well in things that matter to me". A full rational preference belief would be "I want to perform well in things that matter to me, but that does not mean that I must". For a full preference, a negation of the demand is present. This is important because the practitioner needs to know whether the preference is merely a preference, or whether the preference is a precursor to a demand, for example, "I want to perform well in things that matter to me, and therefore I must". That is, people's desires first include wishes and preferences ("I *want to* perform well") but then may also include absolutistic demands ("I *have to* perform well"). So, the architecture of a full rational preference includes the preference and the negation of a demand, whilst an irrational demand (demandingness) includes the preference transformed into a demand (Dryden, 2009a). This delineation is not trivial. Often the athlete will express a partial preference and the demand is implicit. It is our job as the practitioner to elucidate whether the partial preference is just that, or whether a demand is being applied to the preference.

Demandingness is where one turns a preference into an absolutistic demand (Armstrong, 2017). By turning "wants" into "musts", which are exaggerated and unrealistic (Ellis, 2003b), secondary irrational beliefs can quickly follow (e.g., "I want to and therefore I must succeed, else it would be unbearable, and I'd be a useless loser"), which contributes to unhealthy patterns of emotional and behavioural functioning. In REBT, it is when people escalate preferences into demands that UNEs are more likely to occur (Ellis et al., 2010). Human desires are usually healthy and productive but demands (musts, have to's, absolutely shoulds, needs) are often unhealthy and destructive. Ultimately, we are asking, "does a demand logically follow from a preference?" and we are answering, "no, it does not" (e.g., Still, 2010). Ellis (2002b) points out that it is strong desires rather than weak desires that we are more likely to apply demands to. For example, "Because succeeding is so important and desirable for me, then I absolutely must succeed". Ellis (2002b) describes this transferring of wants to musts as grandiose and perfectionistic, because obviously I don't run the universe, so whatever I desire, no matter how strongly I *want* it, doesn't *have to* exist.

A good example of separating 'want' from 'must' is apparent in an interview given to Sky Sports by Jurgen Klopp (Manager of Liverpool Football Club, English Premier League Champions 2020) about an upcoming (important) match against Manchester City Football Club. Here is an excerpt:

INTERVIEWER: Given where you are in the table, the gap is six point right now, you're the team leading the table. For you, is it more of a 'must not lose' as opposed to a 'must-win' game?

KLOPP: (laughing) I am sorry, it is because maybe there are other people who are smarter than me and can see it this, I don't see it like this. For me its 100% a *want to win* game.

INTERVIEWER: *Want* to win…

KLOPP: (nodding head) *Want* to win. 100% with all I have, and erm, this must win 'must' thing I never understood because that doesn't change the chances.

Klopp goes on to reaffirm that "we want to win, and we try everything we can make that happen, which is difficult enough". This philosophy does not appear to have done him any harm, despite the importance of the match (he got a 3-1 victory in the match, and won the premier league title that season).

Transferring a preference into a demand is an example of a non-sequitur, where a conclusion does not follow logically from a previous statement. So, "therefore I must" does not logically follow on from "I want to succeed". Just because you want to succeed, does not mean that you must. Thus, demanding what you prefer is not consistent with reality – it is just not how the world works. Indeed, the "essence of psychological health in REBT theory is rational acceptance of reality" (Ziegler, 2003, p. 28), so beliefs that are inconsistent with reality, i.e., to demand that things be as one would like them to be, is a non-starter. To hold non-sequitur beliefs is to abandon the Stoic ideal of living in accord with reason. Whilst of course it makes sense that an athlete would want to be competent, respected, valued, etc., demanding that they must be competent, respected, valued, etc., (a) does not make it more likely, (b) propels these 'wants' into existential necessities, thus exacerbating the emotional consequences of facing inevitable barriers (As) to these desires, and (c) is empirically false, since there is no rule or empirical law that dictates they 'must' get what they want (Still, 2010). Dryden (2019a) points out that, if the demand "I want X to happen and therefore it must" were true, then it would be impossible for X *not* to be happen, but of course it *is* possible for X not to be happen. In other words, "if something, as a matter of fact, absolutely must, or had to be, a certain way, then that is the way it would be. The *fact* that it is not that way proves the assertion is wrong" (Robb, 2003, p. 36). Athletes who demand success on the basis of their desire to succeed only need to reflect for a few seconds before they can recall a time when they have not succeeded, thus undermining their demand.

> It's an important moment. But it's a game of football, a game we've worked hard to prepare for and a game, if we win, can give us a very good start to our qualifying campaign…But after 36 years the words "must win" leave me rather cold. Most teams go on the field wanting to win. I don't know how you achieve a "must win" other than going out to try and play.
>
> Roy Hodgson, England soccer team manager 2012–2016 (Lawton, 2012)

Resistance to change

Perhaps most importantly, demandingness is considered to be at the very core of psychological disturbance (Dryden, 2019a). Despite the evidence that demandingness is associated with psychological distress (e.g., Turner et al., 2019b; Vîslă et al., 2016), challenging demandingness (musts, have to's, got to's) is a little bit controversial in sport settings. It is a difficult task, with some athletes and coaches, to suggest to them that they do not "HAVE TO" succeed, because it can seem like succeeding is the *only* thing that really matters in sport – so as an athlete or coach, why would I not demand success? Many athletes that I have worked with have held irrational beliefs about competing in sport for as long as they can remember, and many elite athletes have been competing since early childhood (depending on the sport). So, the idea that demandingness is irrational is not an easy pill to swallow for many athletes, even if this belief is evidently hindering their wellbeing and performance. Even when an athlete is clearly in distress because of this belief (and associated As), they can still hold onto their demandingness very tightly. As such, disputing demandingness is better achieved carefully, tactfully, but at the same time, resoundingly. You can leave no doubt in the athlete's mind as to why demandingness is problematic (if it is indeed problematic), and therefore the use of all possible disputation arguments is needed (more about this in Chapter 12 of this book), applied in a collaborative and rigorous manner, like a joint investigation into the validity of demandingness. If you threaten the athlete by too quickly and flippantly rejecting their demandingness, the athlete may nod and agree that the belief is irrational, but will not even achieve intellectual insight (learn arguments for and against iBs and rBs but do not give up iBs and do not believe rBs), never mind the superior and strived for emotional insight (take responsibility for C, and commit to the ongoing challenge of iBs and rehearsal of rBs; e.g., DiGiuseppe et al., 2014).

Conditional vs. unconditional musts

The disputation of demandingness is the source of much misconception surrounding the use of REBT in sport (Turner, 2016b). The REBT practitioner is not on a crusade to destroy all "I must succeed" beliefs, because some demands are 'conditional', whilst some are 'unconditional' (Dryden, 2009b). This is an important distinction because there are legitimate uses of the word 'must' and there are illegitimate uses too. Conditional musts are usually not the targets of disputation in REBT, but unconditional musts are. Ellis (2002a) recognised that *musts* can have some advantages because they could underpin additional effort expenditure over and above the effort expended on a *want*. Conditional musts can be healthy and productive because they accord with reality and may help to attain a goal. Conditional musts realistically account for the probable and real-world consequences of not getting what you want – they are accurate generalisations about the real world that can motivate you. For example, "If I do not work hard, then I probably won't succeed like I want to, so I *have to* work hard to increase my chances of success" or "I must get a place in the team or else I might not be as successful as I want to be" or "we must win the final to be champions". Unconditional (absolutistic) musts do not accord with reality, are unhealthy (emotionally, behaviourally) and hinder goal attainment. Unconditional musts unrealistically imply you must get what you want *just because you want it strongly*, leading to unrealistic overgeneralisations, and bringing about additional distorted/irrational beliefs that reflect the potential consequences of not getting what you want. For example, "I really want to, *and therefore I must*, succeed and if I did not succeed it would be terrible, unbearable, and would mean that I am a complete failure" or "I would so like to get a place in the team, and therefore I absolutely have to, and if I did not succeed it would be the end of the world, I could not stand it, and it would mean that I am a worthless person."

> By making your strong desires into "necessities" you tend to sabotage rather than aid in the achievement of your goals.
>
> (Ellis, 2002a, p. 18)

The present author, alongside many others I imagine, have admittedly in the past mistakenly pursued the disputation of a conditional demand because I didn't fully assess the belief, and missed the fact that the must was being applied conditionally. So, perhaps an example would be useful here. An athlete remarks that, "we must win this game to get the three points", so the REBT practitioner does not challenge them on the irrationality of their utterance. This inference is a logical sequitur, since there is no way to get three points unless the game is won. In other words, this belief accords with a social reality and could be productive (Ellis, 2002a). Another example: an athlete says, "I have to get physically fitter over the summer break, so I can hit the ground running in pre-season". Again, this is not challenged or taken as demandingness, in part because it might be the case that to have a good start to the next season the athlete simply must get fitter. In both examples there is a logical and reasonable condition (to get three points, or to hit the ground running) that underlines the demand. A demand that is unconditional and transferred from a preference ("I want, and therefore I must" = demandingness) is considered to be irrational.

Now, if the athlete is exhibiting a UNE about winning the game, or getting fitter, then it is worth exploring whether there is an *unconditional* demand (demandingness) behind the conditional demand. "The reason or purpose behind a person's conditional 'must' may be an unconditional 'must' in its own right" (Dryden, 2009b, p. 72). 'Musts', especially in sport, can be complicated by multiple conditions that make complete logical sense, and should not always be disputed if one is applying REBT correctly. By erroneously disputing "I have to get fitter over the summer break" you may actually harm the athlete's chances of performing well in the pre-season.

More complicatedly, let's say an athlete believes that "I must wear my lucky socks in order to play well". This would meet the structural and lexiconic criteria of a conditional demand and therefore does not appear to be technically irrational – my playing well is conditional on wearing my lucky socks. So, what do we do here? It is important to recognise that statements like this are logical non-sequiturs, since there is no direct (provable) causal link between 'lucky socks' and playing well, outside of a placebo effect. Part of helping athletes to develop a rational approach to sport is about encouraging scientific thinking and dissuading dogmatic, inflexible ritualistic beliefs. Other examples of conditional musts that are nonsensical include "I must be perfect to play at this level" or "I must give 110% effort to stay in the team". Both statements are lexiconic examples of 'conditional musts', but being perfect and exerting over 100% effort are impossible. However, and very importantly, if these beliefs, conditional or not, are evidently not hindering goal attainment or leading to client suffering, then it is questionable why a practitioner would be focussing on these beliefs as a point of intervention (i.e., disputation, cognitive change) in the first place. Whilst I would not actively encourage such nonsensical beliefs with my clients, and would for sure question the veracity and utility of such beliefs if I became aware of them, I would rarely structure an intervention around them unless they were leading to dysfunction.

No 'buts'

Musts tend to be more problematic if they are derived from a preference. It is the 'want' becoming a 'must' that is self-destructive and dysfunctional and defines "demandingness". Preferences align with our goals, which makes sense because humans tend to move towards that which we desire. But when that which we desire becomes a demand, a must, a have to, the consequences of not getting what we desire becomes a perceived existential threat, and thus is too much to bear, is awful, and shows that we are failures. So, we approach the desire with desperation and panic, and when we don't get what we want, we understandably become emotionally distressed. Dryden (2012c) suggests that a partial preferential belief (e.g., "I really want to be selected for the team") followed by "but I do not have to be" can be considered a full preferential belief. But if the partial preferential belief (e.g., "I really want to be selected for the team") is followed by "and therefore I must be", then this reflects the belief's transformation into demandingness. By making sure the client states the full preferential belief, not just the partial preferential belief, we make it unlikely that demandingness will occur. In other words, don't just let the client articulate a preference without negating the demand.

So, when working with demandingness, the practitioner should consider the preferential derivation of the demand, the conditionality of the demand, and relatedly, the logical validity of the condition if one is present. Ellis (2002a) suggests that irrational, unconditional musts contain no 'buts', whilst rational preferences have 'buts' either stated or implied – "I would like to be selected, but I do not have to be". Irrational demands are absolute – no buts. I encourage practitioners to consider four questions when distinguishing demands:

1. Is the demand absolute (no buts)?
2. Is the demand based on a preference (I *want and therefore* I must)?
3. Is the demand conditional (in order to y, I must x)? If there is a condition, is the condition logically valid (x evidently leads to y)?
4. Is the demand helping or harming goal attainment and/or fulfilment?

If the answers to these questions are yes (a), yes (b), no (c), and 'harming' (d), then it appears that the irrational demandingness belief in question is a very good candidate for disputation (D).

> You are leading the US Open, so what? There is 500 million people watching on TV, so what? If I ever felt myself getting out of that what mattered, what was going to impact hitting a good golf shot, my attitude was, so what? And I think that when it came to the moment on the 18th tee, it was like yeah you've got a great chance to win the US Open. So what? I accept that golf is a game where you are gonna win some, you are gonna lose some.... I knew that *this didn't HAVE to be my time*.... I've accepted I'm gonna win majors, and I'm gonna lose some majors.
>
> Justin Rose about his 2013 US Golf Open win (Ashworth, 2015) (emphasis added)

Frustration intolerance (FI) vs. frustration tolerance (FT)

> Losing, I can't stand it. I can't stand any aspect of it. The taste in your mouth is terrible.
>
> J.J. Watt (American Football player) after a 41-28 defeat to the New England Patriots

Frustration intolerance (FI) beliefs are where a person holds an extreme belief that they cannot stand, tolerate, bear, the adversity they are facing, have faced, or will face (Dryden, 2019a). For example, an athlete might believe that "I cannot stand being left on the bench for the match" or "I can't bear the coach treating me unfairly, its just too tough". In contrast, frustration tolerance (FT) beliefs are where a person holds a flexible belief that it is difficult to tolerate the adversity they are facing or will face, but they can tolerate it and it is worth it to do so (Dryden, 2019a). For example, an athlete might believe that "It is difficult to tolerate being left on the bench for the match, but I can tolerate it and it is worth doing so" or "It is tough to bear the coach treating me unfairly, but I can bear it and it is worth it to do so".

Dryden (2019a) also indicates that FT involves being willing to tolerate the adversity, but the current author suggests that there is an important difference between "I can tolerate" and "I will tolerate". In sport, it might be important to hold a belief that "I will not tolerate the coach treating me this way" *alongside* "I can tolerate the coach treating me this way". In other words, although I *can* tolerate the ill treatment, I chose not to. This *will* to, and *will* not to, tolerate adversity could be functional especially, for example, if the athlete perceives potential abuse from a coach, or a fellow athlete. There is a difference between the ability to tolerate, and the will to tolerate, and athletes should certainly work on their ability to tolerate ALL adversities, but retain the choice to not tolerate adversity (e.g., "I *can* tolerate you treating me this way, but I *will not* tolerate it"). This enables remonstration and activism if appropriate. The fact that the athlete *is* tolerating something is evidence that they *can* tolerate it, but *is* and *can* do not mean *will* or *ought*. This really comes back to an earlier point in this book about changing A. Of course, at times in REBT we can encourage clients to change the situation they are in (or avoid particularly dangerous situations), in other words changing actual or concrete A. But clients will be more equipped to change A if they approach this A change rationally, whereby they are thinking, feeling, and behaving in a functional manner. You can better assert yourself with a transgressor if you are not boiling over with rage (or unhealthy anger). In relation to FT, successful A change might include believing that you *can* tolerate A, but choosing not to tolerate it by taking action to change A.

FI beliefs are non-sequiturs, in the sense that just because something is difficult or tough, does not mean that it is intolerable. Just because an athlete is finding a situation to be difficult or frustrating (i.e., adverse), this does not mean that they *cannot stand* it or *cannot bear* it. It might be the toughest thing they have ever faced, it still doesn't qualify the extreme FI belief. Indeed, often people report that they "cannot stand" what they do not like (DiGiuseppe et al., 2014). When a person holds an FI belief, they believe that if what they desire does not happen, they will die or disintegrate, and or will lose their capacity to experience happiness (Dryden, 2019a). FI beliefs are also clearly factually or empirically false when used to describe past or current adversity. The lack of evidence that an athlete cannot tolerate a past or current adversity lays within the fact of their continued existence made apparent by their presence at the REBT session. In other words, evidence for the FT belief, and against the FI belief, is confirmed by the fact that the athlete is sitting before you, and has obviously tolerated the adversity, on account of them not being deceased. For FI that concerns future adversity (e.g., "my coach is going to scold me for not resting, and I can't stand it when that happens"), the athlete only needs to spend a minute or so recalling tough (perhaps similar) situations of the past to realise that they have stood equal or worse adversities, and are thus capable of standing the upcoming adversity (real or imagined).

One of my favourite articulations of FT comes from George Orwell's 1933 book *Down and Out in Paris and London*. In part 1 of the book, Orwell recounts living in near-extreme poverty in Paris, and remarks (pp. 16–17):

> These three weeks were squalid and uncomfortable, and evidently there was worse coming, for my rent would be due before long. Nevertheless, things were not a quarter as bad as I had expected...there is another feeling that is a great consolation in poverty. I believe everyone who has been hard up has experienced it. It is a feeling of relief, almost pleasure, at knowing yourself at last genuinely down and out. You have talked so often of going to the dogs – and well, here are the dogs, and you have reached them, and you can stand it. It takes off a lot of anxiety.

Is it worth it?

A hallmark of FT beliefs is the notion that the adversity is worth tolerating. It is of course more than likely that by tolerating the adversity the athlete will grow and develop, finding meaning in the adversity that would be unexplored if they were not faced with the adversity. Human beings are capable of tremendous antifragility (Taleb, 2012), which is the property to increase capability and thrive as a result of stressors. I take the stance that whether and to what extent the adversity is worth tolerating is down to the athlete to decide (we can of course help with the decision); lest the athlete push themselves into situations that could result in actual harm. But this should not allay efforts to work towards FT beliefs. Even if the adversity it not worth tolerating (e.g., tolerating the adversity is not advantageous for goal attainment or wellbeing), it is still a good idea for the athlete believe that they *could* or *can* tolerate the adversity if they chose to. That is, it is advantageous to believe that you are capable of tolerating an adversity, whether you decide to tolerate it or not. Indeed, FT beliefs are in part underscored by the belief that you have a choice to tolerate the adversity or not (Dryden, 2019a). By believing that you cannot tolerate the adversity, you are markedly reducing your ability to tolerate it even if you choose to do so, in the spirit of self-defeatism and self-fulfilling prophesy. Non-tolerance reduces one's behavioural repertoire down to avoidance, escape, and attack. Tolerance makes possible engagement, assessment, assertive approach, but also leaves the door open to avoidance and escape if necessary.

FI and anger

Tolerance in FT is not the same as resignation. By helping an athlete to develop high FT I do not encourage them to lie down and roll over at the sight of tough or difficult to tolerate adversity. On the contrary, by developing FT the athlete can take the proper steps to remonstrate or act against a potential wrongdoer in an appropriate and assertive manner, driven by healthy anger rather that unhealthy anger and rage. Of course, rage has its place and was probably useful from an evolutionary perspective (Ellis, 1994), but is no way to conduct oneself in the pursuit of athletic goals or eudaimonia. Research concerning FI indicates that it is positively associated with aggressive expression of anger (Martin & Dahlen, 2004), reduced anger control (Moller & Van der Merwe, 1997), poor social adjustment (Watson et al., 1998), addictive behaviours (Ko et al., 2008), anxiety, depression, and dysfunctional affect (Harrington, 2005a, 2005b). After slapping comedian Chris Rock on stage at the 2022 Oscars Awards Ceremony, Will Smith stated, "My behaviour at last night's Academy Awards was unacceptable and inexcusable. Jokes at my expense are a part of the job, but a joke about Jada's medical condition was too much for me to bear and I reacted emotionally" (BBC News, 2022). "Too much to bear" seems to be especially conducive to anger, a notion that is supported in non-sport (e.g., David et al., 2002) and sport populations (Turner et al., 2019b). There is also a particular link drawn in the literature between high FI and high procrastination (Ellis & Knaus, 1977). Evidence indicates that individuals with discomfort intolerance are more likely to procrastinate on boring, difficult, or demanding tasks (Milgram et al., 1988); which are potential demand characteristics of athletic training and competition, and which are likely to undercut achievement potential (Wilde, 2012). As such, helping athletes to address (challenge and weaken) FI is an important undertaking to the extent that FI underpins emotions and behaviours that can hinder goal attainment.

FT and the pursuit of excellence

For athletes in particular, developing FT believes is important amidst the myriad pain, discomfort, rejection, and failure they face as ubiquitous features of a meaningful athletic pursuit. Believing that you can tolerate these adversities, whilst rationally recognising that they are indeed very tough to tolerate and as a fallible human being you may experience suffering, is a useful, perhaps indispensable, form of barrier self-efficacy (Bandura, 1997). As Michael Jordan (basketball legend) famously said:

> I've missed more than 9000 shots in my career. I've lost almost 300 games. 26 times, I've been trusted to take the game winning shot and missed. I've failed over and over and over again in my life. And that is why I succeed.

He also said that, "Obstacles don't have to stop you. If you run into a wall, don't turn around and give up. Figure out how to climb it, go through it, or work around it" and, "If you quit once it becomes a habit. Never quit!"

These examples from Jordan speak to a commitment and willingness to tolerate certain difficulty and discomfort, and underline the importance of helping athletes to aim for meaningful goals. Taking on the pursuit of a truly meaningful goal will often necessitate the tolerance of much adversity, making tolerance of difficulty and discomfort worthwhile and infused with meaning. If the athlete's goals are not meaningful or ennobling, then there is little reason to tolerate the adversities that appear to thwart goal pursuit. The fulfilment of potential is only achieved through tolerance of difficulty and discomfort; that is in part how we know our goals are meaningful. So not only is FT expressed through articulated beliefs ("it is tough, but I can bear it"), it is also expressed through voluntarily taking on difficult and demanding tasks that could bring about negative emotions. FT can also be expressed through the willingness to fully engage in premeditatio malorum, staying with the adverse image and tolerating the inner discomfort that it begets. Helping an athlete to learn that they can stand discomfort can help them face adversities more functionally, take greater risks, and work harder to maximise their productivity (DiGiuseppe et al., 2014).

Semantics

One of the more interesting features of FI is the commonness of the language that describes it, in everyday conversation. This is where the practitioner needs to be cautious and be sure that when an athlete or coach utters "I can't stand it when…", that we don't jump the gun and assume that they are vocalising an FI belief. For example, an athlete might say,

"I can't stand it when my teammate ignores me at practice" to which we could ask, "When you say, 'I can't stand it', what do you mean here?" The athlete might reply, "I mean, it's difficult to take. I hate it when that happens" (not FI), or they could say, "I mean, its unbearable, I just can't stand it!" (FI). So, with FI it is important to explore the semantic aspects of "can't stand" to ensure that the athlete is indeed transferring something evaluated as "difficult", to a more extreme evaluation of "intolerable". Relatedly, often an FI belief is expressed by remarks such as "it's too tough" or "it's too difficult" where the FI is implied buy not explicitly stated as an "I can't stand". Again, careful questioning here can reveal whether FI or FT is being held by the client.

> If it's endurable, then endure it. Stop complaining.
>
> Marcus Aurelius

> Nothing happens to anyone that he can't endure.
>
> Marcus Aurelius

Stretching FT

Finally, how about issuing a challenge to the athletes we work with to stretch their FT? Perhaps we can ask athletes, "just how much can you tolerate?", "if you worked at it, and really focussed your energy on it, how much tolerance could you develop?", or "why don't we try to find out just how much you can tolerate, before we assume what you can or cannot tolerate?" I bet that you can tolerate more than you think you can. This is not to say that we should encourage athletes to throw themselves into dangerous situations or stoically (small 's') enter into brutal environments just to test and develop their tolerance. But it does mean that we can encourage athletes to take on reasonable challenges that start to push the boundaries of their tolerance. In other words, this is not a call to accept or encourage athlete burnout, but is a suggestion to enable athletes to take on the heaviest weight they *can* carry, and work on *bearing* it, making use of the value placed in a meaningful and sustaining goal. The goal has to be sufficient and worthwhile enough to sustain them and fortify them against the inevitable suffering experienced in pursuit of that goal. This does not mean sacrifice everything in the name of hedonistic glory, as it could be that the biggest load you can carry is raising a family, doing good in your community, lifting those around you out of destitution. Tolerance can be heightened incrementally by pushing yourself, then resting, pushing yourself, resting.

> I've learnt a million things from the day and the years that have followed it…the biggest thing being that when something goes wrong in your life, it doesn't finish you.
>
> Gareth Southgate (Manager of the England Mens Soccer Team, talking about his penalty miss in the 1996 European Championships; Wallace, 2018)

AWFULIZING VS. ANTI-AWFULIZING

> This is not the end of the world. We conceded a goal near the end, and it felt like the end of the world, but it is not the end of the world…I hope I'm not the only person in the stadium who thought: 'This is not the end of the world.' We can work on this…Of course, it is not the best moment for us, because we wasted a lot of energy. Southampton haven't lost away from home, so we had to work hard…You score the goal and you want to win, but it didn't happen for us today. Football is not a fairytale. Sometimes we can write stories like this but it doesn't always happen.
>
> Jurgen Klopp after failing to win in his first three matches in charge of Liverpool Football Club (Agence France-Presse, 2015)

Awfulizing; a belief that the adversity is *so* bad, that it couldn't be any worse (Dryden, 2019a). For a person holding awfulizing beliefs, the adversity is not only bad, but is the worst thing they can imagine. For example, an athlete might believe that, "it would not just be bad, it would be absolutely awful if I was not selected for the game" or "it would be completely terrible, not just bad, if my teammates rejected me". In contrast, anti-awfulizing beliefs are when a person believes that the adversity it is *not* awful, despite perhaps being bad (or perhaps *very* bad); this 'bad' event it is *not* the worst thing they can imagine (Dryden, 2019a). For example, an athlete might believe that, "it would be bad if I was not selected for the game, but certainly not awful" or "it would be inconvenient if my teammates rejected me, but not terrible". Awfulizing is not to be confused with 'catastrophizing', because in REBT awfulizing is an irrational belief whilst catastrophising is a cognitive consequence (Dryden, 2012a). Awfulizing reflects the irrational belief that nothing could be worse, the event in question is 100% bad or worse, no good could possibly come from this bad event, and this event cannot be transcended or surmounted – the event is awful, terrible, the end of the world (Dryden, 2019a). Awfulizing is about "believing that unpleasant or negative events are the worst they could conceivably be" (Neenan & Dryden, 1995, p. 9). In contrast, catastrophising is a distorted cognitive consequence that reflects "a tendency to over-estimate a perceived threat and the corresponding seriousness of its impact" (Waltman & Palermo, 2018; p. 44). It is more reflective of over-estimating the likelihood that something bad will happen, over-estimating how bad it will be or is, and underestimating one's ability to cope with it (Craske et al., 2014; Gellatly & Beck, 2016). In other words, awfulizing is more extreme than catastrophising.

Awfulizing is irrational because it is extreme – it does not allow for the fact that there are things that *could* be worse than the current adversity. Awfulizing is also inconsistent with reality because we cannot prove that the adversity is awful – we can prove that the adversity is bad, it might be very *very* bad (e.g., it might tangibly impede a goal), but we cannot prove that it is more than 100% bad. Just because something is really *really* bad, does not mean that it is awful (Dryden & Branch, 2008). Anti-awfulizing should not be thought of as casually minimising the badness of a very negative event (e.g., "it's not that bad!"), rather, it shows that nothing is truly awful in the universe (Dryden & Branch, 2008). Importantly, the practitioner and client need to be on exactly the same page when it comes to semantics surrounding awfulizing. What does the client mean by "awful" or "terrible"? Do they mean "nothing could be worse", or do they mean "very very bad"? If it is the later, then the client might not be awfulizing, but they could be catastrophising. In helping clients to articulate awfulizing, to aid clarity it is useful to have them include the recognition that the event is *beyond* bad, prior to asserting its awfulness (e.g., "the situation is not just bad, it is awful").

Where is your belief getting you?

For many athletes, the distinction between awfulizing and anti-awfulizing is academic and pointless, especially when they are experiencing emotional disturbance. Let's take, for example, an athlete who becomes injured and is told that their career is over by the team doctor, due to the injury. Whilst the athlete would understandably evaluate the adversity as really bad, and averse to their goal of fulfilling their potential as an athlete, they may also apply an extreme awfulizing evaluation to the adversity, taking it from 'really bad' to 'awful', 'terrible', where 'nothing could be worse'. But of course, it *could* be worse (e.g., they are still alive!), and thus the adversity is not truly "awful". However, this is where the practitioner applies empathy and tact. There is little benefit here in disputing the awfulness of the adversity whilst the athlete is in the midst of undoubted turmoil, where one could *understandably* describe the adversity as "awful". Trying to convince the athlete the adversity is not as bad as they think it is, or not as bad as it possibly could be, is a less than helpful strategy in this situation (DiGiuseppe et al., 2014). The misconstrued and assumed mistreatment of awfulizing beliefs has bolstered some of the misplaced criticisms of REBT – callously telling clients that what they have experienced is 'technically not truly awful' under the fallacious and inaccurate protection of a "it's not the event, but your beliefs that it is awful, that is really causing your emotions" world view. We do not do this in REBT. The REBT practitioner wants more than anything to help the client through difficult times, so would not kick a client when they are down (or at all!), risking the destruction of the therapeutic alliance and also damaging the client's chances of moving on functionally from the adversity.

Awfulizing underpins maladaptive behaviours such as social isolation (Watson et al., 1998), unhealthy anger expression and suppression, and externalised behavioural disorders (Silverman & DiGiuseppe, 2001). Relevant to the injury example, awfulizing is also associated with greater pain (e.g., post-knee surgery; Pavlin et al., 2005), more distress, greater disability, poorer quality of life in response to injury, and is generally negatively related to pain outcomes such as intensity, distress, and functioning (see Schnur et al., 2010, for a review). The unhealthy anxiety and inflated expectations of high pain associated with awfulizing are thought to increase perceptions of pain severity (Sullivan et al., 2001). Suffice it to say, awfulizing should be addressed, but tactfully and carefully.

In cases like the above career ending injury, the current author favours helping the athlete to think about the function or utility of their awfulizing belief, rather than the evidence and logic behind it (e.g., DiGiuseppe et al., 2014). The practitioner can validate the athlete's belief that the adversity is very bad, and ask them to consider whether believing that the adversity is awful is helpful for them to healthily move forward with their life at this time. We can encourage the athlete to consider whether they can adopt a more helpful belief that might serve them better as they begin to move forward after the tragic event. Then, as time passes, we can address the truth and logic of the awfulizing belief – ensuring the full disputation of the irrational belief – with a view to helping the athlete (a) to move on from the event functionally, but also (b) to fortify them against future hardship. The practitioner does this to help reduce the unhealthy negative emotion (UNE), even though at times these conversations can be tough for both client and practitioner. However, just because the athlete holds awfulizing beliefs about the adversity now, it does not mean they will continue to hold awfulizing beliefs over time (Dryden, 2019b). Time-limited irrationality (Neenan & Dryden, 2015) does not necessarily need to be targeted for change, unless it persists, and the client can't get out of believing this way. Another strategy is to work with other core beliefs surrounding the adversity. DiGiuseppe et al. (2014) suggest that clients who experience a severe adversity often hold FI and demandingness beliefs in addition to awfulizing. The practitioner can more tactfully help the client to understand that they are strong enough to bear the significant adversity they have faced, and that if they do so, they might be able to glean some important meaning from it.

Severe adversity notwithstanding, with more minor or 'garden variety' adversities, then the practitioner can more readily apply a variety of disputation arguments (covered later in Chapter 12) to awfulizing. It is best to target awfulizing when the client is clearly applying awfulizing beliefs to adversities that would not be considered truly awful ("the worst thing that could possibly happen") by the vast majority of people. In other words, social consensus would *not* validate and confirm the client's use of "terrible" and "awful" in relation to the adversity. DiGiuseppe et al. (2014) use a good example from Mark Twain: "I've suffered a great many catastrophes in my life. Most of them never happened". This illustrates a good empirical argument against awfulizing, and anti-awfulizing would reflect that some things are bad, but emphasise that they are survivable. Empirically, nothing that *actually* happens, can be as bad what *could* possibly happen. It can always be worse, thus we never max out the potential awfulness of life. Thus, what happens to people in their lives is never awful by comparison with what *could* happen. Human beings have both the gift and the curse of being able to conjure up adversity in our minds, seeing and feeling future potential adversity, and the badness of that adversity is constrained only by the limits of our imagination. So, when working with an athlete who is applying awfulizing to being benched, underperforming, being disrespected by a fellow athlete, for example, we can confidently apply disputation to the awfulizing, but still tread carefully. When doing this, we are not downplaying or undermining the adversity, we are just helping the athlete to avoid evaluating that adversity in an extreme and distorted manner.

Clearly, the severity of an adversity is definitional and in the eye of the beholder, but for sure, some As carry more 'adversity weight' than others. For example, the Holmes and Rahe (1967) Social Readjustment Rating Scale (SRRS) identifies major stressful life events, and each of the 43 stressful events is awarded a 'Life Change Unit' depending on how stressful it was felt to be by a large number of participants. The stressful events are rank ordered (100–0) from greatest to lowest stress. In an updated version of the SRRS (Scully et al., 2000) the top five are death of spouse (100), divorce (58), marital separation (51), personal injury or illness (57), and jail term (50) equal to marriage (50). So when working with athletes, the practitioner should consider the weight of what the athlete has experienced, or will experience, before deciding on the best approach to disputation.

I end this section with a brief snippet of a conversation between comedian Dave Chappelle and late-night talk show host David Letterman (Late Show, 2017). In the conversation, Chappelle puts failure into perspective, and reveals how this perspective helps him take chances:

CHAPPELLE: Oh my god you're a comedian, well what happens if you go out there, and you tell your jokes, and no one laughs?… nothing happens…You get paid the same, you're not gonna die, nothing bad happens. So I keep it all in perspective.

LETTERMAN: Well, good for you, to keep it in perspective, because it's something that I was never able to keep in perspective.

CHAPPELLE: but I'm of the belief that the best comedians bomb hard, when they bomb, they bomb hard, you take chances, sometimes you fall flat sometimes you do great.

DEPRECIATION (GLOBAL EVALUATION) VS. UNCONDITIONAL ACCEPTANCE

> Almost the entire history of Western civilization has been motivated by the dubious proposition that human beings are worthwhile only when they are extrinsically competent, successful, or achieving.
> (Ellis, 1991, p. 147)

> I went through a phase where I thought that only medals would define me or if I didn't have a medal, then I was no-one…you don't need medals to be someone…I am so much more than my medals.
> Ellie Robinson, MBE (English swimmer, multi world record holder; Channel 4 Paralympics, 2021)

In the lead up to the 2018 Football World Cup, Mauricio Macri (President of Argentina) met with the Argentina soccer team. He said to them, "Whatever we Argentinians achieve, we will be happy… it is not true that if one does not become a champion, one is a failure; that is a madness that does not exist anywhere in the world". Alan Burdick at The New Yorker (2018) saw this as an attempt to lower the pressure of expectation and psychological burden on the team, balancing hope against reality, to maybe increase the odds of success. This was smart from an REBT perspective, because captured in Macri's words are sentiments of unconditional acceptance and the negation of depreciation.

Depreciation beliefs are where a person gives themselves, others, or the world, a global negative evaluation (Dryden, 2019a). They evaluate a specific trait, behaviour, or action, according to a standard of desirability or worth, which is plausible, but then *implausibly* apply the evaluation to their entire being (MacInnes, 2004). For example, an athlete might believe that "if I fail to reach my goals, that means I am complete failure" or "if my teammate treats me badly, that means they are a completely bad and rotten person". In other words, not only have I failed, *I am a failure*. Not only did they treat me badly, *they are a completely bad person* for doing so. In contrast, unconditional acceptance beliefs are where a person acknowledges that they, others, and the world, are too complex to merit a global evaluation (Dryden, 2019a). They recognise and understand that although people do bad or stupid things, they cannot be globally rated as bad or stupid, and that the world is full of normal fallible, imperfect human beings (including them!) who will make mistakes (e.g., Szentagotai & Jones, 2010). For example, an athlete might believe that "failing to reach my goal does not make me a complete failure, because my achievements do not define me as a human being" or "my teammate treating me badly does not make them a completely bad person, they are just a normal fallible human being just like everyone else". With acceptance beliefs, it is important that the athlete supplement their evaluation that the adversity is "bad" or "not ideal" with the negation of depreciation ("but that does not make me a failure") and an assertion of acceptance ("I am a fallible human being whether I succeed or not") (Dryden, 2009b).

Acceptance in REBT does not mean resignation to the situation. Condonement is not a requisite of acceptance – we can accept that hunger, poverty, war, suffering, exists in our world without condoning these things. Indeed, by accepting that these things are real it actually can enable us to do something about them (CCBT, 2021). We don't have to like something just because we accept it. Despite our limitations, and amidst the trials and tribulations that befell our ancestors to get us to this point in existence, it is perhaps more appropriate to be grateful for our existence than place any value on the self. There is much about life and the human species that is not perfect, but the capacity to evaluate aspects of our lives evidences our sentient humanness, a fallible aliveness that should call forth our humility and gratitude.

Types of depreciation

As an athlete, perhaps you might choose not to accept failure, but you can *accept yourself* despite this failure. This is important because situations, events, behaviours are rateable, but the whole human being is not. An athlete can recognise a bad performance, whilst recognising that they themselves are not "bad". People are valuable in themselves, even though their behaviours may not always be laudable, so unconditional acceptance does not mean that individuals cannot and do not strive to change or improve their behaviour (e.g., competences, knowledge, way of life; Szentagotai & Jones, 2010). It is possible when working with an athlete who expresses a belief that "I am a bad athlete" or that "I am lazy" or "weak", that we mistakenly treat these beliefs as self-depreciation beliefs. But they are not self-depreciation beliefs, rather, they are examples of role-depreciation and trait-depreciation, respectively (Dryden, 2009b). The athlete is depreciating a part of themselves, not the whole self (e.g., "I am a completely bad person"). A practitioner can of course work with the athlete to dispute the role- or trait-depreciation, but specific REBT would have the practitioner assessing whether this role- or trait-depreciation is underpinned by self-depreciation, and work on disputing that belief as a priority.

Why change?

One criticism of REBT could be that in unconditional acceptance there is the possibility of stagnation and reluctance to change. If I unconditionally accept myself, then why change? Why try to improve? Why not just accept who I am, and stay the same? This again is a confusion between self and role, traits, or behaviours. The focus should be on the improvement of goal-related behaviours (goal as in 'Goals; FG and PG', not just performance related targets). In other words, we are not suggesting that clients accept being a 'bad coach', or an 'inattentive spouse', or a 'low skilled athlete'. Unconditional acceptance is not a proxy for self-efficacy, and athletes can still identify *aspects* of themselves that they do not accept, and thus want to develop competencies within. "I accept myself" is not the same as "I am contented with everything about myself". We can help clients become more skilled, more attentive, more empathetic, etc., because behaviours can be rated, evaluated, and of course can be changed, and we can measure this change. Importantly though, as these behaviours improve, this positive shift does not make the client more worthwhile, or more valuable as a human being.

Human worth

> I never really enjoyed the games. There was too much at stake playing for United. I always struggled in the periods I was out the team or playing badly. I had a feeling of worthlessness. As a footballer you wonder if your team-mates are looking at you and asking the questions you are asking of yourself. Why can't he hit a decent pass? Why's he always injured? What's wrong with him?
>
> Ryan Giggs (Manchester United FC and Wales soccer player)

In hard-line REBT (which the current author ascribes to), human beings are neither valuable nor invaluable – the question of value is inappropriate with regard to a human being (or any being). Ellis (1996c) communicated two main positions on human value. In one view, Ellis tells us that believing "I am good because I exist" is a tautological, unprovable, and un-disprovable supposition, and is in the same class with the statement, "I am bad because I exist". Ellis says

> I do not have intrinsic worth or worthlessness, but merely aliveness. I'd better rate my traits and acts but not my totality or 'self.' I fully accept myself, in the sense that I know I have aliveness, and I choose to survive and live as happily as possible, and with minimum needless pain. I only require this knowledge and this choice – and no other kind of self-rating.
>
> (p. 5)

He does however, also recognise the affective utility in assuming that you have intrinsic value because you are alive rather than assuming that you have no value. But Ellis (1996c) reinforces that "philosophically, it remains an untenable proposition" (p. 5). So, the global evaluation of one's worth as a person is always irrational, because there is no agreed upon standard or science or logic to human rating (Ruggiero et al., 2018). In sum, we can rate acts, deeds, and traits in light of our goals, but we cannot rate our self, being, or totality (Ellis, 1983).

Acceptance is important, but let us not forget the 'unconditionality' of this acceptance. This is vital because it suggests your human worth is not conditional on what you do (or do not do). Rather, there is nothing you can do to increase or decrease your human worth. There is no evidence that you have any intrinsic and inherent worth or value as a human being, and thus, you are not more valuable because you succeed, and you are not less valuable because you fail. Attaching worth to human beings is nonsensical because of the immutability of our humanness, complexity, uniqueness, fallibility, and changeability.

So, REBT has a unique position on human-worth (Dryden, 2019a), underpinned by the notions that humans are human until we die (humanness), that humans are too complex for a single global rating (complexity), that each human is unique (uniqueness), that all humans make mistakes (fallibility), and that humans are constantly in flux (changeability). This position could be applied to the world too, and is nicely captured by Heraclitus (c. 535–475

BC) when he said that, "No person ever steps in the same river twice, for it's not the same river and they are not the same person". Thus, depreciation beliefs are irrational in part because they fail to endorse these positions on human worth. But depreciation is also irrational because it is dysfunctional, in that the tendency to make global evaluations, whilst facilitating rapid judgements about the world, is error prone because it reflects global, stable, and definitive conclusions based on low-frequency behaviours or events (Szentagotai & Jones, 2010). Indeed, "the whole is more than the sum of its parts" (Aristotle, from Metaphysica, tr. 1963). To evaluate the whole based on its parts reflects inaccurate overgeneralising. Evaluate the action/s, not the actor.

It is difficult to imagine what good could come from transferring failure in a task to the global belief that one is a complete failure. The definitiveness of this sentiment leaves no room for self-improvement, and is a non-sequitur that, in athletes, is particularly associated with psychological distress (Mansell, 2021; Turner et al., 2019e). Indeed, in a paper in which practitioners applying REBT in sport were asked which irrational beliefs interfered with performance the most and were most problematic for dealing with major setbacks (Turner et al., 2022a), it was depreciation underpinned by contingent self-worth that rose to the top. In non-athletes, depreciation is associated with range of issues such as defensiveness to negative feedback (Chamberlain & Haaga, 2001a), unhealthy anger expression (Martin & Dahlen, 2004), and has been associated with those who are easily threatened by criticism (Ellis & Dryden, 1997). Literature suggests that depreciation beliefs are a strong predictor of depression (Solomon et al., 2003), anxiety (David et al., 2002), and posttraumatic stress responses (Hyland et al., 2014).

The dangers of self-depreciation are also captured aptly in Malcom Gladwell's book *David and Goliath*, in which there is a brief story about the French artist Jules Holtzapffel. In 19th-century France, the ultimate achievement for a painter was to be selected for The Salon, the premier art show in the world. In 1866, when Holtzapffel was not selected for this coveted accolade, he committed suicide. His suicide note read, "The members of the jury have rejected me. Therefore, I have no talent, and I must die".

Human fallibility

> We need to step away from this ideal that footballers are non-humans just because we idolise their vocation.
>
> Clark Carlisle (ex-Chairman of the PFA)

The notion that athletes, even highly skilled athletes, like all of us are fallible human beings, is not a perspective readily accepted by many, in my experience. Perhaps this is because this level of realism contrasts with the 'bravado' and 'superhuman' narrative (Howells, 2016; Ong et al. 2018; Souter et al., 2018) that surrounds elite athletes. Human fallibility is nothing to dispute or be disappointed about. The *fact* that we are fallible makes our achievements ever more worthwhile and amazing. The fact that human beings, so prone to errors, mistakes, pain, injury, can achieve the things many athletes are capable of achieving is amazing! It is not amazing because it shows infallibility, rather, it is amazing because of and despite the inherent fallibility that besets human beings. It is our potential for bad, that makes the good we do, so good. It is no coincidence that the major religions all include forgiveness rituals – as humans we will often make mistakes and miss the mark (sin).

Just think of the congenital fallibilities human beings possess. Our windpipe is next to our gullet, making choking likely. Wisdom teeth, a vestige of our early ancestors, are not so useful now, but can be the source of pain and illness (such as gum disease and cysts). We have a blind spot in our vision too. Men also have external testicles, whilst obviously serving a purpose (sperm 'prefers' to be at a lower temperature than the rest of the body), are often in harm's way (!). Nathan H. Lents (2018) write that,

> The reality is that evolution is aimless, natural selection is clumsy, and there's no such thing as being perfectly adapted. Our bodies are a mishmash of compromises forged in different eras and by survival forces very different from the ones we now face.

Our bones can break, skin and muscles can tear, and our minds can unhinge – our fallibility is inherent to our species.

It is popular in sport psychology at present to recognise that athletes are not just athletes, but they are of course human beings first and foremost. This is a self-evident truism which nicely fits with REBT. It is important to recognise that Ellis imbedded this philosophy in his work early on, in the 1950s and 1960s, and any consideration of self-compassion and the acceptance of human fallibility, whilst enjoying new popularity, is a recapitulation of Ellisian unconditional acceptance.

I am what I do

> It was become a champion, or probably be broke…For so long I've tied winning to my worth as a person. To anyone that would know me, they know me for being a tennis player. So, like, what am I if I'm not a good tennis player?
>
> Naomi Osaka (professional tennis player, two-time Grand Slam winner, 2021)

There is a tendency, when the stakes are high and the situation is important to us, to wrap our self-worth up with the results of our endeavours. Also, for athletes who develop a strong athletic identity, depreciation might be particularly salient and dangerous. Athletic identity is the degree of strength and exclusivity to which an individual identifies with the athlete role (Brewer et al., 1991), and a person with high athletic identity is more likely to interpret an event in terms of its implications for their athletic functioning (Sparkes, 1998). The notion of exclusivity in athletic identify represents the extent to which an individual's identity and self-worth are determined solely by their athletic performance (Brewer & Cornelius, 2001). A strong exclusive athletic identity could abet emotional disturbance in light of deselection, injury, and retirement, for example (e.g., Brewer et al., 1993; Edison et al., 2021), and athletes are more likely to ruminate and catastrophise in adverse times (Costa et al., 2020). But in contrast, athletic identity could contribute to an emotional connection to sport and have beneficial effects on involvement in physical activity and athletic performance (Babić et al., 2015).

There are consistencies between defining the self on the basis of an athletic pursuit, and the notion of depreciation or global evaluation, such that those who exclusively see themselves as "athletes" who then fail, are more likely to consider *themselves* as complete failures. So if your total self is fused with your athletic pursuit, such that your athlete self is the totality of the self, then it is more likely that failure will be met with depreciation. This is important because as an athlete, you will fail. A lot. If I completely define myself in line with my performance pursuits ("I am an athlete, that is everything I am"), and hold depreciation beliefs ("I am a failure if I fail"), within a context of ubiquitous and inevitable adversity (i.e., failure), then I am in precarious position as a performer with regard to my wellbeing (Turner et al., 2022a). Seemingly as an antidote to athletic identity and depreciation, Ben Foster (Watford and

England goal keeper) in an interview with *The Guardian* (Fisher, 2020) spoke about his breadth of interests and his reluctance to label himself as 'a footballer':

> If you ask me who I am, I would say: 'I'm a father, a husband, I love cycling, I play football for a living, blah, blah, blah' … but the problem comes when straightaway people say: 'I'm a professional footballer.' Come on, mate. You're not – you're a human being first. But that comes with age. And that's the thing you need to get into people's heads, that they are people first. People see them as this commodity, this footballer, but they are a person first and foremost.

I consider depreciation utterances to be an abuse of language because they make us of conjugation of the verb 'to be' in a way that (a) does not reflect reality, (b) is extreme and dogmatic, and (c) is not a helpful or functional way to think. Others, such as D. David Bourland Jr (e.g., Bourland & Johnston, 1997), Albert Ellis (1998 – he also rewrote some of his books in E-prime, which excludes all forms of the verb 'to be'), and Daniel David (2013) have noted that there are particular problems with identity and predication functions (e.g., 'he is an idiot', 'she is bad', 'I am a failure', 'I am stupid') because of structural problems in which the 'map' is confused with the "territory". It is more linguistically clear and logically accurate to state "he behaved idiotically" and "I acted stupidly".

> You are not your behavior.
>
> Your performance is part of you, but certainly not all of you.
>
> (Ellis, 2005b)

Global appreciation?

Whilst depreciation is reflective of global negative evaluation, it could be argued that appreciation beliefs that are global positive evaluations are also irrational. It makes little sense to define oneself as "a complete success" on the basis of positive low-frequency behaviours or events. In REBT it is argued that self-rating in any way is erroneous (Ellis, 1994), because there are no objective bases for arriving at global evaluations of one's self (Sava et al., 2011). Take, for example, Serena Williams: her career singles win rate in Grand Slam finals is 75 (at the time of writing), which means she wins 75% of the time when she is in a Grand Slam final (won 23, lost 10). That's very impressive, and undoubtedly, she is one of the most successful athletes of all time, but we could not describe her as "a complete success", because she loses 25% of Grand Slam finals (10 out of 33). But when she loses, we cannot describe her as a complete failure, because she wins 75% of the time (23 out of 33). So, even with regard to 'positive' or 'desirable' behaviours and events, global evaluation beliefs make little sense. In other words, you are not what you do. Whether global positive evaluations are dysfunctional remains to be fully explored in research, but it could endorse similar inertia and psychological difficulties as depreciation, but through arrogance, complacency, and self-aggrandisation.

Self-esteem

Self-acceptance is often likened to self-esteem, but they are not the same construct, although they can converge upon mental health (e.g., MacInnes, 2006; Sava et al., 2011). Whilst self-acceptance without conditions "secures the stability of an effective philosophy that can weather the vicissitudes of life" (Stephenson et al., 2017, p. 1), self-esteem on the other hand rests on an inaccurate and unstable subjective global rating (positive/favourable or negative/unfavourable) of the self (Popov, 2019; Rosenberg, 1965). In this way, self-esteem is irrational because there is no objective criterion by which one can evaluate the value of human beings (Chamberlain & Haaga, 2001a). In addition, a global self-assessment, such as self-esteem, based on the experience of success and failure, acceptance or rejection by other people, comparison with others, is unstable, and therefore, dysfunctional for mental health (Chamberlain & Haaga, 2001b). MacInnes (2006) found that self-esteem was more closely associated with affect, whilst self-acceptance was more closely linked to psychological wellbeing, and Popov (2019) found that self-acceptance was a stronger predictor of positive mental health outcomes compared to self-esteem. In Baumeister and colleagues' (2013) in-depth review of the evidence concerning self-esteem, they did not find evidence that self-esteem enhancements yield benefits, and they cautioned against the continued widespread efforts to boost self-esteem. They conclude in part that, "the benefits of high self-esteem are far fewer and weaker than proponents of self-esteem had hoped" (p. 38). Ellis understood this, which is in part why he described the proposed mental health advantages of self-esteem, as a myth (Ellis, 2005b). In all, a client who believes that their worth or value as a human being can be inflated or deflated on the basis of their achievements, is potentially on the road to nowhere, and the practitioner should help them work towards unconditional self-acceptance instead.

> I developed a self-limiting belief that my worth as a person was correlated to my performance in the pool.
>
> Lizzie Simmonds (GB Olympic swimmer)

> Some people don't think of athletes as human; they just see them for what they do and their success on the field. The more athletes define themselves by what they do, the more susceptible they are.
>
> Will Heininger (former Michigan football player)

Irrational beliefs as tools

It might be useful to consider irrational beliefs as tools. If they are tools, then what are these tools useful for? They may have been, and may still be, useful for acute life and death situations in which the energy for evasive or combative action was/is needed to avoid death or to survive. But the modern human, particularly in developed countries, rarely faces acute life and death situations. The situations we face now are more likely to be psychologically stressful with danger to esteem, and death of reputation, rather than physical danger and actual death. Irrational beliefs could be a vestige of our pre-civilised past. Indeed, things are getting better for us in the world (objectively, despite how it might *feel*) making irrational beliefs ever more incongruous with the human experience. The dogmatic and extreme rules reflected in irrational beliefs may have provided important and even essential survival tools in early humans, but nowadays, they appear to do more harm than good.

I caution, we should not be so quick to abandon irrational beliefs altogether – we do not want to throw the baby out with the bath water. We should help clients to weaken the irrational beliefs that are demonstrably deleterious to long-range goal attainment and well-being (eudaimonia). Function and pragmatics then, are important when it comes to deciding what is and what is not rational, alongside logical empiricism. But this function needs to be contextualised across time. The belief needs to be useful for the now and future me, not just the 'now me'.

SUMMARY

If we are to develop and express (or apply) our rationality, we must work over a lifetime to think and act against irrationality, and think and act in congruence with rationality. It is not accurate to categorise human beings as rational or irrational, rather, in line with REBT, we can think and act in rational ways, and we can think and act in irrational ways, but these thoughts and actions do not define us. In response to adversity and stressors, human beings are rather adept at thinking and acting in ways that makes things worse. In REBT, we help clients to *not make things worse* first of all, and then we can help them to *make things better*. REBT is designed to help people live longer, minimise their self-defeating proclivities and suffering, but also to "actualize themselves so as to live a more fulfilling and happier existence" (DiGiuseppe et al., 2014, p. 14).

I finish this chapter with a segment of a speech delivered by Brandon Brooks, who at the time of speaking was American football guard for the Philadelphia Eagles of the National Football League. He was speaking at his commencement speech at Miami University. For me, this captures nicely some of the content of this chapter from an athlete's perspective.

> I took being the best very seriously, too seriously in fact. I *demanded excellence* of myself, I *demanded perfection*, no mistakes, no screwups. I wanted to epitomise perfection. I did not want to make mistakes, until I did, and when that did happen, the world wasn't a good place for me…I don't know how many of you know but I have anxiety disorder. I *demanded perfection* of myself and when I failed, when I'm not the superhuman I'm supposed to be, my body and my mind turned on me, where I get tremendously ill for hours and can't play the sport I love. I missed 5 NFL games over my career because I couldn't handle not being perfect. I came to a crossroads where I had to make a decision. I would either cave under the pressure, or get help, persevere and rise to the occasion. I choose the latter because there are no diamonds without pressure…Of all the accomplishments I've had this year, Pro Bowl, Superbowl, I am especially proud of defeating the anxiety that has affected me in the past. I learned through therapy to not worry or care about making a mistake. Why? *Because the best thing about life is, it goes on.* How many times have you thought the worst situation, and *how often has that worst scenario ever came to fruition? Rarely. We're all allowed to make mistakes, to be imperfect, to be human.* Learn that now, listen to someone who knows, learn from your mistakes, keep pushing, trust yourself, and trust the process.
>
> (emphasis added)

CHAPTER 11
Assessing beliefs (B)

Who wins?

DOI: 10.4324/9781003200437-12

The Sword of Damocles story, as told by Cicero in his Tusculanae Disputationes (5.61), sees Damocles, the obsequious courtier pandering to the King, Dionysius. Damocles was telling Dionysius how great he was, owing to his wealth, power, and authority. So, Dionysius offered to trade places with Damocles for a day in order for Damocles to experience this majesty for himself. On accepting this offer, Damocles took his place on the throne. But in a twist of events, Dionysius arranged for a sword, held by a single horsehair, to hang above the throne, now temporally occupied by Damocles. Although being King afford great fortune, a King is always in fear of dangers that might befall them. Damocles begged the King that he be allowed to depart.

Now we know the particulars of the rational and irrational beliefs, we know what we are looking for. So, we can help the client to uncover their irrational beliefs. I say uncover, because oftentimes beliefs are not just sitting on the surface of our awareness waiting to be happened upon and challenged. The Sword of Damocles story is provided above to speak to the author's view of irrational beliefs and how/when they are triggered, and revealed (i.e., catapulted into the client's consciousness). It seems to me that irrational beliefs lay dormant (like the sword suspended above Damocles' head) until we experience (i.e., appraise) a situation that is relevant to and incongruent with an important goal (i.e., G-A incongruence). I use the sword as a metaphor here to capture the self-pressure and danger reflected in irrational beliefs, ready to fall upon us in moments of importance. When we face adversity, the irrational belief becomes salient in influencing emotional and behavioural reactivity, and at that point might be experienced as a declarative and explicit thought. The belief simply isn't relevant to us until we face A, or our Gs are threatened. Beliefs in REBT tend to be *about* A and/or *about* G, and I argue, are triggered by A representing an event (internal or external) that is relevant to incongruent with G. As such, if we want to help clients to access these deeper beliefs, we need to become skilled in bringing these beliefs to the surface – I discuss strategies for doing this in the current chapter. As well as my own applied work, I lean on DiGiuseppe et al. (2014) in this chapter, who provide an extremely comprehensive guide to B assessment.

Speaking to the depth with which irrational beliefs are held, Albert Ellis states that, "People's basic self-disturbing musts and demands are not merely superficially or consciously held, but are often tacit, implicit, and unconscious and are strongly clung to in the 'deep' structures of their minds and bodies" (DiGiuseppe et al., 2014, p. xiv). The way in which these beliefs become implicit and automatic (DiGiuseppe, 1986) is via self-indoctrination, rehearsal, and habit, in the service of cognitive economy, operating quickly and out of our awareness (DiGiuseppe et al., 2014). Some argue (David et al., 2005; DiGiuseppe et al., 2014; Turner, 2016b) that irrational beliefs could be considered as schemas, which are complex structures that represent a person's constructed concepts of reality, and behavioural responses to that reality, and thus are difficult to consciously access and identify. For many of the clients I have worked with, they have held their irrational beliefs for as long as they can remember. This means that they are often not acutely aware of these beliefs, and when they become aware (in our sessions) they are sometimes reticent to question and abandon these beliefs – and so they should be! We should not expect people to so quickly abandon their beliefs, and it is our job to help them to *convince themselves* of the irrationality of these beliefs, with a view to developing rational beliefs. In contrast, I have worked with many clients who do have very good access to their beliefs and seem to be able to articulate them with very little introspection. In other words, don't assume either is the case, and be prepared for both scenarios, and work on a case-by-case basis.

ASKING THE RIGHT QUESTIONS

Because revealing irrational beliefs at least to some extent requires introspection, when we are helping clients to identify their irrational beliefs, we help them go beyond A. Inference chaining, covered in Chapter 6 of this book, can help with this and is probably the 'best' method for revealing, or getting close to, B. But there are other strategies we can employ. When we ask, "what were you thinking when that event occurred?" or "what thoughts were you aware of when in that situation?" – but we could get answers that reflect inferences at A. Therefore, we can encourage the client to think more deeply by asking questions like, "What were you telling yourself about A (client's critical A) that made you feel C (client's UNE)?" In other words, we are helping the client to understand that (a) the A is not causing C, (b) that there is something they have probably not told us that is important, and (c) that it is whatever they were telling themselves *about A* that helped to cause C. There are variations of this enquiry, such as, "what are you telling yourself about the critical A that is leading to C?" or "is there anything you are thinking *about* A that might be *causing* C?" Don't expect a quick answer on this. Some will come straight back to you with an irrational belief (or the echoes of one), some will take a while to ask the question to themselves and let it percolate in their mind a little. If they are struggling, then try some variations of the question.

Another technique, that relates to the questioning above, that I find useful is to present a graphical representation of the ABC aspects of the GABCDE framework and help the client to input their As and Cs into the A and C boxes (as it were). Then they can see that there is something missing in the B box. As you pose the question using this illustration to help the client understand, and perhaps discover and report, this missing link by attempting to introspect on their more deeply held beliefs. This also serves as a nice record of the ABCs that the client can take with them to reflect upon, perhaps tweak, and build upon.

All these questions, including questioning used in inference chaining, are examples of Socratic dialogue which is very useful to encourage self-discovery. Using these approaches, you can help the client to reveal and articulate their irrational beliefs perhaps for the first time, which can trigger a 'light bulb moment' for them, in which they vocalise what has not been vocalised for perhaps a very long time (or ever). It can be a powerful moment, that you can capitalise on by making sure the belief is fully articulated. That is, don't settle for "it is awful to not be approved of", instead, try to encourage the expression of the full preference-demand-awfulizing irrational belief (e.g., "I want to be, and therefore I must be, approved of and it would be awful if I was not") by enquiring further upon what they might be telling themselves about the A (or G of course).

HYPOTHESISING

We can also be more forthright and share some hypotheses about the beliefs with the client. DiGiuseppe et al. (2014) call this "Deductive Hypotheses Driven Assessment" (p. 140). I mentioned in Chapter 4 in this book that the relationship that the practitioner has with the client can be characterised as 'scientists in cahoots' and the notion of formulating hypotheses is in line with this characterisation. The practitioner generates these hypotheses based on their experience and knowledge of REBT (and psychotherapy/applied psychology per se), the client (and people in general), and psychology/psychopathology. Once you have generated a hypothesis, you can share this with the client, but the hypothesis needs to be carefully considered and carefully presented to the client.

When presenting the hypothesis to the client, do so in an inquisitive and genuine manner, expressing your desire and intent to help the client to figure out what they could be telling themselves about A that is helping create to C. This is not a "this is what you are telling yourself, aren't you?" because this is too leading and authoritative. There is no point putting words in the client's mouth because it is *their* beliefs you are trying to locate and work with, not yours. I first formally learnt about this technique whilst studying in New York at the Albert Ellis Institute, and thus follow DiGiuseppe et al.'s (2014) guidance:

1. Use suppositional language, such as "could it be that you are not only believing that being disrespected is *tough*, but that it is also *intolerable*?" Or "do you think that it is possible that performing well is not just preferable to you, but that you *must* perform well?" Or "when you were in that situation, is there a chance that you were thinking that it was terrible or awful, or something like that?"
2. Avoid declarative statements. Try not to say "I don't think you are just saying X to yourself, I think you are actually saying Y". Most athletes do not like to be told what they are thinking.
3. Drop the ego. Remember, you and the client are scientists in cahoots, you are not a Sage or a Guru. Your suggestions might be false, so take an open and non-defensive stance when you present your hypotheses.
4. Seek client feedback. When you present your hypotheses, you are doing so in the form of a question in order to elicit feedback from the client. Whether you are correct, close to correct, or completely incorrect, is decided by the client. This can be in the form of verbal feedback, which is ideal, but can also come in non-verbal forms. Be attentive to body language, tone of voice, eye movement, and any signal that might allude to emotionality. You can quite often tell when you have presented something that the client connects with by observing their reactions to it. You can then reflect this back to the client, for example, "I noticed that when I made that suggestion to you, you grew fidgety in your chair. Why might that be?"

Why would you want to use a Deductive Hypotheses Driven Assessment? Well, say you have an athlete who, after various methods of Socratic dialogue, is not quite able to identify and/or articulate the belief. It might be on their tip of their tongue, they may be skirting around the edge of the belief. Shall we just let them hang there until they happen upon the belief? Or do we make some well-informed suggestions that could push them over the edge? We have all experienced a situation in which somebody said something in such a way that made us think "that's exactly what I believe, but I didn't know I believed it before they just said it". This is what great literature or art stirs up within us, and it sometimes requires an outside perspective to help us realise what we believe. Also, what's the worst that can happen? So long as you have developed a good working alliance with the client, and you have prepared them well for this kind of interaction, then there is little harm in presenting hypotheses to the client with a view to helping them. I have never had a situation where my hypotheses have led to working alliance rupture, but this could happen if the practitioner does not follow the guidance proposed in the four points above. Self-discovery is powerful and should be striven for as the first port of call, but how long are we willing to wait for this self-discovery? In keeping with the brief way in which REBT can be applied, I argue that we should prioritise and create opportunities for self-discovery, but not be afraid of suggestion in the form of collaborative hypothesis venturing and testing. An articulated self-discovered realisation (inside-out) has the benefit of authenticity and ownership for the client, but it is still very powerful when a deeply held belief is revealed to the client from outside-in (i.e., by the practitioner).

Choice

Dryden also developed a technique called the 'Choice-Based Assessment of IBs' (DiGiuseppe et al., 2014) which in my experience is very effective. In this assessment, the practitioner:

1. Asserts the client's preference about A and elicits the client's agreement (e.g., "So it is important for you to be respected by the coach, is that right?").
2. State that the client could hold one of two beliefs that account for the Unhealthy negative emotion (UNE; e.g., unhealthy anger) at C and ask for permission to present them to the client (e.g., "Would it be ok if I suggested two beliefs that you could have been holding at the time you were angry? Can I outline them and then you can tell me which belief, if any, related to your anger?").
3. State the client's C and then present the two beliefs; one demandingness belief, one preference belief (e.g., "At the time when you were angry, was your anger based on a belief that 'It's preferable to be respected by the coach, and therefore I must be,' or is it more of a belief that 'It's preferable to be respected by the coach, but that does not mean that I must be?'".
4. Ask the client which belief they think may have accounted for their UNE (e.g., unhealthy anger).

Obviously, a positive response to the demandingness option means you have probably identified the irrational belief, but a positive response to the preference option means you need to keep on searching and investigating.

What's your story?

One method, that is inspired by Paul Dubois, and shares some characteristics with Dryden's choice-based approach above, encourages the client to consider that they are building a second, and third, story about A. Dubois suggested, "...do not add phobophobia to the phobia that torments you, that would be building a second story to your malady" (Dubois, 1905, p. 367) and "Do not let us build a second story to our sorrow by being sorry for our sorrow" (Dubois, 1909, p. 236). So, we might say to the client:

> Oftentimes we tell ourselves a story in our minds about what happens to us, and this story can be accurate, or it can be inaccurate, and we can take it at face value. But sometimes, we then tell ourselves a second story about that first story, and then we can tell ourselves a third story about the second story, which is often quite unhelpful. In the first story we can say 'my coach ignored me', in the second story we can say 'and that's a bad thing', and in the third story we can say 'but it's not the end of the world, I can certainly tolerate it' or we can say 'and it's terrible to be treated this way and I cannot bear it!' So, when you consider the situation you have described, what are the second and third stories you are telling yourself?

This tri-story idea is also captured by Ellis (1994) when he refers to cold, warm, and hot cognitions, whereby negative warm cognitions generate negative emotions, and rigid and extreme hot cognitions underpin emotional disturbance. In the above example the cold cognition ("my coach treated me badly"), warm cognition ("that's a bad thing"), and hot cognition ("it's terrible, and I cannot bear it!") could underpin unhealthy anger, for example. We can help the client to understand these story layers, and that it is the specific hot cognitions, or third stories, that are most problematic, and we can then help the client to identify their third stories (i.e., irrational beliefs).

TRIGGERING B

Another useful method that we can use to extrapolate the B is to guide the client in the use of imagery. Here, the practitioner asks the client to close their eyes, get relaxed, and imagine in their mind's eye the situation (A) in which they felt the UNE (e.g., unhealthy anger). You can observe body language for signs of engagement and affect to get a sense for whether the client is successful in stirring up the emotion imaginally. Once the client is deeply within this image, ask the client to recall what was going through their mind in that situation. As the event unfolded, what were they telling themselves about the event that was adding fuel to the emotional fire? Some clients might not possess the requisite imagery ability for this activity, so we may need to teach them how to image, or we could apply more sophisticated methods to recreate the situational stimuli (concrete and/or inferred) in order to help access a problematic irrational belief. For example, virtual reality tools (e.g., Spence et al., 2019) can be used to enter clients into very realistic situations that mimic A, such as social-evaluative situations, in order to help trigger emotional reactivity. This can stimulate more deeply held beliefs because we are recreating (as far as we can) the conditions under which this belief is triggered.

In a similar vein, but non-virtually, we can expose the client to a situation that represents A, or gets close to A in terms of demand characteristics, in the session. In-session role play is useful for this purpose, where we enact the A in the room so as to afford greater access to the beliefs shaping the emotion by triggering the beliefs and the emotion purposefully. Care is needed here not to distress the client, but an example might be the enactment of a difficult conversation the client is unhealthy anxious (and thus avoidant) about having with a significant other. The client acts as themselves, and the practitioner takes the place of the other party. The client then attempts the difficult conversation with the other party (the practitioner) so as to elicit the problematic emotion (albeit on a less intense level than would be evinced in the actual situation). This can bring the belief into the client's mind.

Lastly, with some forethought and organisation, we can use video stimuli to trigger emotional reactivity (e.g., Zupan & Eskritt, 2020), ideally the emotion that the client is finding problematic. In reaction to selected emotionally provocative videos, we can encourage the client to report what they were thinking when viewing the videos. In sport, it is often possible to go a step further and use actual performance footage of the client. Based on their felt emotion whilst watching the videos, we can enquire as to the inferences they are making and the beliefs they are applying to the video.

A downside of these triggering B techniques is that they mimic or get close to the A, but they are not the actual A and may not be accurate to the *critical* A. But they can get you into the ballpark in order to facilitate deeper conversations about G, A, and C, and could even stimulate B itself. What would be ideal is being in the actual adverse or activating event with the client in the 'real world', which is more possible when working closely with sports teams. But even if we are there in the moment, we still do not have access to the inferential aspects of A and as such do still need to engage the client in some dialogue about their experiences in order to access and assess B.

Why B?

Why is the REBT practitioner so focussed on Bs? Because they believe that the specific REBT solution to emotional disturbance is to address B. This is about *getting* better, not just *feeling* better. We can help a client to feel better by addressing inferential As. Maybe your teammate did not ignore you on purpose. Maybe your family is not judging you. Maybe your career is not over. Maybe maybe maybe. It is more fruitful to, as discussed in Chapter 6, assume A is true and to uncover and address the beliefs about A, rather than A itself. Inferences at A may or may not be true (e.g., it could be the case that your boss hates you), but irrational beliefs are false by definition (e.g., your boss hating you cannot be intolerable, otherwise you would not be here to tell the tale!), so we are on more solid ground disputing B rather than A.

By addressing B, we reduce the likelihood of emotional disturbance to many possible future As. For example, if the athlete learns that it is not the A that *directly* causes C, but that it is $G - A \times B$ that $= C$, and they can understand and challenge problematic Bs, then they can apply this knowledge to all kinds of goal pursuits and life events. So not only is the B solution elegant (i.e., specific REBT), it is also efficient because it helps the client to apply their critical thinking to the underpinnings of their emotional distress, rather than challenging themselves on every inference (A) they make about the world.

The techniques described here can be used in conjunction and there is no 'correct' or 'best' method, as it depends on the client and the context. But taking shortcuts in assessing B is not advisable, since accurately identifying, and specifying, and then challenging B is crucial for specific REBT. To supplement the discursive assessment methods covered here, I also use various psychometrics to assess irrational beliefs. Clearly, psychometric questionnaires cannot access deeply held beliefs, but are useful for an indication of irrationality, or of a proclivity to endorse irrational beliefs, and as markers of client change as REBT is applied. The irrational performance beliefs inventory (Turner et al., 2018b) was developed for specific use in performance environments, including sport (Turner & Allen, 2018). Also, the Smarter Thinking Profile (smarterthinkingprofile.com; Turner & Wood, 2019b) offers a comprehensive assessment of irrational beliefs and can be completed by clients independently. This profile allows the client to download a report with details about their irrational beliefs across ten performance content areas (achievement, approval, consistency, development, failure, fairness, opportunity, rejection, respect, security).

Control

As can be seen in the ten content areas in the Smarter Thinking Profile, many irrational beliefs are related to aspects of the world that lay across a spectrum of controllability. Some things in life we can fully control, some things we can influence but not fully control, and some things we cannot control at all (e.g., trichotomy of control; Irvine, 2009). For example, whilst it is possible to strongly influence one's 'Development', it is less possible to strongly influence one's 'Opportunity', and almost impossible to strongly influence one's 'Approval'. This is also reflected in the other non-sport measures of irrational beliefs such as the Attitudes and Belief Scale 2 (ABS-2; DiGiuseppe et al., 1988), which includes content areas of achievement, approval, comfort, justice, and control, none of which are fully controllable.

The notion that the things we desire in performance contexts are mostly uncontrollable, is confounded by our demand that these desires be met. The irrational belief "I want to gain approval of people who are important to me, and therefore I must" is bound to be thwarted because one cannot guarantee approval. Wanting something that you cannot control is likely to lead to emotional turmoil especially when rigid demands are applied to the desire, and when extreme evaluations ("it's terrible!") are made about the perceived and actual thwarting of our desires-demands. Epictetus (Epictetus & Dobbin, 2008) knew this. He advised that,

> We are at the mercy of whoever wields authority over the things we either desire or detest. If you would be free, then, do not wish to have, or avoid, things that other people control, because then you must serve as their slave.
>
> (p. 224)

He also asks, "Who, then, is the invincible human being?" and answers, "One who can be disconcerted by nothing that lies outside the sphere of choice" (Discourses, 1.18). He states, "Whenever externals are more important to you than your own integrity, then be prepared to serve them the remainder of your life" (p. 91). By 'externals' he is talking about things that are external to you – things external to your sphere of volition. So, *everything*, apart from your opinion, pursuit, desire, and aversion.

> Whenever I see a person suffering from nervousness, I think, well, what can he expect? If he had not set his sights on things outside man's control, his nervousness would end at once. Take a lyre player: he's relaxed when he performs alone, but put him in front of an audience, and it's a different story, no matter how beautiful his voice or how well he plays the instrument. Why? Because he not only wants to perform well, he wants to be well received – and the latter lies outside his control.
>
> Epictetus (p. 111)

So, when working with clients, it is important to help them to understand that there are aspects of their environment that they cannot control, and to be careful about what they attach their desires (and demands) to. It goes without saying from an REBT perspective that you would help the athlete to reduce their demandingness related to the desires they wish to be fulfilled, but there is also work to do here to help the athlete to delineate what is and what is not within their control. Their choice to hold irrational or rational beliefs is within their control, but to some extent, so too are their desires and inferences. Whilst *specific* REBT is focussed on beliefs at B, the REBT practitioner is not precluded from working with G and A if it is within the client's interest (i.e., *general* REBT), and particularly if they are using the GABCDE framework proactively.

The Control Map

One activity that I developed which can help athletes to understand, or delineate, the extent to which factors that influence their performance are within their control, is called 'The Control Map' (see Turner, 2019b for elaborated detail). This is a practical but desk-based activity that is easy to conduct, and rich in its output for client and practitioner. In The

Control Map, the athlete (or group of athletes) generates a long list of factors that influence their performance, and then decide the extent to which each factor is controllable. Then I work with the athlete to figure out which controllable factors they should focus their work and attention on, and which uncontrollable factors they should either accept (not passively, but matter-of-factly) and/or deploy their attention away from, or work to bring within their sphere of influence. One big takeaway clients usually have is that when it comes to their emotions, they can absolutely work to control them. Not that emotional control is easy – but it is possible with some hard work. Why shouldn't it be hard work? It's a valuable goal that can determine the fulfilment of potential – it is hard but it is worth it. We can work with the individual to help them understand that factors such as emotion can be, in part, controlled, and we can help them develop some emotion regulation competencies aligned with the GABCDE framework.

The Control Map has been used in applied research (e.g., Wadsworth & Hargreaves, 2021), and practitioners often reach out to me to tell me how they have used the activity with great affect. Beth Moulam (Paralympic boccia athlete) blogged about her use of the Control Map with Dr. Andrew Evans:

> One activity I really valued was the control mapping at an individual level. So much so, that I have used it again in my personal life. We looked first at factors that affected our performance, then the control we had over each. The next step was to rank these as being those closest to us, and easiest to control. Finally, identifying factors outside of our control, which we just had to live with.

In tying the Control Map to the assessment of irrational beliefs, the activity of understanding the important factors that influence performance is fertile ground for the application of irrationality. Athletes often disturb themselves about the factors they deem to be vital for their performance, and if those factors are not within their sphere of influence, then the combination of low control and high irrationality applied to those factors is a recipe for high emotionality. This task stimulates further conversation about where athletes might be applying their irrationality and proactively engages athletes in seeking out self-limiting beliefs that might beset the attainment or optimisation of their self-identified performance factors. We can go beyond the traditional remedial approach to REBT by engaging athletes in conversations concerning their progression and development across the performance factors, helping them to be mindful of the rigid and extreme rules and ideas they might apply to those factors and the adversity they will undoubtedly face.

Is it a "belief"?

In unearthing irrational beliefs with clients, it is important to be aware that you will probably dig up many distorted cognitions and ideas that could be classified as irrational on the basis of an REBT definition. But before we take seriously these cognitive events and dispute them, we need to make sure that the client actual believes and endorses what they are reporting. As already mentioned, some thoughts are just fleeting irrationalities that are reflections of the many thoughts and ideas that pass through our minds, like shooting stars across the sky. Just because we hear irrationality (i.e., language that matches the four core irrational beliefs of REBT) this does not necessarily mean that the client *believes* or *endorses* this irrationality. In my experience, some athletes (particularly young athletes) verbally project the irrationality that characterises the climate in which they toil. In other words, they have been conditioned to regurgitate the irrational mantras expounded by key stakeholders in their sport career – such as coaches, parents, fellow athletes, the media, etc. The client might parrot "it is terrible, intolerable, to fail" or "failing means you are a failure" because they have heard a leader in their sport say it, or because they believe it to be the 'right thing to say' in matters of performance. I do not blame athletes for this – we all do this in some manner – often parroting political doctrines due to media brainwashing. So, it is important to address this with clients and try to go beyond what might just be a rehearsed rhetoric. When clients articulate irrationality, we can ask "do you really believe that?" and can even ask them to rate between 1 and 10 the extent to which they do truly believe it (1 = *do not believe*, 10 = *totally believe*). There is no sense in working with a belief that is not *really* endorsed. The same goes for rationality. An athlete may want to present themselves as rational, and thus might articulate rational beliefs. But if they do not really endorse this rationality, or do not really believe in that rational way, then we need to know so that we can increase their endorsement of this rationality.

What to do with B

In the next chapter I cover the disputation (D) of B. But what do we do in the immediate present when the client's B is revealed and articulated? In my practice, I write the irrational beliefs down on paper in front of the client, or a flipchart or whiteboard if one is available (which it usually is when I am working inside a sports facility). There is evidence that thought suppression may paradoxically and counterproductively increase the frequency with which the targeted thought intrudes consciousness (e.g., Rassin et al., 2000; Wegner et al., 1987), and can increase acute autonomic nervous system activity and over time inhibition can serves as a cumulative stressor, increasing the probability of psychosomatic disease (Pennebaker & Susman, 1988). Further, expressing thoughts about an event, rather than suppressing these thoughts, can help with habituation (Roemer & Borkovec, 1994) and is associated with both immediate and long-term health benefit (Pennebaker, 1989). But these anti-suppression effects notwithstanding, I encourage the client to write their B down for five important reasons. First, it externalises the B from within the client and is a commitment to articulating the belief accurately and fully. The focus of the session in that moment is not on the client themselves, but on the belief, which can be assuring for the client and is a less confrontational position to dispute from. Second, it facilitates distancing the client from the irrational beliefs (e.g., Collard, 2019; Hofmann et al., 2010) so that they, or we, can more openly apply a critical and analytical approach to the belief. The client is often less precious about the belief when it doesn't just exist in their own minds, but is out in the real world on paper. Third, it makes the irrational belief seem more real to have it presented in written form, and as such, the client views the belief as a more tangible phenomenon than if it was just a purely psychological event. The client can interact with the belief on paper in a way that they could not if it was just in their mind – then can rip it, throw it away, put a line through it, etc. Forth, the actual writing down of the belief leads to adjustment and refinement as together we figure out exactly how the belief is to be articulated. You may try various versions of the same belief to make sure that the wording is correct and accurate to what the client believes in their own language. Finally, the client can take this belief with them away from the session and work on challenging and disputing it, once we have done some disputation in the session. So, I recommend writing the belief down because this subtle approach to belief articulation can aid belief conceptualisation, clarity, and disputation.

SUMMARY

In this chapter I have covered ways in which the practitioner can assess B in order to help the client identify the irrational belief/s that is/are underpinning their UNE/s. These techniques are really designed for one main purpose, to help the client to become cognisant of philosophies, rules, and ideas that mediate the relationship between A and C. Some techniques reflect direct questions and postulations that are discussed with the client, whilst others are less direct. But the goal is the same: to clearly and unambiguously articulate the irrational beliefs that are underpinning the client's dysfunctional emotions and maladaptive behaviours. I have also touched upon the notion of control as a way to help clients understand what they can and cannot control in relation to their performance, and how this relates to their irrational beliefs. Next, we move onto addressing irrational beliefs, which in REBT, is known as Disputation (D).

Chapter 12
Disputation (D)

"Yours, and only yours: We suffer under this burden".

DOI: 10.4324/9781003200437-13

> With practice, we can learn to monitor our thoughts and challenge the irrational ideas that cause unhealthy emotions and psychosomatic symptoms.
>
> (Dubois and Gallatin, 1906)

> The greatest weapon against stress is our ability to choose one thought over another.
>
> (William James, 1842–1910)

According to Donald Robertson and R. Trent Codd (2019), "The goal of ancient Stoic therapy wasn't the suppression of unhealthy emotions but their transformation into healthy emotions by modification of the underlying beliefs from irrational to rational ones" (p. 46); much like what is proposed and articulated in REBT. It is the challenging of irrational, and rational, beliefs that I tackle in this chapter. But before we enter the rough terrain of disputation (D), it is important to emphasise that only a rudimentary and unsophisticated REBT practitioner is obsessed with irrational beliefs and hellbent on disputation at all costs. Of course, an important aspect of specific REBT is the finding and disputing of irrational beliefs, and research evidence in sport supports this approach (e.g., Jordana et al., 2020). This can only be meaningfully achieved with the commitment of the client to working on weakening their irrational beliefs and strengthening their rational beliefs. But a more sophisticated REBT practitioner recognises that they need to help clients to also consciously take, and profoundly imbibe, a philosophy of acceptance (of the self, others, and the world) in several cognitive, emotional, and behavioural ways (Ellis, 2005a). Also, the REBT practitioner stresses a focus on goals and values (see Chapter 8), and pragmatically helps the client to work towards those goals and values (e.g., Ellis, 2005a). So, far from being an entirely remedial approach focussed on 'fixing' faulty ideas, REBT is a proactive approach to helping clients fulfil their potential. With this important edification in mind, I now move on to exploring disputation in detail.

Disputation is a collaborative (client-practitioner) argument, or a debate, focussed on challenging the client's ideas, not the client themselves. As such, the practitioner should ensure that the client is ready for disputation. That is, it is a good idea to prepare the client for these challenges to their ideas, and make sure they understand what this will entail (Dryden & Branch, 2008). Part of the preparation for disputation is developing a strong working alliance (see Chapter 4) which should be graced with good rapport, an agreed direction of travel for the work, and of course, a detailed idea of the Gs, As, Bs, and Cs. But in addition, it is advisable to explain to the client what disputation is, why it 'needs' to take place, and how they can facilitate the process (i.e., "try to be inquisitive, open, and honest"). The client may have held and harnessed their irrational beliefs for many years, and these axioms which have guided their lives may be deep rooted and entrenched; "people get unbelievably upset when you poke them in the axioms" (Peterson, 2017).

In disputation, what we do not want to do, and do not try to do, is help the client to develop meta-irrational beliefs. That is, do not encourage musts *about* musts (e.g., I must not demand fairness, I must not use the word 'must'). Rather, we help the client to develop more flexible beliefs, such as preference and acceptance beliefs, rather than merely judging and denigrating irrational beliefs. In REBT, it is not the suppression of irrational beliefs that is the focus of the work, but the application of empirical, logical, and functional ideas to one's beliefs in service of greater human functioning. If we become too dogmatic about not holding irrational beliefs, we risk saddling the client with another problem, which is often presented as anger or guilt surrounding the holding of irrational beliefs.

> First give up all fear concerning the illness itself; do not add phobophobia to the phobia that torments you, that would be building a second story to your malady.
>
> (Dubois, 1905, p. 367)

D IS ALSO FOR 'DIFFICULT'

> Knowledge or insight into one's irrational behavior only partially, if at all, helps one change it.
>
> (Ellis, 1976, p. 33)

Whilst the GABC elements of the framework have laid some vital groundwork for the REBT work, D is where the major intervention takes place (Turner & Barker, 2014a). D is where the opportunity for real philosophic change can be instigated, and E (Effective New Belief; Chapter 13) is where this real change can be made habitual. A core rationale for undertaking disputation with the client, is that because the aetiology of irrational beliefs to some degree is natural (e.g., biological basis; Ellis, 1976; Ruth, 1992), and to some degree learnt and rehearsed by the client probably over a long period of time (DiGiuseppe et al., 2014), then these beliefs need to be vigorously unlearnt, and rational beliefs need to be rehearsed instead, so that they become habitual. Ultimately, society drives irrationality, and we as humans develop irrational beliefs as a function of our biological tendency to do so. So, clients are not usually going to give their irrational beliefs up willingly. Ellis (1976) believed not only that the capacity to be irrational is innate, but also innate is the difficulty in modifying or extinguish said irrationality (i.e., "modification-elimination difficulty"; Ruth, 1992, p. 6). Thus, helping clients to dispute, weaken, and abandon their irrational beliefs requires great effort and attention from client and practitioner. The D of 'Disputation' can also be the D of 'Difficult'.

In the early 20th century, Paul Dubois recognised this too. Dubois was saying in the 1900s some of what Ellis would say in the 1950s and 1960s, and with regard to the control of our emotions (i.e., hygienic moral advice), Dubois states:

> I often hear people to whom I give this hygienic moral advice answer me with vivacity: "but I can not do it; I have always been like this; it is my temperament". I do not doubt it. The temperament is precisely that innate disposition which we show from birth, which education often exaggerates, and which always forms the foundation of our moral personality. But by rational education of ourselves we modify our ideas and our sentiments and we make our temperament of a noble character.
>
> (Dubois, 1906, p. 57)

Ellis also recognised that;

> humans have a strong tendency to needlessly and severely disturb themselves, and that, to make matters much worse, they also are powerfully *predisposed* to unconsciously and habitually prolong their mental dysfunctioning and to fight like hell against giving it up.
>
> (Ellis, 1987c, p. 365)

Ellis' core argument was that all humans at some point believe, think, and act in ways that are self-destructive, reflecting the illogicality of holding such beliefs, thoughts, and behaviours (Sharf, 1996). This is evident across all known social and cultural groups. He argues that all societal and cultural institutions promote demandingness, awfulizing, frustration intolerance, and depreciation to greater or lesser extents. Furthermore, irrational beliefs are exacerbated by those around us to whom we look for guidance on how to live our lives (Sharf, 1996). Even when society dissuades certain self-destructive behaviours, we are resistant to rationality and constantly think and act in ways that are contrary to the development of humanity. We give up many erroneous beliefs as we develop and mature, but irrational beliefs maintain.

So, disputation is often difficult because it is a complicated process in which the client confronts and challenges a long and tightly held belief on the basis of empirical fact, logical consistency, functional utility, and heuristic value, and then instantiates a new belief that is resilient to these scientifically informed tests (e.g., DiGiuseppe, 1986). We have to be mindful of the fact that not everybody can or will think critically about their thoughts and beliefs. We often take it for granted as psychologists or psychotherapists that people monitor their internal dialogue and assess its meaning and veracity, but scientific thinking is hard. That is in part why we have to *train* to be scientists.

Emotion regulation

So, irrational beliefs are often stubbornly held, but fortunately, "most people have considerable ability to think, to think about their thinking, and to think about thinking about their thinking… they can change" (Ellis, 1994, p. 138). This is evidenced in the corpus of sport literature that demonstrates that with REBT, irrational beliefs can be meaningfully reduced across a broad range of athletic populations, with focussed one-to-one and group work (e.g., Jordana et al., 2020). In effect, we human beings are capable of meta-cognition, which allows us to achieve what Ellis is talking about in the statement above. When placed within Gross' process model of emotion regulation (Gross, 2014), D and E align with cognitive change activity (DiGiuseppe et al., 2014). The whole G-E 'process' is relevant to cognitive change, or cognitive restructuring, which is "structured, goal-directed, and collaborative intervention strategies that focus on the exploration, evaluation, and substitution of the maladaptive thoughts, appraisals, and beliefs that maintain psychological disturbance" (Clark, 2014, p. 2). D and E then most heavily represent the substitution aspect of cognitive restructuring, but exploration and evaluation continue to take place as we dispute at D and offer new rational beliefs at E.

This disputation, or reappraisal/cognitive change, process is a highly cognitively complex strategy. It is widely recognised that there are a number of brain systems (cortical and subcortical) that are implicated in cognitive change, which draws on a variety of different higher cognitive processes, such as language and memory, for example (Ochsner et al., 2012; Moodie et al., 2020). Cognitive change also has an underlying neural basis, with several brain regions implicated in the regulation of emotion (Botvinick et al., 2004; Miller, 2000; Wager et al., 2004; Wager & Smith, 2003), namely, the pre-frontal cortex (PFC) and the amygdala (Davidson et al., 2007; Ochsner et al., 2002; Wang et al., 2017). Furthermore, there are various brain regions that are modulated as a result of cognitive change (amygdala, ventral striatum, ventromedial PFC, insula; Ochsner et al., 2012). In a meta-analysis by Buhle et al. (2014) it was found from the corpus of evidence that cognitive change activates the dorsomedial PFC, dorsolateral PFC, ventrolateral PFC, and posterior parietal lobe. This supports a psychological model of reappraisal which emphasises the role of domain-general cognitive control processes in the cognitive regulation of emotion (e.g., Ochsner & Gross, 2008).

In a recent study (Steward et al., 2022), participants were trained in the use of Socratic questioning to challenge negative self-beliefs. Then, participants completed a cognitive restructuring task during which they were presented with common negative self-belief statements (e.g., "I think that I'm a failure") that they had to cognitively restructure (challenge). It was found that cognitive restructuring negative self-belief statements elicited prominent activation of default mode network (DMN) regions associated with self-directed thought, lateral PFC cognitive control regions, and subcortical hubs including the mediodorsal thalamus (MD) and head of the caudate. The MD had an excitatory effect on the PFC and caudate during cognitive restructuring, and the medial PFC demonstrated a reciprocal excitatory effect on the MD. The authors suggest that the MD has a central role in mediating higher-order cognition by integrating and sustaining activity across widespread frontal regions. In other words, here in this study is an indication of the neural network changes that might be involved in the kind of cognitive restructuring we undertake in REBT. These studies of cognitive change sit alongside studies that have specifically examined the effects of CBT on brain activity. Clark and Beck (2010) note that, for anxiety disorders, CBT has been found to increase activity in the ventral and dorsal anterior cingulate cortex (ACC) and the medial PFC (implicated in higher-order executive cognitive functions), and the right ventrolateral cortex, and decrease activity in the amygdala, hippocampus, periaqueductal grey, and the anterior and medial temporal cortex. As such, the effects of CBTs are in part to do with their impact upon higher-order executive functions such as problem-solving, cognitive reappraisal, and self-referential thinking. Neurobiologically, it is the top-down regulation by which rational thinking leads to a reduced emotional response and the regulation of negative emotional states (Jokić-Begić, 2010).

Owing to the implication of the several brain regions discussed thus far, cognitive change is a highly effective emotion regulation strategy which has the benefit of being able to alter an emotion episode before the emotion is evinced (antecedent focussed; Gross, 1998). It also has longer-lasting effects (Kross & Ayduk, 2008) compared to attention-focussed strategies (e.g., distraction; Ochsner & Gross, 2005; Silvers et al., 2013) in part because it involves an active change in how one represents the affective meaning of that stimulus (Ochsner et al., 2012). Fortunately, cognitive change is a highly studied phenomenon in the field of emotion regulation, in part because it is examinable using laboratory (functional magnetic resonance imaging; fMRI) protocols, and also because the core idea of cognitive change is central to many forms of therapy, including CBTs (Buhle et al., 2014).

> I will go much further and say that all thought being necessarily bound to the physical or the chemical phenomena of which the brain is the seat, the slavery is still more complete and that all the most elevated manifestations of thought, all our intellectual and moral life, depend above all on the state of the brain.
>
> (Dubois, 1906, p. 10)

So, there are some very good reasons as to why cognitive change seems to be a particularly effective emotion regulation strategy. CBT interventions such as REBT alter brain functioning associated with problem-solving, self-referential, and relational processing, and the regulation of affect (Jokić-Begić, 2010). The evidence of neural bases for cognitive change, alongside the evidence that cognitive change is the most demonstrably effective emotion regulation strategy (e.g., Boehme et al., 2019; McRae et al., 2010), provides some very good reasons as to why we would have a distinct focus on cognitive change within REBT.

Who knows how long human beings have been able to regulate emotions in this way (cognitive change), but the fact that there are brain systems that facilitate this ability indicates that it has been possible since we developed a more elaborated PFC, since the PFC is implicated in the conscious regulation of emotion. It is not like the Stoics invented emotion regulation – they articulated the cognitive control of emotions probably better than it had been articulated before them – but they were observing and reporting (and teaching of course) what was already possible and active in human beings.

Cognitive change in REBT (i.e., disputation) is not a one-time deal. The client is specifically educated and trained in the principles of disputation so that they can execute cognitive change perpetually into the future across many events and emotions. The client practices and rehearses this cognitive change strategy to become skilled in it, and the practitioner supports them in the process of applying cognitive change to specific irrational beliefs. But in addition, and more importantly, whilst for sure there is a focus on helping clients to appraise and process specific events in line with rational principles, there is also a focus on helping them to develop a rational philosophy of life. This rational philosophy enables them to approach all manner of events with an already instilled rational lens through which to view adversity. Indeed, CBTs like REBT works with and influences top-down brain regulation, and as such, the changes made by a client are potentially permanent and generalised to different areas of life (Jokić-Begić, 2010). So in the moment, it is less that clients consciously engage in cognitive change, and more that their wholesale approach to adversity is conducive to a rational interpretation thus enabling an implicit antecedent-focussed emotion regulation strategy that is less deliberative the more they indoctrinate themselves in rationality. Remember Ellis' 'gene for efficiency'? The idea that investing in rationality so that future adversities can be approached and reacted to adaptively speaks to this efficiency. The client is unlearning their irrationality so that such a top-down deliberative cognitive change process might not always be needed in the face of particular adversities. It is thought by some (see Collerton, 2013, for a critical discussion) that the learning that takes place as part of CBT-based interventions is subject to the principles of experience-dependent plasticity which govern learning (e.g., Kleim & Jones, 2008).

Therefore, working on disputation meaningfully over the life course can have important implications for emotion regulation, and subsequent mental and physical health (Wang et al., 2021). Disputation represents the first major part of this cognitive change or restructuring activity and should be applied as systematically as possible for two main reasons. First, systematic disputation is more likely to ensure that the client's irrational beliefs are comprehensively challenged and pilloried. Second, whilst undergoing disputation, the client is learning how to challenge their beliefs beyond the confines of the work you are doing together. Disputation is an important life-skill that stretches beyond the specifics of the issues that the client is currently experiencing. Therefore, it is important to teach the client the how, what, when, and why of disputation, in the interest of helping them develop their meta-cognitive abilities.

Scientists in cahoots

In disputation, the nature of the relationship between practitioner and client is important, and as was stressed earlier in this book, should be characterised in part by a 'scientists in cahoots' approach to the client's issues. Beck and colleagues (e.g., Beck et al., 1975; 1985) refer to this therapeutic relationship as 'collaborative empiricism', which is considered a critical element in the effectiveness of CBT per se (e.g., Kuyken et al., 2009). Clark (2014) indicates that collaborative empiricism involves the practitioner and client sharing their expertise in order to resolve the client's issues. The client is an expert in their lived experience, and the practitioner is an expert in the human change process, so they can work together in the cognitive change process to ensure the best solutions are arrived at for the client. In REBT, the practitioner encourages the client to be critical about their ideas and beliefs, and to question the veracity, logic, and usefulness of their internal states (i.e., inferences, beliefs, emotions), with an acute focus on irrational beliefs for specific REBT to be achieved.

Raymond DiGiuseppe (1986) invokes the Kuhnian hypotheticodeductive model (Kuhn, 1977) to inform the practice of REBT and specifically the disputation process. DiGiuseppe points out that clients are more likely to abandon their irrational beliefs if (a) considerable tension is caused by a great deal of disconfirming empirical evidence for the belief, (b) new problems exist for which the belief cannot help them, and (c) an alternative, and superior, belief becomes available. As such, disputation should be imbued with this scientific approach to beliefs and belief change, such that clients can learn to recognise dis-confirming evidence for their irrational beliefs, to realise that their irrational beliefs do not help them attain their eudaimonic goals, and to generate and strengthen alternative rational beliefs that do help them. DiGiuseppe warns that if we only challenge the client's existing beliefs then meaningful change may fail because the client has no better belief to replace the irrational one.

As mentioned in Chapter 11 (assessing B), one method I have found important for successful disputation is to encourage the client to externalise the irrational beliefs so that I can separate the beliefs from the individual (i.e., "you are not your beliefs"). This can aid the scientific approach to the irrational belief in part because it is more palatable for the client to challenge their beliefs rather than themselves. It is *the belief* that is challenged and disputed, not *the individual* holding the belief. The belief can be physically written down in order to provide a tangible expression of the beliefs to which we can target our disputes. By helping the client to understand that they are not their beliefs, and that their beliefs are not precious, we can more rigorously dispute the beliefs and help the client to understand that their beliefs can be challenged just like anything else in this world. One could describe this as 'cognitive distancing' (Robertson, 2013), which is the process of gaining distance from thoughts, which allows for greater objectivity and the distinction between thoughts and reality (Collard, 2019; Hofmann et al., 2010).

The ability for athletes to dispute their irrational beliefs and develop rational beliefs has been evidenced in many research articles (e.g., Jordana et al., 2020) and book chapters (e.g., Turner & Bennett, 2018), across a wide spectrum of ages, sports, and cultures. The following content provides some guidance on the ways in which disputation can be conducted with athletes. None of these methods are prescriptions and they do not need to be used in isolation.

Start at C

> If thou are pained by any external thing, it is not the thing that disturbs thee, but thine own judgment about it. And it is in thy power to wipe out this judgment now.
>
> Marcus Aurelius

Think about any meaningful journey (an actual one, not a metaphorical one). You decide where you want to go (which is usually underpinned by a *why* too), and then you decide how you are going to get there. This logic can be applied to disputation, and we can ask the client, "How would you like to feel? How would you like to behave? What feelings and actions would serve your goals most effectively?" We can use the information we already have about the unhealthy negative emotion (UNE) to help here, "Currently, you say you are experiencing unhealthy anxiety concerning A. But how do you *want* to feel about A?" The client might say they want to feel 'relaxed', and between you, you will need to figure out whether being relaxed is the most functional approach to A or not. This can be done by figuring out the *why*. But usually, healthy anxiety (rather than no anxiety at all) captures the gravity of the A whilst holding some functional, realistic, helpful tenets (e.g., preparation, focus). So, client and practitioner arrive at a position where there is a want and a will to move from a specific UNE (i.e., current location), to a specific healthy negative emotion (HNE; i.e., desired destination).

Then, we can ask the client, given what they now know about the GABC aspects of the framework, what they think is the best option to getting from UNE to HNE. For example, we might say

> Let's say you want to go from this unhealthy anxiety you are experiencing, to experiencing healthy anxiety. Knowing what you now know about the GABCs of REBT, what do you think is the best way to get from the UNE to the HNE?

Obviously, what you are looking for here is an intimation that the client recognises that their irrational belief (B) could be changed, and if the client suggests that A needs to change, you can converse about the upsides and downsides of this approach. Ultimately, client and practitioner should arrive at the position that to get from UNE to HNE, a good solution might be irrational belief change (although, 'change' is not quite accurate here, because we don't change the belief per se, but we do weaken it and offer up a new belief), and that there is a method we can apply to help this journey to take place. We can then explain disputation, detail the steps we can take, and then importantly, get the client's permission to go ahead with disputation. The client may have a range of irrational beliefs that have been identified, so just focus on one at a time, and get the client's direction and approval when deciding which to focus on and in what order (e.g., Dryden, 2019b).

Some final points before I go on – in specific REBT disputation is applied *only* to the irrational and rational beliefs, not to Gs, As or Cs. In terms of ordering, I have found it preferable to dispute the irrational belief/s, develop rational alternative belief/s, and then dispute the rational alternative beliefs (DiGiuseppe, 1991a). This is known as consecutive (IB then RB) disputation (Dryden, 2019b).

Disputation arguments

> Anger will cease and become more controllable if it finds that it must appear before a judge every day.
> (Seneca, 1928; in Seneca & Campbell, 2004)

If you have read even just some of the volumes of practical works concerning REBT, you will have undoubtedly come across the empirical (true or false?), logical (sensical or nonsensical?), and pragmatic (helpful or unhelpful?) disputation arguments. Without doubt, they are the most commonly written about and recommended arguments in the REBT canon, and thus, I will cover these first. These arguments are predicated on the notion that irrational beliefs are false (and could not be true), nonsensical (inconsistent with reality), and unhelpful (self-destructive). Irrational beliefs boast no empirical evidence in support of their veracity, reflect illogical non-sequiturs, and hinder goal attainment. In contrast, rational beliefs are true, sensical, and helpful. Rational beliefs boast empirical evidence in support of their veracity (or at least *could* be true), reflect logical sequiturs, and aid goal attainment. So, the empirical, logical, and pragmatic disputation arguments are indelibly tied to the defining features of irrational and rational beliefs. Practically, the practitioner is asking the client to (a) posit some evidence attesting to the truth or falsity of the belief (empirical), (b) consider whether the target belief (both irrational and rational) is logical or not, and (c) consider the functionality or helpfulness of the target belief (Dryden & Branch, 2008; Neenan & Dryden, 1999b). That is, the practitioner *asks*, not tells. Scientists *in cahoots* (alliance or partnership), remember. Disputation largely applies logical-empirical methods of science (Dryden & Branch, 2008). As DiGiuseppe et al. (2014) advise, "One of the most important tools in cognitive disputation is the use of questions" (p. 163). In that spirit, I offer some of the questions that work well for me, and I focus on demands ("I want it, therefore I must have it"), since there are comprehensive guidelines available elsewhere covering all kinds of belief types (e.g., DiGiuseppe et al., 2014; Dryden, 2019b; Dryden & Branch, 2008; Ellis, 1994; Neenan & Dryden, 1999b).

Empirical

- Where is the evidence that you MUST get what you want?
- Where is it written that you MUST get what you want?
- Can you provide some data or evidence to support your demand?
- Is there a rule somewhere that dictates that you MUST get what you want?
- What universal law exists that says you MUST get what you want?
- Have there been times when you didn't get what you wanted? So how can your demand to get what you want be true?
- What things MUST you have or do in life? (client answers usually: air, water, food, sleep). Does being approved of by the coach fit into the same category as these musts and have to's?
- Has your demand ensured that you always get what you want? Is there evidence that you do not get what you want, even when you demand it?
- Is it possible that, despite your demand, you might not get what you want?
- Is it consistent with reality, that because you want something, then you MUST have it? Is that how the world works?
- What data can you use to support your demand?
- If your MUST is true, then whenever you use it, you would get what you want. Is this always the case?

Logical

- You said that you want X, *and therefore*, you MUST have it. Is that good logic?
- So, when you want something, you get to demand it? Is this how the world really works?
- Does it follow that just because you want something, then you HAVE TO have it?
- How do you get from *wanting* X, to *demanding* X?

- If you heard someone else making a similar argument that because they wanted something, that it must be, would you be convinced?
- Where is the logic in saying that because you want something, then you MUST have it?
- Can you explain to me how you get from wanting X, to demanding X?
- Why do you *have to* have it, just because you *want* it?
- I see why you might WANT it, but does that necessarily mean that you MUST have it?
- You might want it more than anything else in the world, but does that mean you get to demand it?
- If you faced an opponent, and they demanded it the same as you, do you both get to have it?
- Are you some sort of omnipotent Monarch? In your life, do you just demand things and then automatically get them?

Pragmatic

- Where has your belief that you "MUST have it" got you?
- Has demanding that you MUST have it helped you to achieve your goals?
- Is demanding that you MUST have it helping you or hindering you?
- How has *demanding* you get what you want, actually helped you to get what you want?
- How is your demand that you MUST get it working for you?
- If your demand that you MUST have it was helping you, do you think you would have asked for my help?
- "Whatever I want, I must get". Where will that command get you?
- Is it worth it for you to hold on to the belief that "I must get what I want"?
- When you demand that you get what you want, how do you feel? … And is that feeling helpful to you?
- What happens to you when you demand that you MUST have what you want?
- If you were to list all the ways this demand has helped you vs. hindered you, which list would be longest?
- If you didn't demand that you MUST get what you want, would that really stop you from getting what you want?

The pragmatic dispute is particularly powerful, in part because it speaks to the utilitarian in people, and uselessness is a real blow for any idea. Also, DiGiuseppe et al. (2014) found that therapists said that this pragmatic, or functional, dispute was most effective. The lists above are not prescriptive or exhaustive, but give an idea of the way in which practitioners can approach disputation arguments. There are other arguments you can use too. *Semantic arguments* ask the client to define the specific terms they use (e.g., must, awful, unbearable, failure) with a view to gaining clarity on language use, and also highlighting the logical

Figure 12.1 Client belief disputation.

inconsistency of their language. This can help to elucidate to the client how extreme the belief truly is. For example, the client might indicate that by "awful" they mean "the worst thing imaginable" which might help them to see how fallacious this idea is. By using a semantic question such as "when you say 'intolerable', what do you actually mean by the word 'intolerable'?" you can stimulate some thought in the client about the extremeness of their belief (Figure 12.1).

Paradoxical arguments, or reverse disputing, involves humorously and exaggeratedly strong-manning the client's irrational beliefs. You can also add a sarcastic tone to this method. The target of the humour is always the client's irrational belief, and not the client, and the practitioner needs to have a good understanding of the client's sense of humour before using this method. When pitched correctly, the client will see how irrational and nonsensical the belief is. For example, you could say "My God you're right! You simply *MUST* get what you want! *How dare* the world deny you of the things you want, your majesty!" Or,

> You're right! It is not only awful, but I do not see how you are going to survive. That is the worst news I have ever heard! This is so horrendous that I cannot bear to talk about it. Let's talk about something else, quick!
>
> (e.g., DiGiuseppe et al., 2014; Walen et al., 1992)

This argument can also be tied to pragmatic arguments with clients who are stubbornly holding on to their irrational beliefs, whereby the practitioner paradoxically suggests the client keep believing what they believe (irrationally) and see where it gets them, or have the client project into the future where this belief might lead. The client will usually assert "but that belief is not working for me", and thus the disputation can continue.

Another way to use this paradoxical argument is to not use humour, but to use deadpan exaggeration (which suits me fine, due to my Midland English accent!). This can elicit a defence response from the client who will often *correct the practitioner* for *their* faulty utterance. For example, you could say "You're right, not getting what you want sounds completely unbearable", and the client would respond, "well when you put it like that it sounds a little over the top". You can also *play the fool*, which involves adopting a confused demeanour whilst verbalising how you cannot understand how one can rate the whole self on the basis of one failure, for example. You could say, "I don't get it. If one failure makes you a complete failure, then one success makes you a complete success, right? That doesn't sound right does it?" Finally, an argument that works well with athletes is what I call the 'Ravizza argument' (named after Ken Ravizza, pioneering sport psychologist). Ken would ask, "are you that bad of an athlete that you have to feel great to perform well?" I would ask "are you that bad of an athlete that you have to *demand* that the world be as you *want* it to be" or "are you that desperate an athlete that you need to *demand* success instead of *wanting* it?" These questions are rarely used in a serious tone, and I would almost always be animated and light when using disputes like this – my tone is used in the disputation to highlight the ludicrousness of the belief. However, whether you are playing the fool, using paradoxical stances, or inflecting your questions with humour, questions usually centre around empiricism, logic, and pragmatics.

> When you think things are so terrible for you, he [Ken Ravizza] was able to give you a perspective to make you feel like what you're going through is not really anything bad at all.
>
> Justin Turner (Dodgers third baseman; Staff, 2018)

As with anything in life, disputation can be done badly. It is important not to be pedantic or condescending when using disputation arguments. A nice example of pedantry in disputation is captured in The Office (US version) in the fifth episode of season nine (Wiki Targetted, 2013). In the episode, Andy has gotten his a cappella group to come and perform at the office for Halloween. Jim and Pam have a disagreement, and Jim tries to change the subject:

JIM: Its Halloween, you *have to* sing Monster Mash
PAM: Oh you HAVE TO Jim? You literally have to?
JIM: (long pause) Erm.
PAM: Just. I'm saying, what would happen if they didn't sing it? Would they go to jail? (pause) Would they be shot?
JIM: OK. We'll just forget it.
PAM: No no. I'm interested. I think everybody is interested in why they HAVE TO sing it!
JIM: Because its Halloween. So if you're gonna sing at a concert, it's a good idea to throw that one in.
PAM: No no. It's a good idea to brush your teeth, but you HAVE TO, erm, feed your children, send them to school, all things you can't do if you just keep singing Monster Mash!
KEVIN: (to camera) it turns out, Pam really really hates Monster Mash.

Of course, Pam makes some good points (!), but approaching disputation in this way, is likely to damage the working alliance, and damage the client's confidence in debating and sharing with you.

Given the breadth of available arguments, the practitioner selects the appropriate questions/statements based on their knowledge of the client and their issues (including their Gs, As, Bs, and Cs), their rapport with the client, and on their confidence in applying the arguments. Don't dig yourself a hole with your disputation, because you will confuse yourself, and your client! Also, timing is very important in disputation, and due to the meta-cognitive nature of what we are asking the client to do, it is advisable to allow the client time to process the questions you pose and consider their response. This might mean there are some silent pauses in the conversation, which the practitioner should embrace. It is also important that the practitioner encourages the client to answer the *actual* question, rather than answering the question they *want* to answer. Don't let them wriggle out of these disputations, which they may do because they are uncomfortable or defensive of their long-held belief. The practitioner need not rush, and it is better to execute disputation rigorously and thoroughly rather than see it as tick box exercise. What the client learns here, in terms of the ability to dispute, they can apply to the rest of their lives.

Socratic comparison

> If it is not right, do not do it, if it is not true, do not say it.
>
> (Marcus Aurelius, Meditations, Book 12, p. 60)

In my experience, the disputation arguments are very effective in helping the client to work against their irrational beliefs. However, usually I will not rely solely on these arguments to dispute irrational beliefs. Socratic comparison starts to help the client to understand the differences in truth, logic, and function between rational and irrational beliefs by providing examples for them to grapple with, or by using their own rational and irrational beliefs, to compare and contrast. One of the reasons that these comparison tasks work well is because they create some cognitive dissonance (e.g., Festinger, 1957, 1962) in the client, whereby the contradictory nature of the rational vs. irrational beliefs leads to psychological discomfort. The client is motivated to reduce this dissonance, and therefore the process of instantiating rational beliefs is aided through the desire for internal consistency. There are three activities associated with this method: belief sorting task, a tale of two clients, and paired components rating.

Belief sorting task

This activity involves the client sorting rational beliefs from irrational beliefs, via the use of ten cards with rational beliefs printed on five of them, and irrational beliefs printed on five others. The cards are jumbled up, and the client is set the task of sorting them into two columns – an irrational column and a rational column – and to talk through their decisions as they go (don't let them just guess). The practitioner does not help the client to do this, but engages the client in dialogue concerning their decision-making. The practitioner can gauge the client's understanding and critical abilities. When I have used this in a group context, I do so to get the group thinking about disputation and cue the group with three criteria to help them make their decisions: evidence, logic, pragmatics. But when I use this in one-to-one work, it would normally be used as a start-of-session warm-up following a session in which disputation had taken place. Even though the beliefs on the cards might not fully relate to the client's beliefs, the process of identifying and evaluating rational and irrational beliefs is an important life skill the client can learn. It is also fun! If the client makes some mistakes, it is a good opportunity to correct them and discuss why rational beliefs are rational, and why irrational beliefs are irrational.

A tale of two clients

Similar to the sorting task, this activity helps the client to compare rational and irrational beliefs. But 'a tale of two clients' goes a little further and attempts to help the client to understand the UNE and HNE consequences (C) of the beliefs. To do this, I have prepared two narratives (Figures 12.2 and 12.3), or stories, that portray the same tale, but with the character of each narrative using different internal dialogue. In narrative 1, the character uses rational internal dialogue. In narrative 2 the character uses irrational internal dialogue. But all other elements are identical. Having read both stories, the client then answers several questions concerning the cognitive, emotional, and behavioural consequences of the stories. The stories can be seen below, and the questions are:

- Which character is using more true, logical, and pragmatic internal dialogue?
- Which character is more motivated?
- Which character is more anxious?
- Which character is more likely to fulfil their potential?

Narrative 1 (rational elements in bold)

Jenny wakes up at 7am to prepare. She gets a shower, has her breakfast, and leaves to start her journey. Today is a big day. Today she will take her final exam, the exam she has been building up to take throughout her entire degree. As she makes her way to the exam room in the University, she starts to think about the importance of the exam ***"I really want to do well in this exam"*** *she muses,* ***"it's so important, I so want to get a good grade"****. She continues to think about how her performance will go and images of failure start to creep into her mind. "****It would be really bad if I didn't do well****, it would damage my career prospects" she thinks, while she pictures herself getting writer's block in the exam. Jenny arrives at the exam room and checks her phone one last time. Her best friend has text her: "Make me proud" she says.* ***"It would be painful to let her down"*** *Jenny says to herself,* ***"It would be difficult to take letting my family down as well"****. With this, the importance of the occasion intensifies, and she starts to get into exam mode. The big stage awaits, probably the biggest stage she has approached in her academic studies to date. "This is it" she thinks, "Failure here might damage my career prospects". She has spent her studies trying to reach this point,* ***"I want more than anything to pass this exam"*** *she says to herself,* ***"failure would be a really bad, it would be difficult to bear"****. Jenny takes a seat at her exam desk. Palms sweating, heart racing, her future awaits her.*

Figure 12.2 Rational exam narrative.

Narrative 2 (irrational elements in bold)

Jenny wakes up at 7am to prepare. She gets a shower, has her breakfast, and leaves to start her journey. Today is a big day. Today she will take her final exam, the exam she has been building up to take throughout her entire degree. As she makes her way to the exam room in the University, she starts to think about the importance of the exam ***"I have to do well in this exam"*** *she muses,* ***"it's so important, I have to get a good grade"****. She continues to think about how her performance will go and images of failure start to creep into her mind.* ***"It would be terrible if I didn't do well, absolutely awful for my career prospects"*** *she thinks, while she pictures herself getting writer's block in the exam. Jenny arrives at the exam room and checks her phone one last time. Her best friend has text her: "Make me proud" she says.* ***"I couldn't bear letting her down"*** *Jenny says to herself,* ***"I couldn't stand letting my family down either"****. With this, the importance of the occasion intensifies, and she starts to get into exam mode. The big stage awaits, probably the biggest stage she has approached in her academic studies to date. "This is it" she thinks,* ***"Failure here would make me a failure"****. She has spent her studies trying to reach this point,* ***"I must pass this exam"*** *she says to herself,* ***"failure would be a catastrophe, I don't think I could stand it"****. Jenny takes a seat at her exam desk. Palms sweating, heart racing, her future awaits her.*

Figure 12.3 Irrational exam narrative.

The narratives include simplified irrational beliefs, rather than full preferences and preference-demand beliefs. This is done to facilitate flow and make it more real, and should not be presented to the client as a perfect model of rational and irrational beliefs. I have applied this activity many times with clients, and nine times out of ten the client considers the rational character to be using more true, logical, and pragmatic internal dialogue, to be more motivated, less anxious, and more likely to fulfil their potential. If the client does not answer in this way, then a constructive conversation can be had about the differences and what has led them to answer in the way that they have. In my teaching I have had students construct their own self-narratives using narrative 1 (rational) as a template, in preparation for an exam. It is important that clients realise that with all other details fixed, there are multiple ways of thinking, and that they can choose to think rationally.

Paired components rating

In this approach the practitioner questions paired components of the client's irrational belief and rational belief, at the same time (Neenan & Dryden, 1999b). This activity has clients consider their irrational beliefs in comparison to the rational alternative. As you can see in

	Rational "I want to succeed, but I do not have to"	Irrational "I want to succeed, and therefore I have to"
Which belief is true and which is false?		
Which belief is sensible/logical and which doesn't make sense or is illogical?		
Which belief is helpful and which is unhelpful?		
Which of the two beliefs do you want to strengthen and act on?		

Figure 12.4 Paired components rating disputation task.

Figure 12.4, the client's irrational belief is in the middle column, and the identified rational belief is in the right column next to it. The practitioner then asks the client:

- Which belief is true and which is false?
- Which belief is sensible/logical and which doesn't make sense or is illogical?
- Which belief is helpful and which is unhelpful?
- Which of the two beliefs do you want to strengthen and act on?

The client then places a tick in the box that reflects their answer. As with previous methods, engage the client in discussion as to their decision-making, and ensure that they are clear in their reasons for their answers. No need to rush. Each irrational belief identified with the client (e.g., demands, awfulizing, etc.) should be submitted to this comparison separately, but variations of the task are put forth by Neenan and Dryden (1999b). This activity helps the work to move towards strengthening the rational belief, and importantly, provides some rationale for doing so.

Another type of comparison task I like to use is what I call the 'multiple yous' task. In this activity you have the client imagine that there are multiple versions of themself ('multiple yous') in the future; you A and you B. Here is the twist though – you A holds irrational beliefs about the self, others, the world, whereas you B holds rational beliefs about the self, others, the world. Then I ask the client to run a simulation in their head for 'you A' and 'you B' sequentially. How does life pan out for you A if irrational beliefs are maintained and left to prosper? In contrast, how does life pan out for you B if rational beliefs are developed, strengthened, and maintained? This is a very abstract task, but does clearly highlight to the client that they are at a crossroads at this point in time and they get to decide which of these 'yous' they want to embody.

PRACTICAL TASKS TO HELP WITH EVIDENCE AND LOGIC DISPUTES

With some clients, there is opportunity to engage them in some practical tasks that can demonstrate the irrationality of irrational beliefs more powerfully than arguments and comparison alone. These activities work well in group contexts, but also on a one-to-one level, and take very little preparation. The present author tends to use two particular tasks, one for awfulizing, and one for depreciation. The activities are; the badness scale, and big I little i. I will detail these activities here briefly.

The badness scale

Since the beginning of my foray into REBT in sport, the badness scale (Ellis et al., 1997) has been a staple of the disputation canon (Turner et al., 2014, 2015). This interactive activity is used to help clients dispute awfulizing beliefs, and can be used at one-to-one and group levels. The proliferation of the badness scale in sport is no doubt attributable to the often brief nature of the work undertaken in sport settings. In conducting the badness scale, in a group setting the client/s are asked to write down 'bad' life and sport events on post-it notes (one event per post-it note). They should generate around 10–15 events. Then, they are asked to add them to the badness scale in relation to how bad the event is. The badness scale, pictorially, is a scale that runs from 0% (not bad at all) at the bottom, to 100% (worst thing imaginable) at the top. Think of a circus high striker, with a big bell at the top with '100%' written on it. Debate is encouraged about where events should be placed, and I have noted some patterns in clients' responses. Often, athletes place sport events such as "being deselected" and "giving away a penalty in the last minute of a cup final" at around the 50–70% mark on the scale. More noxious life events, such as losing a loved one, contracting a terminal illness, getting a career-ending injury, are usually placed towards the top of the scale at the 90–100% mark. This task when used in this way illustrates two main points. First, believing that sport failure and setbacks are 'awful' is evidently illogical, because the placement of these events on the badness scale reflects moderate badness. Second, even when things get really bad, it still cannot be 'awful' because the scale maxes out at 100% – there is no 101% (i.e., constituting 'awful'). This limit of badness is made more tangible by the visual aid of the badness scale.

In a one-to-one setting, I use the client's actual As on the badness scale. We can also use some possible or hypothetical bad events to help to compare and contrast the badness of the client's As with the badness of other As. At a one-to-one level this process is more discursive than in a group setting, and the outcomes of the task are threefold. First, you can gauge to what extent the client is indeed awfulizing about their A. How adamant are they that their

A is the worst thing they can imagine? Second, when you challenge the client to try to imagine a worse A than what they have experienced, they will succeed, which leaves them in a predicament. "If my current A is at the very top of the badness scale, then where do I put this worse A?" Thus, the client has to move their current A down on the badness scale, which helps them to gain some perspective concerning the badness or 'awfulness' of their current A. Third, as with the group level method, even when things get really bad, the client can see that it still cannot be 'awful' because the scale maxes out at 100%. The practitioner should exercise caution when using the badness scale, and when disputing awfulizing per se, as per my previous guidance (Chapter 10) – I advise against this task when the client has clearly experienced a culturally agreed upon catastrophe.

Big I little i

The activity is used to dispute depreciation beliefs, and again, is an interactive task. The Big I little i technique (Lazarus, 1977) involves drawing a big outline of letter I that fills a side of paper. Then, the practitioner askes the athlete to think back over the past year, and to verbalise something they did badly (e.g., failed at, transgressed, fell below their standards). A little i is written somewhere within the Big I, and is labelled with the 'bad' behaviour. Then, the athlete is asked to think about and to verbalise something they did well (e.g., succeeded at, met their standards, put in lots of effort on a task). Again, a little i is written somewhere within the Big I, and is labelled with the 'good' behaviour. This continues alternately for five 'bad' things and five 'good' things (one can also include neutral or average little i's; S. Palmer, personal communication, April 26, 2022). The practitioner would of course ensure that the A that triggered the depreciation belief is included. Once this is complete, we now have a big letter I with ten small letter i's inside it, each associated with a 'good' or 'bad' behaviour. The client and practitioner then reflect on the task, and how it might relate to the notion of depreciation. There are four main takeaway points here for the client. First, it is not logical to describe oneself in totality as 'good' or 'bad', 'a success' or 'a failure', because they do many 'good' things, and many 'bad' things. The *part* cannot define the *whole*. Second, the client can see visually that they have done some good things, and that their depreciation belief might be biasing them towards overemphasising and ruminating upon the bad things they do. They are a complex human being that does good and bad things, and the good should not be discounted or overshadowed by the bad. Third, when also applied to other-depreciation and world-depreciation, the client realises that the world is a complex place and whilst human *behaviours* can be rated (i.e., good or bad), the self, the world, and others, cannot be rated. Finally, the 'bad' does not erase the 'good' and vice versa. Even when we act badly, we still have the capacity to act properly, and even when we act well, we can still miss the mark from time to time. Ultimately, we are helping the client to understand that a single failure or even a series of failures is not an adequate or appropriate basis upon which a human can be evaluated – an act can be labelled, but a person cannot be (Collard, 2019).

For an interactive resource that is very much like a big I little i task, you can access a fascinating infographic by Luke Knox of ESPN (n.d.) called "Serena's Grand Slam History". This infographic is an image of tennis player Serena Williams made up of 346 tiles, each representing a Grand Slam match. When you hover over a tile, it gives you the match details and whether Williams won or lost the match. I have used this to help athletes understand that even the best of the best have had many losses in their careers.

Disputation styles

In much of the REBT literature, the style of disputation is boiled down to two main approaches: socratic vs. didactic. But it is common to use a range or combination of styles that suit the client, and the particular stages of the work (Dryden, 2019b), and practitioners are encouraged to be creative (DiGiuseppe et al., 2014). Indeed, there are also humorous and metaphoric styles (e.g., Beal et al., 1996; DiGiuseppe, 1991b; DiGiuseppe et al., 2014). Disputation styles are covered extensively and excellently elsewhere, so I will not labour the point, and the two styles that I would use most often are the Socratic vs. didactic styles, which can be used in conjunction.

Socratic

The practitioner asks the client focussed, open, and meaningful questions, many of which are illustrated earlier in this section, concerning the empirical, logical, and pragmatic status of their irrational and rational beliefs. An excellent discussion can be found in DiGiuseppe et al. (2014, pp. 171–173). This style is preferable to engender client self-discovery and practitioner-client collaboration. One of the ways in which we can execute this style is to humbly act as though the client can actually teach us something we don't know. This is of course a truism, because we really know almost nothing about the client and therefore we should approach them with an inquisitive frame of mind thus allowing and encouraging them to explain to us what they believe and the foundations for these beliefs. Within the context of disputation, this means we can act as if we do not understand the empirical, logical, and pragmatic foundations of the beliefs they hold. With an irrational belief like "I want, therefore I must, be respected by my peers" we might question the logic of the belief by saying to the client "I don't quite understand here. Please explain to me how you get a must from a want" or "help me to figure this out. How are you going from 'want' to 'must'?"

Didactic

The practitioner tells the client, using short explanations and examples, why their irrational beliefs are irrational, and their rational beliefs are rational (e.g., Neenan & Dryden, 1999b). This is really a form of psychoeducation (e.g., Sarracino et al., 2017), a method often used in the sport research when time is of the essence or the work is conducted in a group format (e.g., Turner & Davis, 2019). This style is also useful with clients who cannot engage with Socratic disputing (Dryden, 2019b). Dryden (2009a, 2009b) suggests that this style is used in short chunks, using visual aids, in the client's language, with the practitioner checking for client understanding as they go.

The Smarter Thinking App

Practitioners tasked with the provision of psychology in the 21st century have at their disposal a multitude of resources that can aid service delivery. Our clients are evermore engaged with digital technology, particularly those born after 1982 (called 'Millennials'; Monaco & Martin, 2007), and almost all of them have Smartphones (Muir, 2015). Smartphones are accessible, mobile, and easy to operate, and are becoming more affordable to own. Therefore, alongside Andrew Wood, I developed "The Smarter Thinking App" (Turner & Wood, 2019a) for

Smartphone and tablet users that digitises the disputation of irrational beliefs, and development of rational beliefs. Apps are software programs developed to run on a computer or mobile device to accomplish a specific purpose (Wallace et al., 2012). The App helps users to gain clarity about the adversity they face (A), their beliefs about that adversity (B), their unhealthy negative emotions to the adversity (C), and facilitates the disputation (D) of irrational beliefs. The App helps clients weaken irrational beliefs and strengthen rational beliefs (E) to promote healthy negative emotions. The App applies the three main arguments of evidence, logic, and pragmatics, and does so by engaging the client in Socratic questioning. The App also includes some elements of didactic suggestion, especially regarding the promotion of new rational beliefs.

The App can be used as often as the client wants, allowing for repeated familiarisation and rehearsal of REBT, which would help the client to more accurately use REBT in their daily life. The Smarter Thinking App is not a stand-alone REBT intervention, and should be used as a supplementary aid for helping athletes engage with the GABCDE framework, digitising a vital cognitive homework assignment that can serve as self-help if the user is familiar with REBT. Thus, an athlete's usage of the App can be supported and reviewed by the practitioner. The Smarter Thinking App has a very specific function; to help performers such as athletes learn and use REBT in their careers and lives.

Summary

In this section I have covered ways in which the practitioner can dispute (D) clients' irrational and rational beliefs (B), in order to help them learn the skills of questioning and challenging their beliefs, and to help the client address their current UNEs. I have touched upon how disputation can be applied, the styles that characterise disputation, and some of the practical activities I would often use. I have also introduced The Smarter Thinking App, which is a free resource available on Android and Apple platforms. Next, I move onto discussing the development and strengthening of effective new rational beliefs (E), which is the next logical step after successful disputation.

CHAPTER 13
Effective new beliefs (E)

The claiming. The wielding. The capturing.

DOI: 10.4324/9781003200437-14

In April of 2019, Rory McIlroy gave some interviews in the lead up to the Masters at Augusta (The Masters, 2019). The content below is taken from the interviews (Cannizzaro, 2019; Jackson, 2019; Jones, 2019). The alignment of McIlroy's attitude with the key tenets of REBT, namely, the rational beliefs, is marked, and illustrates how a highly elite athlete can adopt rationality in the face of pressure.

Demandingness

I think there's a difference between a personal desire and a need, and I think I've separated those two.

I would have said a couple of years ago, 'I need to win a Masters. I need a green jacket'. But now it's, 'I want to. I want to win it. And I'd love to win it', but if I don't then I'm okay with that. And I think that is the difference.

Maybe some people will say that I'm not motivated enough. Believe me, I am motivated to make the most of what I have and to put my name among some of the greats of our game. *Author note: a preference to succeed does not reflect low motivation, just different motivation (Davis & Turner, 2020).*

So, have I a desire to do it? Yes. Do I have a need to do it? No.

Frustration tolerance

I'm going to try my ass off here, and I'm probably not going to win, but as long as you can take the positives from it and you move on to the next tournament and the next tournament and the next tournament and you keep going with what you want to do and you keep learning.

I've had 10 years of learning at Augusta, some tough times. And if one day I'm able to get that green jacket at the end of 72 holes, all of those experiences will have played a part in helping me do that. *Author note: it is worth it to struggle.*

Anti-awfulizing

I would dearly love to win this tournament again one day, if it doesn't happen this week that's totally fine, ill come back next year.

Acceptance

Not living and dying by results, not getting caught up in trying to play perfect golf, a little more acceptance, a change in attitude which has been one of the biggest keys to how I've played.

There's ways to help you achieve your goals that aren't just about the result…its not as if I'm coming not to try and win the golf tournament. But the big thing is, I am not my score. I am not my results. Its perspective, its perception.

In golf you fail. My win percentage since I turned pro is probably around 10 per cent, which is pretty good for golf. So knowing nine times out of 10 that you're going to fail, that is freeing, as well. That's freedom. *Author note: failure is just evidence that I am a fallible human being.*

It's not being defined by your wins and losses, that's the key. That's the secret of being freed up and not buying into narratives and not living and dying with every golf tournament or every shot. I think that's very important.

I don't define myself by who I am as a golfer anymore. I'm very comfortable with who I am as a person and very comfortable with who I am as a golfer. *Author note: win or lose in golf, I accept myself as a human being.*

McIlroy also hinted towards long-term, rather than short-term, fulfilment with statements such as "Its not just about one week, this is a lifelong journey of trying to improve and learn and try to master my craft. Its to make the most of the next 20 years of my career" and

> winning tournaments, getting to world No 1 and all those accolades, it's a by-product of doing all the little things right. And I feel like I'm doing the little things right. And step by step they will add up to all that stuff that other people find important.

But McIlroy did not always approach golf in this way, he had to work hard to develop this approach. So how do we as practitioners help our clients to develop this rational approach to life? This is the focus of E, and the focus of this chapter.

Developing rational beliefs

Some of the work necessary for E has already been started in D. Depending on the methods that the practitioner uses in D, rational alternative beliefs may have been posited, and perhaps even disputed. Remember, in REBT we are not *changing* the irrational beliefs per se; rather, we are weakening the conviction in irrational beliefs, and strengthening the conviction in rational beliefs. Disputation is applied to both irrational and rational beliefs, using in essence the same arguments. There are variations in how much E is done alongside D, but I consider E to be explicitly about clearly defining new rational beliefs, and helping the client to strengthen their conviction in, and application of, rational beliefs. When helping the client to develop their effective new rational beliefs at E, the following considerations are useful:

1. As client and practitioner, will you collaboratively decide on the new beliefs? Or will the practitioner take a more didactic approach, and suggest the 'proper' new beliefs? If there is time and client inclination, the former is preferred in order to ensure ownership of the new beliefs and to ensure the client's choice of precise words is considered.
2. How comprehensive will the new beliefs be? Whilst it is more appealing to instantiate the belief that "I can tolerate it" because it is snappy and short, it does not capture the full rational belief ("It is tough, but I can tolerate it, and it is worth it to do so"). The latter is preferred, even though it is more long-winded. Accuracy is vital here, because it is important that the belief to which the client will commit is aligned with the core tenets of rationality laid out in REBT. But *over time*, the client can shorten this belief so long as the essence is still captured and the client understands the deep rationality that underpins their shorter and catchier self-talk. For example, the client can use symbolic language that more efficiently captures their rational beliefs.
3. Is it worth recapping the G-D steps that have been taken? Given the often long and winding conversations that can take place in REBT (although we try not to let this happen), despite its structured and focussed nature, it could be advantageous to go back through what has been covered. This can ensure the client, and the practitioner, is clear on why the E stage is to be executed at this point.
4. Is the client ready? I often try to ensure that E is started in a new session, rather than at the end of a session. This allows the client to reflect meaningfully on how we have arrived at this point, and assuming that D has just taken place, it is worth allowing D to sink in before beginning E.

Once we venture into E, we can help the client to steelman the rational beliefs, rehearse them meaningfully, and plan on their integration into their lives. This requires ongoing effort from the client, and they can anticipate and plan for some backsliding into their old ways of thinking even as they strengthen their conviction and commitment to the effective new belief over time.

There are various reasons why E needs special attention. First, as DiGiuseppe et al. (2014) highlight, people continue to believe in theories that they know are wrong until they discover better ideas (e.g., Kuhn, 1962). In other words, it is not enough to just highlight that irrational beliefs are faulty and that rational beliefs might be better, we need to work with the client to internalise these 'better' rational ideas. Clients might be able to quickly understand the effective new beliefs, and also experience some of the short-term benefits of holding them, but committing to internalising these beliefs and holding them long term is a more difficult task. Ideally, the effective new beliefs should be automatised, such that they inform the client's natural and habitual healthy response to adversity. This automatisation requires rehearsal, repetition, and reinforcement, just like the automatisation of a physical skill.

> When modifications and/or eliminations of certain irrationalities do occur, changes in the frequency, intensity, and duration of these irrationalities are often short-lived, thus resulting in regression, relapse, and/or newly acquired and invented ones.
>
> (Ellis, 1976, in Ruth, 1992, p. 6)

It is not a good idea to try to obliterate irrational beliefs, and then leave a void, because irrational beliefs can creep back in and fill the void. We need to help the client to develop convincing arguments for their rational beliefs that render the irrational beliefs surplus to requirements and fill the gap that disputation leaves. Also, because people often have rational beliefs alongside irrational beliefs (Ellis, 2002a), it is advantageous to ensure that when rational beliefs are developed, they negate the irrational belief as well as state clearly the rational elements (e.g., "I want to, *but I do not have to*") (DiGiuseppe et al., 1988). The best way to construct a rational belief is to negate the irrational belief. In this way, we integrate the irrational within the rational such that we do not deny or ignore the irrational aspects, but recognise and explicitly counter them. We say "it is bad, *but not terrible*" or "I want, *but I do not have to*", for example. Table 12.1 in DiGiuseppe et al. (2014, p. 222) is useful for further guidance on this.

The second reason why E needs special attention is because we are striving for *emotional* insight, not just *intellectual* insight. On completion of D the client may have developed some intellectual insight into the nature of rational and irrational beliefs, the key differences between them (as it pertains to the client's particularly issues), and the way disputation can be used per se (Dryden, 2018). The client acknowledges that their beliefs are underpinning their unhealthy negative emotions (UNE). But *intellectual* insight is usually not enough alone to impact the client's emotions and behaviours in a meaningful way, and the client has not yet made a consistent effort to change (Ellis, 1963). Indeed, the client may still truly believe the irrational beliefs, and whilst they can see why the rational beliefs are indeed more constructive, they will only lightly believe these rational beliefs. Thus, we need to help the client to work towards *emotional* insight to facilitate meaningful change, which involves the client committing to the rational beliefs and committing to the work that is required for meaningful change (Ellis, 1963). In other words, D and E should be life skills that the client can commit to over the life course, rather than remedial short-term techniques that are forgotten about as soon as the REBT work ceases with the client. Thus, we should follow Epictetus' (Epictetus & Dobbin, 2008, p. 127) advice:

> Every habit and faculty is formed or strengthened by the corresponding act – walking makes you walk better, running makes you a better runner. If you want to be literate, read, if you want to be a painter, paint. Go a month without reading, occupied with something else, and you'll see what the result is. And if you're laid up a mere ten days, when you get up and try to walk any distance you'll find your legs barely able to support you. So if you like doing something, do it regularly; if you don't like doing something, make a habit of doing something different. The same goes for moral inclinations. When you get angry, you should know that you aren't guilty of an isolated lapse, you've encouraged a trend and thrown fuel on the fire.

In other words, if you want to develop rational beliefs, then you must work to believe rationally, and work against believing irrationally. In an interview with Michael Bernard, Ellis considered whether the set techniques used to strengthen the degree of endorsement in the new rational beliefs should be subsumed under 'E', or whether 'F' was required (Bernard, 2009). In either case there is certainly a strong case for helping the client develop some skills, beyond disputation, to reinforce their rational beliefs in the real world. Like Ellis, I subsume F under E in this section, and see rational reinforcement as very much an important part of E. In other words, rather than seeing E as just the development of new rationale beliefs, I also see it as the strengthening and committing to this new rationality. Because the task of committing to new beliefs long term can be beset with procrastination, fatigue, loss of interest, and low self-efficacy, the practitioner works hard to collaboratively design and develop ways in which the client can achieve emotional insight. Creativity and tailoring to the client are stressed (Dryden, 2019b), and whilst I cover some techniques in this section, the practitioner should work closely with the client to figure out what types of activities will fit the client's temperament and circumstances. As with disputation, a combination of methods should be used.

> Stoics argued that humans are first and foremost thinking creatures, capable of exercising reason. Although we share many instincts with other animals, our ability to think rationally is what makes us human…It allows us to evaluate our thoughts, feelings, and urges and to decide if they're good or bad, healthy or unhealthy. We therefore have an innate duty to protect our ability to reason and to use it properly.
>
> (Robertson, 2019a, p. 38)

Rehearsal of rational beliefs

Rational cue cards

It is important that the new rational beliefs are constructed to be technically accurate to REBT, but also written in the client's language as much as possible (DiGiuseppe et al., 2014). By that, I mean that the rational beliefs should reflect preferences, anti-awfulizing, FT, and/or unconditional acceptance, but should be written in words that the client understands and connects with. That is, because language is symbolic, a short phrase can be assigned to a full rational belief. One client of mine developed the rational belief "I want hit a good chip shot every time, but I don't have, and I could tolerate it if I did not", and abstracted the belief to the statement "just f***ing do it", or "JFDI" for short. He would use this in practice and in competitions. This, for the client, seemed to capture the cognitive, emotive, and behavioural approach he wanted to take for chip shots that freed him up to express himself on the course. This has echoes of Jos Buttler writing 'f*** it' on every bat he owns (Sealey, 2018).

Producing cue cards with the rational beliefs, abstracted or full, printed or written on them is a useful strategy for helping the client to internalise the rational beliefs. Ten cue cards can be placed in ten different areas that the client will frequently visit. For example, the client can place one in their kit bag, wallet, purse, bedside draw, glove compartment in car, etc. The idea here is to have the client place the cue cards in places where they will happen upon them, therefore seeing and reading (even unconsciously) the rational beliefs frequently and unavoidably. This is not a long-term strategy, but serves as a short-term way of helping the client to remember and rehearse the rational beliefs until they believe that it has been internalised. The same type of activity can be achieved using a Smartphone by setting up a calendar alarm each day with the rational belief as the title of the appointment. Clients can also use the Smarter Thinking App (Turner & Wood, 2019a) to access their chosen rational beliefs to aid reflection and internalisation.

Rational beliefs jar

Different to the above, this activity involves producing many variations of the rational belief, each worded slightly differently. Fifty small slips of paper with ten rational beliefs printed on them (5 slips per rational beliefs) are produced, folded up, and put into a jar (or any suitable container). Each day, the client picks three slips of paper out of the jar, reads the rational beliefs to themselves, and spends just a minute repeating it to themselves (out loud or in their head). The random nature of their selection and the active engagement in the process help the client to focus on the activity and the rehearsal of the belief. This activity is more deliberate than the cue cards task, but in total takes about three minutes per day (1 minute per slip) to complete. Very low time and effort investment, but this activity can help with the internalisation of the rational beliefs and has the client deliberatively investing time in repeating rational beliefs to themselves as mantras.

This activity can also be modified to include both rational *and* irrational beliefs for the purposes of stimulating disputation within sessions. The client selects a slip, and decides whether it is rational or irrational, and explains their thinking using evidence, logic, and pragmatics. This is a form a Socratic comparison but is more driven by the client. This can be a fun challenge in sessions to test the client's disputation skills too.

Athlete Resilience Credo

A credo is "a set of beliefs, which expresses a particular opinion and influences the way you live" (Dryden, 2007, p. 219). Specifically, the Rational Resilience Credo was developed by Dryden (2007) as a set of rational beliefs born from REBT theory, promoting an ideal resilient response to adversity. In 2016, I adapted the credo to suit the audience with whom I apply the credo, i.e., athletes. I developed the Athlete Rational Resilience Credo (ARRC; Turner, 2016a), based on Dryden's (2007) credo, but adapted it to an athlete audience. The ARRC has been used in research to support the application of REBT (Chrysidis et al., 2020; Deen et al., 2017). In Figure 13.1, I present a further adapted credo (Turner, 2020b) that is briefer that the one presented by Turner (2016a).

The ARRC comprises one paragraph for each of the core rational beliefs; paragraph one covers preferences, and paragraphs two, three, and four cover anti-awfulizing, FT, and unconditional acceptance, respectively. The ARRC assertively promotes the four core rational beliefs, which has three main advantages. The ARRC gives a clear indication of

As an athlete and a human being, I have many desires or "wants". Some of these desires are very strong as I am driven to be the best athlete I can possibly be. However, I recognize that no matter how strong my desires are this does not mean that I "have to" or "must" have my desires met. I may want to be successful, perform consistently, be secure in my team, and keep developing my skills, but I know that these desires do not "have to" be met. I accept that from time to time my desires will not be met. It's OK that I feel upset and disappointed when my desires are not met, as this shows that I care about my sport and my achievement within it. My upset feelings are normal, and they can motivate me to work hard towards my desires, knowing full well that demanding that these desires are met is rigid, nonsensical, and fruitless. Not having my wants met provides me with opportunities to grow as a person, fully accepting that unfavourable events are valuable even though they lead to negative feelings.

I recognize that when my desires are not met, I fail, face setbacks, this is bad and unfortunate but not terrible or the end of the world. No matter how bad it is to not have my desires met, I know that worse things could and have happened to me, none of which are truly awful. It is bad not to be successful, not to perform consistently, not be secure in my team, and not to keep developing my skills, but I know that none of this is truly awful. Further, if I am not given opportunities, this certainly is not the end of the world. Even though I might feel upset and my goal attainment may be hindered, I can distinguish inconvenience from catastrophe. I accept that bad things will happen, and that's OK as this provides me with valuable opportunities to grow as a person.

Not having my desires met is very tough and difficult to tolerate. But I know I can tolerate this, because not getting what I want will not kill me or cause so much pain that I disintegrate. Even if my strongest desires are not met it is not unbearable. To not be successful, to not perform consistently, to not be secure in my team, and to not keep developing my skills, is very hard but I know that I can certainly stand this. Although I may feel frustrated and upset and my goal attainment may be hindered, I know that I have the capacity to tolerate failure, setbacks, and being let down. Importantly, I accept that facing tough situations that do not meet my desires is OK as this provides me with valuable opportunities to grow as a person. Ultimately, being able to tolerate adversity is worthwhile because of the strength it gives me to face future adversity. However, just because I can tolerate adversity, it does not mean that I will tolerate it. I can pick my battles, and I if I know something is wrong, I can protest and remonstrate.

If I fail to reach a goal, or if I face an obstacle, I recognize that this is bad, but it says nothing about me as a person. I know that failing does not make me a failure, that stumbling on the way to a goal does not make me useless and does not mean I am worthless. Similarly, succeeding does not mean I am a success, a smooth path to my goal does not mean I am perfect, and does not make me a worthy person. I am able to distinguish between my own behaviour, and me as a total human being. I am not what I do. As a human being, my worth cannot be judged or rated, and does not depend on my success or failure in sport. When I fall short, it just shows that I am a fallible human being just like all other humans. Sometimes I succeed, sometimes I fail, and that's fine. It's OK to feel upset when I fail, face setbacks, or am let down. These feelings can motivate me to work on aspects of myself that are hindering me. No matter how bad things are, I realize that sport and life is a mixture of good and bad events, and that the bad events test me and provide valuable opportunities to grow as a person.

Figure 13.1 The athlete rational credo (Turner, 2020b).

what athletes can aim for in terms of achieving a rational philosophy of life, focusses on the utility of beliefs, rather than changes in G or A, which promotes B–C connections and dissuades A–C connections, and it is written in the first person – rather than speaking to the athlete, as the athlete reads it, they speak to *themselves*.

I suggest three main methods of using the ARRC with clients. First, clients can work to internalise the full credo by reading and rehearsing each day – they could even audio record the credo on their Smartphone to listen to. Practice makes permanent. Second, the client can select chunks of text that are most germane to their issues and/or goals for use as self-talk – they could create some cue cards with shorter sections on them. Third, clients can produce their own ARRC using the generic ARRC as a template. This creates some ownership over the ARRC, can be written using the client's idiosyncratic language, and encourages critical engagement in REBT – the client has to properly understand and be able to articulate REBT in order to create their credo.

Rational self-talk

Of course, the strategies covered thus far in this chapter all make use of self-talk in one way or another. Rational self-talk, or rational self-statements, have been used in past research to formulate rational conditions in which the participants are provided with a set of rational statements to rehearse and use on approach to a task. Early experimental researchers showed that participants using rational self-statements, as opposed to irrational self-statements, demonstrated less motor skill execution errors, and better behavioural efficiency (Bonadies & Bass, 1984; Kombos et al., 1989; Schill et al., 1978). For example, participants approaching a mirror-tracing task who were given 'irrational' self-talk statements (e.g., "If I don't perform perfectly well next time, it will prove I'm stupid") recorded the most errors in the task, and performed slower than the 'rational' self-talk group (e.g., "Mistakes don't mean I'm stupid"; Schill et al., 1978, p. 4). In a more contemporary study, Wood et al. (2017) used rational and irrational self-statement conditions (as well as a control condition) to examine the effects of self-talk on golf-putting accuracy (Experiment 1), and hazard perception, visual search behaviour, and persistence during a breath-holding task (Experiment 2). However, type of self-talk did not appear to affect performance outcomes, possibly owing to the novice status of the performers who took part in the study.

So subsequently, we examined the effects of irrational and rational self-statements on pressurised golf-putting performance, importantly with skilled golfers and in the field (i.e., on the golf course) rather than in the laboratory (Turner et al., 2019c). In this study a within-subjects cross-over design was used; all participants completed golf putting performances across three sessions. Session 1 saw participants complete a baseline (no self-talk) performance. Participants then self-selected their self-talk condition in session 2 by selecting one of two sealed envelopes. One envelope contained rational self-talk instructions, and the other contained irrational self-talk instructions (see Figure 13.2). The contents of each envelope were unknown to the experimenter until all data had been collected. In session 3 participants used the alternate self-talk they had not selected in session 2.

After controlling for the participants playing ability (i.e., baseline scores) data showed that the golfers who adopted rational self-statements recorded higher putting accuracy compared to when engaging with irrational alternatives. The golfers also reported that the rational self-talk was more usable and helpful for their putting performance. The inclusion of a meaningful and stressful scenario, with skilled performers, provided a more accurate method by which to

Rational self-talk	Irrational self-talk
I want to sink this putt but that doesn't mean I must	I want to sink this putt and therefore I must
If I don't succeed in this task, it will be bad but not awful	If I don't succeed in this task it would be awful
If I don't succeed in this task, I will not like it, but I will be able to stand it	I would not be able to stand failing in this task
If I fail to sink this putt then I will have failed, but that would not make me a failure	If I miss this putt, it would make me a failure

Figure 13.2 Rational and irrational self-talk (adapted from Turner et al., 2019c).

examine the effects of irrational and rational self-talk on skilled performance, compared to previous research.

So, rational self-talk or self-statements can be used on approach to a task in order to maximise task execution. Dryden (2019a) suggests, and I agree, that encouraging the client to actually face their As whilst rehearsing their rational beliefs is a very powerful technique. When encouraging the client to do this, it is important they refrain from avoiding the A or removing themselves from A before they have successful regulated their emotion by using the rational belief. This mixture of behavioural intent to face A and not avoid it, and the cognitive strategy of using the rational beliefs, creates a powerful inoculation effect against the threat of A. For example, perhaps a coach is unhealthily anxious about making mistakes in their pre-match team talk (A), so has been avoiding them (C) and letting the assistant coach do them. The coach has an irrational belief that "I must not make mistakes in the team talk, and if I do make mistakes it shows how useless I am". I would encourage the coach to rehearse the belief that "I would prefer not to make mistakes in the team talk, but if I do make mistakes, it is not ideal, but it doesn't mean that I am useless, it just shows I am fallible like everyone else!" whilst forthrightly taking responsibility for all pre-match team talks. Face the A, with the rational B.

A modification of this technique (more purely behavioural) would be to have the client enter into the commitment of taking responsibility for all pre-match team talks, without the rehearsal of the rational belief. Just like the story about Albert Ellis in New York Botanical Gardens that opened this book, by acting differently, you can think differently. The exposure to A and encouragement to 'stay in there' (Dryden, 2019b) are sometimes known as 'flooding' (e.g., Ellis, 1980b; Turner et al., 2020b), and can help the client to realise that the situation is not as bad as they thought it was, and that if they do make mistakes, nobody really notices or cares. Even if people do notice and care, the client will notice that they are still capable of coaching successfully, and are thus not "useless". These experiences will help the client to develop and reinforce the rational belief because they have gathered empirical evidence to disprove the irrational belief, and prove the rational belief. So, this technique can help the client to re-appraise A (i.e., inferential A change), and/or develop rational beliefs; either way, they are able to face the situation forthrightly. Seneca said, "It's not because things are difficult that we do not dare; it is because we do not dare that things are difficult" (Letter to Lucilius, letter 104, section 26) and the client will realise that the more they voluntarily face

A, the more than will be able to face many other As. We can support the client in facing A, and ensure that this homework task is negotiated and set carefully, so that the client feels supported and understands the purpose of this task within the work being done.

Self-talk strategies are considered one of the most widely used, and effective approaches for the enhancement of athletic performance (Van Raalte et al., 2016). Variations of self-talk have been categorised into a taxonomy that includes: valence (i.e., positive, negative, & neutral), overtness (i.e., spoken out loud), systems one (i.e., rapid & autonomous) and two (i.e., slow and consciously monitored), and grammatical form (Van Raalte & Vincent, 2017). Researchers have highlighted the importance of function over valence (i.e., positive vs. negative) when employing self-talk strategies with athletes. Thus, it appears negative self-talk can help or hinder performance (Weinberg, 2018), by enhancing or down-regulating confidence and promoting goals and engagement (Hardy et al., 2009; Latinjak et al., 2014), a notion reflected within the central tenets of REBT. Indeed, Latinjak et al. (2014) suggest that goal-directed self-talk should be classified in terms of functionality (facilitative/ debilitative) instead of valence (positive/negative), a notion that fits the binary theory of emotional distress (BTED) in REBT, with its focus on the function of belief and emotion rather than valence.

In sum, on approach to an adversity, one way in which clients can implement their rational beliefs is via the use of rational self-talk, specifically devised for use in those moments (Turner et al., 2019d). Helping the client to get into the habit of doing this can be achieved in session, where the practitioner can rehearse with the athlete when they will use their self-talk, and what their self-talk will contain (e.g., Chrysidis et al., 2020). A final point to make with regard to self-talk is to not underestimate the utility of evocation and intonation (DiGiuseppe et al., 2014). When the client uses the rational beliefs, and when you help them to reinforce the rational beliefs, it is often useful to annunciate the key words like 'must' vs. 'want', for example. Is it often the case that clients think that their rational beliefs should reflect calm and balance, which can be the case, but is not always true (depends on the desired or required emotional arousal). For example, on facing an important event, it is fine to express the passion in wanting to perform well by evocatively expressing that "I REALLY WANT to perform well, but I do not HAVE TO". The words in capital letters can be higher or lower in pitch, louder, slowed down, and/or enunciated. This can work out loud, or in the client's head. Don't be afraid to use expletives too (!) if the client is game (Figure 13.3).

Imagery

The client rehearses the new rational beliefs whilst they imagine themselves facing the adversity (Dryden, 2019b). The client does this until they can experience the healthy negative emotions (HNEs). The practitioner may need to help the client develop their imagery skills first, but for some emotions, such as anxiety, the client is often quite apt at foreseeing their demise in light of A. Do not expect the client to be able to do this perfectly at first, and you can guide them in and out of imagery and build up to being able to experience HNEs via the rational belief. Importantly, this method is helping the client to develop their self-efficacy in using their rational beliefs in the face of the adversity, and getting them used to feeling negative but healthy emotions as a result. In addition, Rational Emotive Imagery (REI; Maultsby, 1971) is an oft-used technique in REBT (Ellis & Harper, 1975; Hickey & Doyle, 2018; Hymen & Warren, 1978), which is a form of mental practice or rehearsal of thinking, feeling and behaving exactly the way you want (Maultsby, 1984). REI involves the client

Figure 13.3 Client rational beliefs.

imagining the A and its associated UNE, and then changing the UNE to the HNE. The client then reports to the practitioner how they were able to go from UNE to HNE – if it was achieved by changing A, the client does this exercise again. The exercise continues until the client can change UNE to HNE by only changing their beliefs from irrational to rational. Once this is achieved, the client can practise this technique independently, now able to rehearse cognitive change in the service of the HNE. It is recommended that clients undertake REI for ten minutes, four or more times per day, but also more informally when they have time and opportunity (Wirga et al., 2020).

Chadha et al. (2019) point out that REI shares some characteristics with other forms of imagery more typically used in sport settings. For example, motivational general arousal (MG-A) imagery can be used to enhance an athlete's overall affective experiences and interpretation of pre-competitive symptoms (e.g., Mellalieu et al., 2009). Both REI and MG-A imagery focus upon the emotional experiences associated with emotion (Vadocz et al., 1997), but in MG-A imagery it is more typical for the athlete to imagine arousal-reducing images (e.g., quiet place). In REI, as discussed, the client is encouraged to alter their irrational beliefs in order to alter their emotion, specifically, from UNE to HHE. Chadha et al. (2019) also encourage the convergence of REI and MG-A imagery with Lazarus' (1999) cognitive appraisal theory (covered in Chapter 2). For example, knowing anger stems from a core relational theme of 'misdemeanour against me and mine' (other blame), and appraisal components high goal relevance, and high goal incongruence, other/world-accountability, and/or self-accountability (see Figure 5.1), it is possible to have the client imagine the A to include these elements. Then, they can practise applying their rational belief in these types of situations in the service of healthy anger (HNE) as opposed to unhealthy anger (UNE).

A good knowledge of theory can reveal useful applied techniques. Whilst sport literature offers some very useful modes of imagery, such as MG-A imagery, for a specific REBT solution the focus should remain on belief change, rather than G and A change or direct C change.

If then plans

Implementation intentions were posited by Dr. Peter M. Gollwitzer, Professor of Psychology at New York University, and are more commonly known as 'if-then plans', which are specific plans that identify both an appropriate goal-directed response and a suitable situation in which to initiate that response ("If situation *Y* arises, then I will perform goal directed behavior *Z*!"; Webb & Sheeran, 2007). This technique is quite simple and can be used to help clients to utilise the GABCDE framework out in the real world (e.g., Bishop, 2000), but from my experience is most useful for rehearsing the new rational beliefs (E). In implementation intentions, the 'if' part could reflect the A (adversity, barrier, obstacle) that could thwart a goal (G), or it could reflect the goal (G) itself. The 'then' part reflects the functional response to the A or G. In our case when using REBT, the 'then' part is where we inject the client's newly developed rational beliefs.

For example, on approaching a competitive situation in which performing well is your aim (G), you could say "IF I feel unhealthily anxious before the competitive, THEN I will remind myself that although I really want to perform well, that doesn't mean that I have to". Or, in situations where you are faced with social conflict (A), you could say "IF I am treated with disrespect by my teammate, THEN I will reaffirm to myself that being treated with disrespect is tough, but I can tolerate it and it is worth it to do so". The client can make these if-then plans broader too, to reflect their fundamental goals (FGs; see Chapter 8). For example, "IF I want to fulfil my potential as a human being, THEN I will remind myself each day that although life is difficult and challenging, I can bear it and it is worth it to do so". Or,

> IF I want to maintain my healthy emotional disposition, THEN each day I will tell myself that I am a fallible human being that sometimes succeeds, and sometimes fails, and that my self-worth is not contingent on this success and failure.

Implementation intentions are more useful for clients than just assuming or expecting that they will apply their rational beliefs in relevant situations. If-then plans give them a strategy and well, a plan (!), with which to go forthrightly into the real world. It is then less likely that they will be caught off guard in the face of an A, and slip back into their old irrationalities. A meta-analysis by Gollwitzer and Sheeran (2006) revealed that the overall effect size (across 8,461 participants) of forming implementation intentions on goal achievement was medium-large (d =.65). They also found that implementation intentions were effective for the initiation of goal striving, the shielding of goal pursuit from unwanted influences, disengagement from failing courses of action, and conservation of capability for future goal striving. The benefit of integrating REBT principles into the implementation intentions is that the THEN component is controllable by the client. It can even be applied to REBT itself, for example, "IF I find myself demanding the things that I want, THEN I will challenge my thinking with truth, logic, and pragmatics". There are of course many potential IF's and many possible THEN's, so you can help the client to formulate and test these if-then plans in session, and encourage them to apply them as homework assignments. As the client practises this planning more frequently, they will develop more confidence in applying their new rational beliefs across a range of situations. They feel prepared for the As that await them, and the As they themselves bring forth.

Debate and role play

One very useful way to help the client to reinforce their rational beliefs is to have the client defend them. For example, you can engage the client in a debate concerning the rational beliefs in which you (the practitioner) argue *against* the rational belief, and they (the client) argue *for* the rational belief. You can also reverse these roles so that the client is *against* the rational belief, and the practitioner is *for* the rational beliefs (DiGiuseppe et al., 2014). Indeed, the client can make use of an intrapersonal dialogue between two parts of the self, rational vs. irrational, to promote commitment to the rational (Dryden, 2018). One way to do this is to have the client argue both for *and* against using a two-chair technique (Dryden, 2019b). When the client sits in one chair they argue *against* the rational belief, and when they sit in the other chair (physically opposite to the client), they argue *for* the rational belief. The practitioner moderates the 'debate' and encourages both sides to use the principles of evidence, logic, and pragmatics. Whichever format is selected, the practitioner should take sufficient time to set this up properly, and to help the client reflect on the meaning of this work after it has been completed. What we are doing here is encouraging the independent utilisation of disputation, and at the same time bolstering the client's commitment to the rational beliefs.

How do we know E is working?

> A rational being can turn each setback into raw material and use it to achieve its goal.
>
> Marcus Aurelius

The client may be able to comprehend that their irrational beliefs are hindering them, and that rational beliefs would better serve them. They may be able to very articulately grasp the differences between irrational and rational beliefs, and understand disputation. But, as many writers have noted, comprehension alone may not be sufficient to engender emotional and/or behavioural change (e.g., Kinney, 2000). One of the hallmarks of the client truly believing the tenets of REBT is that the client demonstrates *emotional* insight on top of their *intellectual* insight. This emotional insight can be demonstrated in many ways by the client, chief of which are a) the assumption of responsibility for thoughts, feelings, and actions, b) the clear and strong recognition that they can do something about their irrational beliefs and the long-term commitment to doing something about their irrational beliefs, c) the *independent* disputation of irrational beliefs and the acting against the irrational beliefs, and d) the spontaneous formulation of and commitment to rational beliefs in the face of adversity. In brief, emotional insight is evident when a client acknowledges that their beliefs and behaviours are self-defeating, and then makes consistent and deliberate efforts to effect substantive change, promoting a true philosophical restructuring (Kinney, 2000). Or as Ellis (1963) puts it, "Where the client with intellectual-insight…thinks it would be desirable if he believed the right things, he does not actually believe them. The person with emotional insight truly believes, is committed, and therefore acts" (p. 126).

The client may report some cognition-emotion mismatch (Stott, 2007), which is frequently reported in the application of cognitive behavioural therapies (Dryden, 2012d). That is, the client may experience some disassociation between their rational thoughts vs. how they *feel* about themselves. Feel is italicised here because when the client says 'feel' they are not alluding to an emotion per se. It is more likely that they are alluding to a more deeply held belief. For example, an athlete may say: "I know that I'm not a failure if I have not met my standards, but I still feel like a complete failure". What the client might be indicating here is that they can endorse the rational *thought* but not the rational *belief*. We want to move the client from mere rational *cognition* towards deeply held rational *philosophies*.

Intellectual insight can be captured nicely by psychometrics and self-reports, and can be demonstrated in session using debate and other Socratic methods. I like to use an irrational vs. rational belief conviction scales, whereby clients give a rating to their irrational beliefs, and their rational beliefs, indicating the extent to which they *truly* believe each. For example, Figure 13.4 is a scale I use with clients that has them report their endorsement of an irrational/rational belief, frequency with which the belief/s enters into conscious thought, and how helpful the belief/s was for them in that moment. This can be done as soon as the rational beliefs are formulated, and the aim is to help the client increase their true conviction in the rational beliefs, and reduce their true conviction in the irrational beliefs as the work takes place. Endorsement of A–C vs. B–C thinking can be measured using the

Rational/irrational beliefs self-rating form

Instructions:
Please enter your *irrational* belief (iB) here____________________
Please enter your alternate *rational* belief (rB) here____________________
Then complete the questions below by indicating your answers on the scales.

	To what extent to agree with the belief?				
	Strongly disagree	Disagree	Neither agree or disagree	Agree	Strongly agree
Your iB	1	2	3	4	5
Your rB	1	2	3	4	5
	How often does the belief appear in conscious thought?				
	Never	Rarely	Sometimes	Often	A lot
Your iB	1	2	3	4	5
Your rB	1	2	3	4	5
	How helpful was the belief in the moment?				
	Very unhelpful	A little unhelpful	Neither helpful or unhelpful	A little helpful	Very helpful
Your iB	1	2	3	4	5
Your rB	1	2	3	4	5

Figure 13.4 The rational/irrational beliefs self-rating form.

cognitive-mediation beliefs questionnaire (CMBQ; Turner et al., 2021) – since REBT is endorsing of B–C thinking, scores in B–C thinking should increase through REBT work, whilst scores in A–C think should reduce.

Intellectual insight is really best demonstrated at the level of behaviour. Is the client forthrightly taking on the A that typically gives rise to their Bs and UNEs? Is the client actively engaging socially? Is the client taking on new challenges? Is the client employing healthy coping strategies to deal with life's many challenges? Is the client acting against the irrational belief? Given that we have a concept of what behavioural tenets help define HNEs, the practitioner can assess the expression of these behaviours, or action tendencies, to help infer whether emotional insight is being achieved (or worked towards). For example, in the sport literature performance measures are often obtained to mark shifts (hopefully improvements) in some sport-relevant performance parameter (e.g., Maxwell-Keys et al., 2022; Wood et al., 2016, 2018a).

To help the client achieve emotional insight, practitioners should not over rely on cognitive methods in their work (DiGiuseppe et al., 2014; Kinney, 2000). The use of emotive, imaginal, and behavioural methods is important here (e.g., Robb et al., 1999), and these activities can be done both in and out of sessions (see Chapter 4). For example, REI can be practitioner led, but the client can also apply this technique independently, so long as they have learnt it properly in-session. Flooding, or 'stay in there' techniques can be applied by the client out in the real world, or by using imagery, and can powerfully demonstrate that a feared stimulus is not 'awful' and the client can in fact 'tolerate' the adversity (DiGiuseppe et al., 2014).

DOUBLETHINK: RATIONAL *BELIEFS* AND IRRATIONAL *SELF-TALK*

In the last two chapters, I have talked about D and E in terms of disputing irrational and rational beliefs, and strengthening rational beliefs. Whilst research has indicated that rational self-talk is advantageous for optimal performance (e.g., Turner et al., 2019d), there remains little evidence to directly suggest that irrational self-talk is directly harmful for athletic performance. Instead, recent anecdotal reports (Wood et al., 2017) point towards a more complex and nuanced insight into the operationalisation of irrational self-talk on performance. For example, in the golf study I covered earlier in this chapter (Turner et al., 2019c), golfers performed better when using rational self-talk compared to irrational self-talk, but when they used irrational self-talk, they still showed performance improvements from baseline (just not as much as for those using rational self-talk). This aligns with my experience working across a range of settings, whereby in some situations, especially situations which might benefit from intense and acute deployment of effort and attention, the language of irrational beliefs *can sometimes* provide an impassioned motivational quality that could spur on performance. That is, for some who operate in a high-performance environment, the adoption of extreme and dogmatic self-talk may help, rather than hinder, success in the short term.

This brings into question the importance of the 'function' argument in disputation, and in the definition of irrationality in REBT per se. If the irrational belief is helpful for my short-term goals, why would I give it up? If it is helpful, how can it be irrational? The key question here, is '*helpful for what?*' In my earlier comments on eudaimonia vs. short-term pleasure, I made the point that primary goals (PGs) should not be placed above fundamental goals (FGs) in a goal hierarchy, because short-term hedonism should not be placed above long-term fulfilment. So, even when the irrational belief is helpful in the short term, the practitioner should be very careful in promoting irrational beliefs, and should strongly dissuade the client from applying irrational beliefs unilaterally to their vocational endeavours. That is, it is one thing using a belief like "I must stay in front of my competitor" or "failure in this moment would be the worst thing ever" during the heat of performance, and it is another thing to use demanding and awfulizing beliefs on a day-to-day basis in relation to athletic life per se (e.g., "I must have a glittering career, and it would be awful if I did not"). In other words, not every irrational *thought* is an irrational *belief*, and there is a temporal dimension that goes along with a belief that is different to a thought (i.e., time-limited irrationality; Neenan & Dryden, 2015), whereby a thought is short term and potentially fleeting, and a deeply held belief is longer-term and more stable (i.e., schema; DiGiuseppe et al., 2014; Turner, 2016b).

As a result of this performance paradox, I have proposed (Turner, 2016b, 2019a) that irrational self-talk in the moment vs. irrational beliefs per se can live together under the Orwellian concept of 'doublethink'; "…the power of holding two contradictory beliefs in one's mind simultaneously, and accepting both of them" (Orwell, 1949, p32). Orwell goes on to describe doublethink in the following way: "To tell deliberate lies while genuinely believing in them, to forget any fact that has become inconvenient, and then when it becomes necessary again, to draw it back from oblivion for just so long as it is needed…" (Orwell, 1949, p. 32). That is, a client can forget any fact or belief that has become inconvenient in the moment, and then draw it back only when it is needed. For example, an ultra-runner may hold deeply rational beliefs ("I want to succeed in sport, but that does not mean that I have to"), yet employ irrational self-talk (i.e., "I must finish this race, otherwise it would be terrible") during the most arduous stages of a race. Accordingly, the irrational self-talk in this case could aid the athlete in pushing themselves over the line, thus facilitating their performance. So, in doublethink, it is possible to use irrational self-talk in acute situations where performance gains might be possible, and at the same time, hold rational beliefs about the self, others, and the world. It is possible to momentarily abscond the rational beliefs from consciousness, and bring into focus irrational self-talk, in the service of acute performance. Irrational and rational ideas can be used as tools to be used judiciously. This is about choice, in the moment, as to what is most helpful in a given situation, and the self-talk used to aid a performance does not need to reflect deeply held beliefs. Ellis (1976) also recognised this ability to engage in doublethink, citing a

> basic human tendency to have two contradictory beliefs at the same time – an "intellectual" one which you lightly and occasionally hold and an "emotional" one which you vigorously and consistently hold, and which you therefore usually tend to act upon. This tendency to have simultaneously contradictory beliefs again seems part of the human condition.
>
> (p. 33)

This cognitive dissonance (e.g., Festinger, 1957) must be managed carefully by the athlete, but can be momentarily ignored because the irrational belief is producing the desired outcome of acutely enhanced performance. The skill here is for the athlete to choose when to use irrational thought for the purposes of performance, a choice that relies on their meta-cognitive ability (Metcalfe & Shimamura, 1994) to recognise the thought, decide whether the thought is helpful in the moment, whilst also knowing that the thought is irrational. Novak Djokovic, professional tennis player with 20 Grand Slam singles titles (at the time of writing), gives a nice example of this dissonance, saying that "Tennis is my life, obviously; I need to focus, I need to win. But it's not the only thing. I'm not going to play forever" (Wilbon, 2012). Here, Djokovic expresses the rigid need to succeed, but also expresses a non-extreme belief that tennis is not the only thing. Clients who are unable to relinquish their irrational thoughts when they depart from the field of play may find it difficult to endorse rational beliefs, and therefore may be at risk from the many deleterious mental health outcomes associated with irrational beliefs (Turner, 2016b).

This idea that irrationality could lead to favourable outcomes aligns with Bret Weinstein's concept of metaphorical truth. Weinstein (PowerfulJRE, 2017) posits that,

> I have a category that I call 'literally false, metaphorically true'. These are ideas that aren't true in the factual sense, but they are true enough that if you behave as if they are true, you come out ahead of where you would be if you behaved according to the fact that they're not true.

Weinstein uses the example of the belief that 'everything happens for a reason', which whilst false, is a helpful belief if a tragedy befalls you (e.g., you may be open to opportunities by not being preoccupied with your misfortune). As applied to irrational beliefs, they are literally false (empirically and logically invalid) but in acute performance situations could be beneficial. This is clearly all about context (timing) and function.

However, I have some cautionary instruction here. Whilst history tells us that many goals have been achieved because the individual was able to push past their perceived limits, it is debatable whether this is an appropriate way to engage with our endeavours. Bullying oneself into pushing past safe physical and psychological limits using irrational self-talk could have deleterious effects on mental (e.g., depression) and physical (e.g., illness) health (e.g., Turner et al., 2022b), even if the human capability to override innate warning systems is lauded culturally and in the media. It is important for clients to keep their eyes on the prize – eudaimonia – not short-term pleasure or happiness. In the interest of eudaimonia, the client may execute their wisdom by being able to flexibly choose when to apply irrationality in the service of short-term gains, but only if this short-term gain (PG) is part of the long-term pursuit of fulfilment (FG). Clients should not sacrifice the long-term, for the short-term.

Furthermore, in sport research there is some evidence that irrational beliefs can be helpful for skill execution in low pressure situations, but a hinderance in high pressure situations. Mesagno et al. (2020) investigated 'choking' (skill performance decrement in an anxiety-producing situation, compared to when that same skill is performed at a "normal" standard in low-pressure situations; Mesagno & Hill, 2013) in relation to irrational beliefs. Mesagno and colleagues had experienced Australian football players complete the aforementioned irrational performance beliefs inventory (iPBI; Turner & Allen, 2018) prior to taking part in an Australian football set shot experiment across low- and high-pressure conditions. Data indicated that performance tended to increase with increasing irrational beliefs under low-pressure, but decrease with increasing irrational beliefs under high-pressure. This effect was evident only for athletes who had choked under high-pressure (whose performance score declined by more than 15 points from base levels). Therefore, under high acute pressure, it might be risky for performers to hold or utilise irrational beliefs, but under low acute pressure, for some athletes, holding or utilising irrational beliefs might be helpful for performance.

In a similar vein, Morgulev and Galily (2018) analysed three decades of N.B.A. playoff performances and found that teams did worse in must-win situations than when the stakes were low or were equal for both teams. Speaking to Alan Burdick at The New Yorker, one of the authors (Galily) said that, "We thought it would help when you have your back against the wall…You need to win or your season is ended; it's a great incentive to play at your best. But we learned that the opposite is true". So, ultimately there is a complexity in the utility of irrational beliefs when it comes to performance under pressure.

I am suggesting here that in some situations it may be appropriate and advantageous to use irrational self-talk, despite its falsehood. This strategy can be used effectively and safely on four conditions. First, the client understands that their irrational self-talk, no matter how useful acutely, is indeed false and illogical. Second, the client understands that the irrational self-talk is only being used acutely for specific identifiable benefits. Third, the client is able to relinquish this irrational way of thinking as soon as the acute situation has ceased. Fourth, the athlete has an undergirding foundation of rationality that supports their movement towards their PGs and especially their FGs. Whilst there is no hard evidence for this doublethink phenomenon as applied to REBT, anecdotally I see it a lot with the clients I work with, and future researchers should consider investigating it empirically. Whether or not irrational self-talk can be used acutely in a functional way, practitioners should be very careful about promoting irrational beliefs due to their demonstrable perniciousness.

Remember the two dials from Chapter 2? I said that rationality and irrationality could be viewed as two separate dials (Figure 13.5 a,b) on a sound system, like bass and treble. Bass and treble are separate, but interact, and can be adjusted independently, just like irrational and rational beliefs. Irrational and rational beliefs are not at opposite ends of the same continuum (Bernard, 2009), they are separate, but interacting. In relation to doublethink and the flexible and context-specific utilisation of rational/irrational beliefs, in some situations you might need to amplify the irrational beliefs and dial down the rational beliefs. In other situations, you might need to amplify rational beliefs and dial down the irrational beliefs. Balance is key. It is not that we are *changing* the irrational *to* rational. We are not *swapping* the bass *for the* treble. We are dialling down the bass (i.e., irrational beliefs), and dialling up the treble (i.e., rational beliefs). The bass will always be there – it is a ubiquitous aspect of human nature – but so will the treble. We can help clients to become skilled mixers by teaching them skills that will help them to dial down the bass and dial up the treble when warranted, or dial up the bass and dial down the treble when warranted. We can work with clients to understand the appropriate rational/irrational mix for particular situations, and for their engagement with life per se.

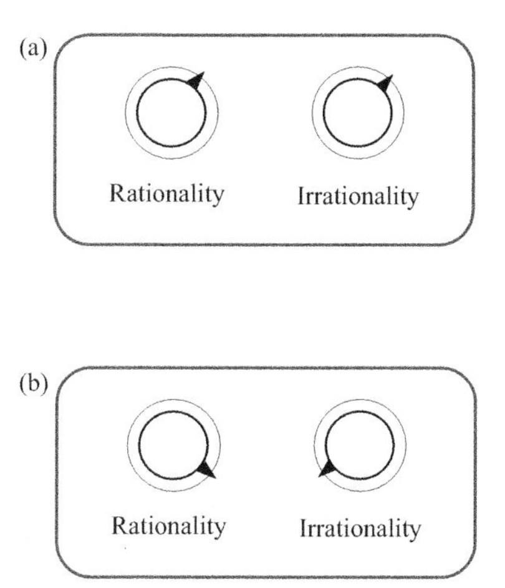

Figure 13.5b (a) Rational/irrational frequency dials. (b) High rationality and low irrationality on the rational/irrational frequency dials.

Caring less

Some clients, often coaches of the athletes I have worked with, worry about rationality. Some believe that by being more rational, it means that you will become an unemotional, unmotivated, dispassionate, robot. There is this sense that irrationality and the emotional heat that it generates is somehow tied to how much an athlete cares about winning, and thus, the removal of this irrationality will in some way damage performance. How can they win if they don't care? Indeed, there is a misconception that wanting instead of demanding, not viewing failure as the end of the world, tolerating life's vicissitudes, and not defining yourself by your pursuits, is disadvantageous for performance in part because of reductions in motivation (Atkinson, 2014).

This is obviously a very simplistic, and frankly worrying, view of REBT, emotion, and motivation. None of these concerns are borne out by the data, and in my applied work I have never had an athlete suffer from emotional or motivational deficits through my work with them. Also, we have evidence that rationality, not irrationality, is more conducive to athletic performance especially under pressure (e.g., Mesagno et al., 2020; Turner et al., 2019c). Also, research has shown that it is not that rational beliefs reduce the *quantity* of motivation per se, rather it is more accurate to say that rational beliefs change the *quality* of one's motivation. Applied papers have shown that through REBT athletes report increases in more self-determined forms of motivation regulation (more autonomous, less controlled motivation) (Chrysidis et al., 2020; Davis & Turner, 2020; Turner & Davis, 2019; Wood et al., 2020). Research has also shown that the combination of irrational beliefs and less autonomous (more controlled) motivation is a potential risk factor for poor mental and physical health in athletes (Turner et al., 2022b).

So, it is not the case that encouraging rational beliefs leads to lack of motivation, and we are not teaching athletes to care less. We are not teaching them to be passive. We are not minimising their desires for success, goal attainment, fulfilment of potential. We are merely enabling a balanced and healthy approach to those goals, shifting a desperate and panicked 'must' to a more measured but equally passionate *want*. We can help them to care appropriately about those goals, and ensure that they do not sacrifice their wellbeing on the altar of athletic success.

> ...when it came to the moment on the 18th tee, it was like yeah you've got a great chance to win the US Open. So what?...I knew that *this didn't HAVE to be my time*...I've accepted I'm gonna win majors, and I'm gonna lose some majors.
>
> Justin Rose about his 2013 US Golf Open win (Ashworth, 2015) (emphasis added)

Finishing the work – making oneself redundant

As a reminder, here are the main stages of REBT:

1. Develop and strengthen the working alliance.
2. Establish the aims of the work, agree on a target problem, and a way forward.
3. Assess C – establish the existence of UNEs and HNEs concerning the target problem.
4. Assess A – establish the inference/s concerning the target problem that is/are triggering irrational beliefs (B).

5. Assess G – establish how and to what extent A impedes G in the target problem. Also, support and encourage eudaimonic goals.
6. Teach the B–C connection – educate the athlete in the idea of cognitive mediation.
7. Assess B – establish the existence and nature of irrational beliefs (iB) and rational beliefs (rB).
8. Teach the athlete about iBs and rBs, and how to distinguish between them.
9. Ensure client is able to see the connection between their Gs, As, Bs, and Cs.
10. Disputation (D) – challenge and weaken irrational beliefs.
11. Effective New Belief (E) – develop, challenge, strengthen, and commit to rational beliefs.
12. Ensuring redundancy – client becomes their own 'practitioner'.

When finishing the work with a client we of course need to have ameliorated the issue for which they sought our help. But also, through REBT we should be encouraging the client to become their own therapist (Dryden et al., 2010), in effect making ourselves as practitioners redundant. In REBT we help the client to learn, develop, strengthen, and refine particular ideas and skills that facilitate their progression towards fulfilment. The client has only really learnt an idea or skill when they can apply that idea and skill independently. The client may demonstrate learning in sessions where there is an intense repetition of disputation and rational belief rehearsal. But has the client *retained* this learning to the extent that they can dispute beliefs as they emerge in life, away from the practitioner? The goal should be to ensure the client understands and can apply REBT by themselves, and that emotional insight is either partially achieved or can be worked towards by the client autonomously. The practitioner and client should see emotional insight on the horizon.

For me to be confident that the client can independently apply REBT, I need to be able to answer the following questions positively:

1. Does the client understand, and can they accurately articulate each element of, the GABCDE framework?
2. Does the client endorse B–C thinking over A–C thinking?
3. Does the client understand, and can they demonstrate the application of, the differences between irrational and rational beliefs?
4. Can the client generate rational beliefs?
5. Does the client understand, and can they recognise in themselves, UNEs and HNEs?
6. Can the client apply disputation rigorously and accurately?
7. Does the client have a plan for committing to their new rational beliefs?
8. Is the client properly, and rationally, oriented towards their FGs?
9. Does the client's behaviour indicate the expression of HNEs rather than UNEs?

I can of course ask the above questions to the client directly, and we can obviously discuss each question, but these questions are more for me, and my answers are based on the client's progress and articulation of REBT in the sessions and in their homework. One effective way for me to be able to answer some of these questions is for the client to act as my psychologist and take me through one of my issues. The issue I choose will be something minor and will reflect a fairly innocuous life quibble, but I will try to be as honest as I can with the client in my articulation of my issue. It is the client's job to apply REBT with me as best they can, attempting to cover the main tenets of what they have learnt with my issue as a case example. Clearly, I am not expecting advanced level psychology work here, but I am looking for their ability to demonstrate their understanding in line with some of the above questions (not all questions are relevant to this task). If I notice deficits in their understanding, I can discuss this with the client to make sure these deficits are addressed forthrightly.

Lastly, I recap everything that we have done in our work together, for the client. I try to provide a brief summary of what was covered and the extent to which we have done what we said we were going to do – in other words, I am verbally reflecting on the extent to which the aims of the work have been met. This is really to make sure that we have been as comprehensive as we can in our work, and to provide an opportunity for the client to flag anything they are still unclear on. It also provides them with some final clarity and motivation to continue to work towards rationality. I would end my work with the client by informing them that I am confident in their capacity to move forward positively, but that support is here if they need it. Of course, if the practitioner so wishes, at this point we can use psychometrics (including for example the iPBI) to assess pre-post REBT shifts in irrational beliefs.

A Hero's Journey

One of the ways I think about the work done in REBT is that it is congruent with 'The Hero's Journey' – the monomythic pattern proposed by Joseph Campbell (2008) in which a hero embarks on a treacherous adventure and claims victory before returning home – triumphant – but changed. The narrative structure of 'The Hero's Journey' helps us to better understand and utilise (i.e., communicate) the GABCDE framework which is at the heart of the REBT change process. One of the potential problems with the use of metaphor is the assumption of shared (client-practitioner) meaning (DiGiuseppe & Muran, 1992). But using 'The Hero's Journey' as a metaphor assuages this issue somewhat due to its ubiquity in story telling (including books, movies, video games). It is likely that the client's favourite film follows 'The Hero's Journey', at least in part. We can of course use the analogy of 'The Hero's Journey' with clients to help them to make sense of the figurative journey they have been on through their work with the practitioner. 'The Hero's Journey' is deeply imbedded within our culture and our psyche, reflecting an archetypal narrative that has become somewhat of a cliché in story telling – in part because it is appealing, powerful, and marketable. This is, I believe, partly why the GABCDE framework is so compelling and useful, because it aligns with the way we have been making sense of the world through stories and narratives for a long time.

Analogies or metaphors can also serve as memorable overarching rhetorical depictions of the change process itself. In other words, we can abstract out important features of REBT enabling the client to better understand, engage with, and utilise its core features. Stories and analogies can be essential tools in the therapeutic process, because they can provide practitioners with a way to communicate complex psychological ideas to clients (Killick et al., 2016). It is argued within literature that the use of metaphor can be a vital component of CBT (e.g., Blenkiron, 2010; Stott et al., 2010). Creative activities, such as stories and metaphor, can facilitate the explanation of complex ideas relevant to therapeutic change in manner that is potential fun and engaging (Killick et al., 2016). The use of stories and parables can be used as metaphors in REBT (Wessler & Wessler, 1980), and can be employed to instigate client paradigm shift (DiGiuseppe & Muran, 1992). One such paradigm shift might include a move from non-autonomous emotion regulation, to autonomous emotional regulation, through a greater harnessing of emotional responsibility. Enabling a client to move from a position of emotional victimhood (i.e., "emotions are something that happen to me and I don't have a say in my emotions") to emotional responsibility (i.e., "I can shape my emotions, they do not simply happen to me") is an important part of REBT.

We can use 'The Hero's Journey' in the REBT work we do, to illustrate the GABCDE framework to clients (e.g., athletes, coaches) and help them make sense of the work we have done together. Some clients can better connect with REBT, and most other ideas, when it is presented as a journey or story. 'The Hero's Journey' dramatises the client's (and practitioner's) experience applying REBT, giving it a narrative meaning that illustrates the importance of the work, whilst providing a structure that can mark progress and guide the work. To my knowledge, this Hero's Journey analogy has not been used in connection with the GABCDE framework in the past, so I cannot present evidence to the reader that it in some way enhances the effectiveness of REBT. All I can really say is that it helps me and the people I work with to connect with, and better understand, the REBT process – which can't be bad.

The full extent to which REBT and specifically the GABCDE framework aligns with 'The Hero's Journey' is not within the remit of the current book (I have written/spoken about it in detail elsewhere). But for the present purposes, I present Figure 13.6 as a mapping from the stages of 'The Hero's Journey' to the elements of the GABCDE framework. I hope the reader finds it stimulating and encourages them to understand how 'The Hero's Journey' and REBT can sit side by side for client communication and comprehension purposes.

Stage of Hero's Journey	**Related aspects of REBT**
The ordinary world	Assessment and initial establishment of Gs, As, and Cs.
Call to adventure	Preparing client to undertake deeper analysis.
Refusal of the call	Client resistance to deeper analysis and or change.
Meeting the mentor	Client and practitioner prepare to cross the threshold to deeper analysis together.
Crossing the threshold	Deeper analysis of G, A, and C, and recognition of B. Psychoeducation in the GABC aspects of the framework.
Tests, allies, and enemies	Establishing critical A, and clearly defining B(s).
Approach the Dragon's Den	Distillation of work completed, and preparing for D.
The ordeal	D as part of cognitive change.
The reward	Development and reinforcement of rational beliefs (E)
The road back	Strengthening and imbedding of rational beliefs (E).
The resurrection	New functional and healthy approach to, or response to, A.
The return	Client independence. Practitioner redundance.

Figure 13.6 Summary of the alignment between the REBT GABCDE framework and 'The Hero's Journey'.

SUMMARY

In this chapter we have taken a detailed look at the effective new beliefs (E) element of the GABCDE framework. If you and the client are successful in this element, then the client will likely be able to move into the future with the skills to pursue Gs and face As with rationality. Because of this, the client has markedly enhanced their proclivity to experience HNEs in pursuit of their goals, and as a result, has also enhanced the likelihood of attaining those goals. The client can apply the skills of disputation and rational belief strengthening to fortify themselves against the vicissitudes of life. The work for the client is not over, of course. Only continued commitment to rationality and constant work against irrationality will secure long-term fulfilment and psychological health. As Morpheus says to Neo in *The Matrix* film, "I can only show you the door. You're the one that has to walk through it".

CHAPTER 14
Closing remarks

For your sins, I command thee.

DOI: 10.4324/9781003200437-15

What's it all about then – this REBT malarky? In this book, I have tried to present what REBT is, some of the evidence that underpins REBT's effectiveness, and have put forth how REBT *can be* practised in sport and performance settings. I have also tried to make clear that whilst REBT is no panacea, it is remarkably flexible and thus can help us as practitioners to approach a broad range of client issues. By linking REBT to emotion regulation science, psychological skills training, and by offering the interdependent GABC(DE) framework, I hope I have been able to demonstrate to the reader that REBT is not insula or niche. I also hope I have helped the reader to see that the underpinnings of REBT can be found in both ancient and modern works of philosophy and science.

I did not invent REBT, nor have I been a part of its development over the years, so I believe I can be *somewhat* objective when it comes to REBT. Like any approach to psychology, REBT has its limitations. Frankly, some of the *perceived* limitations of REBT are based on a poor understanding of REBT (e.g., that REBT only focusses on beliefs and belief change). Other limitations are grounded in a philosophical debate often between advocates of second- and third-wave psychotherapies (e.g., Collard, 2019, and see volume 23, issue 2, 2005 in the *Journal of Rational-Emotive and Cognitive-Behavior Therapy*). There are some excellent debates concerning REBT in the literature (see volume 14, issue 1, 1996 in the *Journal of Rational-Emotive and Cognitive-Behavior Therapy*) – it's not like REBT has had an easy ride (nor should it have!). But in my mind, I have come across one main limitation or difficulty in applying REBT in my practice, which I will touch upon here.

Why can't we be friends?

It isn't obvious how REBT could be applied to help practitioners work with *group dynamics* issues within a team. Of course, we can deliver group REBT (e.g., Vertopolous & Turner, 2017), but there isn't much in REBT that *expressly* enables us to help groups bond or gel directly. It isn't really a framework that offers team building activities for the sake of team building. When working with an REBT framework (GABCDE) I have to think more flexibly and laterally about my approach in order to develop group-level content or strategies that foster belongingness, cohesion, and collaboration. That is not to say that REBT does not have a social outlook or is not informed by social psychology, which it is (Ellis, 2003c). Ellis proposed in 1976 that irrationality has a biological basis but that there is also a vital social component to our sustained irrationality. The very process of REBT, the discursive and mostly Socratic interaction between client and practitioner speaks to the capacity for the *social* to influence the *personal*. In other words, through REBT people can unlearn their irrationality through discursive exchange.

But there are various ways in which REBT can enable group bonding and can influence group dynamics. This is in part because each element of the GABCDE framework is relevant to what one might call the social domain. Goals and values (G) are a) informed socioculturally and b) can be formed around, and about, social factors (Ellis, 1994). To the first point, many of our important goals only make sense within a social context – a goal of becoming a successful athlete makes little sense without the social fabric that surrounds sport, providing the infrastructure for competition, the societal valuing of athletic competence, and the potential tangible rewards for attainment. To the second point, goals can be formed about relationships both in and out of sport. We are social creatures and REBT is expressly encouraging of social wellbeing and utility. Adversity (A) is also highly relevant to the social domain. The concrete adversities we face often occur within a social context and our inferences are often socially informed. That is, many As emanate from content areas of approval, rejection, acceptance, and treatment of and by others, for example. The social setting is generative of As in part because our goals (Gs) can be socially derived. Our perceptions of A are also culturally mediated – for some cultures some 'As' might not be 'As' (i.e., might not be adverse) at all. When one looks at the irrational beliefs, it is clear that we can form beliefs about social aspects of life ("I must be approved of, I must be loved, I must be accepted"). But also, we can learn our beliefs from people around us via narratives and rituals (Seitz et al., 2018).

Because of the social basis for many Gs, As, and Bs, then it stands to reason that our cognitive, emotional, and behavioural consequences (Cs) are socially relevant. Emotions have a social purpose and activate behaviour that can influence our interaction with the social environment (e.g., van Kleef et al., 2016). As such, the experience and expression of Cs can influence our interactions with others via our behaviour. Unhealthy anxiety, guilt, and shame could lead to withdrawal from and avoidance of others (specific individual and/or entire social groups). Unhealthy anger can lead to outward aggression towards others, even if those people are not the antagonists. Those who enact unhealthy negative emotions (UNEs) such as unhealthy anger may be ostracised and/or demeaned socially. The skills and techniques, and overall philosophy, of disputation (D) and effective new beliefs (E) can be shared and propagated socially (e.g., within a team, a dyadic relationship, in a family). We can work with teams to develop the group's capacity the challenge illogical and unconstructive ideas, and champion logical and constructive ideas. Wilson (2010) states that "For rationalism to succeed, we need to initiate a positive feedback cycle in which rational strategies increase existential security, which in turn favors the cultural evolution of factually rational strategies over their factually irrational alternatives" (p. 70). A social movement towards rationality cannot only be done on an individual basis – although it may start there – it must be done through the shared recognition that rationality is valuable for our survival and wellbeing. Rationality is not just about the selfish drive for self-fulfilment, although it can of course begin there. You are the centre of your world, after all. But, we are networked together as social beings, so by you putting yourself together in the right way (rationally), it is more likely that you will have an additive effect on those around you, who are also networked and can impact others not directly in your line of sight.

Lastly on this point of group dynamics, REBT's perspective on human worth is vital for group functioning. If I have the irrational belief that "when people make mistakes, it makes them completely stupid and bad people" (other-depreciation) then I am unlikely to be able to form strong connections with those people. I am more likely to be antagonised by them, and to avoid them. In REBT, we help clients to develop rational acceptance beliefs whereby amidst the myriad ways in which people can let us down or treat us poorly, we can accept people as what they are – limited and fallible human beings that do good things *and* bad things. Their value is not tied to their actions. This position is more likely to foster social relations because the antagonistic nature of social interaction is reduced somewhat and I am more likely to be able to at least be in the same room as the person/people for whom I previously held other-depreciation beliefs. I can interact with a perceived wrong-doer and form an amicable and potentially mutually advantageous union, so long as I do not view them as wholly worthless. The productive communion between opposing parties defines our democratic political system, which can be corrupted by extreme polarisation. So, if you want to help create and maintain a well-functioning, cohesive, and collaborative team, then it stands to reason that destructive Gs, As, Bs, and Cs are ameliorated, and more constructive Gs, As, Bs, and Cs are realised.

A BROADER PERSPECTIVE

Part of the focus of this book is the applicability of REBT in both its *specific* and *general* forms. Whilst the main thrust of this book is *specific* REBT, I have tried to stress and reiterate throughout that we can apply *general* REBT very flexibly in working with performers. And whilst, from an emotion regulation perspective, I do focus most of my efforts on providing evidence for cognitive change (i.e., disputation), alternate emotion regulation strategies are of course viable and effective. I encourage readers who are exclusively of the *specific* REBT persuasion to think about how coming away from this reductionist view of, or approach to, REBT would aid their practice. What I have tried to do in this book is to highlight the interwoven nature of the GABCDE framework such that each element is up for grabs in terms of helping clients. We can work with G, A, and C directly, which may have an influence on B. But for sure, at the core of REBT is belief change, and I remain vehement (but not inflexibly so) that *specific* REBT should be attempted if possible and necessary. I believe that rationality should be striven for in the clients we work with, and that these striving should be in the service of aiding the client in their pursuit of eudaimonic fulfilment as a human being in the long term. My beliefs concerning the importance of rationality stem from my work applying and studying REBT, but also from my reading of Stoicism, and my identity as a scientist.

REBT is just one of the many psychological approaches to sport and performance psychology one could pursue. Practitioners might be wondering why they should bother with REBT, and what REBT could offer their clients. I hope I have provided a good case for REBT in this book, and I hope this book will prove to be interesting and useful to those who read it. Lastly, I leave you with a quote from Albert Ellis, which I think communicates nicely some of what REBT has to offer.

> REBT tries to go beyond the rest of the CBTs by showing its clients and others that they are constructively able, albeit with considerable work and practice, to make a profound cognitive-emotional-behavioral change, so that if they encounter some of the worst adversities in the present or future, they will still only make themselves moderately anxious and regretful instead of panicked and depressed. Then, REBT again hypothesizes, individuals will be better able to change what they can change, to accept (but still dislike) what they cannot change, and…to have the wisdom to know the difference.
>
> (Ellis, 2003c, p. 17)

Afterword

DOI: 10.4324/9781003200437-16

Since the 1980s one of my major criticisms of sport and exercise psychology has been the focus on basic thinking skills that often have amounted to just positive thinking. Although this may help to facilitate some enhanced performance, this method fundamentally differs from the robust nature of the Rational Emotive Behaviour Therapy (REBT), Training and Coaching approach which elicits performance interfering thoughts (PITs), disputes them, and then works towards developing performance enhancing thoughts (PETs). If an athlete demands that 'I must perform well' and if they don't, its evidence in their mind that 'I'm a total failure'. Just re-writing these irrational beliefs (from an REB theory perspective) without disputing them first may not be sufficient for enduring change. Athletes expect to work and train physically hard at their particular sport in order to improve their personal best, and hopefully win. And if they are given the option to improve their performance by applying 'Smarter Thinking' then it's a no-brainer.

Empathy can help to facilitate personal, coaching, therapy, and training relationships. REBT accepts that high-performance scenarios or Activating Events (or Adversities) are often perceived by people (in this case athletes) as very stressful. In fact, Dr. Albert Ellis included the 'A' for adversity and that's the empathy. However, the key difference is that with the REB perspective, nothing is inherently stressful in itself. It is a particularly Stoical view, of course. However, athletes generally wish to be both physically and psychologically resilient and the G-ABCDE model of emotional management often fits their needs. Through gaining knowledge of their own irrational demanding and secondary beliefs, with the assistance of the practitioner, they can develop rational preferences and goal focussed secondary beliefs. From 'I must perform well, otherwise I'd be a failure, that would be awful and I couldn't stand it' triggering goal blocking, high-performance anxiety, to 'I really strongly prefer to perform well, but if I don't, I can still accept myself, it won't be the end of my world, and I can stand it' triggering goal focussed, high-performance concern. However, this cognitive-emotive transformation is not an easy process for people.

In summary, this book highlights the different steps that are involved to help the athlete on their performance journey. A journey that will often involve gaining insight into their internal cognitive world, facilitated by the practitioner who will assist them in uncovering irrational beliefs, disputing them, and developing new powerful rational beliefs that will help them improve their personal best, without the need to wear their lucky socks!

Professor Stephen Palmer
Founder and Director of the UK Centre for
Rational Emotive Behaviour Therapy
26 April, 2022

References

Abbink, K., & Harris, D. (2019). In-group favouritism and out-group discrimination in naturally occurring groups. *PLoS One, 14*(9), e0221616. https://doi.org/10.1371/journal.pone.0221616
Agence France-Presse. (2015, October 26). *It is Not the End of the World: Jurgen Klopp after Liverpool's Draw*. NDTV Sports. Retrieved from http://sports.ndtv.com/english-premier-league/news/250752-it-is-not-the-end-of-the-world-jurgen-klopp-after-liverpool-s-draw
Aguirre Velasco, A., Cruz, I., Billings, J., Jimenez, M., & Rowe, S. (2020). What are the barriers, facilitators and interventions targeting help-seeking behaviours for common mental health problems in adolescents? A systematic review. *BMC Psychiatry, 20*(1), 293. https://doi.org/10.1186/s12888-020-02659-0
Alberti, R., & Emmons, M. (2001). *Your perfect right: Assertiveness and equality in your life and relationships* (8th ed.). Impact Publishers.
Alegria, K. E., & Cameron, L. D. (2020). Cognitive mediators. In M. Gellman (Ed.), *Encyclopedia of behavioral medicine* (2nd ed., pp. 496–497). Springer International Publishing.
Alexander, R. D. (1987). *The biology of moral systems*. Aldine De Gruyter.
Anderson, C. M., & Putterman, L. (2006). Do non-strategic sanctions obey the law of demand? The demand for punishment in the voluntary contribution mechanism. *Games & Economic Behavior, 54*, 1–24. https://doi.org/10.1016/j.geb.2004.08.007
Andersen, M. B. (2009). The "canon" of psychological skills training for enhancing performance. In K. F. Hays (Ed.), *Performance psychology in action: A casebook for working with athletes, performing artists, business leaders, and professionals in high-risk occupations* (pp. 11–34). American Psychological Association. https://doi.org/10.1037/11876-001
Angel, H. -F., & Seitz, R. J. (2017). Violation of expectation as matter for the believing process. *Frontiers in Psychology, 8*, 772. https://doi.org/10.3389/fpsyg.2017.00772
Armstrong, L. M. (2017). Rational emotive therapy. In V. Zeigler-Hill & T. Shackelford (Eds.), *Encyclopedia of personality and individual differences*. Springer. https://doi.org/10.1007/978-3-319-28099-8_996-1
Artiran, M. K., Şimşek, O. F., & Turner, M. (2019). Mediational role of rumination and reflection on irrational beliefs and distress. *Behavioural and Cognitive Psychotherapy, 47*(6), 659–671. https://doi.org/10.1017/S1352465819000031
Artiran, M. K., Simsek, O. F., & Turner, M. J. (2020). REBT with context of basic psychological needs: RESD-A scale. *Behavioural and Cognitive Psychotherapy, 48*(5), 598–614.
Ashworth. (2015, March 16). *'Here, Now' - A Film about Justin Rose* [Video]. YouTube. https://www.youtube.com/watch?v=-xdlx3NlAIg
Atkinson, M. (2014, September). *The Psychologist, 27*.
Aurelius, Marcus. (2014). *The meditations of Marcus Aurelius* (G. Long, Trans.). (Wisehouse Classics Edition). Wisehouse. Kindle Edition.
Austin, J. T., & Vancouver, J. B. (1996). Goal constructs in psychology: Structure, process, and content. *Psychological Bulletin, 120*, 338–375.
Backx, W. (2012). The distinction between quantitative and qualitative dimensions of emotions: Clinical implications. *Journal of Rational-Emotive and Cognitive-Behavior Therapy, 30*, 25–37. https://doi.org/10.1007/s10942-010-0122-0

Babić, V., Sarac, J., Missoni, S., & Sindik, J. (2015). Athletic engagement and athletic identity in top croatian sprint runners. *Collegium Antropologicum, 39*(3), 521–528.
Baggini, J. (2019). *A short history of truth: Consolations for a post-truth world* (Reprint ed.). Quercus Publishing.
Bandura, A. (1977). *Social learning theory*. Prentice Hall.
Bandura, A. (1989). Social cognitive theory. In R. Vasta (Ed.), *Annals of child development. Six theories of child development* (pp. 1–60). JAI Press.
Bandura, A. (1997). *Self-efficacy: The exercise of control*. Freeman.
Bandura, A. (2006). Toward a psychology of human agency. *Perspectives on Psychological Science, 1*, 164–180.
Bar, M., Neta, M., & Linz, H. (2006). Very first impressions. *Emotion, 6*, 269–278.
Barlow, J., Coren, E., & Stewart-Brown, S. (2003). Parent-training programmes for improving maternal psychosocial health. *Cochrane Database of Systematic Reviews, 4*, 1–98. https://doi.org/10.1002/14651858.CD002020.pub2
Barrett, L. F. (2017). The theory of constructed emotion: an active inference account of interoception and categorization. *Social Cognitive and Affective Neuroscience, 12*(1), 1–23, https://doi.org/10.1093/scan/nsw154
Barrett, L. F. (2018). *How emotions are made: The secret life of the brain* (Reprint ed.). Harper Paperbacks.
Baumeister, R. F., Vohs, K. D., Aaker, J. L., & Garbinsky, E. N. (2013). Some key differences between a happy life and a meaningful life. *The Journal of Positive Psychology, 8*(6), 505–516. https://doi.org/10.1080/17439760.2013.830764
Baumeister, R. F., Campbell, J. D., Krueger, J. I., & Vohs, K. D. (2003). Does high self-esteem cause better performance, interpersonal success, happiness, or healthier lifestyles? *Psychological Science in the Public Interest, 4*(1), 1–44. https://doi.org/10.1111/1529-1006.01431
BBC News. (2021, February 19). *Fran Lebowitz: 'Being Offended is Part of Leaving Home'*. https://www.bbc.co.uk/news/av/entertainment-arts-56114783
BBC News. (2022, March 29). *Will Smith Apologises to Chris Rock after Oscars Slap*. Retrieved 1 April 2022, from https://www.bbc.co.uk/news/entertainment-arts-60909487
Beal, D., Kopec, A. M., & DiGiuseppe, R. (1996). Disputing clients' irrational beliefs. *Journal of Rational-Emotive and Cognitive-Behavior Therapy, 14*, 215–229.
Beck, A. T. (1976). *Cognitive therapy and the emotional disorders*. International Universities Press.
Beck, J. S. (1995). *Cognitive therapy: Basics and beyond*. Guilford Press.
Beck, A. T. (2015). Theory of personality disorders. In Aaron T. Beck, D. D. Davis, & A. Freeman (Eds.), *Cognitive therapy of personality disorders* (3rd ed., pp. 19–62). Guilford Press.
Beck, A. T., Emery, G., & Greenberg, R. L. (1985). *Anxiety disorders and phobias: A cognitive perspective*. Basic Books.
Beck, A. T., & Freeman, A. M. (1990). *Cognitive therapy of personality disorders*. Guilford Press.
Beck, A. T., & Haigh, E. A. (2014). Advances in cognitive theory and therapy: The generic cognitive model. *Annual Review of Clinical Psychology, 10*, 1–24. https://doi.org/10.1146/annurev-clinpsy-032813-153734
Beck, A. T., Rush, A. J., Shaw, B. F., & Emery, G. (1979). *Cognitive therapy of depression*. New York: Guilford.
Bellet, B. W., Jones, P. J., & McNally, R. J. (2018). Trigger warning: Empirical evidence ahead. *Journal of Behavior Therapy and Experimental Psychiatry, 61*, 134–141. https://doi.org/10.1016/j/jbtep.2018.07.002
Bellet, B. W., Jones, P. J., Meyersburg, C. A., Brenneman, M. M., Morehead, K. E., & McNally, R. J. (2020). Trigger warnings and resilience in college students: A preregistered replication and extension. *Journal of Experimental Psychology: Applied, 26*(4), 717–723. https://doi.org/10.1037/xap0000270
Bennett, R., & Oliver, J. E. (2019). *Acceptance and commitment therapy: 100 key points and techniques*. Routledge/Taylor & Francis Group.
Bennett-Levy, J., McManus, F., Westling, B. E., & Fennell, M. (2009). Acquiring and refining CBT skills and competencies: Which training methods are perceived to be most effective? *Behavioural and Cognitive Psychotherapy, 37*(5), 571–583. https://doi.oeg/10.1017/S1352465809990270

Bernard, M. E. (1985). A rational-emotive mental training program for professional athletes. In A. Ellis & M. E. Bernard (Eds.), *Clinical applications of rational-emotive therapy* (pp. 227–309). Plenum.

Bernard, M. E. (1998). Validation of the general attitude and belief scale. *Journal of Rational-Emotive & Cognitive-Behavior Therapy, 16*(3), 183–196. https://doi.org/10.1023/A:1024911014579

Bernard, M. E. (2009). Dispute irrational beliefs and teach rational beliefs: An interview with Albert Ellis. *Journal of Rational-Emotive & Cognitive-Behavior Therapy, 27*(1), 67–77. https://doi.org/10.1007/s10942-009-0089-x

Bernard, M. E., & Dryden, W. (2019). *Advances in REBT: Theory, practice, research, measurement, prevention and promotion*. Springer Nature.

Bernard, M. E., Froh, J. J., DiGiuseppe, R., Joyce, M. R., & Dryden, W. (2010). Albert Ellis: Unsung hero of positive psychology. *The Journal of Positive Psychology, 5*(4), 302–310. https://doi.org/10.1080/17439760.2010.498622

Bishop, F. M. (2000). Helping clients manage addictions with REBT. *Journal of Rational-Emotive & Cognitive-Behavior Therapy, 18*, 127–151. https://doi.org/10.1023/A:1007874820119

Blanke, E. S., Brose, A., Kalokerinos, E. K., Erbas, Y., Riediger, M., & Kuppens, P. (2020). Mix it to fix it: Emotion regulation variability in daily life. *Emotion, 20*(3), 473–485. https://doi.org/10.1037/emo0000566

Blau, S., & Fuller, J. R. (2006). Rational-emotive disputing and the five-factor model: Personality dimensions of the Ellis emotional efficiency inventory. *Journal of Rational-Emotive and Cognitive Behavior Therapy, 24*(2), 87–100.

Blenkiron, P. (2010). *Stories and analogies in cognitive behaviour therapy*. Wiley-Blackwell.

Boehme, S., Biehl, S. C., & Mühlberger, A. (2019). Effects of differential strategies of emotion regulation. *Brain Sciences, 9*(9), 225. https://doi.org/10.3390/brainsci9090225

Boekaerts, M., de Koning, E., & Vedder, P. (2006). Goal-directed behavior and contextual factors in the classroom: An innovative approach to the study of multiple goals. *Educational Psychology, 41*, 33–51. https://doi.org/10.1207/s15326985ep4101_5

Bona, E. (2015, September 29). *Bill Shankly Remembered: 11 Brilliant Quotes from Liverpool's Iconic Manager*. Liverpool Echo. Retrieved 31 January 2022, from https://www.liverpoolecho.co.uk/news/liverpool-news/bill-shankly-remembered-11-brilliant-10156199

Bonadies, G. A., & Bass, B. A. (1984). Effects of self-verbalizations upon emotional arousal and performance: A test of rational-emotive theory. *Perceptual & Motor Skills, 59*, 939–948. https://doi.org/10.2466/pms.1984.59.3.939

Bond, J. (2002). Applied sport psychology: Philosophy, reflections, and experience. *International Journal of Sport Psychology, 33*, 19–37.

Bond, F. W., Dryden, W., & Briscoe, R. (1999). Testing two mechanisms by which rational and irrational beliefs may affect the functionality of inferences. *The British Journal of Medical Psychology, 72*(4), 557–566. https://doi.org/10.1348/000711299160121

Bordin, E. S. (1979). The generalizability of the psychoanalytic concept of the working alliance. *Psychotherapy: Theory, Research & Practice, 16*(3), 252–260. https://doi.org/10.1037/h0085885

Botvinick, M. M., Cohen, J. D., & Carter, C. S. (2004). Conflict monitoring and anterior cingulate cortex: An update. *Trends in Cognitive Sciences, 8*(12), 539–546. https://doi.org/10.1016/j.tics.2004.10.003

Bourland, D. D., & Johnston, P. D. (1997). *E-Prime III!: A third anthology*. International Society for General Semantics.

Bowater, D. (2013, May 31). *Escenic*. The Telegraph. Retrieved 12 March 2022, from https://www.telegraph.co.uk/sport/football/teams/brazil/10092710/Brazil-v-England-QPR-goalkeeper-Julio-Cesar-claims-pressure-is-on-Luis-Scolaris-struggling-team.html

Bowman, A., & Turner, M. J. (2022). When time is of the essence: The use of rational emotive behavior therapy (REBT) informed single-session therapy (SST) to alleviate social and golf-specific anxiety, and improve wellbeing and performance, in amateur golfers. *Psychology of Sport and Exercise*. Accepted 15th February 2022.

Boyer, P. (2003). Religious thought and behaviour as by-products of brain function. *Trends in Cognitive Sciences, 7*, 119–124.

Breitmeyer, A. M., & Turner, M. J. (2018). Sport coaching. In M. Bernard & O. David (Eds.), *Coaching for rational living* (pp. 453–470). Springer.
Brenkley, S. (2012, July 18). *Anderson: I Thrive on Pressure Now*. The Independent. http://www.independent.co.uk/sport/cricket/james-anderson-i-thrive-on-pressure-now-7953463.html
Brennan, T. (2002). Telos. *Routledge Encyclopedia of Philosophy*. Taylor and Francis.
Brewer, B. W., van Raalte, J. L., & Linder, D. E. (1991). Construct validity of the athletic identity measurement scale. *Proceedings of the North American Society for the Psychology of Sport and Physical Activity Annual Conference*. Monterey, CA, USA. 13–16 June 1991.
Brewer, B. W., Van Raalte, J. L., & Linder, D. E. (1993). Athletic identity: Hercules' muscles or Achilles heel? *International Journal of Sport Psychology, 24*(2), 237–254.
Brewer, B. W., & Cornelius, A. E. (2001). Norms and factorial invariance of the athletic identity measurement scale. *Academic Athletic Journal, 16*, 103–113.
Brewer, M. B., & Caporael, L. R. (2006). An evolutionary perspective on social identity: Revisiting groups. In M. Schaller, J. A. Simpson, & D. T. Kenrick (Eds.), *Evolution and social psychology* (pp. 143–161). Psychology Press.
Bromberg-Martin, E. S., Matsumoto, M., & Hikosaka, O. (2010). Dopamine in motivational control: Rewarding, aversive, and alerting. *Neuron, 68*(5), 815–834. https://doi.org/10.1016/j.neuron.2010.11.022
Browne, C. M., Dowd, E. T., & Freeman, A. (2010). Rational and irrational beliefs and psychopathology. In D. David, S. J. Lynn, & A. Ellis (Eds.), *Rational and irrational beliefs: Research, theory, and clinical practice* (pp. 149–171). Oxford University Press.
Bruce, M. J., Stasik-O'Brien, S. M., & Hoffmann, H. (2021). Students' psychophysiological reactivity to trigger warnings. *Current Psychology*. https://doi.org/10.1007/s12144-021-01895-1
Buhle, J. T., Silvers, J. A., Wage, T. D., Lopez, R., Onyemekwu, C., Kober, H., Weber, J., & Ochsner, K. N. (2014). Cognitive reappraisal of emotion: A meta-analysis of human neuroimaging studies. *Cerebral Cortex, 24*(11), 2981–2990. https://doi.org/10.1093/cercor/bht154
Bunford, N., Steven, W. E., & Wymbs, F. (2015). ADHD and emotion dysregulation among children and adolescents. *Clinical Child and Family Psychology Review, 18*, 185–217. https://doi.org/10.1007/s10567-015-0187-5
Burdick, A. (2008, June 12). *In Sports, a Must-Win Situation Usually Leads to a Loss*. The New York Times. URL https://www.newyorker.com/science/lab-notes/why-a-must-win-situation-is-a-losing-one
Burdick, A. (2018, June 13). *Why a Must-Win Situation Is a Losing One*. The New Yorker. Retrieved 12 March 2022, from https://www.newyorker.com/science/lab-notes/why-a-must-win-situation-is-a-losing-one
Buschmann, T., Horn, R. A., Blankenship, V. R., Garcia, Y. E., & Bohan, K. B. (2018). The relationship between automatic thoughts and irrational beliefs predicting anxiety and depression. *Journal of Rational-Emotive & Cognitive-Behavior Therapy*, *36*(2), 137–162. https://doi.org/10.1007/s10942-017-0278-y
Campbell, B., & Barone, L. M. (2012). Evolutionary basis of human migration. In M. H. Crawford & B. C. Campbell (Eds.), *Causes and Consequences of Human Migration* (pp. 45–64). Cambridge University Press.
Campbell, J. (2008). *The hero with a thousand faces (The collected works of Joseph Campbell)* (3rd ed.). New World Library.
Cannizzaro, M. (2019, April 7). *How Rory McIlroy is now Dealing with Career Grand Slam Pressure*. New York Post. Retrieved 17 March 2022, from https://nypost.com/2019/04/06/how-rory-mcilroy-is-now-dealing-with-career-grand-slam-pressure/
Carson, S. (2021, July 16). *Naomi Osaka on Netflix Exposes the Cost of the Pressures we Put on Young Athletes*. Inews.Co.Uk. Retrieved 12 March 2022, from https://inews.co.uk/culture/television/naomi-osaka-netflix-documentary-review-1106067
Carver, C. S., & Scheier, M. F. (1998). *On the self-regulation of behavior*. Cambridge University Press.

Carver, C. S., & Scheier, M. F. (2001). *On the self-regulation of behavior*. Cambridge University Press.
Caserta, D. A., Dowd, E. T., Lynn, S. J., David, D., & Ellis, A. (2010). Rational and irrational beliefs in primary prevention and mental health. In D. David, S. J. Lynn, & A. Ellis (Eds.), *The role of rational and irrational beliefs in human functioning and disturbances: Implications for research, theory, and clinical practice*. Oxford University Press.
Castonguay, L. G., Constantino, M. J., McAleavey, A. A., & Goldfried, M. R. (2010). The therapeutic alliance in cognitive-behavioral therapy. In J. C. Muran & J. P. Barber (Eds.), *The therapeutic alliance: An evidence-based guide to practice* (pp. 150–171). The Guilford Press.
CCBT. (2021, June 13). *REBT Helps You Accept Reality – Like It or Not*. College of Cognitive Behavioural Therapies. Retrieved 12 March 2022, from https://www.cbttherapies.org.uk/2021/06/13/rebt-helps-you-accept-reality-like-it-or-not/
Chadha, N., Turner, M. J., & Slater, M. J. (2019). Investigating irrational beliefs, cognitive appraisals, challenge and threat, and affective states in golfers approaching competitive situations. *Frontiers in Psychology*. https://doi.org/10.3389/fpsyg.2019.02295
Chamberlain, J. M., & Haaga, D. A. F. (2001a). Unconditional self-acceptance and responses to negative feedback. *Journal of Rational-Emotive & Cognitive Behavioral Therapy, 19*, 177–189. https://doi.org/10.1023/A:1011189416600
Chamberlain, J. M., & Haaga, D. A. F. (2001b). Unconditional self-acceptance and psychological health. *Journal of Rational-Emotive & Cognitive-Behavior Therapy, 19*, 163–176.
Chan, S., Torous, J., Hinton, L., & Yellowlees, P. (2015). Towards a framework for evaluating mobile mental health apps. *Telemedicine and e-Health, 21*, 1038–1041. https://doi.org/10.1089/tmj.2015.0002
Channel 4 Paralympics [C4 Paralympics]. (2021, August 31). *'The British Public Have Proven to me That You Don't Need Medals to be Someone'* [Tweet]. Twitter. https://twitter.com/C4Paralympics/status/1432630042757058563
Chotpitayasunondh, V., & Turner, M. J. (2019). The development and validation of the Thai-translated irrational performance beliefs inventory (T-iPBI). *Journal of Rational Emotive & Cognitive Behavior Therapy, 37*(2), 202–221. https://doi.org/10.1007/s10942-018-0306-6
Chrysidis, S., Turner, M. J., & Wood, A. G. (2020). The effects of REBT on irrational beliefs, self-determined motivation, and self-efficacy in American football. *Journal of Sports Sciences, 38*(19), 2215–2224. https://doi.org/10.1080/02640414.2020.1776924
Chulef, A. S., Read, S. J., & Walsh, D. A. (2001). A hierarchical taxonomy of human goals. *Motivation and Emotion, 25*, 191–232. https://doi.org/10.1023/A:1012225223418
Cisler, J. M., & Koster, E. H. (2010). Mechanisms of attentional biases towards threat in anxiety disorders: An integrative review. *Clinical Psychology Review, 30*(2), 203–216. https://doi.org/10.1016/j.cpr.2009.11.003
Clark, D. A. (2014). Cognitive restructuring: A major contribution of cognitive therapy. In S. G. Hofmann & D. J. A. Dozois (Eds.), *Cognitive behavioral therapy: A complete reference guide, Vol. 1. CBT general techniques* (pp. 23–45). Wiley-Blackwell.
Clark, D. A., & Beck, A. T. (2010). Cognitive theory and therapy of anxiety and depression: convergence with neurobiological findings. *Trends in Cognitive Sciences, 14*(9), 418–424. https://doi.org/10.1016/j.tics.2010.06.007
Clark, D. M. (2001). A cognitive perspective on social phobia. In W. R. Crozier & L. E. Alden (Eds.), *International handbook of social anxiety: Concepts, research and interventions relating to the self and shyness* (pp. 405–430). Wiley.
Claspell, E. (2010). Cognitive-behavioral therapies. In S. J. Hanrahan & M. B. Andersen (Eds.), *Routledge handbook of applied sport psychology* (pp. 131–140). Routledge.
Collard, J. J. (2019). ACT vs CBT: An exercise in idiosyncratic language. *International Journal of Cognitive Therapy, 12*(2), 126–145. https://doi.org/10.1007/s41811-019-00043-9
Collard, J. J. (2022). Cognitive-behavioural therapy (CBT). In M. J. Turner, M. V. Jones, & A. W. Wood, (Eds.), *Applying Cognitive Behavioural Therapeutic (CBT) Approaches in Sport*. Routledge.
Collerton, D. (2013). Psychotherapy and brain plasticity. *Frontiers in Psychology, 4*, Article 548. https://doi.org/10.3389/fpsyg.2013.00548

Connors, M. H., & Halligan, P. W. (2015). A cognitive account of belief: A tentative road map. *Frontiers in Psychology*, *5*, 1588. https://doi.org/10.3389/fpsyg.2014.01588

Cooper, M., & McLeod, J. (2010). Pluralism: Towards a new paradigm for therapy. *Therapy Today*, November, 10–14. https://static1.squarespace.com/static/596f25c2725e25fb89b3a6f4/t/5c541514eb393164fddb2225/1549014293962/2010+pluralism+TT.pdf

Costa, S., Santi, G., di Fronso, S., Montesano, C., Di Gruttola, F., Ciofi, E. G., Morgilli, L., & Bertollo, M. (2020). Athletes and adversities: Athletic identity and emotional regulation in time of COVID-19. *Sport Sciences for Health*, *16*(4), 609–618. https://doi.org/10.1007/s11332-020-00677-9

Craske, M. G., Treanor, M., Conway, C. C., Zbozinek, T., & Vervliet, B. (2014). Maximizing exposure therapy: An inhibitory learning approach. *Behaviour Research and Therapy*, *58*(1), 10–23. https://doi.org/10.1016/j.brat.2014.04.006

Crawford, T., & Ellis, A. (1989). A dictionary of rational-emotive feelings and behaviors. *Journal of Rational-Emotive & Cognitive-Behavior Therapy*, *7*(1), 3–28. https://doi.org/10.1007/BF02175569

Crum, J. E. (2018). A clinical strategy to strengthen the connection between cognition, emotion, and behavior: From philosophical principles to psychotherapy practice. *Journal of Rational-Emotive & Cognitive-Behavior Therapy*, *37*(3), 241–250. https://doi.org/10.1007/s10942-018-0308-4

Cunningham, R., & Turner, M. J. (2016). Using rational emotive behavior therapy (REBT) with mixed martial arts (MMA) athletes to reduce irrational beliefs and increase unconditional self-acceptance. *Journal of Rational-Emotive & Cognitive-Behavior Therapy*, *34*(4), 289–309.

Cutuli, D. (2014). Cognitive reappraisal and expressive suppression strategies role in the emotion regulation: An overview on their modulatory effects and neural correlates. *Frontiers in Systems Neuroscience*, *8*, Article 175.

Damasio, A. (1994). *Descartes' error: Emotion, reason and the human brain*. Papermac.

Damasio, A. (2003). *Looking for Spinoza joy, sorrow and the feeling brain*. Vintage books.

David, A., Ghinea, C., Macavei, B., & Eva, K. (2005). A search for "hot" cognitions in a clinical and non-clinical context: Appraisal, attributions, core relational themes, irrational beliefs, and their relations to emotion. *Journal of Cognitive-Behavioral Psychotherapy*, *5*, 1–42.

David, D. (2013). E-prime/r-prime and emotion regulation in the context of the binary model of distress: An experimental investigation based on the general semantics framework. *Journal of Cognitive and Behavioral Psychotherapies*, *13*(1), 1–11.

David, D. (2015). Rational emotive behavior therapy. In R. L. Cautin & S. O. Lilienfeld (Eds.), *Encyclopedia of Clinical Psychology*. Wiley-Blackwell.

David, D., Cotet, C., Matu, S., Mogoase, C., & Stefan, S. (2018). 50 years of rational-emotive and cognitive-behavioral therapy: A systematic review and meta-analysis. *Journal of Clinical Psychology*, *74*(3), 304–318. https://doi.org/10.1002/jclp.22514

David, D., & Cramer, D. (2010). Rational and irrational beliefs in human feelings and psychophysiology (pp. 99–114). In D. David, S. J. Lynn, & A. Ellis (Eds.), *Rational and irrational beliefs*. Oxford University Press.

David, D., & DiGiuseppe, R. (2010). Social and cultural aspects of rational and irrational beliefs: A brief reconceptualization. In D. David., S. J. Lynn, & A. Ellis (Eds.), *Rational and irrational beliefs: Research, theory, and clinical practice* (pp. 49–61). Oxford University Press.

David, D., Freeman, A., & DiGiuseppe, R. (2010b). Rational and irrational beliefs: Implications for mechanisms of change and practice in psychotherapy. In D. David, S. J. Lynn, & A. Ellis (Eds.), *Rational and irrational beliefs: Research, theory, and clinical practice* (pp. 195–217). Oxford University Press.

David, D., & Hofmann, S. G. (2013). Another error of Descartes? Implications for the 'third wave' cognitive-behavioral therapy. *Journal of Cognitive and Behavioral Psychotherapies*, *13*(1), 115–124.

David, D., Lynn, S. J., & Ellis, A. (2010a). *Rational and irrational beliefs: Research, theory, and clinical practice* (Illustrated ed.). Oxford University Press.

David, D., Miclea, M., & Opre, A. (2004). The information-processing approach to the human mind: Basics and beyond. *Journal of Clinical Psychology*, *60*(4), 353–368. https://doi.org/10.1002/jclp.10250

David, D., Schnur, J., & Belloiu. A. (2002). Another search for the "hot" cognitions: Appraisal, irrational beliefs, attributions, and their relation to emotion. *Journal of Rational-Emotive & Cognitive-Behavior Therapy*, *20*(2), 93–131.

David, D., Szentagotai, A., Eva, K., & Macavei, B. (2005). A synopsis of rational-emotive behavior therapy (REBT): Fundamental and applied research. *Journal of Rational-Emotive & Cognitive-Behavior Therapy*, *23*, 175–221. https://doi.org/10.1007/s10942-005-0011-0

David, O. A., Canta, A., Salagean, I., Valenza, G., & Mennin, D. S. (2020). The phobic applying for a job: Differential efficacy of reappraising or faking on subjective states, physiological reactions and performance. *Personality and Individual Differences*, *167*, Article 110243. https://doi.org/10.1016/j.paid.2020.110243

David, O. A., Cîmpean, A., Costescu, C., DiGiuseppe, R., Doyle, K., Hickey, M., & David, D. (2021). Effectiveness of outpatient rational emotive behavior therapy over one decade. *American Journal of Psychotherapy*, *74*(4), 157–164. https://doi.org/10.1176/appi.psychotherapy.20200009

Davidson, R. J., Fox, A., & Kalin, N. H. (2007). Neural bases of emotion regulation in nonhuman primates and humans. In J. J. Gross (Ed.), *Handbook of emotion regulation* (pp. 47–68). The Guilford Press.

Davies, M. F. (2006). Irrational beliefs and unconditional self-acceptance. I. Correlational evidence linking two key features of REBT. *Journal of Rational-Emotive & Cognitive-Behavior Therapy*, *24*(2), 113–124.

Davis, H., & Turner, M. J. (2020). The use of rational emotive behavior therapy (REBT) to increase the self-determined motivation and psychological well-being of triathletes. *Sport, Exercise, and Performance Psychology*, *9*(4), 489–505. https://doi.org/10.1037/spy0000191

Deci, E. L., & Ryan, R. M. (2000). The "what" and the "why" of goal pursuits: Human needs and the self-determination of behavior. *Psychological Inquiry*, *11*, 227–268.

Deen, S., Turner, M. J., & Wong, R. (2017). The effects of REBT and credos on irrational beliefs and resilient qualities in athletes, *The Sport Psychologist*, *31*, 249–263.

de Haan, E., Molyn, J., & Nilsson, V. O. (2020). New findings on the effectiveness of the coaching relationship: Time to think differently about active ingredients? *Consulting Psychology Journal: Practice and Research*, *72*(3), 155–167. https://doi.org/10.1037/cpb0000175

Demaree, H. A., Schmeichel, B. J., Robinson, J. L., Pu, J., Everhart, D., & Berntson, G. G. (2006). Up- and down-regulating facial disgust: Affective, vagal, sympathetic, and respiratory consequences. *Biological Psychology*, *71*, 90–99.

Dennison, L., Morrison, L., Conway, G., & Yardley, L. (2013). Opportunities and challenges for smartphone applications in supporting health behavior change: Qualitative study. *Journal of Medical Internet Research*, *15*, 86–113.

De Sousa, R. (2007). Truth, authenticity, and rationality. *Dialectica*, *61*, 323–345. https://doi.org/10.1111/j.1746-8361.2007.01104.x

Devey, A., Turner, M. J., & Artiran, M. (2022). Adolescent soccer athletes' irrational beliefs about basic psychological needs are related to their emotional intelligence and mental health. *Journal of Rational-Emotive & Cognitive-Behavior Therapy*. Accepted 6th May 2022.

DiGiuseppe, R. (1986). The implication of the philosophy of science for rational-emotive theory and therapy. *Psychotherapy: Theory, Research, Practice, Training*, *23*(4), 634–639. https://doi.org/10.1037/h0085668

DiGiuseppe, R. (1991a). Comprehensive cognitive disputing in RET. In M. Bernard (Ed.), *Using rational-emotive therapy effectively: A practitioner's guide*. Plenum.

DiGiuseppe, R. (1991b). A rational emotive model of assessment. In M. E. Bernard (Ed.), *Using rational emotive therapy effectively* (pp. 151–169). Plenum.

DiGiuseppe, R. (1996). The nature of irrational and rational beliefs: Progress in rational emotive behavior theory. *Journal of Rational-Emotive & Cognitive-Behavior Therapy*, *14*, 5–28. https://doi.org/10.1007/BF02238091

DiGiuseppe, R. A., Doyle, K. A., Dryden, W., & Backx, W. (2014). *A practitioner's guide to rational emotive behavior therapy* (3rd ed.). Oxford University Press.

DiGiuseppe, R., Leaf, R., Exner, T., & Robin, M. V. (1988). *The development of a measure of rational/irrational thinking*. Paper presented at the World Congress of Behavior Therapy, Edinburgh, Scotland.
DiGiuseppe, R., & Muran, J. C. (1992). The use of metaphor in rational-emotive psychotherapy. *Psychotherapy in Private Practice, 10*(1–2), 151–165.
DiLorenzo, T. A., David, D., & Montgomery, G. H. (2007). The interrelations between irrational cognitive processes and distress in stressful academic settings. *Personality and Individual Differences, 42*, 765–777.
Dixon, M., Turner, M. J., & Gillman, J. (2017). Examining the relationships between challenge and threat cognitive appraisals and coaching behaviours in football coaches. *Journal of Sports Sciences, 35*(24), 2446–2452.
Dobson, K. S. (2013). The science of CBT: Toward a metacognitive model of change? *Behavior Therapy, 44*(2), 224–227. https://doi.org/10.1016/j.beth.2009.08.003
Dobson, K. S., & Dozois, D. J. A. (2010). Historical and philosophical bases of the cognitive-behavioral therapies. In K. S. Dobson (Ed.), *Handbook of cognitive-behavioral therapies* (3rd ed., pp. 3–38). The Guilford Press.
Dobson, K. S., & Shaw, B. F. (1988). The use of treatment manuals in cognitive therapy: Experience and issues. *Journal of Consulting and Clinical Psychology, 56*, 673–680.
Doubleday, E. K., King, P., & Papageorgiou, C. (2002). Relationship between fluid intelligence and ability to benefit from cognitive-behavioural therapy in older adults: A preliminary investigation. *The British Journal of Clinical Psychology, 41*(4), 423–428. https://doi.org/10.1348/014466502760387542
Dryden, W. (1986). A case of theoretically consistent eclecticism: Humanizing a computer 'addict'. *International Journal of Eclectic Psychotherapy*, 5(4), 309–327.
Dryden, W. (1987). *Current issues in rational-emotive therapy*. Croom Helm.
Dryden, W. (1989). The use of chaining in rational-emotive therapy. *Journal of Rational-Emotive & Cognitive-Behavior Therapy*, 7(2), 59–66. https://doi.org/10.1007/BF01246504
Dryden, W. (1990). *Rational-emotive counselling in action*. SAGE Publications.
Dryden, W. (1994). Reason and emotion in psychotherapy: Thirty years on. *Journal of Rational-Emotive Cognitive-Behavioral Therapy, 12*, 83–99. https://doi.org/10.1007/BF02354606
Dryden, W. (1995). *Preparing for client change in rational emotive behavior therapy*. Whurr.
Dryden, W. (2003). *Rational emotive behaviour therapy: Theoretical developments (Advancing theory in therapy)*. Routledge.
Dryden, W. (2006). *First steps in REBT: A guide to practicing REBT in peer counseling*. Albert Ellis Institute.
Dryden, W. (2007). Resilience and rationality. *Journal of Rational-Emotive & Cognitive-Behavior Therapy, 25*(3), 213–226. https://doi.org/10.1007/s10942-006-0050-1
Dryden, W. (2008). *Distinctive features of rational emotive behaviour therapy*. Brunner-Routledge.
Dryden, W. (2009a). *Skills in rational emotive behaviour counselling and psychotherapy*. Sage.
Dryden, W. (2009b). *How to think and intervene like an REBT therapist* (1st ed.). Routledge.
Dryden, W. (2010). Elegance in REBT: Reflections on the Ellis and Dryden sessions with Jane. *Journal of Rational-Emotive & Cognitive-Behavior Therapy, 28*(3), 157–163.
Dryden, W. (2012a). *The ABCs of REBT revisited: Perspectives on conceptualization*. Springer.
Dryden, W. (2012b). The "ABCs" of REBT III: A study of errors and confusions made by Ellis and Joffe Ellis (2011). *Journal of Rational-Emotive and Cognitive-Behavior Therapy, 30*(3), 188–201. https://doi.org/10.1007/s1094 2–011–0140–6
Dryden, W. (2012c). On rational beliefs in rational emotive behavior therapy: A theoretical perspective. *Journal of Rational-Emotive & Cognitive-Behavior Therapy, 31*(1), 39–48. https://doi.org/10.1007/s10942-012-0158-4
Dryden, W. (2012d). *Cognitive behaviour therapies* (1st ed.). SAGE Publications Ltd.
Dryden, W. (2013). *Rationality and pluralism*. Routledge.
Dryden, W. (2016). *When time is at a premium: Cognitive-behavioural approaches to single session therapy and very brief coaching*. Rationality Publications.

Dryden, W. (2017). Rational emotive behaviour therapy. In C. Feltham, T. Hanley, & L. A. Winter (Eds.), *The SAGE handbook of counselling and psychotherapy* (4th ed.). SAGE Publications Ltd.
Dryden, W. (2018). *Very brief therapeutic conversations* (1st ed.). Routledge.
Dryden, W. (2019a). The distinctive features of rational emotive behavior therapy. In M. Bernard & W. Dryden (Eds.), *Advances in REBT* (pp. 23–46). Springer. https://doi.org/10.1007/978-3-319-93118-0_8
Dryden, W. (2019b). Rational emotive behavior therapy: Assessment, conceptualisation and intervention. In M. Bernard & W. Dryden (Eds.), *Advances in REBT*. Springer, Cham. https://doi.org/10.1007/978-3-319-93118-0_8
Dryden, W. (2019c). Rational emotive behaviour therapy and the working alliance. In M. Bernard & W. Dryden (Eds.), *Advances in REBT*. Springer. https://doi.org/10.1007/978-3-319-93118-0_8
Dryden, W. (2020). *Single-session therapy and its future: What SST leaders think (routledge focus on mental health)*. Routledge.
Dryden, W. (2021a). *New directions in rational emotive behaviour therapy*. Routledge.
Dryden, W. (2021b). *Reason to change: A rational emotive behaviour therapy workbook* (2nd ed.). Routledge.
Dryden, W. (2022). *The REBT therapist's pocket companion* (2nd ed.). Albert Ellis Institute.
Dryden, W., Beal, D., Jones, J., & Trower, P. (2010). The REBT competency scale for clinical and research applications. *Journal of Rational-Emotive & Cognitive-Behavior Therapy*, *28*(4), 165–216. https://doi.org/10.1007/s10942-010-0111-3
Dryden, W., & Branch, R. (2008). *The fundamentals of rational emotive behaviour therapy: A training handbook* (2nd ed.). Wiley.
Dryden, W., & David, D. (2008). Rational emotive behavior therapy: Current status. *Journal of Cognitive Psychotherapy*, *22*(3), 195–209. https://doi.org/10.1891/0889-8391.22.3.195
Dryden, W., & Ellis, A. (1988). Rational-emotive therapy. In K. S. Dobson (Ed.), *Handbook of cognitive-behavioral therapies*. Guilford.
Dryden, W., & Neenan, M. (1995). *Dictionary of rational emotive behavior therapy*. Wiley.
Dryden, W., & Neenan, M. (2020). *Rational emotive behaviour therapy: 100 key points and techniques* (3rd ed.). Routledge.
Dryden, W., & Still, A. (2012). *The historical and philosophical context of rational psychotherapy: The Legacy of Epictetus*. Routledge.
Dubois, P. (1905). *The psychic treatment of nervous disorders: The psychoneuroses and their moral treatment* (pp. 367–368). Funk & Wagnalls.
Dubois, P. (1906). *The influence of the mind on the body* (L. B. Gallatin, Trans, 5th ed.). Funk & Wagnalls.
Dubois, P. (1909). *Psychic treatment of nervous diseases* (6th ed.). Funk & Wagnalls Company.
Dubois, P., & Boyd, H. H. (1909). *Self-control and how to secure it: (L'Éducation de Soi-Même). Authorized Translation by Harry Hutcbeson Boyd*. Leopold Classic Library.
Edison, B. R., Christino, M. A., & Rizzone, K. H. (2021). Athletic identity in youth athletes: A systematic review of the literature. *International Journal of Environmental Research and Public Health*, *18*(14), 7331. https://doi.org/10.3390/ijerph18147331
Elko, K. P., & Ostrow, A. C. (1991). Effects of a rational-emotive education program on heightened anxiety levels of female collegiate gymnasts. *The Sport Psychologist*, *5*, 235–255.
Elliott, R., Jobber, D., & Sharp, J. (1995). Using the theory of reasoned action to understand organizational behaviour: The role of belief salience. *British Journal of Social Psychology*, *34*(2), 161–172. 10.1111/j.2044–8309.1995.tb01055.x
Ellis, A. (1962). *Reason and emotion in psychotherapy*. Lyle Stuart.
Ellis, A. (1963). Toward a more precise definition of "emotional" and "intellectual" insight. *Psychological Reports*, *13*(1), 125–126. https://doi.org/10.2466/pr0.1963.13.1.125
Ellis, A. (1973). *Humanistic psychotherapy: The rational-emotive approach*. McGraw-Hill.
Ellis, A. (1976). The biological basis of human irrationality. *Journal of Individual Psychology*, *32*(2), 145–168.
Ellis, A. (1977). Rejoinder: Elegant and Inelegant RET. *The Counseling Psychologist*, *7*(1), 73–82. https://doi.org/10.1177/001100007700700110

Ellis, A. (1979). Is rational-emotive therapy stoical, humanistic, or spiritual? *Journal of Humanistic Psychology, 19*(3), 89–92. https://doi.org/10.1177/002216787901900314
Ellis, A. (1980a). The fact of mental illness. *Rational Living, 15*, 25–30.
Ellis, A. (1980b). Rational-emotive therapy and cognitive behavior therapy: Similarities and differences. *Cognitive Therapy and Research, 4*(4), 325–340.
Ellis, A. (1983). *The case against religiosity*. Institute for Rational Emotive Therapy.
Ellis, A. (1987a). Yes, how reasonable is rational-emotive therapy? *Review of Existential Psychology and Psychiatry, 19*, 135–139.
Ellis, A. (1987b). The impossibility of achieving consistently good mental health. *American Psychologist, 42*, 364–375.
Ellis, A. (1987c). On the origin and development of rational-emotive theory (pp. 148–175). In W. Dryden (Ed.), *Key cases in psychotherapy*. New York University Press.
Ellis, A. (1988). *How to stubbornly refuse to make yourself miserable: About anything - yes, anything!* (p. 11). Little, Brown Book Group. Kindle Edition.
Ellis, A. (1991). Achieving self-actualization: The rational-emotive approach. *Journal of Social Behavior & Personality, 6*(5), 1–18.
Ellis, A. (1994). *Reason and emotion in psychotherapy* (2nd ed.). Carol Publishing Group.
Ellis, A. (1995). Changing rational emotive therapy (RET) to rational emotive behaviour therapy (REBT). *Journal of Rational-Emotive and Cognitive-Behavior Therapy, 13*(3), 85–89.
Ellis, A. (1996a). *How to stubbornly refuse to make yourself miserable about anything--yes, anything*. Lyle Stuart Inc.
Ellis, A. (1996b). The humanism of rational emotive behavior therapy and other cognitive behavior therapies. *The Journal of Humanistic Education and Development, 35*(2), 69–88. https://doi.org/10.1002/j.2164-4683.1996.tb00356.x
Ellis, A. (1996c). *REBT diminishes much of the human ego* (Rev. ed.). Albert Ellis Institute.
Ellis, A. (1997). Using rational emotive behavior therapy techniques to cope with disability. *Professional Psychology: Research and Practice, 28*(1), 17–22. https://doi.org/10.1037/0735-7028.28.1.17
Ellis, A. (1998). Albert Ellis, Shaun Blau (Eds.), *The Albert Ellis reader: A guide to well-being using rational emotive behavior therapy*. Citadel Press.
Ellis, A. (2001). *Feeling better, getting better, staying better: Profound self-help therapy for your emotions*. Impact.
Ellis, A. (2002a). *Overcoming resistance: A rational emotive behavior therapy integrated approach* (2nd ed.). Springer Publishing Co.
Ellis, A. (2002b). The role of irrational beliefs in perfectionism. In G. L. Flett & P. L. Hewitt (Eds.), *Perfectionism: Theory, research, and treatment* (pp. 217–229). American Psychological Association. https://doi.org/10.1037/10458-009
Ellis, A. (2003a). Similarities and differences between rational emotive behavior therapy and cognitive therapy. *Journal of Cognitive Psychotherapy, 17*(3), 225–240. https://doi.org/10.1891/jcop.17.3.225.52535
Ellis, A. (2003b). Early theories and practices of rational emotive behavior therapy and how they have been augmented and revised during the last three decades. *Journal of Rational-Emotive & Cognitive-Behavior Therapy, 21*(3/4), 219–243.
Ellis, A. (2003c). The relationship of rational emotive behavior therapy (REBT) to social psychology. *Journal of Rational-Emotive & Cognitive-Behavior Therapy, 21*(1), 5–20. https://doi.org/10.1023/A:1024177000887
Ellis, A. (2004). *The road to tolerance: The philosophy of rational emotive behaviour therapy*. Prometheus.
Ellis, A. (2005a). Can rational-emotive behavior therapy (REBT) and acceptance and commitment therapy (ACT) resolve their differences and be integrated? *Journal of Rational-Emotive & Cognitive-Behavior Therapy, 23*(2), 153–168. https://doi.org/10.1007/s10942-005-0008-8
Ellis, A. (2005b). *The myth of self-esteem: How rational emotive behavior therapy can change your life forever (psychology)*. Prometheus.
Ellis, A. (2006, May 24). *Ask Dr. Ellis - REBT Network: Albert Ellis | Rational Emotive Behavior Therapy*. REBT Network. http://www. rebtnetwork.org/ask/may06.html

Ellis, A. (2019). *How to stubbornly refuse to make yourself miserable about anything—yes, anything!* Little, Brown Book Group.
Ellis, A., David, D., & Lynn, S. J. (2010). Rational and irrational beliefs: A historical and conceptual perspective. In D. David, S. J. Lynn, & A. Ellis (Eds.), *Rational and irrational beliefs: Research, theory, and clinical practice* (pp. 3–22). Oxford University Press.
Ellis, A., & DiGiuseppe, R. (1993). Are inappropriate or dysfunctional feelings in rational-emotive therapy qualitative or quantitative? *Cognitive Therapy and Research*, *5*, 471–477
Ellis, A., & Dryden, W. (1997). *The practice of rational emotive behavior therapy* (2nd ed.). Springer Publishing Co.
Ellis, A., Gordon, J., Neenan, M., & Palmer, S. (1997). *Stress counselling: A rational emotive behavior approach*. Cassell.
Ellis, A., & Harper, R. A. (1975). *A new guide to rational living*. Prentice-Hall.
Ellis, A., & Knaus, W. J. (1977). *Overcoming Procrastination.* Institute for Rational Living.
Ellis, A., & MacLaren, C. (1998). *Rational emotive behavior therapy: A therapist's guide*. Impact Publishers.
Engels, G. I., Garnefski, N., & Diekstra, R. F. (1993). Efficacy of rational-emotive therapy: A quantitative analysis. *Journal of Consulting and Clinical Psychology*, *61*(6), 1083–1090.
Entman, R. M. (1989). How the media affect what people think: An information processing approach. *The Journal of Politics*, *51*(2), 347–370. https://doi.org/10.2307/2131346
Epictetus., & Dobbin, R. (2008). *Discourses and selected writings (Penguin classics)* (1st ed.). Penguin Classics.
Escadi, C., Oyeoku, E. K., Onuigbo, L. N., Otu, M. S., Nwefuru, B. C., & Edeh, N. C. (2019). Rational-emotive behavior therapy program for trauma-specific beliefs among undergraduate students: Testing the effect of a group therapy. *Global Journal of Health Science 11*(8).
Evans, A. L., Turner, M. J., Pickerin, R., & Powditch, R. (2018). The effects of rational and irrational coach team talks on the cognitive appraisal and achievement goal orientation of varsity football athletes. *International Journal of Sports Science & Coaching*, *13*(3). https://doi.org/10.1177/1747954118771183
Everett, J. A. C., Faber, N. S., & Crockett, M. (2015). Preferences and beliefs in ingroup favoritism. *Frontiers in Behavioral Neuroscience*, *9*, Article 15.
Falkingham, K. (2019, July 14). *I Heard 'Novak' for 'Roger' - Djokovic*. BBC Sport. Retrieved 9 March 2022, from https://www.bbc.co.uk/sport/tennis/48984899
Faustino, B., & Vasco, A. B. (2021). Emotional schemas mediate the relationship between emotion regulation and symptomatology. *Current Psychology*, https://doi.org/10.1007/s12144-021-01560-7
Festinger, L. (1957). *A theory of cognitive dissonance*. Stanford University Press.
Festinger, L. (1962, October). Cognitive dissonance. *Scientific American*, *207*(4), 93–106.
Finley, R. D. (1979). The spiritual poverty of rational-emotive therapy. *Journal of Humanistic Psychology*, *19*(3), 83–87.
Fisher, B. (2020, September 11). *Ben Foster: 'I Want to be a Cyclist after Football. The Alps, Vuelta, Giro'*. Watford | The Guardian. Retrieved 12 March 2022, from https://amp.theguardian.com/football/2020/sep/10/ben-foster-watford-cyclist-after-football-the-alps-vuelta-giro?__twitter_impression=true
Ford, B. Q., & Gross, J. J. (2018). Emotion regulation: Why beliefs matter. *Canadian Psychology/Psychologie Canadienne*, *59*(1), 1–14. https://doi.org/10.1037/cap0000142
Forgas, J. P., Goldenberg, L., & Unkelbach, C. (2009). Can bad weather improve your memory? An unobtrusive field study of natural mood effects on real-life memory. *Journal of Experimental Social Psychology*, *45*(1), 254–257.
Franken, R. E. (1994). *Human motivation* (3rd ed.). Brooks/Cole Publishing Company.
Frankl, Viktor E. (1992). *Man's search for meaning* (p. 12). Ebury Publishing. Kindle Edition.
Frankl, V. E. (2000). *Man's search for meaning: An introduction to Logotherapy* (Rev. ed.). Beacon Press.
Frede, D. (2003). Stoic determinism. In B. Inwood (Ed.), *The Cambridge companion to the stoics* (pp. 179–205). Cambridge University Press. https://doi.org/10.1017/CCOL052177005X.008
Frijda, N. (1986). *The emotions*. Cambridge University Press.
Frijda, N. (1988). The laws of emotion. *American Psychologist*, *43*, 349–358.

Frijda, N. H., Manstead, A. S. R., & Bem, S. (2000). The influence of emotions on beliefs. In N. H. Frijda, A. S. R. Manstead, & S. Bem, S. (Eds.), *Emotions and beliefs how feelings influence thoughts* (pp. 1–9). Cambridge University Press.

Friston, K. (2010). The free-energy principle: A unified brain theory? *Nature Reviews Neuroscience, 11*, 127–138. https://doi.org/10.1038/nrn2787

Garcés, M., & Finkel, L. (2019). Emotional theory of rationality. *Frontiers in Integrative Neuroscience, 13*, 11. https://doi.org/10.3389/fnint.2019.00011

Gellatly, R., & Beck, A. T. (2016). Catastrophic thinking: A transdiagnostic process across psychiatric disorders. *Cognitive Therapy and Research, 40*(4), 441–52. https://doi.org/10.1007/s10608-016-9763-3

Gewirth, A. (2009). *Self-fulfillment*. Princeton University Press.

Gilbert, D. T., Pinel, E. C., Wilson, T. D., Blumberg, S. J., & Wheatley, T. P. (1998). Immune neglect: A source of durability bias in affective forecasting. *Journal of Personality and Social Psychology, 75*, 617–638.

Gladwell, M. (2013). *David and Goliath: Underdogs, misfits, and the art of battling giants*. Little, Brown and Co.

Goldin, P. R., McRae, K., Ramel, W., & Gross, J. J. (2008). The neural bases of emotion regulation: Reappraisal and suppression of negative emotion. *Biological Psychiatry, 63*, 577–586.

Gollwitzer, P. M., Wieber, F., Meyers, A. L., & McCrea, S. M. (2010). How to maximize implementation intention effects. In C. R. Agnew, D. E. Carlston, W. G. Graziano, & J. R. Kelly (Eds.), *Then a miracle occurs: Focusing on behavior in social psychological theory and research* (pp.137–161). Oxford Press.

Gollwitzer, P. M., & Sheeran, P. (2006). Implementation intentions and goal achievement: A meta-analysis of effects and processes. In M. P. Zanna (Ed.), *Advances in experimental social psychology, Vol. 38* (pp. 69–119). Elsevier Academic Press. https://doi.org/10.1016/S0065-2601(06)38002-1

Gonzalez, J. E., Nelson, J. R., Gutkin, T. B., Saunders, A., Galloway, A., & Shwery, C. S. (2004). Rational emotive therapy with children and adolescents a meta-analysis. *Journal of Emotional and Behavioral Disorders, 12*(4), 222–235.

Gould, S. J. (2002). *The structure of evolutionary theory*. Belknap Press of Harvard University Press.

Grabe, M. E., Zhou, S., & Barnett, B. (2001). Explicating sensationalism in television news: Content and the bells and whistles of form. *Journal of Broadcasting and Electronic Media, 45*, 635–655. https://doi.org/10.1207/s15506878jobem4504_6

Grant, M., Salsman, N. L., & Berking, M. (2018). The assessment of successful emotion regulation skills use: Development and validation of an English version of the emotion regulation skills questionnaire. *PLoS One, 13*(10), e0205095. https://doi.org/10.1371/journal.pone.0205095

Gross, J. J. (1998a). The emerging field of emotion regulation: An integrative review. *Review of General Psychology, 2*(3), 271–299. https://doi.org/10.1037/1089-2680.2.3.271

Gross, J. J. (1998b). Antecedent- and response-focused emotion regulation: Divergent consequences for experience, expression, and physiology. *Journal of Personality and Social Psychology, 74*(1), 224–237. https://doi.org/10.1037/0022-3514.74.1.224

Gross, J. J. (2014). Emotion regulation: Conceptual and empirical foundations. In J. J. Gross (Ed.), *Handbook of emotion regulation* (pp. 3–20). The Guilford Press.

Gross, J. J. (2015a). Emotion regulation: Current status and future prospects. *Psychological Inquiry, 26*(1), 1–26. https://doi.org/10.1080/1047840X.2014.940781

Gross, J. J. (2015b). The extended process model of emotion regulation: Elaborations, applications, and future directions. *Psychological Inquiry, 26*(1), 130–137.

Gross, J. J., & Thompson, R. A. (2007). Emotion regulation: Conceptual foundations. In J. J. Gross (Ed.), *Handbook of emotion regulation* (pp. 3–24). The Guilford Press.

Haaga, D. A., DeRubeis, R. J., Stewart, B. L., & Beck, A. T. (1991). Relationship of intelligence with cognitive therapy outcome. *Behaviour Research & Therapy, 29*(3), 277–281. https://doi.org/10.1016/0005-7967(91)90118-m

Hadot, P. (2002). *What is Ancient Philosophy?*. Harvard University Press.

Hadot, P., & Chase, M. (2002). *What is ancient philosophy?* (New ed.). Belknap Press: An Imprint of Harvard University Press.
Halasz, G. (2004). In conversation with Dr Albert Ellis. *Australasian Psychiatry*, *12*(4), 325–333. https://doi.org/10.1080/j.1440-1665.2004.02121.x
Halligan, P. W. (2006). Beliefs: Shaping experience and understanding illness. In P. W. Halligan & M. Aylward (Eds.), *The power of belief: Psychosocial influence on illness, disability and medicine* (pp. 11–26). Oxford University Press.
Halligan, P. W. (2007). Belief and illness. *Psychologist*, *20*, 358–361.
Hardy, J., Roberts, R., & Hardy, L. (2009). Awareness and motivation to change negative self-talk. *The Sport Psychologist*, *23*(4), 435–450.
Harrington, N. (2005a). Dimensions of frustration intolerance and their relationship to self-control problems. *Journal of Rational-Emotive & Cognitive-Behavioral Therapy*, *23*, 1–20. https://doi.org/10.1007/s10942-005-0001-2
Harrington, N. (2005b). It's too difficult! Frustration intolerance beliefs and procrastination. *Personality and Individual Differences*, *39*, 873–883. https://doi.org/10.1016/j.paid.2004.12.018
Harris, S. (2006). *The end of faith*. Amsterdam University Press.
Hayes, S. C., Levin, M. E., Plumb-Vilardaga, J., Villatte, J. L., & Pistorello, J. (2013). Acceptance and commitment therapy and contextual behavioral science: Examining the progress of a distinctive model of behavioral and cognitive therapy. *Behavior Therapy*, *44*(2), 180–198. https://doi.org/10.1016/j.beth.2009.08.002
Hayes, J. P., Morey, R. A., Petty, C. M., Seth, S., Smoski, M. J., McCarthy, G., et al. (2010). Staying cool when things get hot: Emotion regulation modulates neural mechanisms of memory encoding. *Frontiers in Human Neuroscience*, *4*, 230.
Headington Institute. (2020, September 5). *How You Think About Stress Matters*. Retrieved 31 January 2022, from https://www.headington-institute.org/resource/how-you-think-about-stress-matters/
Healy, L., Tincknell-Smith, A., & Ntoumanis, N. (2018). Goal setting in sport and performance. In *Oxford research encyclopedia of psychology*. doi: 10.1093/acrefore/9780190236557.013.152
Hendriks Vettehen, P., & Kleemans, M. (2017). Proving the obvious? What sensationalism contributes to the time spent on news video. *Electronic News*, *12*(2), 113–127. https://doi.org/10.1177/1931243117739947
Herbert, J. D., & Forman, E. M. (2013). Caution: The differences between CT and ACT may be larger (and smaller) than they appear. *Behavior Therapy*, *44*(2), 218–223. https://doi.org/10.1016/j.beth.2009.09.005
Hewstone, M., Rubin, M., & Willis, H. (2002). Intergroup bias. *Annual Review of Psychology*, *53*, 575–604. https://doi.org/10.1146/annurev.psych.53.100901.135109
Hickey, M., & Doyle, K. A. (2018). Rational emotive behavior therapy. In A. Vernon & K. A. Doyle (Eds.), *Cognitive behavior therapies: A guidebook for practitioners* (pp. 109–142). American Counseling Association.
Höchli, B., Brügger, A., & Messner, C. (2018). How focusing on superordinate goals motivates broad, long-term goal pursuit: A theoretical perspective. *Frontiers in Psychology*, *9*, Article 1879. https://doi.org/10.3389/fpsyg.2018.01879
Hofmann, S. G., Asmundson, G. J., & Beck, A. T. (2013). The science of cognitive therapy. *Behavior Therapy*, *44*(2), 199–212. https://doi.org/10.1016/j.beth.2009.01.007
Hofmann, S. G., Sawyer, A. T., & Fang, A. (2010). The empirical status of the 'new wave' of cognitive behavioral therapy. *Psychiatric Clinics of North America*, *33*(3), 701–710. https://doi.org/10.1016/j.psc.2010.04.006
Holiday, R. (2019, March 29). *Premeditatio Malorum*. Daily Stoic. Retrieved 14 October 2022, from https://dailystoic.com/premeditatio-malorum/
Holmes, T. H., & Rahe, R. H. (1967). The Social Readjustment Rating Scale. *Journal of Psychosomatic Research*, *11*(2), 213–218. https://doi.org/10.1016/0022-3999(67)90010-4
Hooper, A. (2020, January 19). *Lizzie Simmonds: 'Who Am I and What is My Purpose?'* SportSpiel. Retrieved 12 March 2022, from https://sportspielonline.com/2019/09/29/lizzie-simmonds-who-am-i-and-what-is-my-purpose/

Horvath, A. O., & Greenberg, L. S. (1989). Development and validation of the working alliance inventory. *Journal of Counseling Psychology*, *36*, 223–233. https://doi.org/10.1037/0022-0167.36.2.223

Howells, K. (2016, August 23). *'Super-Human' Athletes are at Risk from the Post-Olympic Blues – Here's Why*. The Conversation. Retrieved 12 March 2022, from https://theconversation.com/super-human-athletes-are-at-risk-from-the-post-olympic-blues-heres-why-64266

Howlett, J. R., & Paulus, M. P. (2015). The neural basis of testable and non-testable beliefs. *PLoS ONE*, *10*, e0124596. https://doi.org/10.1371/journal.pone.0124596

Hoyt, M. F. (2011). Foreword. In A. Slive & M. Bobele (Eds.), *When one hour is all you have: Effective therapy for walk-in clients* (pp. xix–xv). Zeig, Tucker, & Theisen.

Huang, J., & Bargh, J. (2014). The selfish goal: Autonomously operating motivational structures as the proximate cause of human judgment and behavior. *Behavioral and Brain Sciences*, *37*(2), 121–135. https://doi.org/10.1017/S0140525X13000290

Huguet, A., Rao, S., McGrath, P. J., Wozney, L., Wheaton, M., Conrod, J., & Rozario, S. (2016). A systematic review of cognitive behavioral therapy and behavioral activation apps for depression. *PLoS One*, *11*, 1–19. https://doi.org/10.1371/journal.pone.0154248

Humphrey, J., & Hughes, D. (2020, September 21). *E23- Jonny Wilkinson: How a Mental Health Crisis Led to a Life of Exploration | The High Performance Podcast on Acast*. Acast. Retrieved 27 March 2022, from https://play.acast.com/s/the-high-performance-podcast/jonnywilkinson-howamentalhealthcrisisledtoalifeofexploration

Hutchinson, G. T., & Chapman, B. P. (2005). Logotherapy-enhanced REBT: An integration of discovery and reason. *Journal of Contemporary Psychotherapy*, *35*, 145–155. https://doi.org/10.1007/s10879-005-2696-x

Hyland, P., Shevlin, M., Adamson, G., & Boduszek, D. (2014). Modelling the structure of the Attitudes and Belief Scale 2: Toward the development of an abbreviated version. *Cognitive Behaviour Therapy*, *43*, 60–71.

Hymen, S. P., & Warren, R. (1978). An evaluation of rational-emotive imagery as a component of rational-emotive therapy in the treatment of test anxiety. *Perceptual and Motor Skills*, *46*(3), 847–853. https://doi.org/10.2466/pms.1978.46.3.847

Ierodiakonou, K. (2015). How feasible is the Stoic conception of eudaimonia? In Ø. Rabbås, E. K. Emilsson, H. Fossheim, & M. Tuominen (Eds.), *The quest for the good life* (pp. 183–196). Oxford University Press. https://doi.org/10.1093/acprof:oso/9780198746980.003.0010

Irvine, W. B. (2009). *A guide to the good life: The ancient art of stoic joy.* Oxford University Press.

Irving, P., & Dickson, D. (2006). A re-conceptualization of Rogers' core conditions: Implications for research, practice and training. *International Journal for the Advancement of Counselling*, *28*, 183. https://doi.org/10.1007/s10447-005-9000-3

Jackson, K. (2019, March 27). *Rory McIlroy Will not be Defined by Wins and Lossesahead of WGC-Match Play*. Sky Sports. Retrieved 17 March 2022, from https://www.skysports.com/golf/news/12176/11676065/rory-mcilroy-will-not-be-defined-by-wins-and-losses-ahead-of-wgc-match-play

Jha, A. (2018, February 14). *Where Belief is Born*. The Guardian. Retrieved 21 March 2022, from https://www.theguardian.com/science/2005/jun/30/psychology.neuroscience

Johns, M. J., Inzlicht, M., & Schmader, T. (2008). Stereotype threat and executive resource depletion: Examining the influence of emotion regulation. *Journal of Experimental Psychology: General*, *137*, 691–705.

Jokić-Begić, N. (2010). Cognitive-behavioral therapy and neuroscience: Towards closer integration. *Psychological Topics*, *19*, 235–254.

Jooste, J., Wolfson, S., & Kruger, A. (2022). Irrational performance beliefs and mental well-being upon returning to sport during the COVID-19 pandemic: A test of mediation by intolerance of uncertainty. *Research Quarterly for Exercise and Sport*. https://doi.org/10.1080/02701367.2022.2056117

Jones, B. R. (2019, April 8). *Rory: Id Love to Win Masters but I Dont Need to Any More*. Belfast Telegraph. Retrieved 17 March 2022, from https://www.belfasttelegraph.co.uk/sport/golf/masters/rory-id-love-to-win-masters-but-i-dont-need-to-any-more-37991659.html

Jones, P. J., Bellet, B. W., & McNally, R. J. (2020). Helping or harming? The effect of trigger warnings on individuals with trauma histories. *Clinical Psychological Science*, *8*(5), 905–917. https://doi.org/10.1177/2167702620921341

Jordana, A., Turner, M. J., Ramis, Y., & Torregrossa, M. (2020). A systematic mapping review on the use of rational emotive behavior therapy (REBT) with athletes. *International Review of Sport and Exercise Psychology*. https://doi.org/10.1080/1750984X.2020.1836673

Kashdan, T., & Biswas-Diener, R. (2014). *The power of negative emotion: How anger, guilt, and self doubt are essential to success and fulfillment*. Oneworld Publications.

Kazantzis, N., Whittington, C., & Datillio, F. (2010). Meta-analysis of homework effects in cognitive and behavioral therapy: A replication and extension. *Clinical Psychology: Science and Practice*, *17*(2), 144–156.

Kendall, P. C., & Ingram, R. E. (1989). Cognitive-behavioral perspectives: Theory and research on depression and anxiety. In P. C. Kendall & D. Watson (Eds.), *Anxiety and depression: Distinctive and overlapping features* (pp. 27–53). Academic Press.

Kelly, G. (1955). *The Psychology of Personal Constructs*. W. W. Norton.

Kelly, T. (2003). Epistemic rationality as instrumental rationality: A critique. *Philosophy and Phenomenological Research*, *66*, 612–640. https://doi.org/10.1111/j.1933-1592.2003.tb00281.x

Kern, A. (2020). Human life, rationality and education. *Journal of Philosophy of Education*, *54*, 268–289.

Kerr, J. H. (1993). An eclectic approach to psychological interventions in sport: Reversal theory. *The Sport Psychologist*, *7*(4), 400–418. https://journals.humankinetics.com/view/journals/tsp/7/4/article-p400.xml

Khantzian, E. J. (1985). The self-medication hypothesis of addictive disorders: Focus on heroin and cocaine dependence. *The American Journal of Psychiatry*, *142*, 1259–1264.

Killick, S., Curry, V., & Myles, P. (2016). The mighty metaphor: A collection of therapists' favourite metaphors and analogies. *The Cognitive Behaviour Therapist*, *9*, E37. https://doi.org/10.1017/S1754470X16000210

King, A., Barker, J. B., Turner, M. J., & Plateau, C. (2022). The socialisation of irrational beliefs in sport. *Journal of Rational-Emotive and Cognitive-Behavioral Therapy*. https://doi.org/10.1007/s10942-022-00460-4.

Kinney, A. (2000). The intellectual-insight problem: Implications for assessment and rational-emotive behavior therapy. *Journal of Contemporary Psychotherapy*, *30*, 261–272. https://doi.org/10.1023/A:1004142732449

Kinsella, C. (2017, May 6). *Ryan Giggs Admits He 'Never Really Enjoyed' Playing Professional Football*. JOE.Ie. Retrieved 12 March 2022, from https://www.joe.ie/sport/ryan-giggs-admits-never-really-enjoyed-playing-professional-football-587355

Kleim, J. A., & Jones, T. A. (2008). Principles of experience-dependent neural plasticity: implications for rehabilitation after brain damage. *Journal of speech, language, and hearing research: JSLHR*, *51*(1), S225–S239. https://doi.org/10.1044/1092-4388(2008/018)

Klein, G. (2014, August 1). *Performing a Project Premortem*. Harvard Business Review. Retrieved 24 March 2022, from https://hbr.org/2007/09/performing-a-project-premortem

Knaus, W. (2006). *Rational Emotive Education. Theory into Practice*. New York: REBT Network. Retrieved on 20th May, 2016 from http://doi.org/10.1080/00405847709542709

Knight, C. J., Harwood, C. G., & Sellars, P. A. (2018). Supporting adolescent athletes' dual careers: The role of an athlete's social support network. *Psychology of Sport and Exercise*, *38*, 137–147. https://doi.org/10.1016/j.psychsport.2018.06.007

Knox, L. (n.d.). *Infographic: Serena's Grand Slam History*. ESPN.Com. Retrieved 16 March 2022, from https://www.espn.com/espn/feature/story/_/id/17365694/interactive-look-serena-williams-346-grand-slam-matches#:%7E:text=A%20remarkably%20consistent%20performer%2C%20Serena, Martina%20Navratilova%20and%20Chris%20Evert.

Ko, C. H., Yen, J. Y., Yen, C. F., Chen, C. S., & Wang, S. Y. (2008). The association between Internet addiction and belief of frustration intolerance: The gender difference. *Cyberpsychology & Behavior: The Impact of the Internet, Multimedia and Virtual Reality on Behavior and Society*, *11*(3), 273–278. https://doi.org/10.1089/cpb.2007.0095

Kobylińska, D., & Kusev, P. (2019). Flexible emotion regulation: How situational demands and individual differences influence the effectiveness of regulatory strategies. *Frontiers in Psychology, 10*, Article 72. https://doi.org/10.3389/fpsyg.2019.00072

Kombos, N. A., Fournet, G. P., & Estes, R. E. (1989). Effects of irrationality on a trail making performance task. *Perceptual and Motor Skills, 68*, 591–598. http://doi.org/10.2466/pms.1989.68.2.591

Koole, S. L. (2009). The psychology of emotion regulation: An integrative review, *Cognition and Emotion, 23*(1), 4–41. https://doi.org/10.1080/02699930802619031

Kreibig, S. D., Gendolla, G. H., & Scherer, K. R. (2010). Psychophysiological effects of emotional responding to goal attainment. *Biological Psychology, 84*(3), 474–487. https://doi.org/10.1016/j.biopsycho.2009.11.004

Kring, A. M. (2008). Emotion disturbances as transdiagnostic processes in psychopathology. In M. Lewis, J. M. Haviland-Jones, & L. Feldman (Eds.), *Handbook of emotions* (pp. 691–708). Guilford Press.

Kring, A. M., & Werner, K. H. (2004). Emotion regulation in psychopathology. In P. Philippot & R. S. Feldman (Eds.), *The regulation of emotion* (pp. 359–385). Lawrence Erlbaum Associates, Inc.

Kross, E., & Ayduk, O. (2008). Facilitating adaptive emotional analysis: Distinguishing distanced-analysis of depressive experiences from immersed-analysis and distraction. *Personality and Social Psychology Bulletin, 34*, 924–938.

Kuhn, T. (1977). *The essential tension: Selected studies tradition and changes*. The University of Chicago Press.

Kuhn, T. S. (1962). *The structure of scientific revolutions*. University of Chicago Press.

Kuyken, W., Padesky, C. A., & Dudley, R. (2009). *Collaborative case conceptualization: Working effectively with clients in cognitive-behavioral therapy.* Guilford Press.

Lang, A., Newhagen, J., & Reeves, B. (1996). Negative video as structure: Emotion, attention, capacity, and memory. *Journal of Broadcasting & Electronic Media, 40*, 460–477. https://doi.org/10.1080/08838159609364369

Larner, C., Morris, T., & Marchant, D. (2007). The management of directional trait anxiety in competitive sports with rational-emotive behavior therapy. *Paper Presented at the European Congress of Sport Psychology.* Available at: http://www.fepsac.com/congresses/congress_2007

Late Show [CBS]. (2017, June 5). *Dave Chappelle Interview on David Letterman (2014)* [Video]. YouTube. https://www.youtube.com/watch?v=kXv39gQ_YEg

Latinjak, A. T., Zourbanos, N., López-Ros, V., & Hatzigeorgiadis, A. (2014). Goal-directed and undirected self-talk: Exploring a new perspective for the study of athletes' self-talk. *Psychology of Sport and Exercise, 15*, 548–558.

Lawton, M. (2012, October 16). *Poland v England: Roy Hodgson Acid Test: MATT LAWTON.* Mail Online. Retrieved 25 March 2022, from https://www.dailymail.co.uk/sport/football/article-2218275/Poland-v-England-Roy-Hodgson-acid-test-MATT-LAWTON.html

Lazarus, A. A. (1977). Towards an egoless state of being. In A. Ellis & R. Grieger (Eds.), *Handbook of rational-emotive therapy*. Springer Publishing Company.

Lazarus, A. A. (1995). REBT: A sign of evolution or devolution? An historical perspective. *Journal of Rational-Emotive & Cognitive-Behavior Therapy, 13*(2), 97–100. https://doi.org/10.1007/bf02354455

Lazarus, R., & Folkman, S. (1984). *Stress, appraisal, and coping*. Springer.

Lazarus, R. S. (1991). *Emotion and adaptation*. Oxford University Press.

Lazarus, R. S. (1995). Cognition and emotion from the RET viewpoint. *Journal of Rational-Emotive & Cognitive-Behavior Therapy, 13*(1), 29–54. https://doi.org/10.1007/BF02354556

Lazarus, R. S. (1999). *Stress and emotion: A new synthesis.* Springer Publishing Co.

Leary, M. R., & Cottrell, C. A. (2013). Evolutionary perspectives on interpersonal acceptance and rejection. In C. N. DeWall (Ed.), *The Oxford handbook of social exclusion* (pp. 9–19). Oxford University Press.

Lega, L. I., & Ellis, A. (2001). Rational emotive behavior therapy (REBT) in the new millennium: A cross-cultural approach. *Journal of Rational-Emotive & Cognitive-Behavior Therapy, 19*(4), 201–222. https://doi.org/10.1023/A:1012537814117

Lents, N. H. (2018, May 18). *Evolution's Worst Mistake? How About External Testicles?* Undark Magazine. Retrieved 12 March 2022, from https://undark.org/2018/05/18/wilo-lents-human-errors/

Levis, D. J. (2009). The prolonged CS exposure techniques of implosive (flooding) therapy. In W. T. O'Donohue & J. E. Fisher (Eds.), *General principles and empirically supported techniques of cognitive behavior therapy* (pp. 370–380). John Wiley.
Livni, E. (2018, December 21). *Daniel Kahneman Explains Why Most People Don't Want to be Happy*. Quartz. Retrieved 10 March 2022, from https://qz.com/1503207/a-nobel-prize-winning-psychologist-defines-happiness-versus-satisfaction/
Lizza, R. (2020, July 27). *Americans Tune in to 'Cancel Culture' — and Don't Like What They See*. POLITICO. https://www.politico.com/news/2020/07/22/americans-cancel-culture-377412
Longman, J. (2021, July 28). *Simone Biles Rejects a Long Tradition of Stoicism in Sports*. New York Times. https://www.nytimes.com/2021/07/28/sports/olympics/simone-biles-mental-health.html#:~:text=Biles%20was%20widely%20embraced%20as,courage%20to%20acknowledge%20her%20vulnerability.&text=As%20a%20subscriber%2C%20you%20have,articles%20to%20give%20each%20month.
Lukianoff, G., & Haidt, J. (2017, July 31). *How Trigger Warnings Are Hurting Mental Health on Campus*. The Atlantic. https://www.theatlantic.com/magazine/archive/2015/09/the-coddling-of-the-american-mind/399356/
Lukianoff, G., & Haidt, J. (2019). *The coddling of the American mind: How good intentions and bad ideas are setting up a generation for failure*. Penguin Books.
Lyons, L. C., & Woods, P. J. (1991). The efficacy of rational-emotive therapy: A quantitative review of the outcome research. *Clinical Psychology Review, 11*(4), 357–369.
Macey, D. A., Ryan, K. M., Springer, N. J., Akira, S. I., Clegg, L., Conaway, C., Foss, K. A., Fox, C., Freeman, C. P., & Good, J. E. (2014). *How Television Shapes Our Worldview*. Adfo Books.
MacInnes, D. (2004). The theories underpinning rational emotive behaviour therapy. *International Journal of Nursing Studies, 41*, 685–695.
Macinnes, D. L. (2006). Self-esteem and self-acceptance: An examination into their relationship and their effect on psychological health. *Journal of Psychiatric and Mental Health Nursing, 13*(5), 483–489.
Mack, D. E., Wilson, P. M., Oster, K. G., Kowalski, K. C., Crocker, P. R., & Sylvester, B. D. (2011). Well-being in volleyball players: Examining the contributions of independent and balanced psychological need satisfaction. *Psychology of Sport and Exercise, 12*(5), 533–539.
Madden, M. (2015, February 18). *Dusting 'Em Off: Bob Dylan - Bob Dylan*. Consequence. Retrieved 10 March 2022, from https://consequence.net/2012/03/dusting-em-off-bob-dylan-bob-dylan/
Mahmoodi Kahriz, B., Bower, J. L., Glover, F. M. G. Q., & Vogt, J. (2019). Wanting to be happy but not knowing how: Poor attentional control and emotion-regulation abilities mediate the association between valuing happiness and depression. *Journal of Happiness Studies, 21*(7), 2583–2601. https://doi.org/10.1007/s10902-019-00193-9
Mahoney, M. J. (1974). *Cognition and behavior modification* (1st ed.). Ballinger Pub. Co.
Mansell, P. C. (2021). Stress mindset in athletes: Investigating the relationships between beliefs, challenge and threat with psychological wellbeing. *Psychology of Sport and Exercise, 57*.
Marlow, C. (2009). Creating positive performance beliefs: The case of a tenpin bowler. In B.Hemmings & T. Holder (Eds.), *Applied sport psychology: A case-based approach* (pp. 65–87). John Wiley & Sons Ltd.
Martin, R. C., & Dahlen, E. R. (2004). Irrational beliefs and the experience and expression of anger. *Journal of Rational-Emotive & Cognitive-Behavior Therapy, 22*, 3–20. https://doi.org/10.1023/B:JORE.0000011574.44362.8f
Maslow, A. H. (1943). A theory of human motivation. *Psychological Review, 50*(4), 370–396.
The Masters. (2019, April 9). *Rory McIlroy -2019 Masters Interview* [Video]. YouTube. https://www.youtube.com/watch?v=bQRk8F6XjKI
Mathews, A., & MacLeod, C. (2002). Induced processing biases have causal effects on anxiety. *Cognition and Emotion, 16*(3), 331–354.
Matweychuk, W., DiGiuseppe, R., & Gulyayeva, O. (2019). A comparison of REBT with other cognitive behavior therapies. In M. E. Bernard & W. Dryden (Eds.), *Advances in REBT: Theory, practice, research, measurement, prevention and promotion* (pp. 47–77). Springer Nature. https://doi.org/10.1007/978-3-319-93118-0_3

Maultsby, M. C. (1975). *Help yourself to happiness trough rational self-counseling*. Institute for Rational Living.
Maultsby, M. C., Jr. (1984). *Rational behavior therapy*. Prentice Hall.
Maultsby, M., Jr. (1971). Rational emotive imagery. *Rational Living, 6*(1), 24–27.
Mauss, I. B., Tamir, M., Anderson, C. L., & Savino, N. S. (2011). Can seeking happiness make people unhappy? Paradoxical effects of valuing happiness. *Emotion, 11*, 807–815.
Maxwell-Keys, C., Wood, A. G., & Turner, M. J. (2022). Developing decision making in Rugby Union match officials using rational emotive behavior therapy (REBT). *Psychology of Sport and Exercise, 58*. Accepted 2nd November 2021.
May, R. (1975). *The courage to create*. W. W. Norton.
McCauley, K. (2012, March 23). *Brad Friedel In 'Giving A Crap About Things Other Than Football' Shocker*. Cartilage Free Captain. Retrieved 25 March 2022, from https://cartilagefreecaptain.sbnation.com/2012/3/23/2896508/brad-friedel-interview-quotes-tottenham-hotspur
McDowell, J. (2010). Towards a reading of Hegel on action in the 'reason' chapter of the phenomenology. In A. Laitinen & C. Sandis (Eds.), *Hegel on action* (pp. 166– 184). Palgrave-Macmillan.
McEachrane, M. (2009). Capturing emotional thoughts: The philosophy of cognitive-behavioral therapy. In Y. Gustafsson, C. Kronqvist, & M. McEachrane (Eds.), *Emotions and understanding: Wittgensteinian perspectives*. Palgrave-Macmillan.
McKay, R. T., & Dennett, D. C. (2009). The evolution of misbelief. *Behavioral and Brain Sciences, 32*, 493–561.
McCrae, R. R., & Costa, P. T. (1987). Validation of the five-factor model of personality across instruments and observers. *Journal of Personality and Social Psychology, 52*(1), 81–90. https://doi.org/10.1037/0022-3514.52.1.81
McRae, K., Hughes, B., Chopra, S., Gabrieli, J. D. E., Gross, J. J., & Ochsner, K. N. (2010). The neural bases of distraction and reappraisal. *Journal of Cognitive Neuroscience, 22*, 248–262. https://doi.org/10.1162/jocn.2009.21243
Meijen, C., Turner, M., Jones, M. V., Sheffield, D., & McCarthy, P. (2020). A theory of challenge and threat states in athletes: A revised conceptualization. *Frontiers in Psychology, 11*, 126. https://doi.org/10.3389/fpsyg.2020.00126
Mellalieu, S. D., Hanton, S., & Thomas, O. (2009). The effects of a motivational general-arousal imagery intervention upon preperformance symptoms in male rugby union players. *Psychology of Sport & Exercise, 10*, 175–185. https://doi.org/10.1016/j.psychsport.2008.07.003
Memon, Z. A., & Treur, J. (2010). On the reciprocal interaction between believing and feeling: An adaptive agent modelling perspective. *Cognitive Neurodynamics, 4*(4), 377–394.
Merzenich, M. M., & Sameshima, K. (1993). Cortical plasticity and memory. *Current Opinion in Neurobiology, 3*, 187–196.
Mesagno, C., Buchanan, E., Tibbert, S. J., & Turner, M. J. (2020). An initial investigation into irrational beliefs and choking under pressure. *Journal of Applied Sport Psychology, 33*(6), 569–589.
Mesagno, C., & Hill, D. M. (2013). Choking under pressure debate: Is there chaos in the brickyard? *International Journal of Sport Psychology, 44*, 288–293.
Metcalfe, J., & Shimamura, A. P. (1994). *Metacognition: Knowing about knowing*. MIT Press.
Michalski, R. L., & Shackelford, T. K. (2010). Evolutionary personality psychology: Reconciling human nature and individual differences. *Personality and Individual Differences, 48*(5), 509–516. https://doi.org/10.1016/j.paid.2009.10.027
Michel-Kröhler, A., & Turner, M. J. (2022). Link between irrational beliefs and important markers of mental health in a German sample of athletes: Differences between gender, sport-type and performance level. *Frontiers in Psychology, Movement Science and Sport Psychology*. 13:918329. doi: 10.3389/fpsyg.2022.918329.
Milgram, N. A., Sroloff, B., & Rosenbaum, M. (1988). The procrastination of everyday life. *Journal of Research in Personality, 22*(2), 197–212. https://doi.org/10.1016/0092-6566(88)90015-3
Miller, E. K. (2000). The prefrontal cortex and cognitive control. *Nature Reviews Neuroscience, 1*, 59–65.

Miller, W. R., & Rollnick, S. (2013). *Motivational interviewing: Helping people change* (3rd ed.). Guilford Press.

Milton, J., Newton, T., Addison, J., Barrow, S., Marvell, A., Vertue, G., Hayman, F., … Tonson, J and R. (1749). *Paradise lost: A poem, in twelve books*. London: Printed for J. and R. Tonson and S. Draper in the Strand.

Mobbs, D., Hagan, C. C., Dalgleish, T., Silston, B., & Prévost, C. (2015). The ecology of human fear: Survival optimization and the nervous system. *Frontiers in Neuroscience, 9*, 55. https://doi.org/10.3389/fnins.2015.00055

Mobini, S., & Grant, A. (2007). Clinical implications of attentional bias in anxiety disorders: An integrative literature review. *Psychotherapy: Theory, Research, Practice, Training, 44*(4), 450–462.

Moller, A. T., & Van der Merwe, J. D. (1997). Irrational beliefs, interpersonal perception and marital adjustment. *Journal of Rational-Emotive & Cognitive-Behavior Therapy, 15*, 260–290.

Moodie, C. A., Suri, G., Goerlitz, D. S., Mateen, M. A., Sheppes, G., McRae, K., Lakhan-Pal, S., Thiruchselvam, R., & Gross, J. J. (2020). The neural bases of cognitive emotion regulation: The roles of strategy and intensity. *Cognitive, Affective & Behavioral Neuroscience, 20*(2), 387–407. https://doi.org/10.3758/s13415-020-00775-8

Moore, R. H. (1983). Inference as '/~ in RET. *British Journal of Cognitive Psychotherapy, 1*(2), 17–23.

Moors, A., Ellsworth, P. C., Scherer, K. R., & Frijda, N. H. (2013). Appraisal theories of emotion: State of the art and future development. *Emotion Review, 5*(2), 119–124. https://doi.org/10.1177/1754073912468165

Monaco, M., & Martin, M. (2007). The millennial student: A new generation of learners. *Athletic Training Education Journal, 2*(2): 42–46. doi: https://doi.org/10.4085/1947-380X-2.2.42

Monroe, S. M., & Kelley, J. M. (1997). Measurement of stress appraisal. In S. Cohen, R. C. Kessler, & L. U. Gordon (Eds.), *Measuring stress: A guide for health and social scientists* (pp 122–147). Oxford University Press, Inc.

Morgulev, E., & Galily, Y. (2018). Choking or delivering under pressure? The case of elimination games in NBA playoffs. *Frontiers in Psychology, 9*, 979. https://doi.org/10.3389/fpsyg.2018.00979

Morris, T., Spittle, M., & Watt, A. P. (2005). *Imagery in sport*. Human Kinetics Books.

Moulam, B. (2022, March 4). *Stepping Back*. Beth Moulam. Retrieved 13 March 2022, from https://www.bethmoulam.com/stepping-back/

Muir, R. (2015). *A Record 91% of UK Millennials Own a Smartphone; Apple Devices Secure 78% Video Ad Completion Rate*. Retrieved from https://www.exchangewire.com/blog/2015/07/16/a-record-91-of-uk-millennials-own-a-smartphone-apple-devices-secure-78-video-ad-completion-rate/

Mundie, S. (presenter), & O'Sullivan, R. (guest). (2022, April 22). Does success = happiness? - Ronnie O'Sullivan. *Life Lessons: From Sport and Beyond*. Apple Podcasts. https://podcasts.apple.com/gb/podcast/dont-tell-me-the-score/id1564063336?i=1000558337457

Murguia, E., & Díaz, K. (2015). The philosophical foundations of cognitive behavioral therapy: Stoicism, Buddhism, Taoism, and Existentialism. *Journal of Evidence-Based Psychotherapies, 15*(1), 37–50.

Navarrete, C. D., Kurzban, R., Fessler, D. M. T., & Kirkpatrick, L. A. (2004). Anxiety and intergroup bias: Terror management or coalitional psychology? *Group Processes & Intergroup Relations, 7*(4), 370–397.

Neenan, M. (2009). *Developing resilience: A cognitive-behavioural approach*. Routledge/Taylor & Francis Group.

Neenan, M., & Dryden, W. (1996). The intricacies of inference chaining. *Journal of Rational-Emotive and Cognitive-Behavior Therapy, 14*(4), 231–243.

Neenan, M., & Dryden, W. (1999a). When laddering and the downward arrow can be used as adjuncts to inference chaining in rebt assessment. *Journal of Rational-Emotive & Cognitive-Behavior Therapy, 17*, 95–104. https://doi.org/10.1023/A:1023000914421

Neenan, M., & Dryden, W. (1999b). *Rational emotive behaviour therapy: Advances in theory and practice*. Whurr.

Neenan, M., & Dryden, W. (2010). *Rational emotive behaviour therapy in a nutshell.* SAGE Publications.

Neenan, M., & Dryden, W. (2015). *Cognitive behaviour therapy: 100 key points and techniques* (2nd ed.). Routledge/Taylor & Francis Group.

Neimark, J. (2019, October 9). *How We Won the Hominid Wars, and All the Others Died Out.* Discover Magazine. Retrieved 10 March 2022, from https://www.discovermagazine.com/the-sciences/how-we-won-the-hominid-wars-and-all-the-others-died-out

Nejati, M., Farsi, A., Motesharcie, E., & Turner, M. J. (2022). The Persian irrational performance beliefs inventory (iPBI-Persian): Translation, confirmatory factor analysis, and test-retest reliability, in Iranian athletes. *Journal of Rational-Emotive & Cognitive-Behavior Therapy.* Accepted 21st April 2021.

Nelson-Jones, R. (2006). *Theory and practice of counselling and therapy* (4th ed.). Sage Publications Ltd.

Nettle, D. (2006). The evolution of personality variation in humans and other animals. *American Psychologist, 61*(6), 622–631. https://doi.org/10.1037/0003-066X.61.6.622

Niedenthal, P. M. (2007). Embodying emotion. *Science, 316,* 1002–1005

Ochsner, K. N., & Gross, J. J. (2005). The cognitive control of emotion. *Trends in Cognitive Sciences, 9*(5), 242–249. https://doi.org/10.1016/j.tics.2005.03.010

Ochsner, K. N., & Gross, J. J. (2008). Cognitive emotion regulation: Insights from social cognitive and affective neuroscience. *Current Directions in Psychological Science, 17*(2), 153–158. https://doi.org/10.1111/j.1467-8721.2008.00566.x

Ochsner, K. N., Bunge, S. A., Gross, J. J., & Gabrieli, J. D. (2002). Rethinking feelings: an FMRI study of the cognitive regulation of emotion. *Journal of cognitive neuroscience, 14*(8), 1215–1229. https://doi.org/10.1162/089892902760807212

Ochsner, K. N., Ray, R. R., Cooper, J. C., Robertson, E. R., Chopra, S., Gabrieli, J. D. E., & Gross, J. J. (2004). For better or for worse: Neural systems supporting the cognitive down– and up–regulation of negative emotion. *Neuroimage, 23,* 483–499.

Ochsner, K. N., Silvers, J. A., & Buhle, J. T. (2012). Functional imaging studies of emotion regulation: A synthetic review and evolving model of the cognitive control of emotion. *Annals of the New York Academy of Sciences, 1251*(1), E1–E24. https://doi.org/10.1111/j.1749-6632.2012.06751.x

Ong, C. W., McGregor, P., & Daley, C. (2018). The boy behind the bravado: Player advanced safety and support in a professional football academy setting. *Sport and Exercise Psychology Review, 14*(1), 65–79.

Oltean, H. R., & David, D. O. (2018). A meta-analysis of the relationship between rational beliefs and psychological distress. *Journal of Clinical Psychology, 74*(6), 883–895. https://doi.org/10.1002/jclp.22562

Oltean, H. R., Hyland, P., Vallières, F., & David, D. O. (2019). Rational beliefs, happiness and optimism: An empirical assessment of REBT's model of psychological health. *International journal of psychology: Journal International de Psychologie, 54*(4), 495–500. https://doi.org/10.1002/ijop.12492

Ortner, C. N., Ste Marie, M., & Corno, D. (2016). Cognitive costs of reappraisal depend on both emotional stimulus intensity and individual differences in habitual reappraisal. *PloS ONE, 11*(12), e0167253. https://doi.org/10.1371/journal.pone.0167253

Orwell, G. (1933). *Down and out in Paris and London.* Martin Secker & Warburg Ltd.

Orwell, G. (1949). *Nineteen eighty-four.* Martin Secker & Warburg Ltd.

Palmer, S. (2009). Inference chaining: A rational coaching technique. *Coaching Psychology International, 2*(1), 11–12.

Park, A. (2021, July 22). *How Olympians Are Fighting to Put Athletes' Mental Health First.* Time. https://time.com/6082203/tokyo-olympics-mental-health/

Pavlin, D. J., Sullivan, M. J., Freund, P. R., & Roesen, K. (2005). Catastrophizing: A risk factor for postsurgical pain. *The Clinical Journal of Pain, 21*(1), 83–90. https://doi.org/10.1097/00002508-200501000-00010

Pekrun, R. (2006). The control-value theory of achievement emotions: Assumptions, corollaries, and implications for educational research and practice. *Educational Psychology Review, 18,* 315–341.

Pelusi, N. M. (2003). Evolutionary psychology and rational emotive therapy. In W. Dryden (Ed.), *Rational emotive behaviour therapy: Theoretical developments*. Brunner Routledge.

Pennebaker, J. W. (1989). Confession, inhibition, and disease. In L. Berkowitz (Ed.), *Advances in experimental social psychology, Vol. 22* (pp. 211–244). Academic Press. https://doi.org/10.1016/S0065-2601(08)60309-3

Pennebaker, J. W., & Susman, J. R. (1988). Disclosure of traumas and psychosomatic processes. *Social Science & Medicine, 26*(3), 327–332. https://doi.org/10.1016/0277-9536(88)90397-8

Peterson, J. B. (2017, May 20). *Biblical Series I: Introduction to the Idea of God* [Video]. YouTube. https://www.youtube.com/watch?v=f-wWBGo6a2w&feature=youtu.be

Peterson, J. B., Doidge, N., & Van, S. E. (2018). *12 rules for life: An antidote to chaos*. Random House Canada.

Pierson, H., & Hayes, S. C. (2007). Using acceptance and commitment therapy to empower the therapeutic relationship (pp. 205–228). In P. Gilbert & R. Leahy (Eds.), *The therapeutic relationship in cognitive behavior therapy*. Routledge.

Pigliucci, M. (2019, April 25). *Marcus Aurelius – the Unemotional Stoic?* IAI TV - Changing How the World Thinks. Retrieved 8 March 2022, from https://iai.tv/articles/marcus-aurelius-the-unemotional-stoic-auid-1227

Pinker, S. (2021). *Rationality: What it is. Why it seems scarce. Why it matters*. Viking.

Poczwardowski, A., Sherman, C. P., & Ravizza, R. (2004). Professional philosophy in the sport psychology service delivery: Building theory and practice. *The Sport Psychologist, 18*, 445–463. https://doi.org/10.1123/tsp.18.4.445

Popov, S. (2019). When is unconditional self-acceptance a better predictor of mental health than self-esteem? *Journal of Rational-Emotive & Cognitive-Behavior Therapy, 37*, 251–261 (2019). https://doi.org/10.1007/s10942-018-0310-x

PowerfulJRE. (2017). *Joe Rogan Experience #1006- Jordan Peterson & Bret Weinstein* [Video]. YouTube. URL https://www.youtube.com/watch?v=6G59zsjM2UI

Prapavessis, H., & Grove, J. R. (1998). Self-handicapping and self-esteem. *Journal of Applied Sport Psychology, 10*, 175–184.

Rakovshik, S. G., & McManus, F. (2010). Establishing evidence-based training in cognitive behavioral therapy: A review of current empirical findings and theoretical guidance. *Clinical Psychology Review, 30*(5), 496–516. https://doi.org/10.1016/j.cpr.2010.03.004

Rassin, E., Merckelbach, H., & Muris, P. (2000). Paradoxical and less paradoxical effects of thought suppression: A critical review. *Clinical Psychology Review, 20*(8), 973–995. https://doi.org/10.1016/s0272-7358(99)00019-7

Raue, P. J., & Goldfried, M. R. (1994). Therapeutic alliance in cognitive-behavior therapy. In A. O. Horvath & L. S. Greenberg (Eds.), *The working alliance: Theory, research and practice* (pp. 131–152). Wiley.

Ray, R. D., McRae, K., Ochsner, K. N., & Gross, J. J. (2010). Cognitive reappraisal of negative affect: Converging evidence from EMG and self-report. *Emotion, 10*, 587–592.

Reinboth, M., & Duda, J. L. (2006). Perceived motivational climate, need satisfaction and indices of well-being in team sports: A longitudinal perspective. *Psychology of Sport and Exercise, 7*(3), 269–286.

Richards, J. M., Butler, E., & Gross, J. J. (2003). Emotion regulation in romantic relationships: The cognitive consequences of concealing feelings. *Journal of Social and Personal Relationships, 20*, 599–620.

Ritter, W. (1930). Is man a rational animal? *Human Biology, 2*(4), 457–472. Retrieved September 18, 2020, from http://www.jstor.org/stable/41447045

Robb, H. (2003). REBT: Thinking it through once more. In W. Dryden (Ed.), *Rational emotive behaviour therapy: Theoretical developments* (pp. 35–54). Routledge.

Robb, H., Backx, W., & Thomas, J. (1999). The use of cognitive, emotive and behavioral interventions in rational emotive behavior therapy when clients lack "emotional" insight. *Journal of Rational-Emotive & Cognitive Behavior Therapy, 17*(3), 201–209.

Robb, H., & Ciarrochi, J. (2005). Some final, gulp, "words" on REBT, ACT & RFT. *Journal of Rational-Emotive & Cognitive-Behavior Therapy, 23*(2), 169–173. https://doi.org/10.1007/s10942-005-0009-7

Robertson, D. (2010). *The philosophy of Cognitive-Behavioural Therapy (CBT): Stoic philosophy as rational and cognitive psychotherapy*. Karnac.
Robertson, D. (2013, January 18). *Cognitive Distancing in Stoicism*. Donald Robertson. Retrieved 14 March 2022, from https://donaldrobertson.name/2013/01/18/cognitive-distancing-in-stoicism/
Robertson, D. (2018, March 15). *Why everything isn't totally indifferent to Stoics*. Donald J. Robertson. Retrieved 31 August 2022, from https://donaldrobertson.name/2018/03/17/why-everything-isnt-totally-indifferent-to-stoics/
Robertson, D. J. (2019a). *How to think like a roman emperor: The stoic philosophy of marcus aurelius*. St. Martin's Press.
Robertson, D. (2019b). *The philosophy of cognitive-behavioural therapy (cbt): Stoic philosophy as rational and cognitive psychotherapy* (2nd ed.). Routledge.
Robertson, D. J. (2021a, February 23). *The Difference between stoicism and Stoicism - Stoicism — Philosophy as a Way of Life*. Medium. https://medium.com/stoicism-philosophy-as-a-way-of-life/the-difference-between-stoicism-and-stoicism-907ee9e35dc5
Robertson, D. J. (2021b, September 4). *What do the Stoic Virtues Mean?* Donald Robertson. Retrieved 10 March 2022, from https://donaldrobertson.name/2018/01/18/what-do-the-stoic-virtues-mean/
Robertson, D. J. (2021c, December 11). *The Stoic Virtues and Code of Honor - Stoicism — Philosophy as a Way of Life*. Medium. https://medium.com/stoicism-philosophy-as-a-way-of-life/the-stoic-virtues-and-code-of-honor-2141ceae095f
Robertson, D., & Codd, R. T. (2019). Stoic philosophy as a cognitive-behavioral therapy. *The Behavior Therpist, 42*(2), 33–60.
Roemer, L., & Borkovec, T. D. (1994). Effects of suppressing thoughts about emotional material. *Journal of Abnormal Psychology, 103*(3), 467–474. https://doi.org/10.1037//0021-843x.103.3.467
Rogers, C. R. (1957). The necessary and sufficient conditions of therapeutic personality change. *Journal of Consulting Psychology 21*(2), 95–103. https://doi.org/10.1037/h0045357
Rogers, C. R. (1961). *On becoming a person: A therapist's view of psychotherapy*. Houghton Mifflin.
Roseman, I. J., & Smith, C. A. (2001). Appraisal theory: Overview, assumptions, varieties, controversies. In K. R. Scherer, A. Schorr, & T. Johnstone (Eds.), *Appraisal processes in emotion: Theory, methods, research* (pp. 3–19). Oxford University Press.
Rosenberg, M. (1965). *Society and the adolescent self-image*. Princeton University Press. 10.1515/9781400876136
Ruggiero, G. M., Spada, M. M., & Caselli, G. (2018). A historical and theoretical review of cognitive behavioral therapies: From structural self-knowledge to functional processes. *Journal of Rational-Emotive Cognitive-Behavioral Therapy, 36*(4), 378–403. https://doi.org/10.1007/s10942-018-0292-8
Ruiz, M. (2021, July 14). *Netflix's 'Naomi Osaka' Explores the Mental Toll of Being a Champion*. Vogue. Retrieved 14 October 2022, from https://www.vogue.com/article/naomi-osaka-docuseries-netflix-review
Russell, B. (1950). *Unpopular essays*. George Allen & Unwin.
Russell, B. (2022). *On the value of scepticism*. Haldeman-Julius.
Ruth, W. J. (1992). Irrational thinking in humans: An evolutionary proposal for Ellis' genetic postulate. *Journal of Rational-Emotive & Cognitive-Behavior Therapy, 10*(1), 3–20. https://doi.org/10.1007/BF01245738
Ruth, W. (1993). Evolutionary psychology and rational emotive therapy: Time to open the floodgates. *Journal of Rational Emotive and Cognitive Behavior Therapy, 11*(winter), 4.
Ryan, R. M., & Martela, F. (2016). Eudaimonia as a way of living: Connecting Aristotle with self-determination theory. In J. Vittersø (Ed.), *International handbooks of quality-of-life. Handbook of eudaimonic well-being* (pp. 109–122). Springer International Publishing. https://doi.org/10.1007/978-3-319-42445-3_7
Sachs, O., & Hirsch, J. (2008). A neurology of belief. *Annals of Neurology, 63*, 129–130.
Salamone, J. D., & Correa, M. (2012). The mysterious motivational functions of mesolimbic dopamine. *Neuron, 76*(3), 470–485. https://doi.org/10.1016/j.neuron.2012.10.021

Salovey, P., Detweiler-Bedell, B. T., Detweiler-Bedell, J. B., & Mayer, D. (2010). Emotional intelligence. In M. Lewis, J. M. Haviland-Jones & L. Feldman-Barrett (Eds.), *Handbook of emotions* (pp. 533–547). Guilford Press.

Samar, S. M., Walton, K. E., & McDermut, W. (2013). Personality traits predict irrational beliefs. *Journal of Rational-Emotive and Cognitive Behavior Therapy*, *31*, 231–242. https://doi.org/10.1007/s10942-013-0172-1

Sapolsky, R. M. (2007). Stress, stress-related disease, and emotional regulation. In J. J. Gross (Ed.), *Handbook of emotion regulation*. Guilford Press.

Sarracino, D., Dimaggio, G., Ibrahim, R., Popolo, R., Sassaroli, S., & Ruggiero, G. M. (2017). When REBT goes difficult: Applying ABC-DEF to personality disorders. *Journal of Rational Emotive and Cognitive Behavior Therapy*, *35*, 278–295. https://doi.org/10.1007/s10942-016-0258-7

Sathyanarayana Rao, T. S., Asha, M. R., Jagannatha Rao, K. S., & Vasudevaraju, P. (2009). The biochemistry of belief. *Indian Journal of Psychiatry*, *51*(4), 239–241. https://doi.org/10.4103/0019-5545.58285

Sava, F. A. (2009). Maladaptive schemas, irrational beliefs, and their relationship with the five-factor personality model. *Journal of Cognitive and Behavioral Psychotherapies*, *9*(2), 135–147.

Sava, F. A., Maricutoiu, L. P., Rusu, S., Macsinga, I., & Virgă, D. (2011). Implicit and explicit self-esteem and irrational beliefs. *Journal of Cognitive-Behavioral Psychotherapy and Research*, *11*, 97–111.

Scheff, T. J. (2007). Catharsis and other heresies: A theory of emotion. *Journal of Social, Evolutionary, and Cultural Psychology*, *1*(3), 98–113. http://dx.doi.org/10.1037/h0099826

Schill, T., Monroe, S., Evans, R., & Ramanaiah, N. (1978). The effects of self-verbalizations on performance: A test of the rational-emotive position. *Psychotherapy*, *15*, 2–7. https://doi.org/10.1037/h0085835

Schopenhauer, A. (1850). *Essays and aphorisms*. Penguin Books Ltd. Kindle Edition.

Schnur, J. B., Montgomery, G. H., & David, D. (2010). Irrational and rational beliefs and physical health. In David, A. Ellis, & S. J. Lynn (Eds.), *Rational and irrational beliefs: Research, theory and clinical practice* (pp. 253–264). Oxford University Press.

Schwitzgebel, E. (2010). Belief. In E. N. Zalt (Ed.), *The Stanford Encyclopedia of Philosophy*. Stanford University.

Scully, J. A., Tosi, H., & Banning, K. (2000). Life event checklists: Revisiting the social readjustment rating scale after 30 years. *Educational and Psychological Measurement*, *60*(6), 864–876. https://doi.org/10.1177/00131640021970952

Sedley, D. (1998). The goal. Stoicism. *Routledge Encyclopedia of Philosophy*. Taylor and Francis. https://doi.org/10.4324/9780415249126-A112-1

Sealey, L. (2018, June 5). England star Jos Buttler explains why he writes 'f*** it' on every bat he owns. *The Metro*. Retrieved from https://metro.co.uk/2018/06/05/new-england-test-hero-jos-buttler-explains-writes-f-every-bat-owns-7605949/

Seitz, R. J., & Angel, H.-F. (2020). Belief formation—A driving force for brain evolution. *Brain and Cognition*, *140*, Article 105548. https://doi.org/10.1016/j.bandc.2020.105548

Seitz, R. J., Paloutzian, R. F., & Angel, H. F. (2016). Processes of believing: Where do they come from? What are they good for? *F1000Research*, *5*, 2573. https://doi.org/10.12688/f1000research.9773.2

Seitz, R. J., Paloutzian, R. F., & Angel, H. F. (2018). From believing to belief: A general theoretical model. *Journal of Cognitive Neuroscience*, *30*(9), 1254–1264. https://doi.org/10.1162/jocn_a_01292

Seneca, L. A., & Campbell, R. (2004). *Letters from a Stoic: Epistulae Morales ad Lucilium (Classics S.)* (New ed.). Penguin.

Sharf, R. S. (1996). *Theories of psychotherapy and counseling: Concepts and Cases*. Brooks/Cole Publishing Company.

Shea, D. (2016). Basic tenets of rebt/cbt. In *Cognitive behavioral approaches for counselors* (pp. 21–38). SAGE Publications, Inc. https://doi.org/10.4135/9781483393650.n5

Sheen, T. (2015, December 24). *Manchester United 'Must Win' Against Stoke on Boxing Day, Says Under-Pressure Louis van Gaal*. The Independent. Retrieved from http://www.independent.co.uk/sport/

football/premier-league/louis-van-gaal-manchester-united-must-win-against-stoke-says-under-pressure-manager-a6785446.html
Sheldon, K. M. (2002). The self-concordance model of healthy goal-striving: When personal goals correctly represent the person. In E. L. Deci & R. M. Ryan (Eds.), *Handbook of self-determination research* (pp. 65–86). University of Rochester Press.
Sheldon, K. M., & Elliot, A. J. (1999). Goal striving, need satisfaction, and longitudinal well-being: The self-concordance model. *Journal of Personality and Social Psychology*, *76*(3), 482–497. https://doi.org/10.1037/0022-3514.76.3.482
Sheppes, G., & Gross, J. J. (2013). Emotion regulation effectiveness: What works when. In H. Tennen, J. Suls, & I. B. Weiner (Eds.), *Handbook of psychology: Personality and social psychology* (pp. 391–405). John Wiley & Sons, Inc.
Sheppes, G., Scheibe, S., Suri, G., Radu, P., Blechert, J., & Gross, J. J. (2014). Emotion regulation choice: A conceptual framework and supporting evidence. *Journal of Experimental Psychology. General*, *143*(1), 163–181. https://doi.org/10.1037/a0030831
Shermer, M. (2011). *The believing brain: From ghosts and gods to politics and conspiracies---how we construct beliefs and reinforce them as truths*. Times Books.
Si, G., & Lee, H. (2008). Is it so hard to change? The case of a Hong Kong Olympic silver medallist. *International Journal of Sport and Exercise Psychology*, *6*, 319–330.
Sille, R., Turner, M. J., & Eubank, M. (2020). "Don't be stupid, stupid!": Cognitive-behavioral techniques to reduce irrational beliefs and enhance focus in a youth tennis player. *Case Studies in Sport and Exercise Psychology*, *4*, 40–51.
Silverman, S., & DiGiuseppe, R. (2001). Cognitive-behavioral constructs and children's behavioral and emotional problems. *Journal of Rational-Emotive & Cognitive-Behavioral Therapy*, *19*, 119–134. https://doi.org/10.1016/j.chiabu.2008.05.007
Silvers, J. A., Buhle, J. T., & Ochsner, K. N. (2013). The neuroscience of emotion regulation: Basic mechanisms and their role in development, aging and psychopathology. In K. N. Ochsner & S. M. Kosslyn (Eds.), *The handbook of cognitive neuroscience*. Oxford University Press.
Smith, C. A., & Kirby, L. D. (2009). Putting appraisal in context: Toward a relational model of appraisal and emotion. *Cognition and Emotion*, *23*(7), 1352–1372. https://doi.org/10.1080/02699930902860386
Smith, C. A., & Lazarus, R. S. (1993). Appraisal components, core relational themes, and the emotions. *Cognition and Emotion*, *7*(3–4), 233–269. https://doi.org/10.1080/02699939308409189
Smith, M. I. (2011). Rapid processing of emotional expressions without conscious awareness. *Cerebral Cortex*, *22*, 1748–1760.
Şoflău, R., & David, D. O. (2016). A meta-analytical approach of the relationships between the irrationality of beliefs and the functionality of automatic thoughts. *Cognitive Therapy and Research*, *41*(2), 178–192. https://doi.org/10.1007/s10608-016-9812-y
Solomon, A., Arnow, B. A., Gotlib, I. H., & Wind, B. (2003). Individualized measurement of irrational beliefs in remitted depressives. *Journal of Clinical Psychology*, *59*, 439–455. https://doi.org/10.1002/jclp.10081
Soroka, S., & McAdams, S. (2015). News, politics, and negativity. *Political Communication*, *32*, 1–22. https://doi.org/10.1080/10584609.2014.881942
Souter, G., Lewis, R., & Serrant, L. (2018). Men, mental health and elite sport: A narrative review. *Sports Medicine - Open*, *4*(1), 57. https://doi.org/10.1186/s40798-018-0175-7
Sparkes, A. C. (1998). Athletic identity: An Achilles' heel to the survival of self. *Qualitative Health Research*, *8*(5), 644–664. https://doi.org/10.1177/104973239800800506
Spence, S. H., March, S., & Donovan, C. L. (2019). New technologies to deliver CBT: Computer and web-based programs, mobile applications, and virtual reality. In L. J. Farrell, T. H. Ollendick, & P. Muris (Eds.), *Innovations in CBT for childhood anxiety, OCD, and PTSD: Improving access and outcomes* (pp. 73–105). Cambridge University Press. https://doi.org/10.1017/9781108235655.005
Spörrle, M., Strobel, M., & Tumasjan, A. (2010). On the incremental validity of irrational beliefs to predict subjective wellbeing while controlling for personality factors. *Psicothema*, *22*, 543–548.

Sprenkle, D. H., & Blow, A. J. (2004). Common factors and our sacred models. *Journal of Marital and Family Therapy*, *30*(2), 113–129. https://doi.org/10.1111/j.1752-0606.2004.tb01228.x

Staff, A. B. (2018, October 5). *Sports Psychology Pioneer Ravizza Dies*. Athletic Business. Retrieved 16 March 2022, from https://www.athleticbusiness.com/leadership/news/15154750/sports-psychology-pioneer-ravizza-dies

Stanovich, K. E. (2004). *The robot's rebellion: Finding meaning in the age of Darwin*. University of Chicago Press.

Stanovich, K. E. (2012). On the distinction between rationality and intelligence: Implications for understanding individual differences in reasoning. In K. Holyoak & R. Morrison (Eds.), *The Oxford handbook of thinking and reasoning* (pp. 343–365). Oxford University Press.

Stanovich K. E. (2018). How to think rationally about world problems. *Journal of Intelligence*, *6*(2), 25. https://doi.org/10.3390/jintelligence6020025

Stefan, S., Cristea, I. A., Szentagotai Tatar, A., & David, D. (2019). Cognitive-behavioral therapy (CBT) for generalized anxiety disorder: Contrasting various CBT approaches in a randomized clinical trial. *Journal of Clinical Psychology*, *75*(7), 1188–1202. https://doi.org/10.1002/jclp.22779

Stephens, W. O. (n.d.). Stoic ethics. *Internet Encyclopedia of Philosophy*. Internet Encyclopedia of Philosophy and Its Authors. Retrieved 23 April 2022, from https://iep.utm.edu/stoiceth/

Stephenson, E., Watson, P. J., Chen, Z. J., & Morris, R. J. (2017). Self-compassion, self-esteem, and irrational beliefs. *Current Psychology*, *37*(4), 809–815. https://doi.org/10.1007/s12144-017-9563-2

Steward, T., Kung, P. H., Davey, C. G., Moffat, B. A., Glarin, R. K., Jamieson, A. J., Felmingham, K. L., & Harrison, B. J. (2022). A thalamo-centric neural signature for restructuring negative self-beliefs. *Molecular Psychiatry*, Advance online publication. https://doi.org/10.1038/s41380-021-01402-9

Stich, S. P. (1990). *The fragmentation of reason*. MIT Press.

Still, A. (2010). Rationality and rational psychotherapy: The heart of REBT. In D. David, S. J. Lynn, & A. Ellis (Eds.), *Rational and irrational beliefs: Research, theory, and clinical practice* (pp. 23–48). Oxford University Press.

Still, A., & Dryden, W. (1999). The place of rationality in stoicism and REBT. *Journal of Rational-Emotive and Cognitive-Behavior Therapy, 17*, 143–164.

Still, A., & Dryden, W. (2012). *The historical and philosophical context of rational psychotherapy: The legacy of Epictetus.* Karnac Books.

Stott, R. (2007). When head and heart do not agree: A theoretical and clinical analysis of Rational-Emotional Dissociation (RED) in cognitive therapy. *Journal of Cognitive Psychotherapy*, *21*(1), 37–50. https://doi.org/10.1891/088983907780493313

Stott, R., Mansell, W., Salkovskis, P., Lavender, A., & Cartwright-Hatton, S. (2010). *Oxford guide to metaphors in CBT: Building cognitive bridges*. Oxford University Press.

Sullivan, M. J. L., Thorn, B., Haythornthwaite, J. A., Keefe, F., Martin, M., Bradley, L. A., & Lefebvre, J. C. (2001). Theoretical perspectives on the relation between catastrophizing and pain. *The Clinical Journal of Pain*, *17*(1), 52–64. https://doi.org/10.1097/00002508-200103000-00008

Szentagotai, A. (2006). Irrational beliefs, thought suppression and distress - a mediation analysis. *Journal of Cognitive and Behavioral Psychotherapies*, 6(2), 119–127.

Szentagotai, A., & Freeman, A. (2007). An analysis of the relationship between irrational beliefs and automatic thought in predicting distress. *Journal of Cognitive and Behavioral Psychotherapies*, *7*(1), 1–9.

Szentagotai, A., & Jones, J. (2010). The behavioral consequences of irrational beliefs. In D. David, S. J. Lynn, & A. Ellis (Eds.), *Rational and irrational beliefs in human functioning and disturbances*. Oxford University Press.

Taleb, N. N. (2012). *Antifragile: Things that gain from disorder*. Random House.

Taves, A., & Asprem, E. (2016). Experience as event: Event cognition and the study of (religious) experiences. *Religion Brain and Behavior*, *7*(1), 43–62. https://doi.org/10.1080/2153599X.2016.115037

Team Coco. (2013, January 16). *Rocker Jack White - Serious Jibber-Jabber with Conan O'Brien* [Video]. YouTube. https://www.youtube.com/watch?v=AJgY9FtDLbs&feature=youtu.be

Thomas, L. (2021, December 20). *A Year That Changed How Athletes Think About Mental Health*. The New Yorker. Retrieved 20 March 2022, from https://www.newyorker.com/culture/2021-in-review/a-year-that-changed-how-athletes-think-about-mental-health

Thomas, O., Maynard, I., & Hanton, S. (2007). Intervening with athletes during the time leading up to competition: Theory to practice II. *Journal of Applied Sport Psychology*, *19*(4), 398–418. https://doi.org/10.1080/10413200701599140

Tooby, J., Cosmides, L., Sell, A., Lieberman, D., & Sznycer, D. (2008). Internal regulatory variables and the design of human motivation: A computational and evolutionary approach. *Handbook of Approach and Avoidance Motivation*, *15*, 251–271.

Tóth, R., Turner, M. J., Kökény, T., & Tóth, L. (2022). "I must be perfect": The role of irrational beliefs and perfectionism on the competitive anxiety of Hungarian athletes. *Frontiers in Psychology: section Movement Science and Sport Psychology*. Accepted 18th August 2022.

Trincas, R., Bilotta, E., & Mancini, F. (2016). Specific beliefs about emotions are associated with different emotion-regulation strategies. *Psychology*, *7*, 1682–1699.

Trip, S., Vernon, A., & McMahon, J. (2007). Effectiveness of rational-emotive education: A quantitative meta-analytical study. *Journal of Cognitive and Behavioral Psychotherapies*, *7*(1), 81–93

Trower, P., & Jones, J. (2001). How REBT can be less disturbing and remarkably more influential in britain: A review of views of practitioners and researchers. *Journal of Rational-Emotive & Cognitive-Behavior Therapy*, *19*, 21–30. https://doi.org/10.1023/A:1007891115800

Troy, A. S., Shallcross, A. J., Brunner, A., Friedman, R., & Jones, M. C. (2018). Cognitive reappraisal and acceptance: Effects on emotion, physiology, and perceived cognitive costs. *Emotion*, *18*(1), 58–74. https://doi.org/10.1037/emo0000371

Tullett, A. M., Prentice, M. S., Teper, R., Nash, K. A., Inzlicht, M., & Mcgregor, I. (2013). Neural and motivational mechanics of meaning and threat. In K. D. Markman, T. Proulx, & M. J. Lindberg (Eds.), *The psychology of meaning* (pp. 401–419). American Psychological Association.

Tuning In [Radiocentre]. (2021, November 11). *John Cleese Talks Creativity, Freedom of Speech and blacklisting himself from Cambridge University* [Video]. YouTube. https://www.youtube.com/watch?v=qmQ9_stT2Kc

Turner, M. J. (2013, March). *The Performance Consequences, and Manipulation, of Challenge and Threat States* (Thesis). https://eprints.staffs.ac.uk/2033/1/Turner%20Martin%20James%20PhD%20Thesis.pdf

Turner, M. J. (2014). Smarter thinking in sport. *The Psychologist*, *27*(8), 596–599.

Turner, M. J. (2016a). Proposing a rational resilience credo for athletes. *Journal of Sport Psychology in Action*, *7*(3), 170–181. https://doi.org/10.1080/21520704.2016.1236051

Turner, M. J. (2016b). Rational emotive behavior therapy (REBT), irrational and rational beliefs, and the mental health of athletes, *Frontiers: Movement Science and Sport Psychology*. https://doi.org/10.3389/fpsyg.2016.01423

Turner, M. J. (2016c, February 6). *Human>Performer*. The Smarter Thinking Project. Retrieved 20 March 2022, from https://thesmarterthinkingproject.com/humanperformer/

Turner, M. J. (2019a). REBT in sport. In M. E. Bernard & W. Dryden W (Eds.), *REBT: Advances in theory, research, prevention, promotion*, (pp. 307–335). Springer Press.

Turner, M. J. (2019b, August 16). *Control*. The Smarter Thinking Project. Retrieved 13 March 2022, from https://thesmarterthinkingproject.com/control/

Turner, M. J. (2020b, August 6). *The Olympic Games: The Rational Pursuit of Excellence*. MMU News. Retrieved 1 March 2022, from https://www.mmu.ac.uk/hpsc/news-and-media/news/story/?id=12703

Turner, M. J., & Allen, M. (2018). Confirmatory factor analysis of the irrational Performance Beliefs Inventory (iPBI) in a sample of amateur and semi-professional athletes. *Psychology of Sport and Exercise*, *35*, 126–130. https://doi.org/10.1016/j.psychsport.2017.11.017

Turner, M. J., Allen, M., Slater, M. J., Barker, J. B., Woodcock, C., Harwood, C. G., & McFadyen, K. (2018b). The development and initial validation of the irrational performance beliefs inventory (iPBI). *European Journal of Psychological Assessment, 34*, 174–180.
Turner, M. J., Aspin, G., Didymus, F., Mack, R., Olusoga, P., Wood, A. G., & Bennett. R. (2020a). One case, five approaches: The application of psychotherapeutic approaches in sport psychology. *The Sport Psychologist, 34*(1), 71–83. https://doi.org/10.1123/tsp.2019-0079
Turner, M. J., Aspin, G., & Gillman, J. (2019e). Maladaptive schema as a potential mechanism through which irrational beliefs relate to psychological distress in athletes. *Psychology of Sport & Exercise, 44*, 9–16. https://doi.org/10.1016/j.psychsport.2019.04.015
Turner, M. J., & Bennett, R. (2018). *Rational emotive behaviour therapy in sport and exercise.* Routledge.
Turner, M. J., & Barker, J. B. (2013). Examining the efficacy of rational-emotive behavior therapy (REBT) on irrational beliefs and anxiety in elite youth cricketers. *Journal of Applied Sport Psychology, 25*(1), 131–147.
Turner, M. J., & Barker. J. B. (2014a). Using rational emotive behavior therapy with athletes. *The Sport Psychologist, 28*(1), 75–90.
Turner, M. J., & Barker, J. B. (2014b). *Tipping the balance: The mental skills handbook for athletes.* UK: Bennion Kearny.
Turner, M. J., Carrington, S., & Miller, A. (2019b). Psychological distress across sport participation groups: The mediating effects of secondary irrational beliefs on the relationship between primary irrational beliefs and symptoms of anxiety, anger, and depression. *Journal of Clinical Sport Psychology, 13*(1), 17–40.
Turner, M. J., Chadha, N, J., Davis, H., Deen, M. S., Gilmore, H., Jones, J. K., Goldman, S., & Terjesen, M. (2022a). At the coalface: Practitioner perspectives on applying rational emotive behaviour therapy (REBT) in high performance sport. *Journal of Rational-Emotive & Cognitive-Behavior Therapy*. Accepted 2nd May 2022.
Turner, M. J., & Davis, H. (2019). Exploring the effects of rational emotive behaviour therapy (REBT) on the irrational beliefs and self-determined motivation of triathletes. *Journal of Applied Sport Psychology, 31*(3), 253–272. https://doi.org/10.1080/10413200.2018.1446472
Turner, M. J., Ewen, D., & Barker, J. B. (2020b). An idiographic single-case study examining the use of rational emotive behavior therapy (REBT) with three amateur golfers to alleviate sport performance phobias. *Journal of Applied Sport Psychology, 32*(2), 186–204.
Turner, M. J., & Jones, M. V. (2014). Stress, emotions and athletes' positive adaptation to sport: Contributes from a transactional perspective. In R. Gomes, R. Resende, & A. Albuquerque (Eds.), *Positive human functioning from a multidimensional perspective, Vol. 1* (pp. 85–111). Nova Science.
Turner, M. J., & Jones, M. V. (2018). *Arousal Control in Sport.* Oxford Research Encyclopedia of Psychology. https://doi.org/10.1093/acrefore/9780190236557.013.155
Turner, M. J., Jones, J., & Wood, A. G. (2018a). Applying the REBT cognitive disputation technique to the binary theory of emotional distress. *Effective Scientist-Practitioner, 1*(1), 46–64.
Turner, M. J., Kirkham, L., & Wood, A. G. (2019c). Teeing up for success: The effects of rational and irrational self-talk on the putting performance of amateur golfers. *Psychology of Sport & Exercise, 38*, 148–153. https://doi.org/10.1016/j.psychsport.2018.06.012
Turner, M. J., Miller, A., Youngs, H., Barber, N., Brick, N. E., Chadha, N. J., Chandler, C., Coyle, M., Didymus, F. F., Evans, A. L., Jones, K., McCann, B., Meijen, C., & Rossato, C. J. L. (2022b). "I must do this!": A latent profile analysis approach to understanding the role of irrational beliefs and motivation regulation in mental and physical health. *Journal of Sports Sciences*. https://doi.org/10.1080/02640414.2022.2042124. Accepted 9th February 2022.
Turner, M. J., & Moore, M. (2016). Irrational beliefs predict increased emotional and physical exhaustion in Gaelic football athletes. *International Journal of Sport Psychology, 47*(2), 187–199.
Turner, M. J., Slater, M. J., & Barker, J. B. (2014). Not the end of the world: The effects of rational emotive behavior therapy on the irrational beliefs of elite academy athletes. *Journal of Applied Sport Psychology, 26*(2), 144–156.

Turner, M. J., Slater, M. J., & Barker, J. B. (2015). The season-long effects of rational emotive behavior therapy on the irrational beliefs of professional academy soccer athletes, *International Journal of Sport Psychology*, *5*, 429–451.

Turner, M. J., Slater, M. J., Dixon, J., & Miller, A. (2017). Test-retest reliability of the irrational performance beliefs inventory (iPBI). *European Journal of Sport Science*, *18*(1), 123–129. https://doi.org/10.1080/17461391.2017.1411527

Turner, M. J., & Wood, A. G. (2019a). *The Smarter Thinking App* (Version 1.0.2). [Mobile app]. Google Play Store. https://play.google.com/store/apps/details?id=com.smarterthinkingprofile.smarterthinking&gl=GB

Turner, M. J., & Wood, A. G. (2019b, August 12). *Smarter Thinking | Achieve More by Stressing Less | FREE Profile Report*. Smarter Thinking. Retrieved 9 March 2022, from https://smarterthinkingprofile.com/

Turner, M. J., Wood, A. G., Barker, J. B., & Chadha, N. (2019d). Rational self-talk: A rational emotive behaviour therapy (REBT) perspective. In A. T. Latinjak & A. Hatzigeorgiadis (Eds.), *Self-talk in sport* (pp. 109–122). Routledge.

Turner, M. J., Wood, A. G., Boatwright, D., Chadha, N., Jones, J. K., & Bennett, R. (2021). Assessing beliefs about emotion generation and change: The conceptualisation, development, and validation of the Cognitive Mediation Beliefs Questionnaire (CMBQ). *Psychotherapy Research: Journal of the Society for Psychotherapy Research*, *31*(7), 932–949. https://doi.org/10.1080/10503307.2020.1871524

Turner, M. J., Wood, A. G., & Jones, J. J. (2019a). A response to Philip Hyland, Demetris Katsikis, and Chrysoula Kostogiannis on the debate point concerning the binary theory of emotional distress. *Effective Scientist-Practitioner*, *2*, 60–66.

Urfa, O., & Asci, F. H. (2018). Examination of psychometric properties of the irrational performance belief inventory-2. *Studies in Psychology -Psikoloji Calismalar Dergisi*, *38*(2), 219–236.

Usborne, S. (2021, August 23). *How to Win at Life: What Sports Psychologists can Teach us All*. The Guardian. https://www.theguardian.com/lifeandstyle/2021/aug/21/how-to-win-at-life-what-sports-psychologists-can-teach-us-all

Vadocz, E. A., Hall, C. R., & Moritz, S. E. (1997). The relationship between competitive anxiety and imagery use. *Journal of Applied Sport Psychology*, *9*, 241–253. https://doi.org/10.1080/10413209708406485

Van Bockstaele, B., Atticciati, L., Hiekkaranta, A. P., Larsen, H., & Verschuere, B. (2019). Choose change: Situation modification, distraction, and reappraisal in mild versus intense negative situations. *Motivation and Emotion*. Advance online publication. https://doi.org/10.1007/s11031-019-09811-8

van Kleef, G. A., Cheshin, A., Fischer, A. H., & Schneider, I. K. (2016). Editorial: The social nature of emotions. *Frontiers in Psychology*, *7*, Article 896.

Van Raalte, J. L., & Vincent, A. (2017). Self-talk in sport and performance. In O. Braddick (Ed.), *Oxford research encyclopedia of psychology* (pp. 1–20). https://doi.org/10.1093/acrefore/9780190236557.013.157

Van Raalte, J. L., Vincent, A., & Brewer, B. W. (2016). Self-talk: Review and sport-specific model. *Psychology of Sport and Exercise*, *22*, 139–148.

Veale, D., & Willson, R. (2007). *Manage your mood: Using behavioural activation to overcome depression*. Robinson Publishing.

Vealey, R. S. (2007). Mental skills training in sport. In G. Tenenbaum & R. C. Eklund (Eds.), *Handbook of sport psychology* (3rd ed., pp. 287–309). Wiley.

Vertopolous, V., & Turner, M. J. (2017). Examining the effectiveness of a rational emotive personal-disclosure mutual-sharing (REPDMS) intervention on the irrational beliefs, rational beliefs, and emotions of Greek adolescent athletes. *The Sport Psychologist*, 31, 264–274.

Vîslă, A., Flückiger, C., grosse Holtforth, M., & David, D. (2016). Irrational beliefs and psychological distress: A meta-analysis. *Psychotherapy and Psychosomatics*, *85*(1), 8–15. https://doi.org/10.1159/000441231

Wadsworth, N., & Hargreaves, A. (2021). "A blank slate": Preparing for Tokyo 2021 during COVID-19. *Case Studies in Sport and Exercise Psychology*, *5*(S1), S1-1. https://doi.org/10.1123/cssep.2020-0027

Wager, T. D., Jonides, J., & Reading, S. (2004). Neuroimaging studies of shifting attention: A meta-analysis. *NeuroImage*, *22*(4), 1679–1693. https://doi.org/10.1016/j.neuroimage.2004.03.052

Wager, T. D., & Smith, E. E. (2003). Neuroimaging studies of working memory: A meta-analysis. *Cognitive, Affective & Behavioral Neuroscience*, *3*(4), 255–274. https://doi.org/10.3758/CABN.3.4.255

Wallace, S. (2018, July 2). *How Gareth Southgate Is Using His Own Bitter Failure to End England's Penalty Curse*. The Telegraph. Retrieved 12 March 2022, from https://www.telegraph.co.uk/world-cup/2018/07/02/gareth-southgate-using-bitter-failure-end-englands-penalty-curse/

Wallace, S., Clark, M., & White, J. (2012). 'It's on my iPhone': Attitudes to the use of mobile computing devices in medical education, a mixed methods study. *British Medical Journal*, *2*, 10–24. https://doi.org/10.1136/bmjopen-2012-001099

Walen, S., DiGiuseppe, R., & Dryden, W. (1992). *A practitioner's guide to rational-emotive therapy*. Oxford University Press.

Waltman, S. H., & Palermo, A. (2019). Theoretical overlap and distinction between rational emotive behavior therapy's awfulizing and cognitive therapy's catastrophizing. *Mental Health Review Journal*, *24*(1), 44–50. https://doi.org/10.1108/mhrj-07-2018-0022

Wang, K., Goldenberg, A., Dorison, C. A., Miller, J. K., Uusberg, A., Lerner, J. S., Gross, J. J., Agesin, B. B., Bernardo, M., Campos, O., Eudave, L., Grzech, K., Ozery, D. H., Jackson, E. A., Garcia, E., Drexler, S. M., Jurković, A. P., Rana, K., Wilson, J. P., Antoniadi, M., … Moshontz, H. (2021). A multi-country test of brief reappraisal interventions on emotions during the COVID-19 pandemic. *Nature Human Behaviour*, 10.1038/s41562-021-01173-x. Advance online publication. https://doi.org/10.1038/s41562-021-01173-x

Wang, H. Y., Xu, G. Q., Ni, M. F., Zhang, C. H., Sun, X. P., Chang, Y., & Zhang, B. W. (2017). Neural mechanisms of implicit cognitive reappraisal: Preceding descriptions alter emotional response to unpleasant images. *Neuroscience*, *347*, 65–75. https://doi.org/10.1016/j.neuroscience.2017.01.047

Warwick, M. (2021, December 16). *Concussion and Suicide: A Family's Search for Answers*. BBC Sport. Retrieved 8 March 2022, from https://www.bbc.co.uk/sport/cycling/59639369

Watson, J., Hilliard, R., & Way, W. (2018). *Counseling and communication skills in sport and performance psychology*. Oxford Research Encyclopedia of Psychology. https ://doi.org/10.1093/acrefore/97801 90236 557.013.140.

Watson, P. J., Sherbak, J., & Morris, R. J. (1998). Irrational beliefs, individualism-collectivism, and adjustment. *Personality & Individual Differences*, *24*, 173–179. https://doi.org/10.1016/S0191-8869(97)00168-2

Webb, T. L., & Sheeran, P. (2007). How do implementation intentions promote goal attainment? A test of component processes. *Journal of Experimental Social Psychology*, *43*(2), 295–302. https://doi.org/10.1016/j.jesp.2006.02.001

Wegner, D. M., Schneider, D. J., Carter, S. R., & White, T. L. (1987). Paradoxical effects of thought suppression. *Journal of Personality and Social Psychology*, *53*(1), 5–13. https://doi.org/10.1037/0022-3514.53.1.5

Weil, L. G., Fleming, S. M., Dumontheil, I., Kilford, E. J., Weil, R. S., Rees, G., Dolan, R. J., & Blakemore, S. J. (2013). The development of metacognitive ability in adolescence. *Consciousness and Cognition*, *22*(1), 264–271. https://doi.org/10.1016/j.concog.2013.01.004

Weinberg, R. (2018). Self-talk theory, research, applications: Some personal reflections. *The Sport Psychologist*, *32*, 74–78.

Weinberg, R. S. (2013). Goal setting in sport and exercise: Research and practical applications. *Revista da Educação Física*, *24*, 171–179.

Wenzel, A. (2006). Attentional disruption in the presence of negative automatic thoughts. *Behavioral and Cognitive Psychotherapy*, *34*, 385–395.

Wessler, R. L. (1996). Idiosyncratic definitions and unsupported hypotheses: Rational emotive behavior therapy as pseudoscience. *Journal of Rational-Emotive & Cognitive-Behavior Therapy*, *14*(1), 41–61. https://doi.org/10.1007/bf02238093

Wessler, R., & Wessler, R. (1980). *The principles and practice of rational-emotive therapy*. San Francisco: Jossey-Bass.

Wiki Targeted (Entertainment). (2013, July 28). In *Dunderpedia: The Office Wiki*. https://theoffice.fandom.com/wiki/Here_Comes_Treble_(Episode)

Wilbon, M. (2012). *The Best American sports Writing*. Houghton Mi-in Harcourt Publishing Company.

Wilde, J. (2012). The relationship between frustration intolerance and academic achievement in college. *International Journal of Higher Education*, *1*, 1–8. https://doi.org/10.5430/ijhe.v1n2p1

Wilde, O. (1891). *The Picture of Dorian Gray*. Retrieved via: http://www.literaturepage.com/read/doriangray-30.html

Willard, D. (2021). *Renovation of the heart: Putting on the character of Christ -20th anniversary edition* (Enlarged ed.). NavPress.

Williams, C. M., Shaw, M. T., Mastroleo, N. R., & Zale, E. L. (2021). Sport-related and psychosocial factors associated with motives and consequences of alcohol and cannabis use among NCAA athletes: A systematic review. *Alcohol and Alcoholism*, agab022, https://doi.org/10.1093/alcalc/agab022

Wills, F., & Sanders, D. (2013). *Cognitive behaviour therapy: Foundation for practice*. SAGE Publications, Inc.

Wilson, D. S. (2010). Rational and irrational beliefs from an evolutionary perspective. In D. David, S. J. Lynn, & A. Ellis (Eds.), *Rational and irrational beliefs: Research, theory, and clinical practice* (pp. 63–72). Oxford University Press.

Wirga, M., DeBernardi, M., Wirga, A., Wirga, M. L., Banout, M., & Fuller, O. G. (2020). Maultsby's rational behavior therapy: Background, description, practical applications, and recent developments. *Journal of Rational-Emotive & Cognitive-Behavior Therapy*, *38*(3), 399–423. https://doi.org/10.1007/s10942-020-00341-8

Wolanin, A. T., & Marks, D. R. (2019). Athlete mental health. In M. H. Anshel, T. A. Petrie, & J. A. Steinfeldt (Eds.), *APA handbook of sport and exercise psychology, Vol. 1. Sport psychology* (pp. 653–674). American Psychological Association. https://doi.org/10.1037/0000123-033

Wolpe, J. (1973). *The practice of behavior therapy*. Pergamon Press.

Wolpe, J. (1990). *The practice of behavior therapy* (4th ed.). Pergamon Press, Inc.

Wood, A., Barker, J. B., & Turner, M. J. (2016). Developing performance using rational emotive behavior therapy (REBT): A case study with an elite archer. *The Sport Psychologist*, *31*(1), 78–87.

Wood, A. G., Barker, J. B., & Turner, M. J. (2017). Rational emotive behaviour therapy to help young athletes build resilience and deal with adversity. In C. J. Knight, C. G. Harwood, & D. Gould (Eds.), *Sport Psychology for Youth Athletes* (pp. 265–276). Routledge.

Wood, A, G., Barker, J. B., Turner, M., & Sheffield, D. (2018a). Examining the effects of rational emotive behavior therapy (rebt) on performance outcomes in elite paralympic athletes. *Scandinavian Journal of Medicine & Science in Sports*, *28*(1), 329–339. https://doi.org/10.1111/sms.12926

Wood, A., Barker, J. B., & Turner, M. J., & Thomson, P. (2018b). Exploring the effects of a single rational emotive behavior therapy workshop in elite blind soccer players. *The Sport Psychologist*, *32*(4), 321–332.

Wood, A., Mack, R., & Turner, M. J. (2020). Developing self-determined motivation and performance with an elite athlete using motivational interviewing in adjunct to rational emotive behaviour therapy. *Journal of Rational-Emotive & Cognitive-Behavior Therapy*, *38*, 540–567.

Wood, A. G., Turner, M. J., Barker, J. B., & Higgins, S. J. (2017). Investigating the effects of irrational and rational self-statements on motor-skill and hazard perception performance. *Sport, Exercise, and Performance Psychology*, *6*(4), 384–400.

Wood, A. G., Turner, M. J., & Barker, J. B. (2019). Bolstering psychological health using rational emotive behaviour therapy. In G. Breslin & G. Leavey (Eds.), *Mental health and well-being interventions in sport: A case study analysis*. Routledge.

Woody, S. R., & Adessky, R. S. (2002). Therapeutic alliance, group cohesion, and homework compliance during cognitive-behavioral group treatment of social phobia. *Behavior Therapy*, *33*, 5–27.
World Data Lab. (n.d.). *World Poverty Clock*. World Poverty. Retrieved 11 March 2022, from https://worldpoverty.io/headline
Yamauchi, R., & Murakoshi, S. (2001). The effect of rational-emotive behavior therapy on female soft-tennis players experiencing cognitive anxiety. *Japanese Journal of Sport Psychology*, *28*, 67–75.
Ziegler, D. J. (2001). The possible place of cognitive appraisal in the ABC model underlying rational emotive behavior therapy. *Journal of Rational-Emotive & Cognitive-Behavior Therapy*, *19*(3), 137–152. https://doi.org/10.1023/A:1011172915691
Ziegler, D.J. (2003). The concept of psychological health in rational emotive behavior therapy. *Journal of Rational-Emotive & Cognitive-Behavior Therapy*, *21*, 21–36. https://doi.org/10.1023/A:1024129117726
Ziegler, D. J., & Leslie, Y. M. (2003). A test of the ABC model underlying rational emotive behavior therapy. *Psychological Reports*, *92*, 235 240.
Zupan, B., & Eskritt, M. (2020). Eliciting emotion ratings for a set of film clips: A preliminary archive for research in emotion. *The Journal of Social Psychology*, *160*(6), 768–789.

Index

Note: *Italic* page numbers refer to figures.

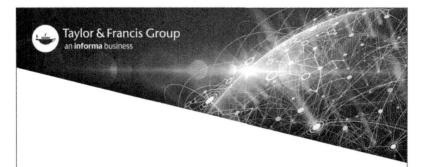